MOBILE SUIT GUNDAM SEED

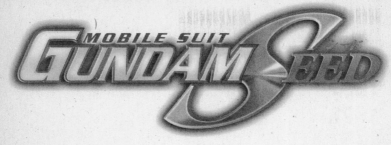

5

ART BY Masatsugu Iwase

ORIGINAL STORY BY
Hajime Yatate AND Yoshiyuki Tomino

TRANSLATED AND ADAPTED BY
David Ury

BY
ign

DEL REY

BALLANTINE BOOKS • NEW YORK

2005 Del Rey Books Trade Paperback Edition

Published in the United States by Del Rey Books, an imprint of The Random House Publishing Group, a division of Random House, Inc., New York.

Del Rey is a registered trademark and the Del Rey colophon is a trademark of Random House, Inc.

Originally published in Japan by Kodansha Ltd., Tokyo.

ISBN 0-345-47795-2

Printed in the United States of America

www.delreymanga.com

1 2 3 4 5 6 7 8 9

Lettered by Foltz Design

Contents

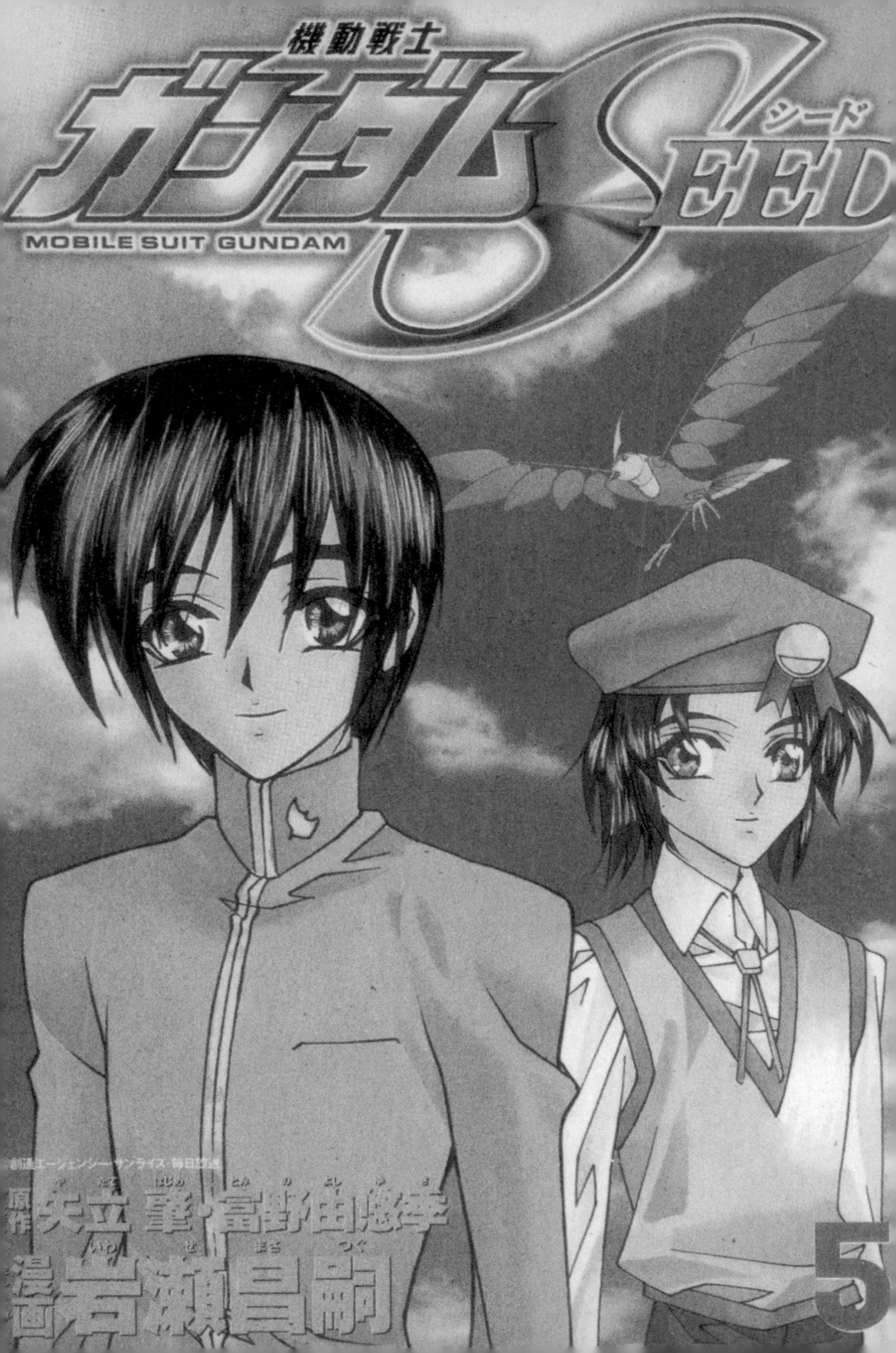
機動戦士
ガンダム SEED
シード
MOBILE SUIT GUNDAM
創通エージェンシー・サンライズ・毎日放送
原作 矢立 肇・富野由悠季
漫画 岩瀬昌嗣
5

機動戦士 ガンダム SEED シード

MOBILE SUIT GUNDAM

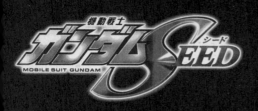

THE STORY SO FAR

GUNDAM AEGIS ATTACHES TO STRIKE AND SELF-DESTRUCTS. KIRA IS BELIEVED TO BE M.I.A., AND A DOWN-TRODDEN ARCHANGEL CREW HEADS FOR THE EARTH ALLIANCE'S MAIN BASE IN ALASKA. THE BADLY INJURED KIRA IS FOUND BY MALCHIO AND BROUGHT TO LACUS OF PLANT. ATHRUN, WRESTLES WITH GUILT AND ANGUISH, BELIEVING THAT HE HAS KILLED HIS OLD FRIEND. "OPERATION SPIT FIRE," ZAFT'S STRATEGY TO DESTROY THE EARTH ALLIANCE, IS SET INTO MOTION. THE ARCHANGEL IS PUT ON THE DEFENSIVE AND A BLOODY BATTLE ENSUES. AFTER LEARNING ABOUT ZAFT'S STRATEGY, LACUS CLYNE INTRODUCES KIRA TO THE NEW MOBILE SUIT, FREEDOM. KIRA LAUNCHES FREEDOM AND HEADS TOWARD ALASKA. BUT KIRA'S ENTRY INTO THE BATTLE DOES LITTLE TO STOP THE DAMAGE. KIRA LEARNS THAT THE EARTH ALLIANCE HAS PLANTED AND ACTIVATED A CYCLOPS BOMB BENEATH THE ALASKA BASE. THE MAJORITY OF BOTH EARTH ALLIANCE FORCES AND ZAFT FORCES ARE WIPED OUT. THE ARCHANGEL CREW, DISTURBED AND ANGERED BY THE EARTH ALLIANCE'S ACTIONS, FLEES TOWARD THE AUBE. THE AUBE REFUSES A DEMAND FROM THE EARTH ALLIANCE THAT IT HAND OVER THE MASS DRIVER. ZAFT COMMANDER CREUSET THEN DEPLOYS HIS FLEET OF NEW MOBILE SUITS AND ATTACKS PANAMA. MEANWHILE, AFTER RECEIVING ORDERS TO TAKE BACK FREEDOM AND DISPOSE OF ALL MEMBERS OF THE CLYNE PARTY, ATHRUN ZALA ENCOUNTERS LACUS CLYNE. ATHRUN LEARNS THAT KIRA IS STILL ALIVE AND HE HEADS TOWARD EARTH IN GUNDAM JUSTICE. HE DECIDES TO JOIN FORCES WITH THE AUBE IN ORDER TO UNDERSTAND WHAT HE "TRULY IS FIGHTING FOR"....

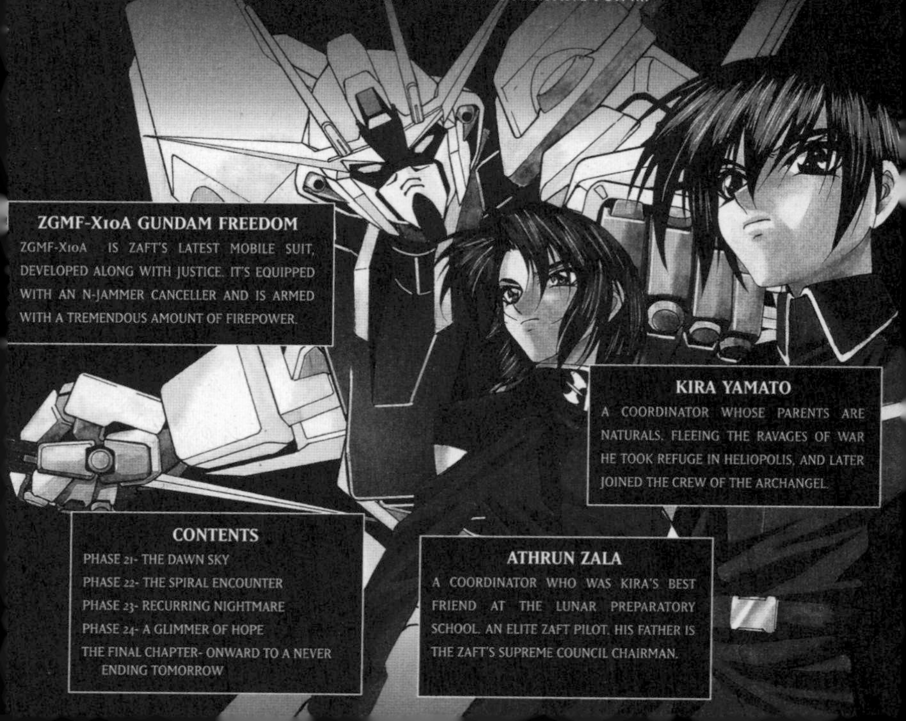

ZGMF-X10A GUNDAM FREEDOM

ZGMF-X10A IS ZAFT'S LATEST MOBILE SUIT, DEVELOPED ALONG WITH JUSTICE. IT'S EQUIPPED WITH AN N-JAMMER CANCELLER AND IS ARMED WITH A TREMENDOUS AMOUNT OF FIREPOWER.

KIRA YAMATO

A COORDINATOR WHOSE PARENTS ARE NATURALS. FLEEING THE RAVAGES OF WAR HE TOOK REFUGE IN HELIOPOLIS, AND LATER JOINED THE CREW OF THE ARCHANGEL.

ATHRUN ZALA

A COORDINATOR WHO WAS KIRA'S BEST FRIEND AT THE LUNAR PREPARATORY SCHOOL. AN ELITE ZAFT PILOT. HIS FATHER IS THE ZAFT'S SUPREME COUNCIL CHAIRMAN.

CONTENTS

PHASE-21 THE DAWN SKY

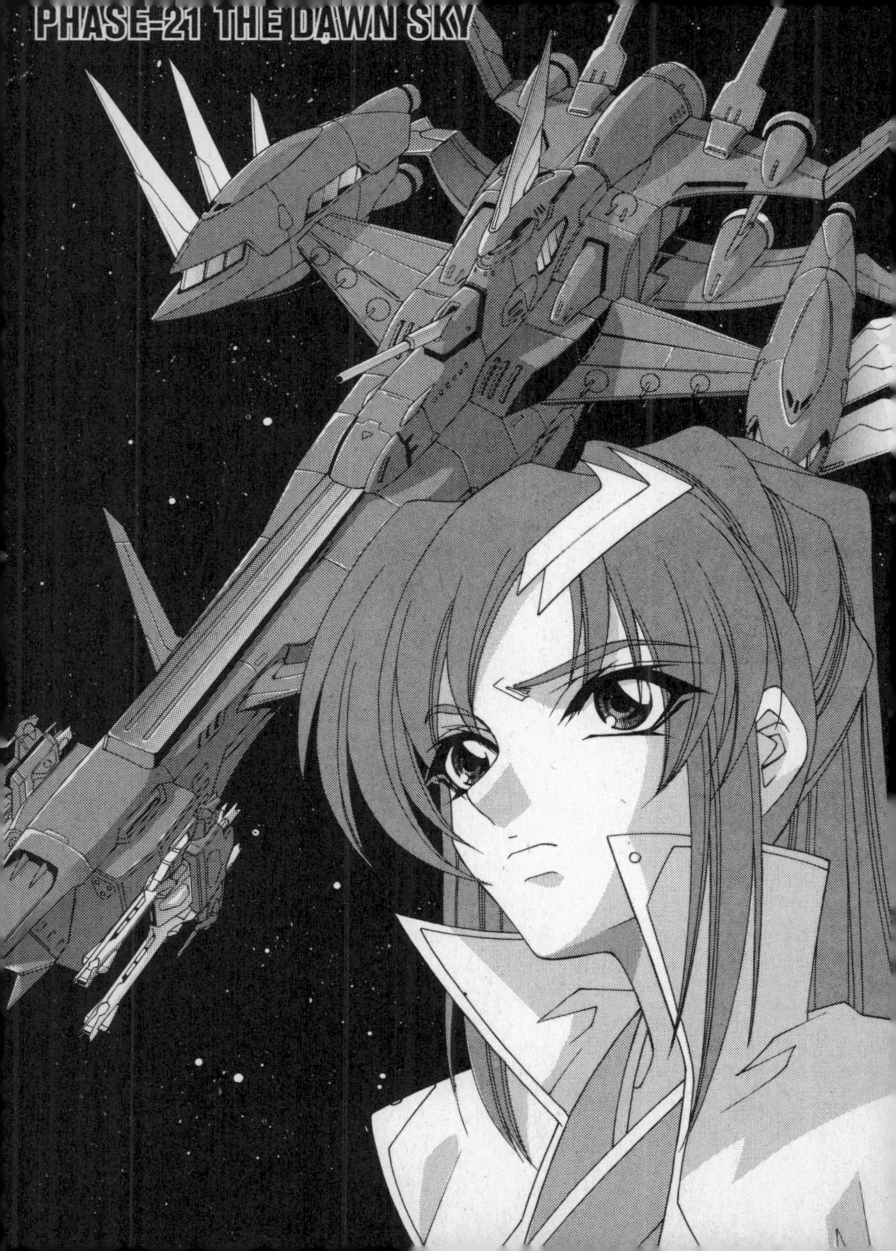

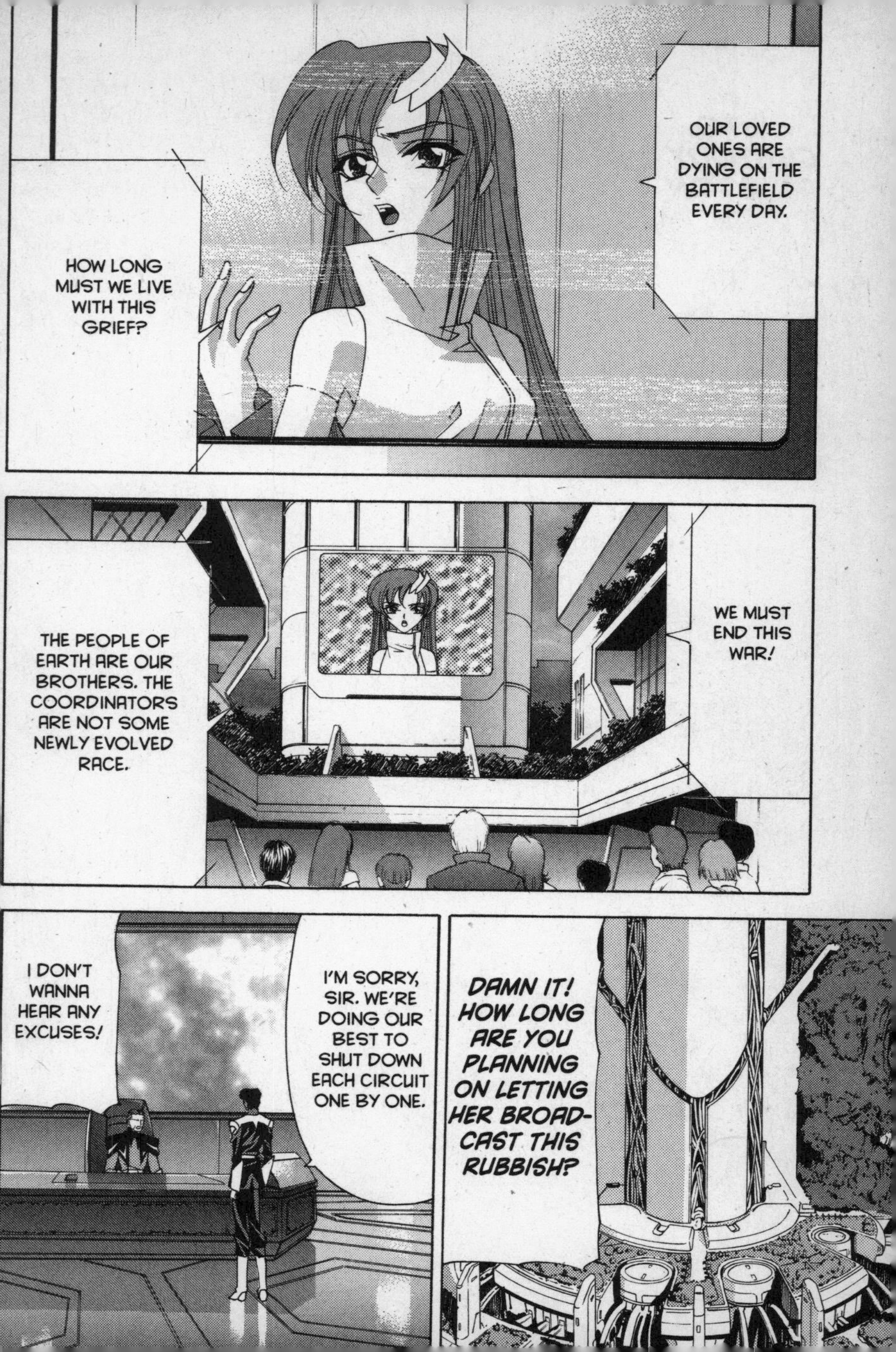
OUR LOVED ONES ARE DYING ON THE BATTLEFIELD EVERY DAY.
HOW LONG MUST WE LIVE WITH THIS GRIEF?
WE MUST END THIS WAR!
THE PEOPLE OF EARTH ARE OUR BROTHERS. THE COORDINATORS ARE NOT SOME NEWLY EVOLVED RACE.
DAMN IT! HOW LONG ARE YOU PLANNING ON LETTING HER BROAD-CAST THIS RUBBISH?
I'M SORRY, SIR. WE'RE DOING OUR BEST TO SHUT DOWN EACH CIRCUIT ONE BY ONE.
I DON'T WANNA HEAR ANY EXCUSES!

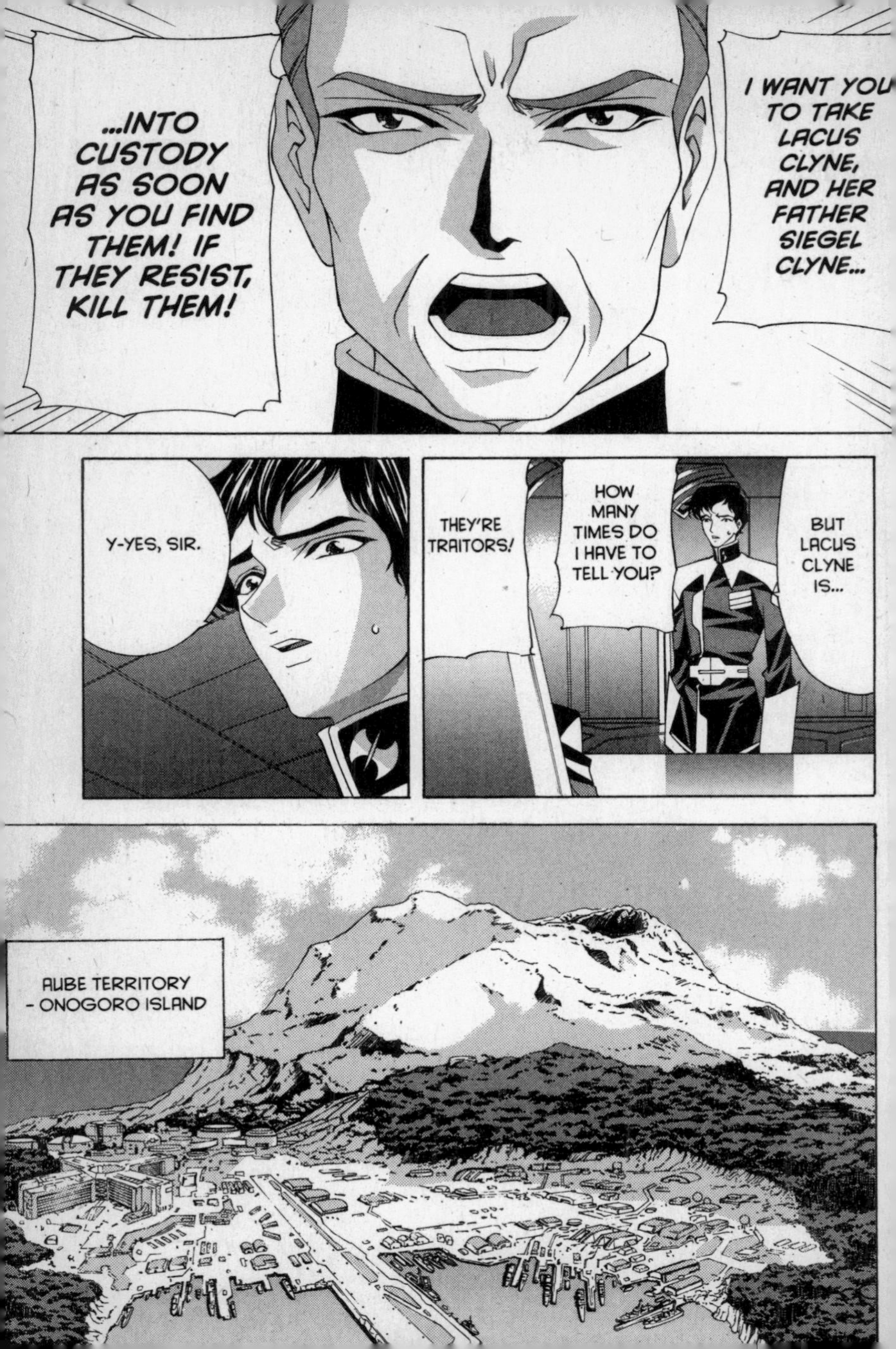
I WANT YOU TO TAKE LACUS CLYNE, AND HER FATHER SIEGEL CLYNE...
...INTO CUSTODY AS SOON AS YOU FIND THEM! IF THEY RESIST, KILL THEM!
BUT LACUS CLYNE IS...
HOW MANY TIMES DO I HAVE TO TELL YOU?
THEY'RE TRAITORS!
Y-YES, SIR.
AUBE TERRITORY - ONOGORO ISLAND

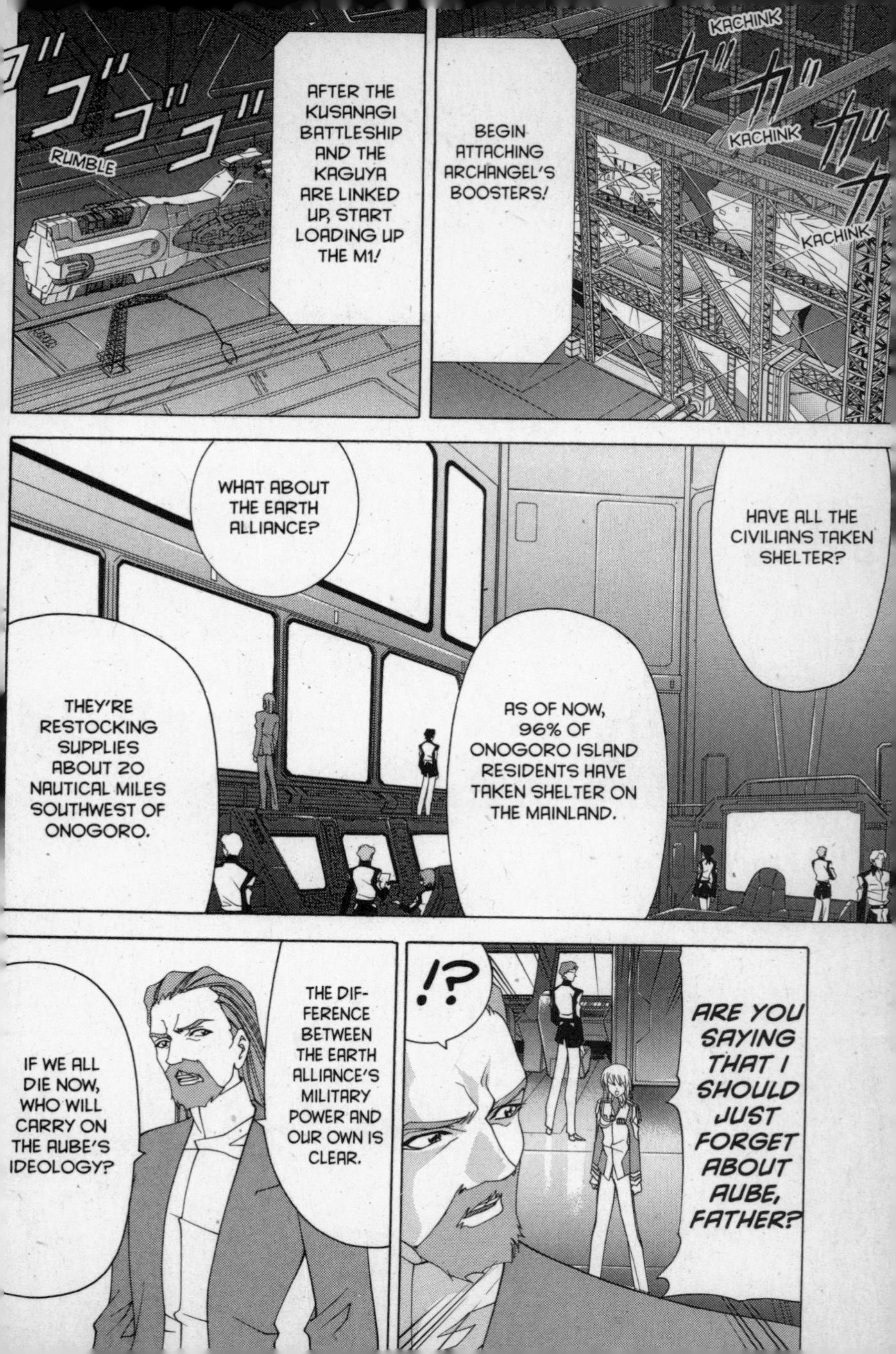
KACHINK
BEGIN ATTACHING ARCHANGEL'S BOOSTERS!
KACHINK
KACHINK
AFTER THE KUSANAGI BATTLESHIP AND THE KAGUYA ARE LINKED UP, START LOADING UP THE M1!
RUMBLE
HAVE ALL THE CIVILIANS TAKEN SHELTER?
AS OF NOW, 96% OF ONOGORO ISLAND RESIDENTS HAVE TAKEN SHELTER ON THE MAINLAND.
WHAT ABOUT THE EARTH ALLIANCE?
THEY'RE RESTOCKING SUPPLIES ABOUT 20 NAUTICAL MILES SOUTHWEST OF ONOGORO.
ARE YOU SAYING THAT I SHOULD JUST FORGET ABOUT AUBE, FATHER?
!?
THE DIF-FERENCE BETWEEN THE EARTH ALLIANCE'S MILITARY POWER AND OUR OWN IS CLEAR.
IF WE ALL DIE NOW, WHO WILL CARRY ON THE AUBE'S IDEOLOGY?

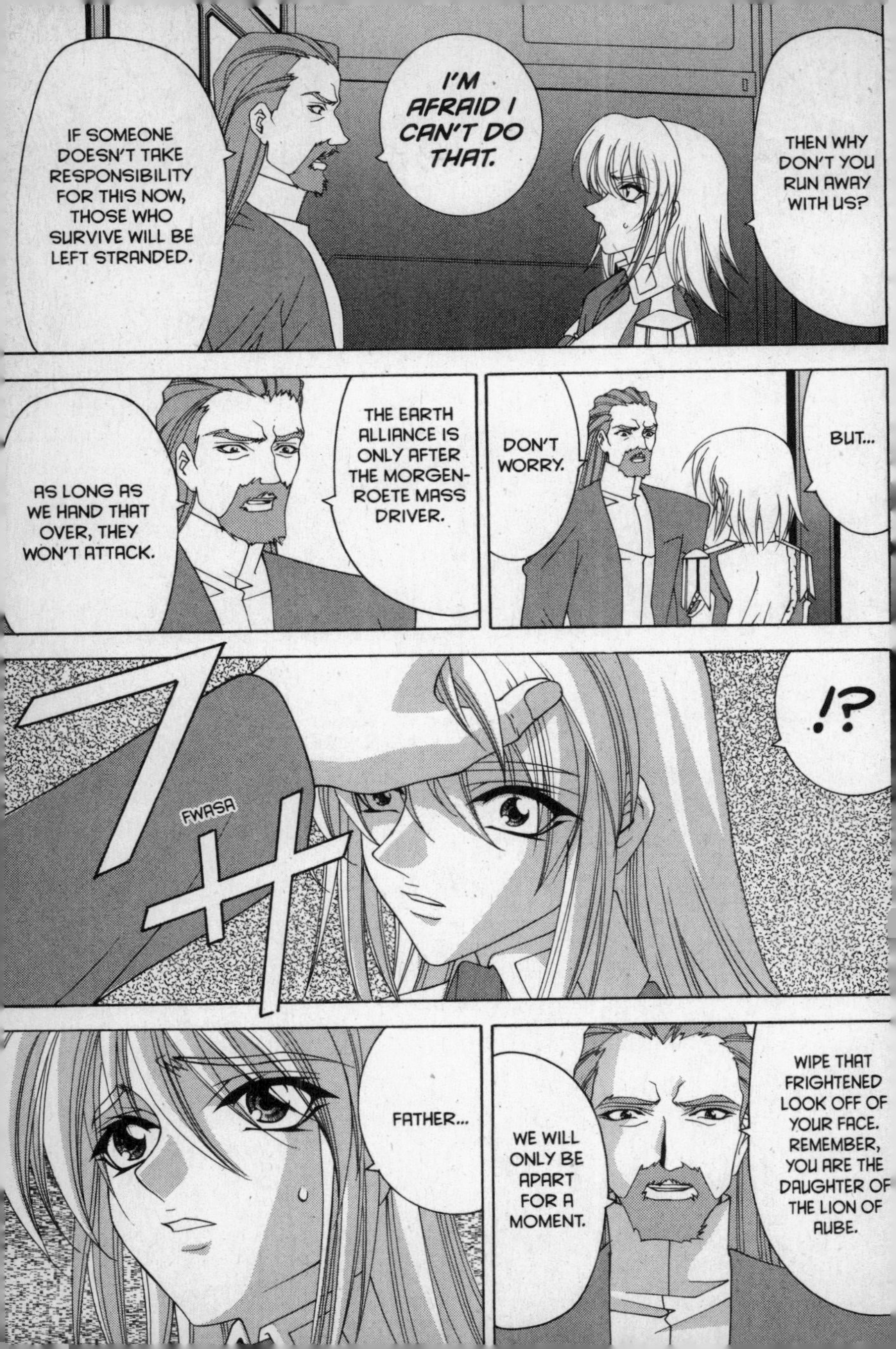
THEN WHY DON'T YOU RUN AWAY WITH US?
I'M AFRAID I CAN'T DO THAT.
IF SOMEONE DOESN'T TAKE RESPONSIBILITY FOR THIS NOW, THOSE WHO SURVIVE WILL BE LEFT STRANDED.
BUT...
DON'T WORRY.
THE EARTH ALLIANCE IS ONLY AFTER THE MORGEN-ROETE MASS DRIVER.
AS LONG AS WE HAND THAT OVER, THEY WON'T ATTACK.
!?
FWASA
WIPE THAT FRIGHTENED LOOK OFF OF YOUR FACE. REMEMBER, YOU ARE THE DAUGHTER OF THE LION OF AUBE.
WE WILL ONLY BE APART FOR A MOMENT.
FATHER...

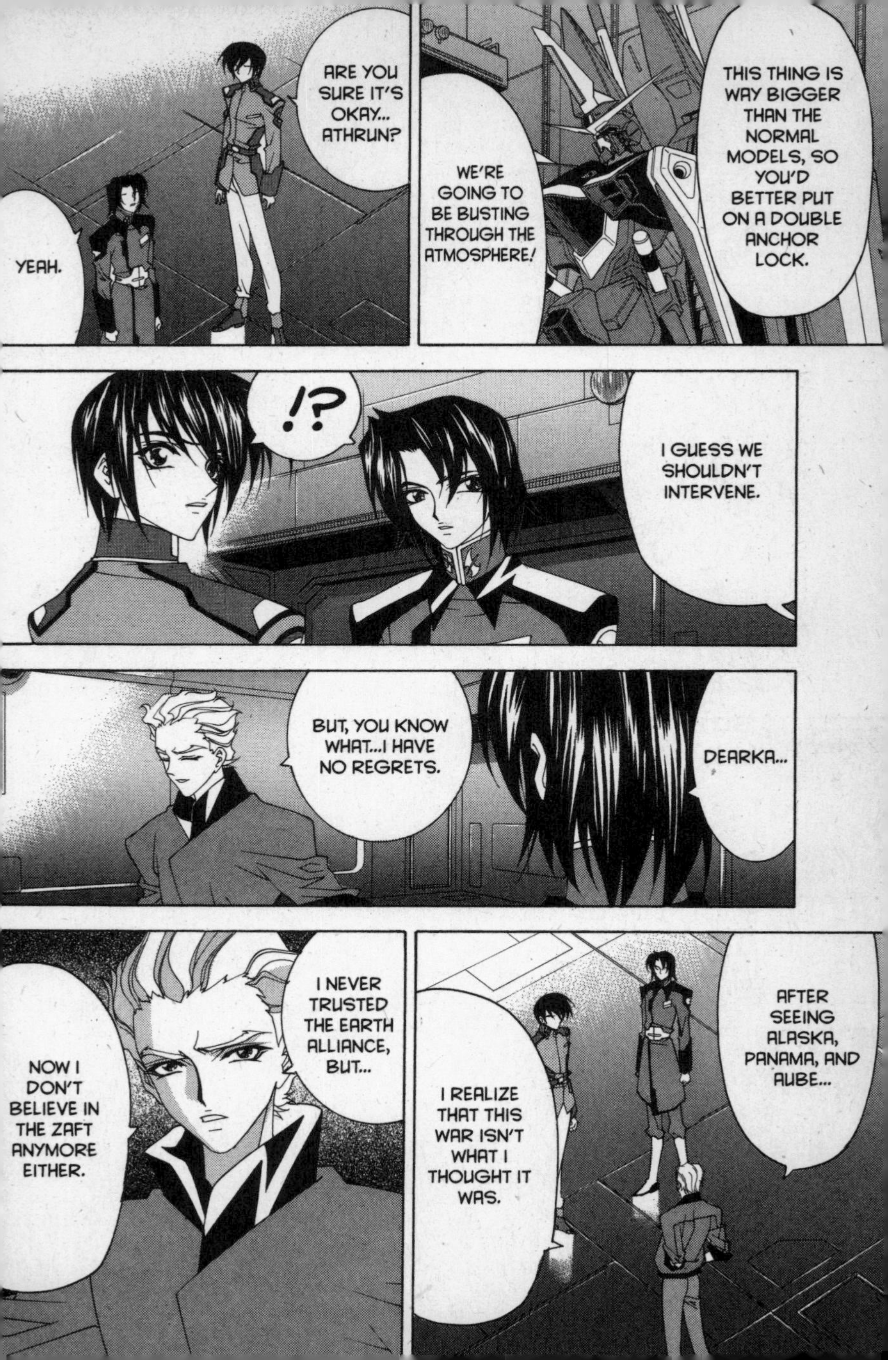

THIS THING IS WAY BIGGER THAN THE NORMAL MODELS, SO YOU'D BETTER PUT ON A DOUBLE ANCHOR LOCK.
WE'RE GOING TO BE BUSTING THROUGH THE ATMOSPHERE!
ARE YOU SURE IT'S OKAY... ATHRUN?
YEAH.
I GUESS WE SHOULDN'T INTERVENE.
!?
DEARKA...
BUT, YOU KNOW WHAT...I HAVE NO REGRETS.
AFTER SEEING ALASKA, PANAMA, AND AUBE...
I REALIZE THAT THIS WAR ISN'T WHAT I THOUGHT IT WAS.
I NEVER TRUSTED THE EARTH ALLIANCE, BUT...
NOW I DON'T BELIEVE IN THE ZAFT ANYMORE EITHER.

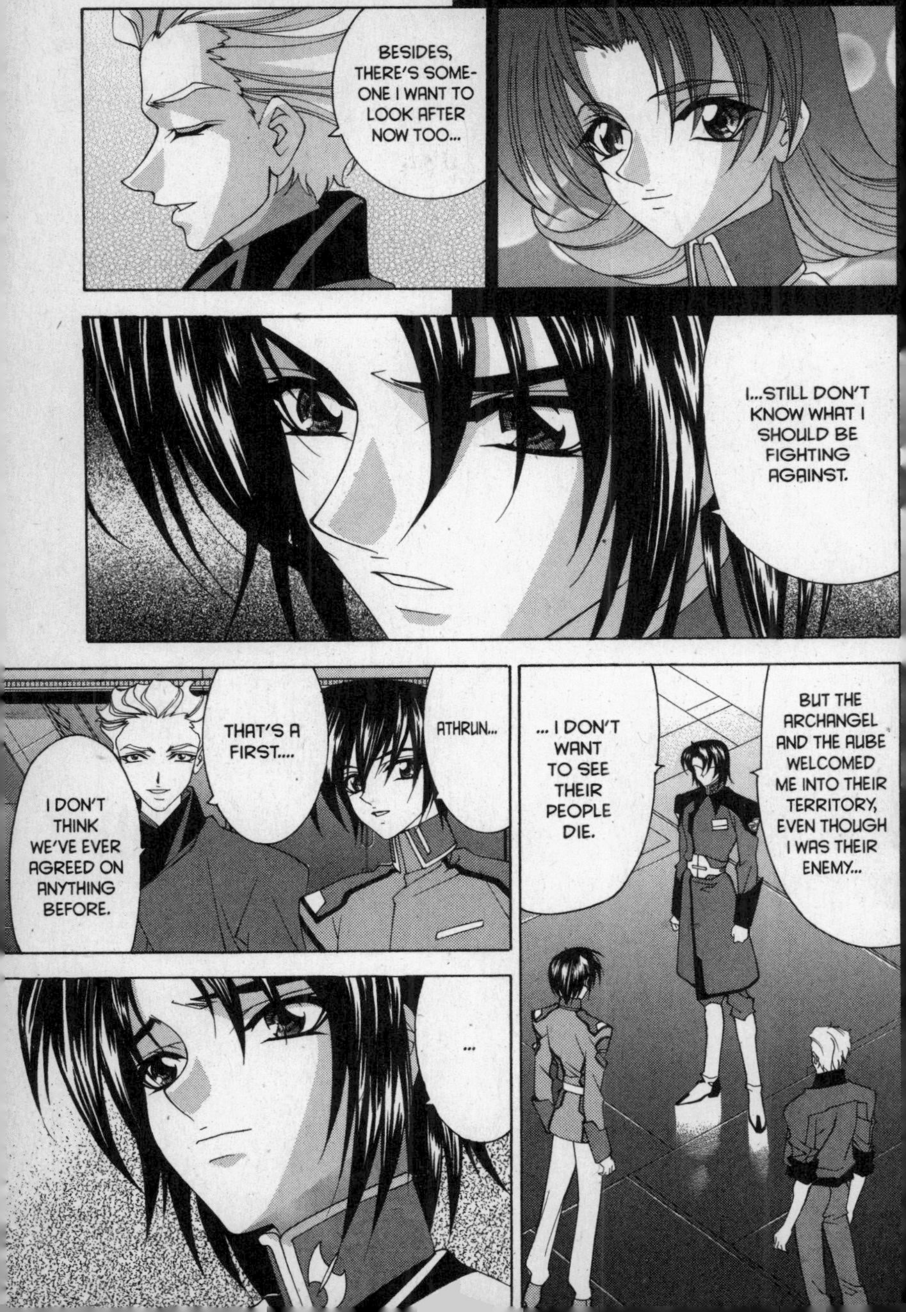
BESIDES, THERE'S SOME-ONE I WANT TO LOOK AFTER NOW TOO...
I...STILL DON'T KNOW WHAT I SHOULD BE FIGHTING AGAINST.
BUT THE ARCHANGEL AND THE AUBE WELCOMED ME INTO THEIR TERRITORY, EVEN THOUGH I WAS THEIR ENEMY...
... I DON'T WANT TO SEE THEIR PEOPLE DIE.
ATHRUN...
THAT'S A FIRST....
I DON'T THINK WE'VE EVER AGREED ON ANYTHING BEFORE.
...

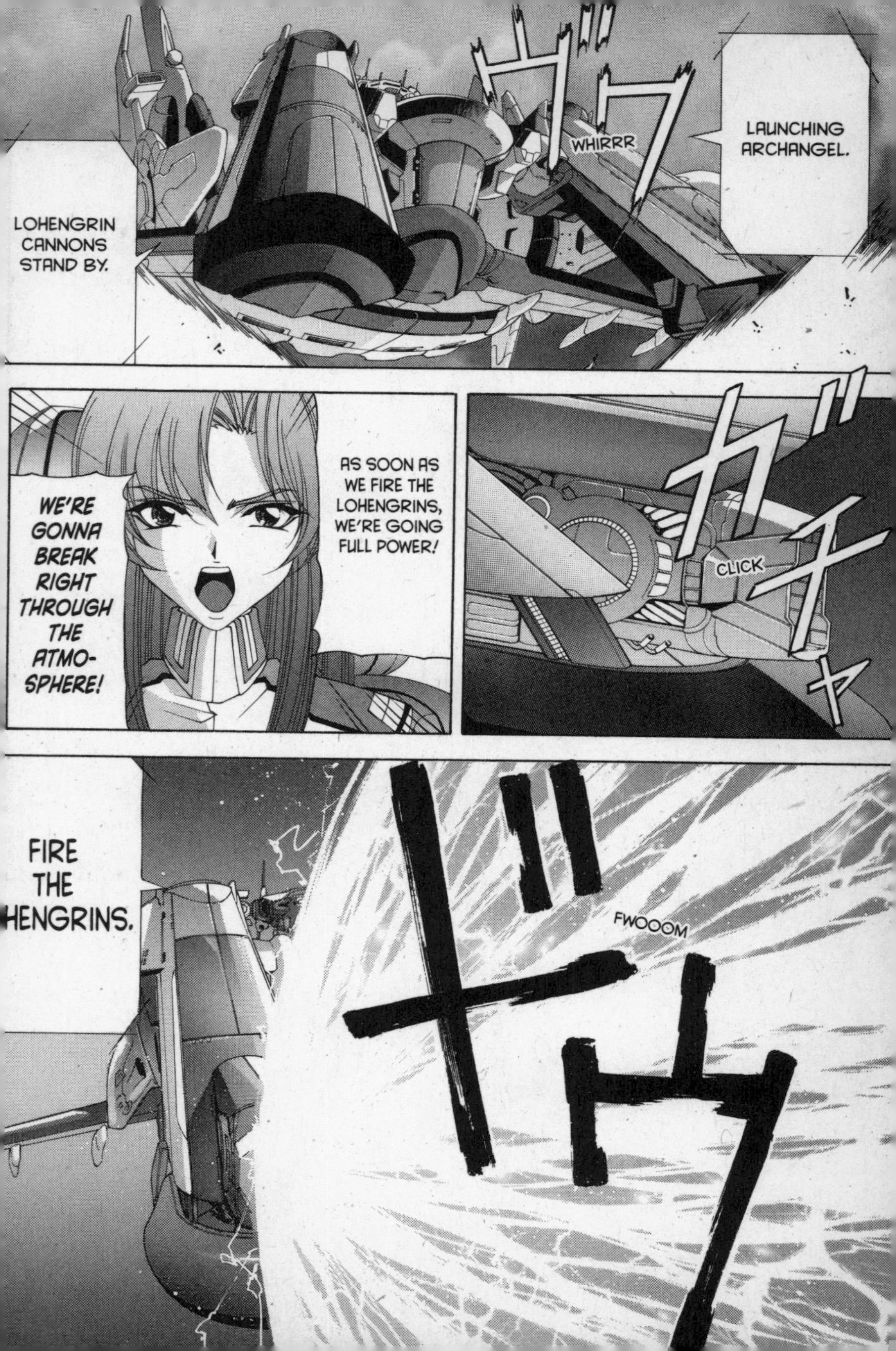

LAUNCHING ARCHANGEL.
WHIRRR
LOHENGRIN CANNONS STAND BY.
CLICK
AS SOON AS WE FIRE THE LOHENGRINS, WE'RE GOING FULL POWER!
WE'RE GONNA BREAK RIGHT THROUGH THE ATMOSPHERE!
FIRE THE
HENGRINS.
FWOOOM

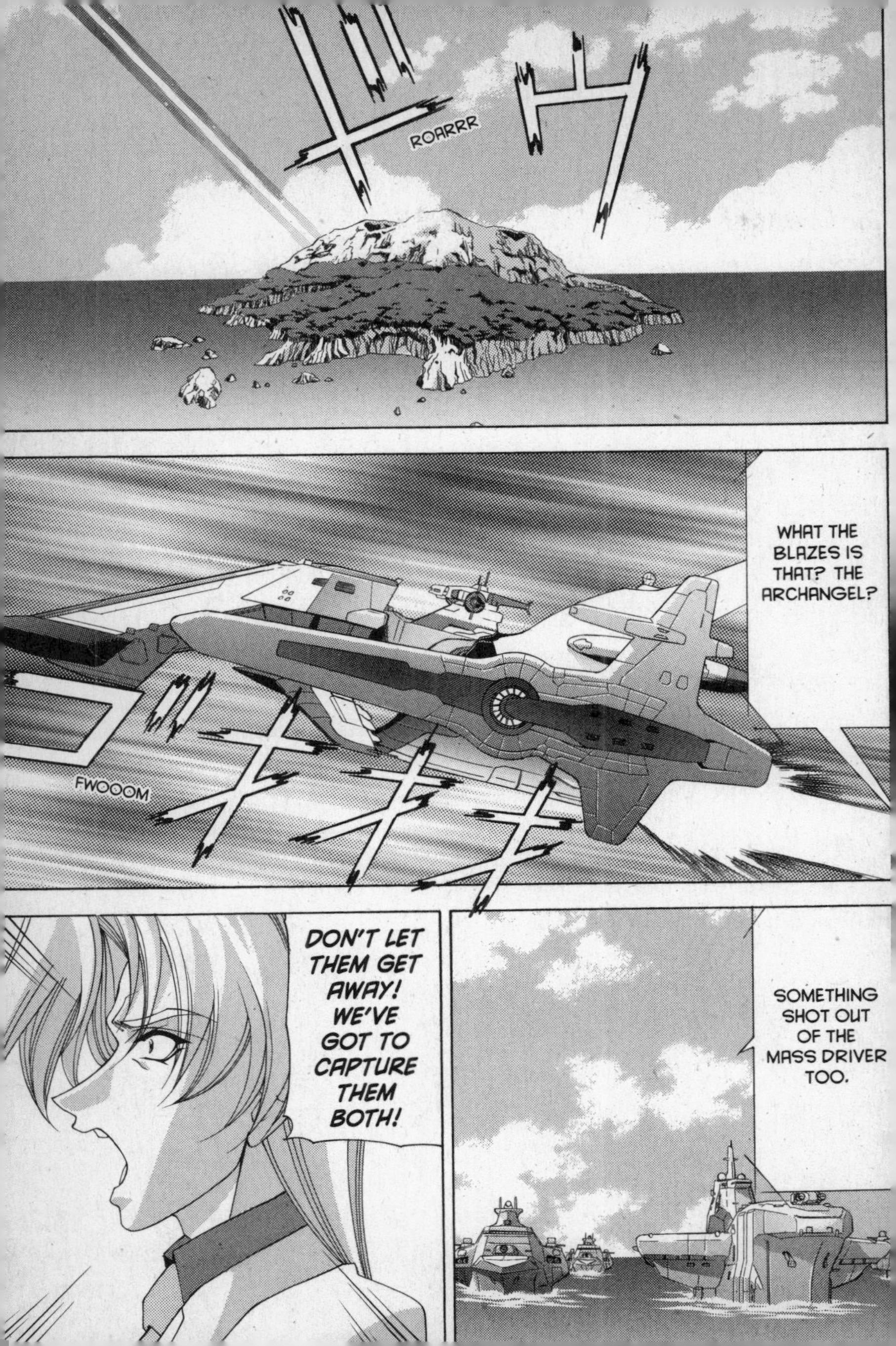
ROARRR
WHAT THE BLAZES IS THAT? THE ARCHANGEL?
FWOOOM
SOMETHING SHOT OUT OF THE MASS DRIVER TOO.
DON'T LET THEM GET AWAY! WE'VE GOT TO CAPTURE THEM BOTH!

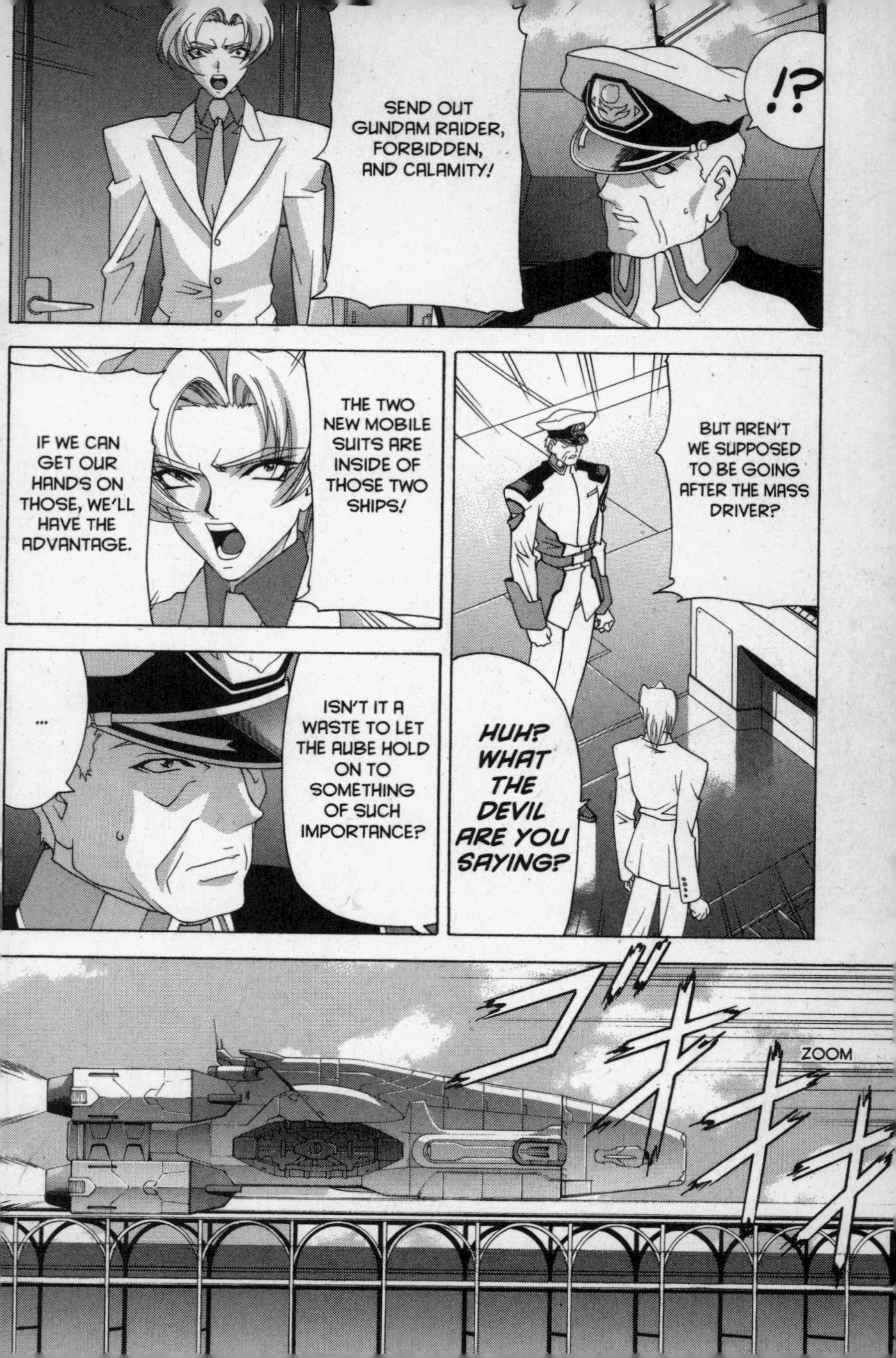
SEND OUT GUNDAM RAIDER, FORBIDDEN, AND CALAMITY!
!?
BUT AREN'T WE SUPPOSED TO BE GOING AFTER THE MASS DRIVER?
THE TWO NEW MOBILE SUITS ARE INSIDE OF THOSE TWO SHIPS!
IF WE CAN GET OUR HANDS ON THOSE, WE'LL HAVE THE ADVANTAGE.
HUH? WHAT THE DEVIL ARE YOU SAYING?
ISN'T IT A WASTE TO LET THE AUBE HOLD ON TO SOMETHING OF SUCH IMPORTANCE?
...
ZOOM

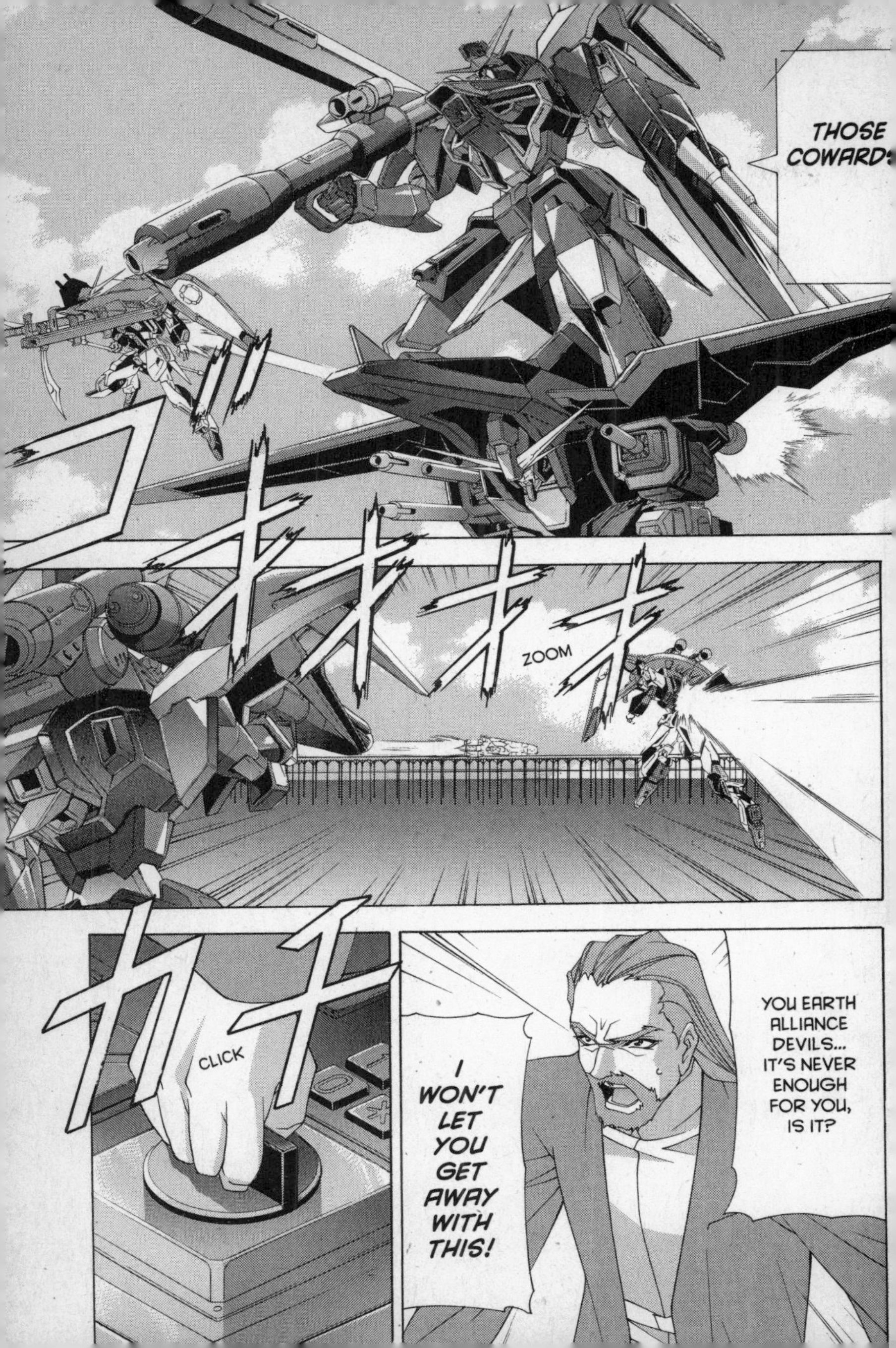
THOSE COWARDS
ZOOM
YOU EARTH ALLIANCE DEVILS... IT'S NEVER ENOUGH FOR YOU, IS IT?
I WON'T LET YOU GET AWAY WITH THIS!
CLICK

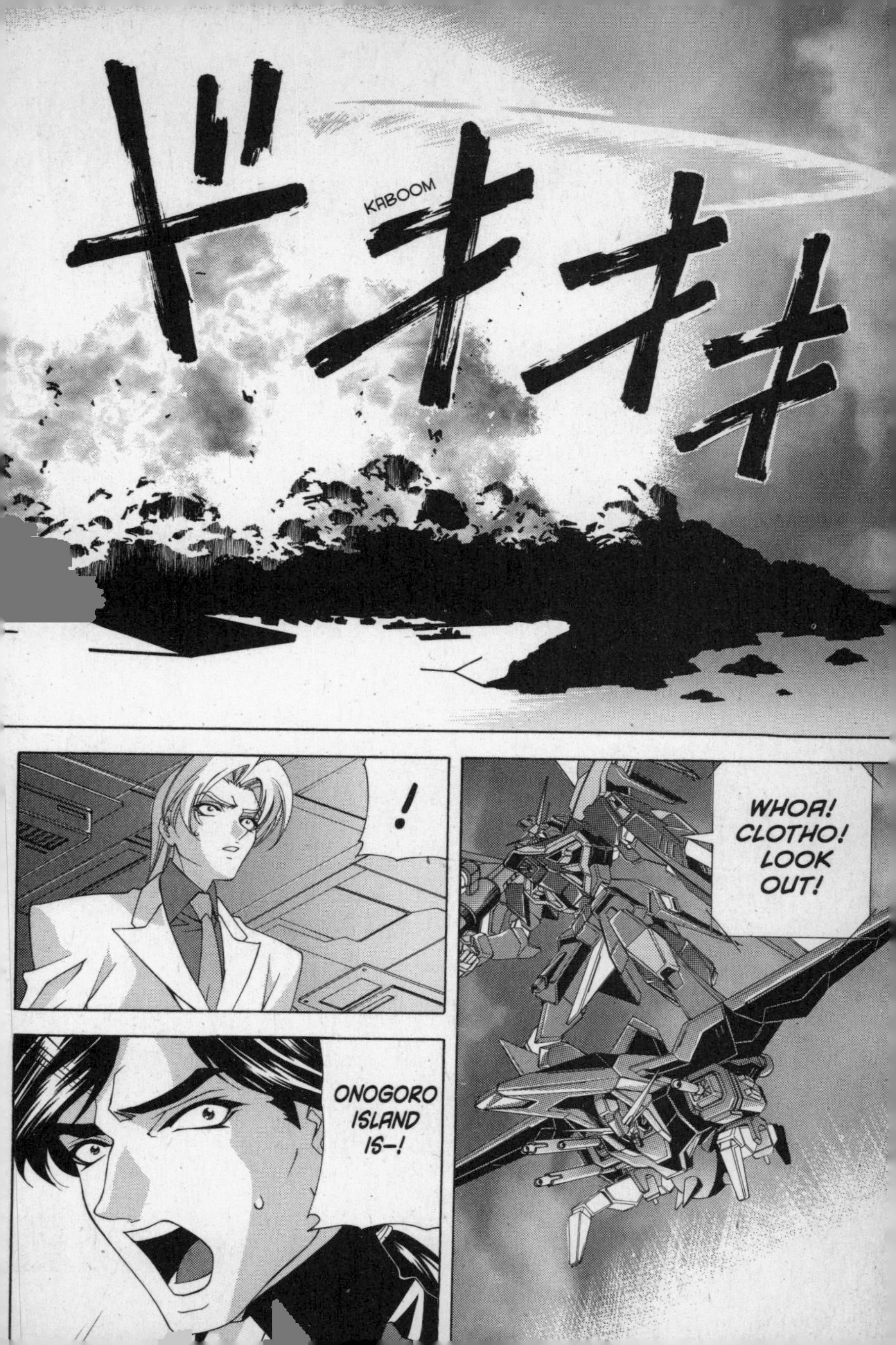
ザオオォ
KABOOM
WHOA! CLOTHO! LOOK OUT!
!
ONOGORO ISLAND IS-!

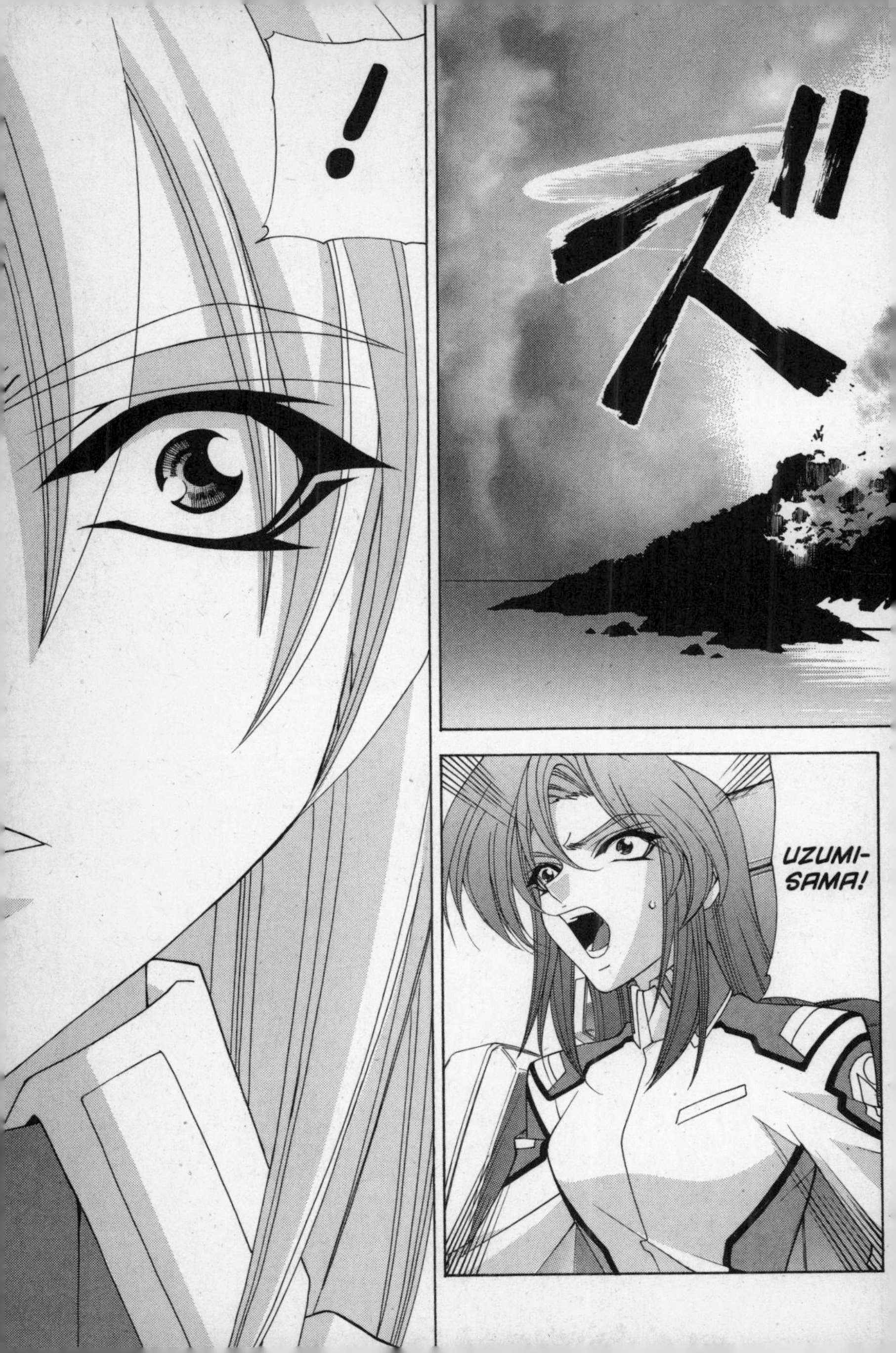
ズ
UZUMI-SAMA!
!

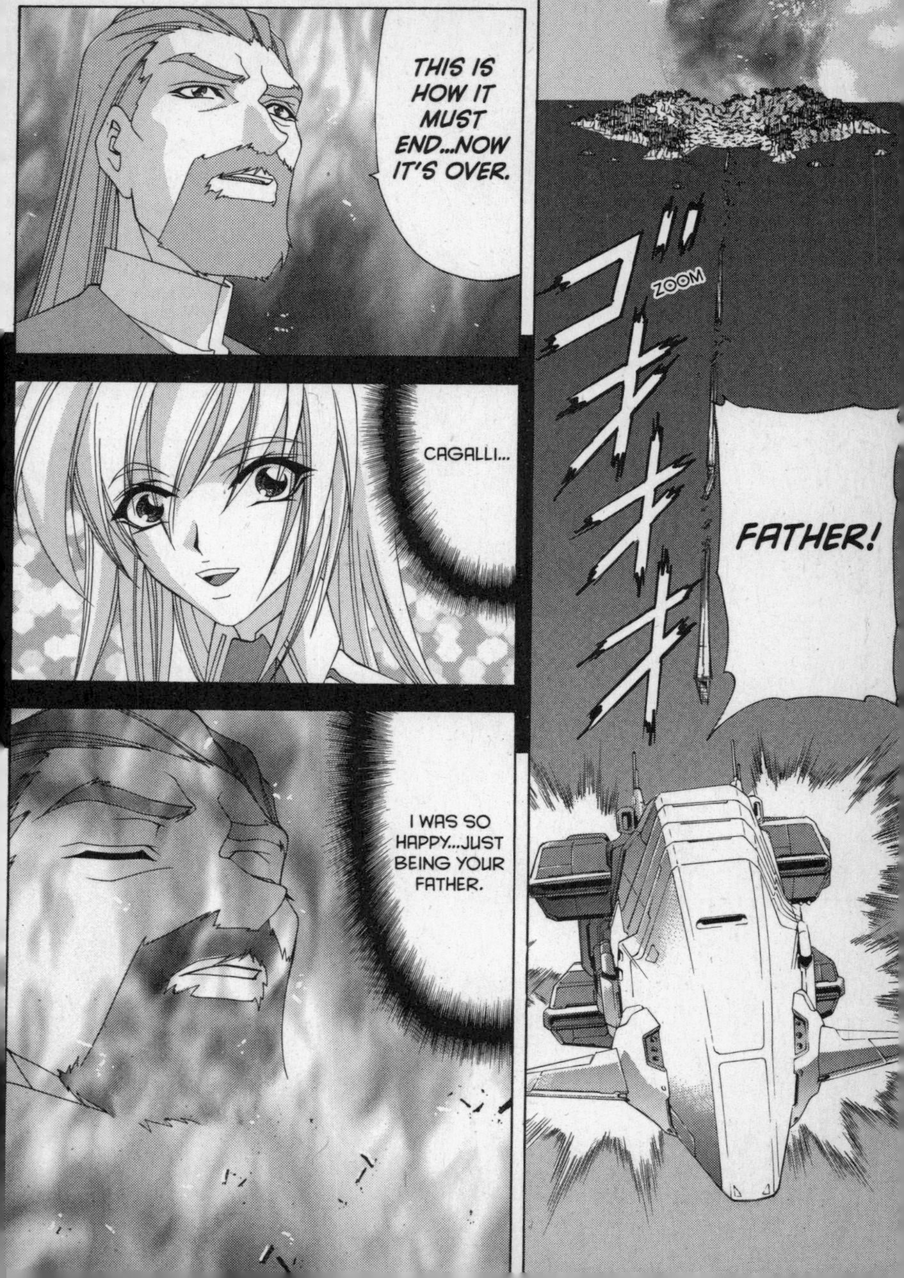
ゴォォォ
ZOOM
FATHER!
THIS IS HOW IT MUST END...NOW IT'S OVER.
CAGALLI...
I WAS SO HAPPY...JUST BEING YOUR FATHER.

ROAR

YOU...
NARA
ATHHA
UZUMI...

I'LL NEVER
GIVE UP.

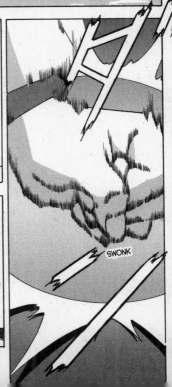

SWONK

HMMPH!

CONTACT
GENERAL
SUTHERLAND!
WHAT'S
GOING ON
IN VICTORIA?

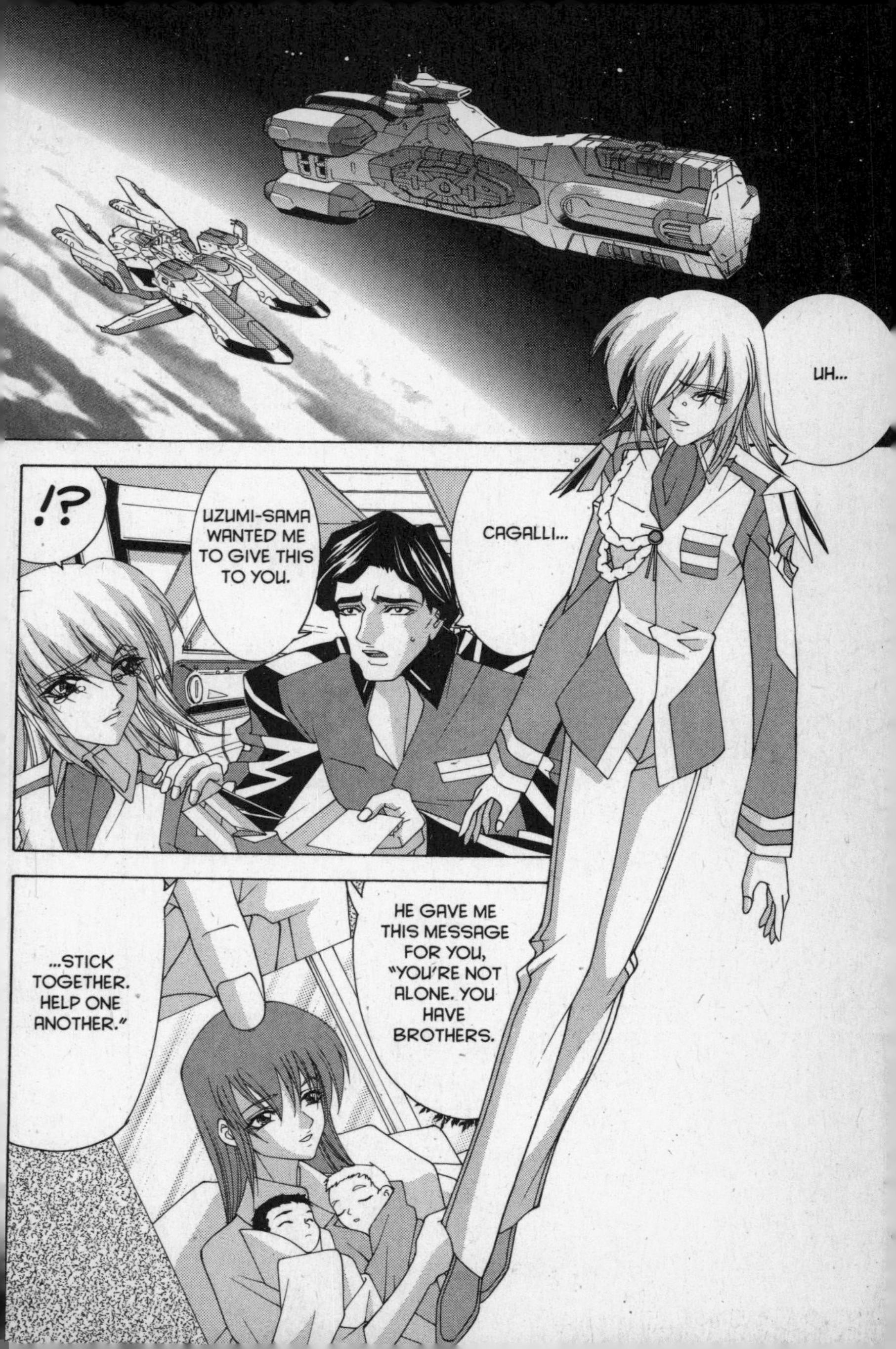
UH...
CAGALLI...
UZUMI-SAMA WANTED ME TO GIVE THIS TO YOU.
!?
HE GAVE ME THIS MESSAGE FOR YOU, "YOU'RE NOT ALONE. YOU HAVE BROTHERS.
...STICK TOGETHER. HELP ONE ANOTHER."

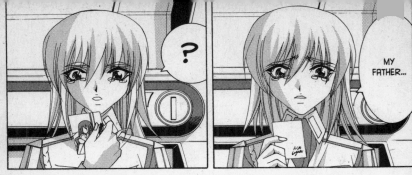

MY FATHER...
?
!?
Kira Cagalli
WHA- WHAT THE--?
WE CAN'T USE THE KUSANAGI BATTLESHIP UNTIL WE GET IT COMPLETELY LINKED UP.
LAUNCH ALL MOBILE SUITS IMMEDIATELY, AND PUT THEM ON THE LOOKOUT!

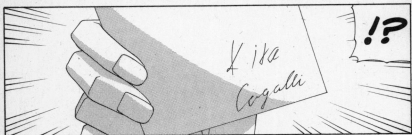

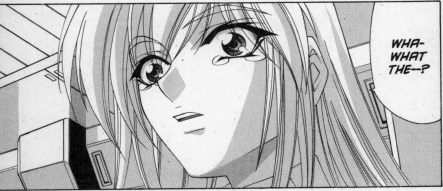

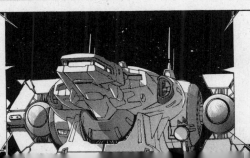

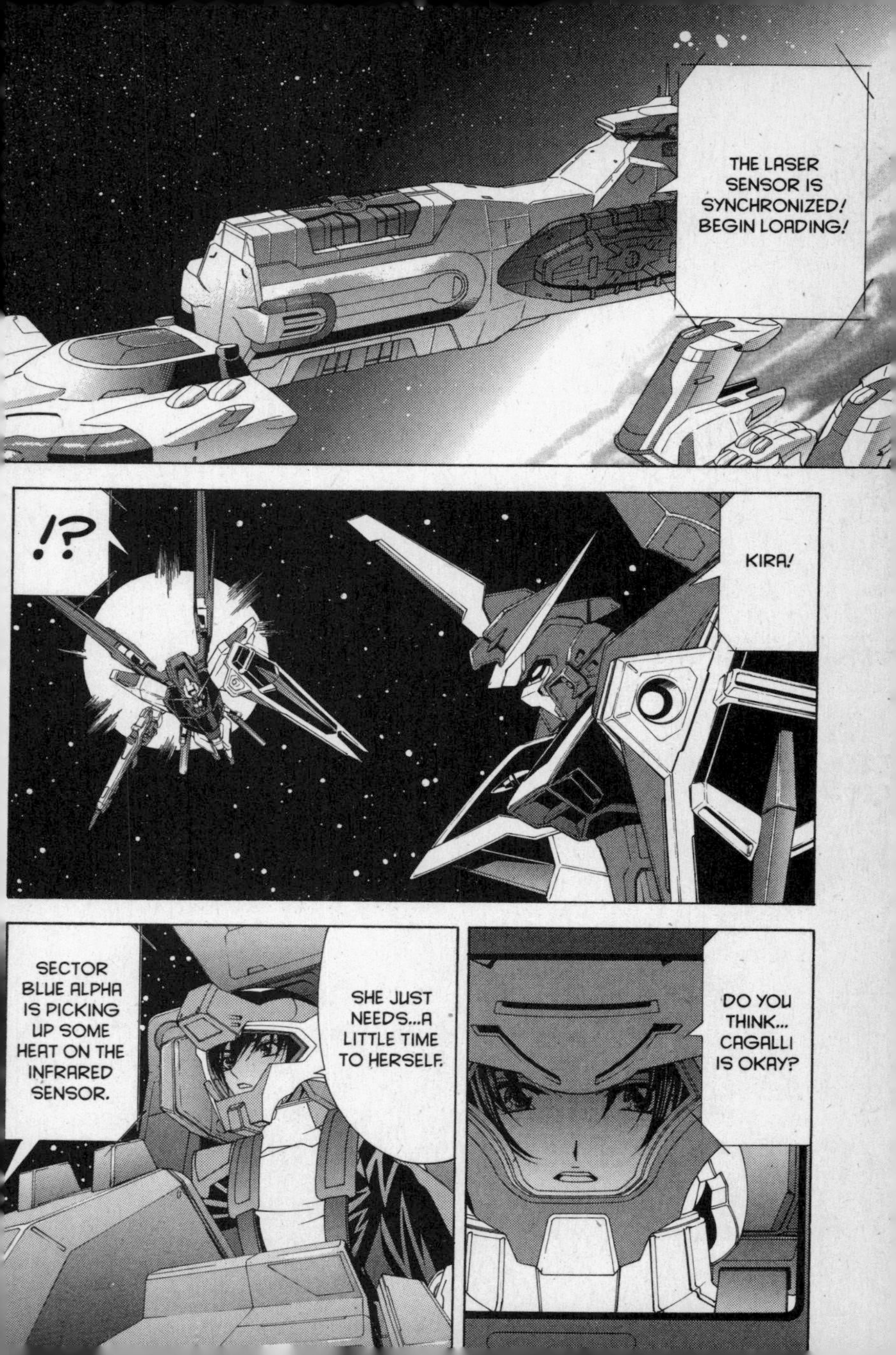
THE LASER SENSOR IS SYNCHRONIZED! BEGIN LOADING!
KIRA!
!?
DO YOU THINK... CAGALLI IS OKAY?
SHE JUST NEEDS...A LITTLE TIME TO HERSELF.
SECTOR BLUE ALPHA IS PICKING UP SOME HEAT ON THE INFRARED SENSOR.

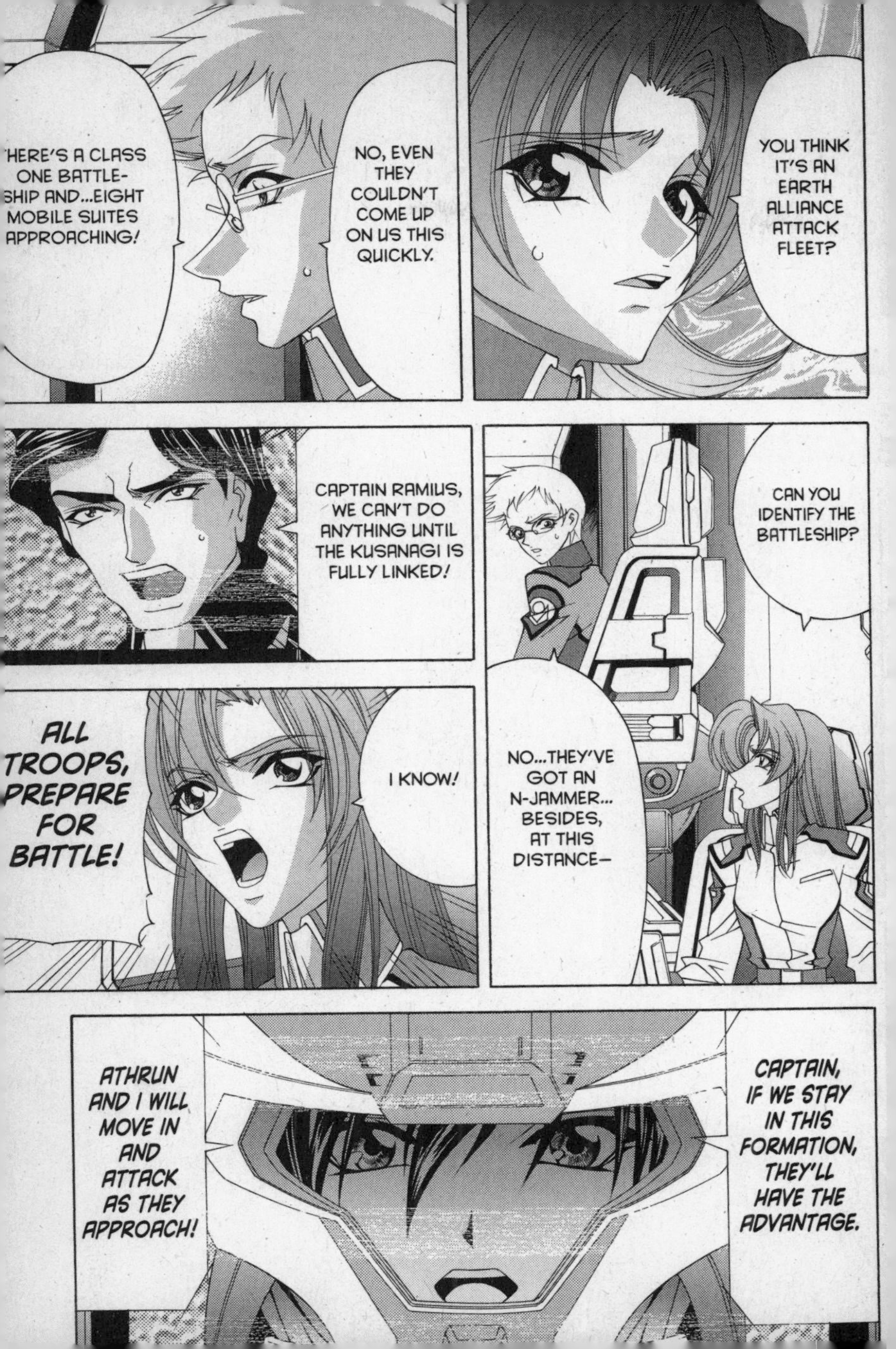
YOU THINK IT'S AN EARTH ALLIANCE ATTACK FLEET?
NO, EVEN THEY COULDN'T COME UP ON US THIS QUICKLY.
THERE'S A CLASS ONE BATTLE-SHIP AND...EIGHT MOBILE SUITES APPROACHING!
CAN YOU IDENTIFY THE BATTLESHIP?
NO...THEY'VE GOT AN N-JAMMER... BESIDES, AT THIS DISTANCE–
CAPTAIN RAMIUS, WE CAN'T DO ANYTHING UNTIL THE KUSANAGI IS FULLY LINKED!
I KNOW!
ALL TROOPS, PREPARE FOR BATTLE!
CAPTAIN, IF WE STAY IN THIS FORMATION, THEY'LL HAVE THE ADVANTAGE.
ATHRUN AND I WILL MOVE IN AND ATTACK AS THEY APPROACH!

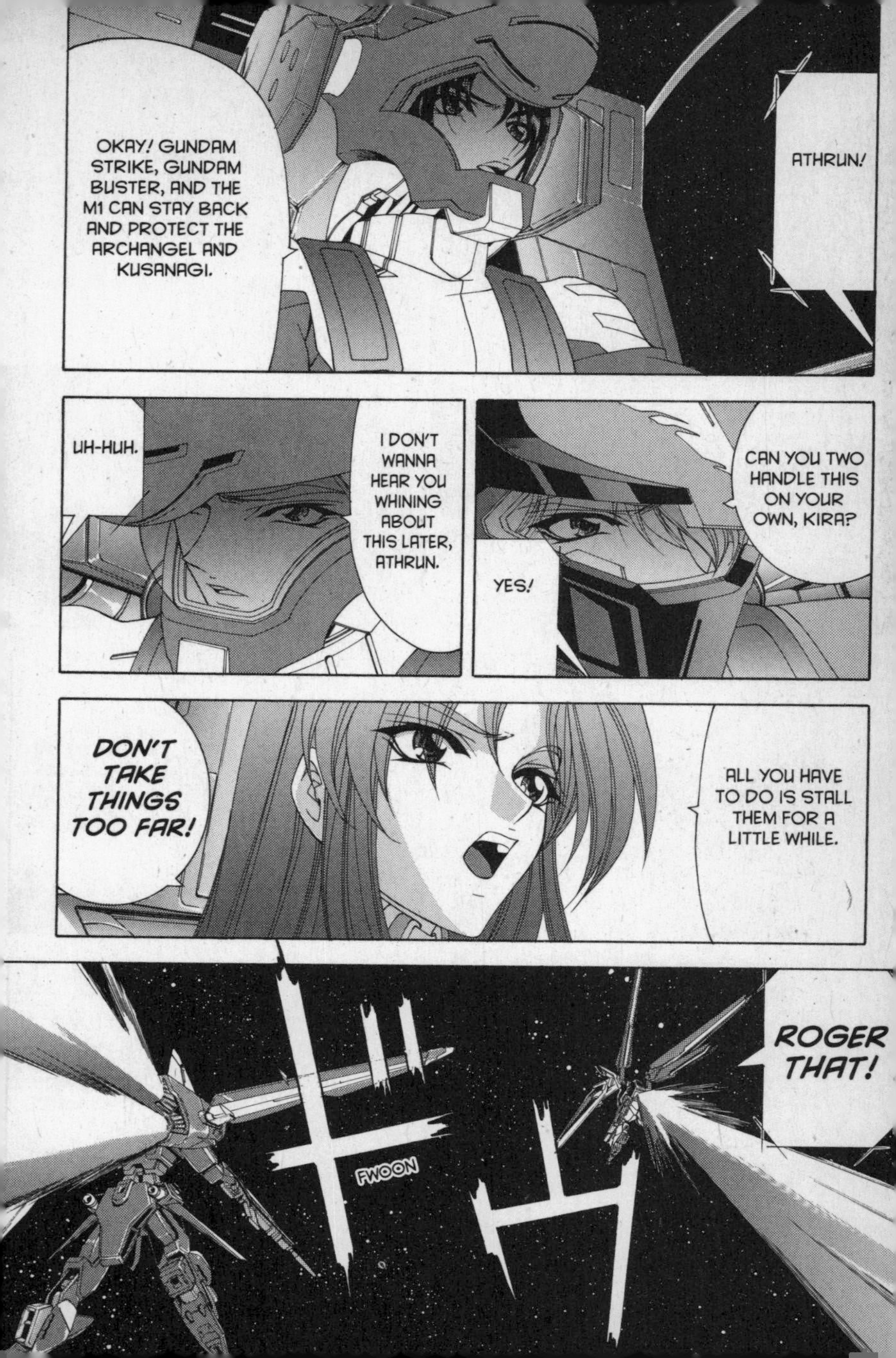
ATHRUN!
OKAY! GUNDAM STRIKE, GUNDAM BUSTER, AND THE M1 CAN STAY BACK AND PROTECT THE ARCHANGEL AND KUSANAGI.
CAN YOU TWO HANDLE THIS ON YOUR OWN, KIRA?
YES!
I DON'T WANNA HEAR YOU WHINING ABOUT THIS LATER, ATHRUN.
UH-HUH.
ALL YOU HAVE TO DO IS STALL THEM FOR A LITTLE WHILE.
DON'T TAKE THINGS TOO FAR!
ROGER THAT!
FWOON

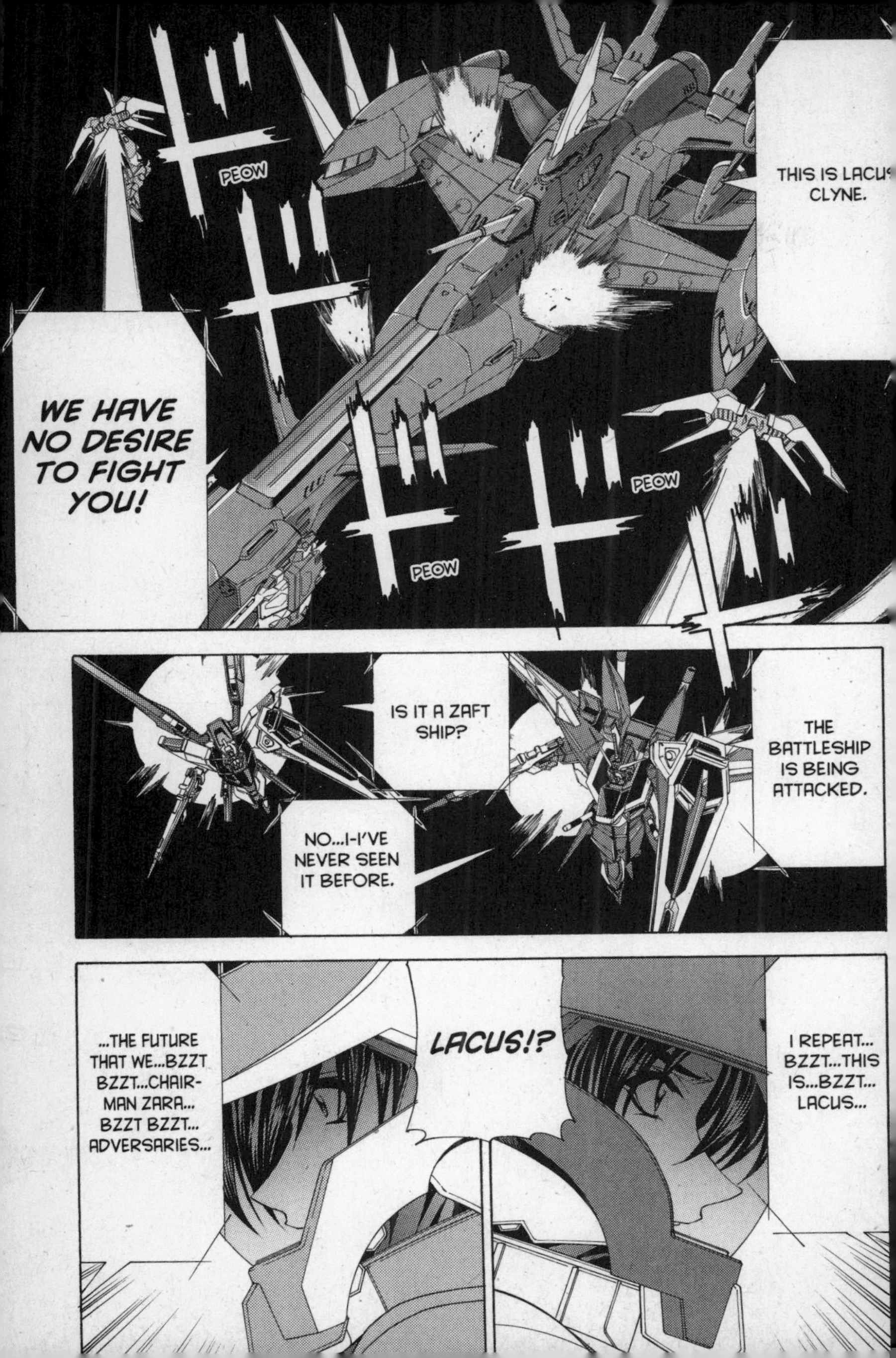
THIS IS LACUS CLYNE.
PEOW
PEOW
PEOW
WE HAVE NO DESIRE TO FIGHT YOU!
THE BATTLESHIP IS BEING ATTACKED.
IS IT A ZAFT SHIP?
NO...I-I'VE NEVER SEEN IT BEFORE.
I REPEAT... BZZT...THIS IS...BZZT... LACUS...
LACUS!?
...THE FUTURE THAT WE...BZZT BZZT...CHAIR-MAN ZARA... BZZT BZZT... ADVERSARIES...

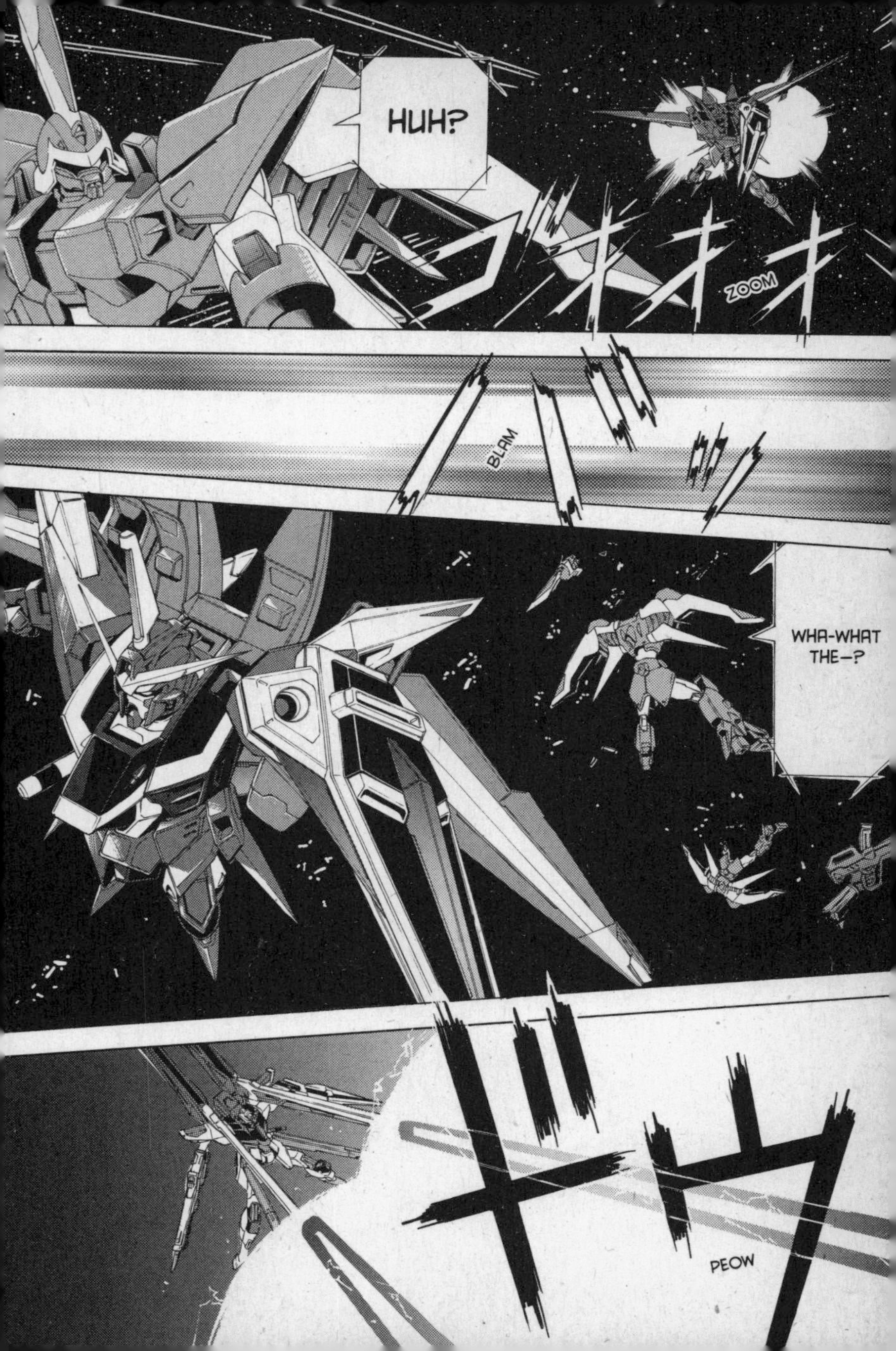
HUH?
ZOOM
BLAM
WHA-WHAT THE—?
PEOW

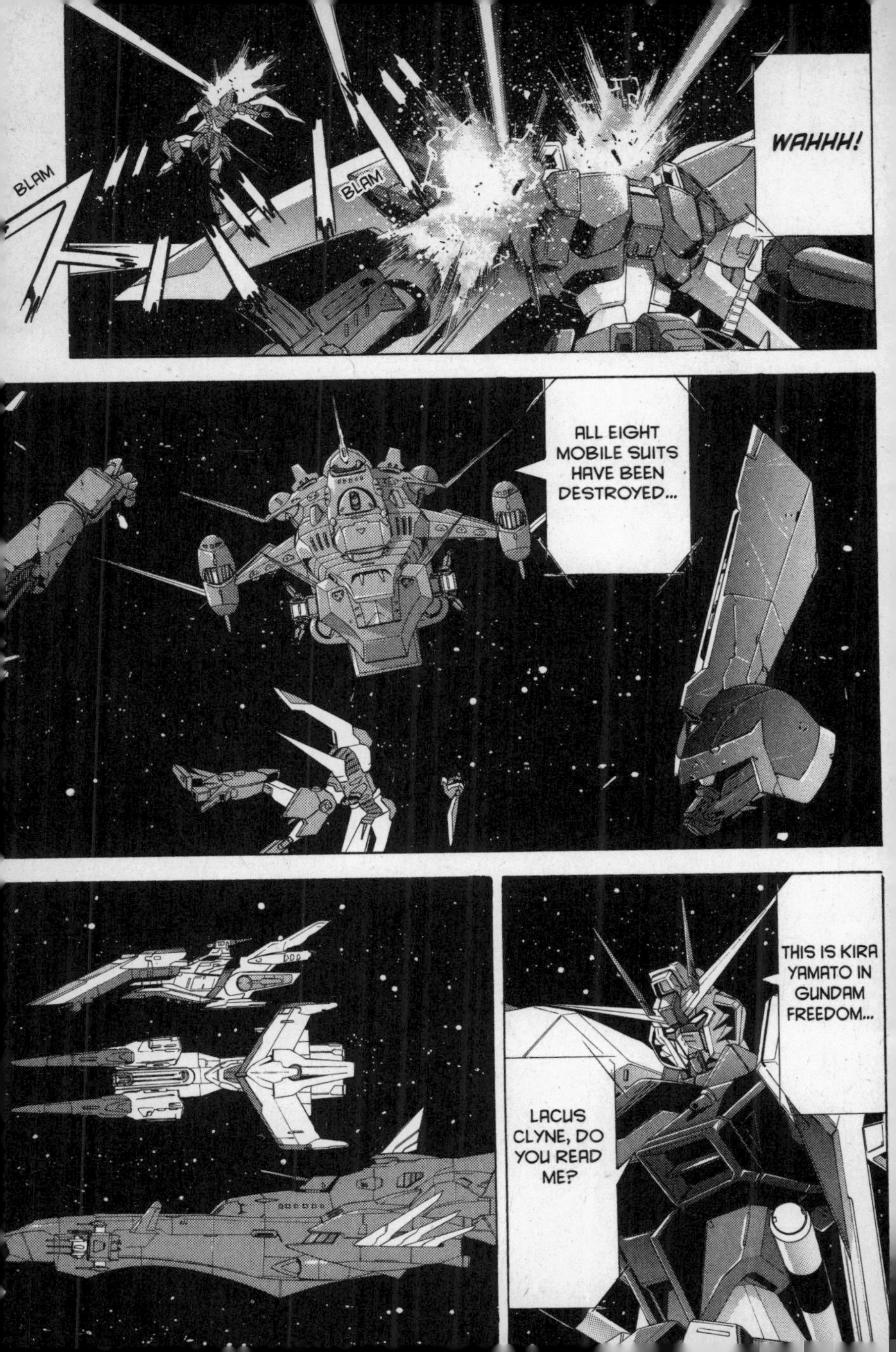
WAHHH!
BLAM
BLAM
ALL EIGHT MOBILE SUITS HAVE BEEN DESTROYED...
THIS IS KIRA YAMATO IN GUNDAM FREEDOM...
LACUS CLYNE, DO YOU READ ME?

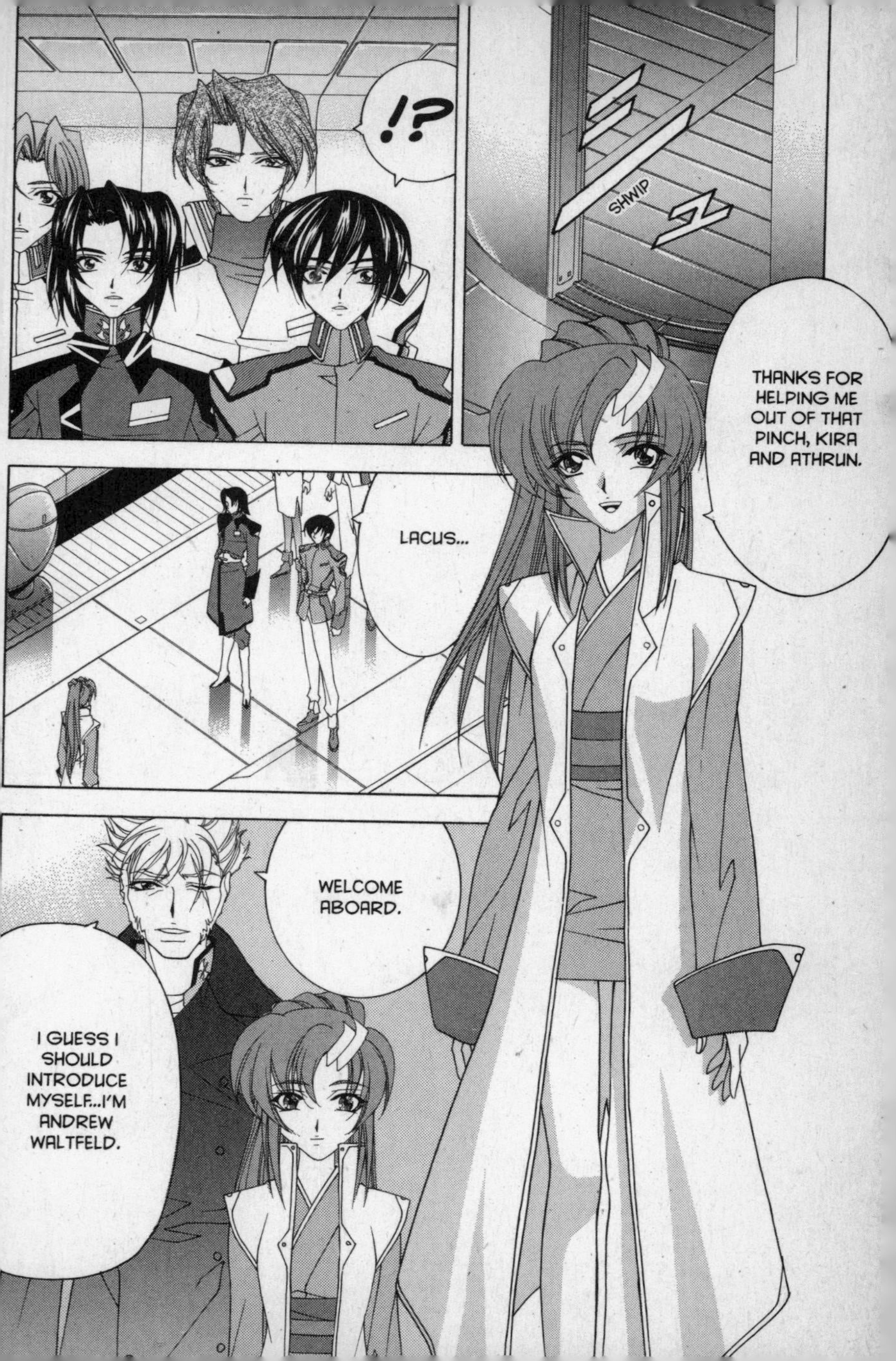
SHWIP
!?
THANKS FOR HELPING ME OUT OF THAT PINCH, KIRA AND ATHRUN.
LACUS...
WELCOME ABOARD.
I GUESS I SHOULD INTRODUCE MYSELF...I'M ANDREW WALTFELD.

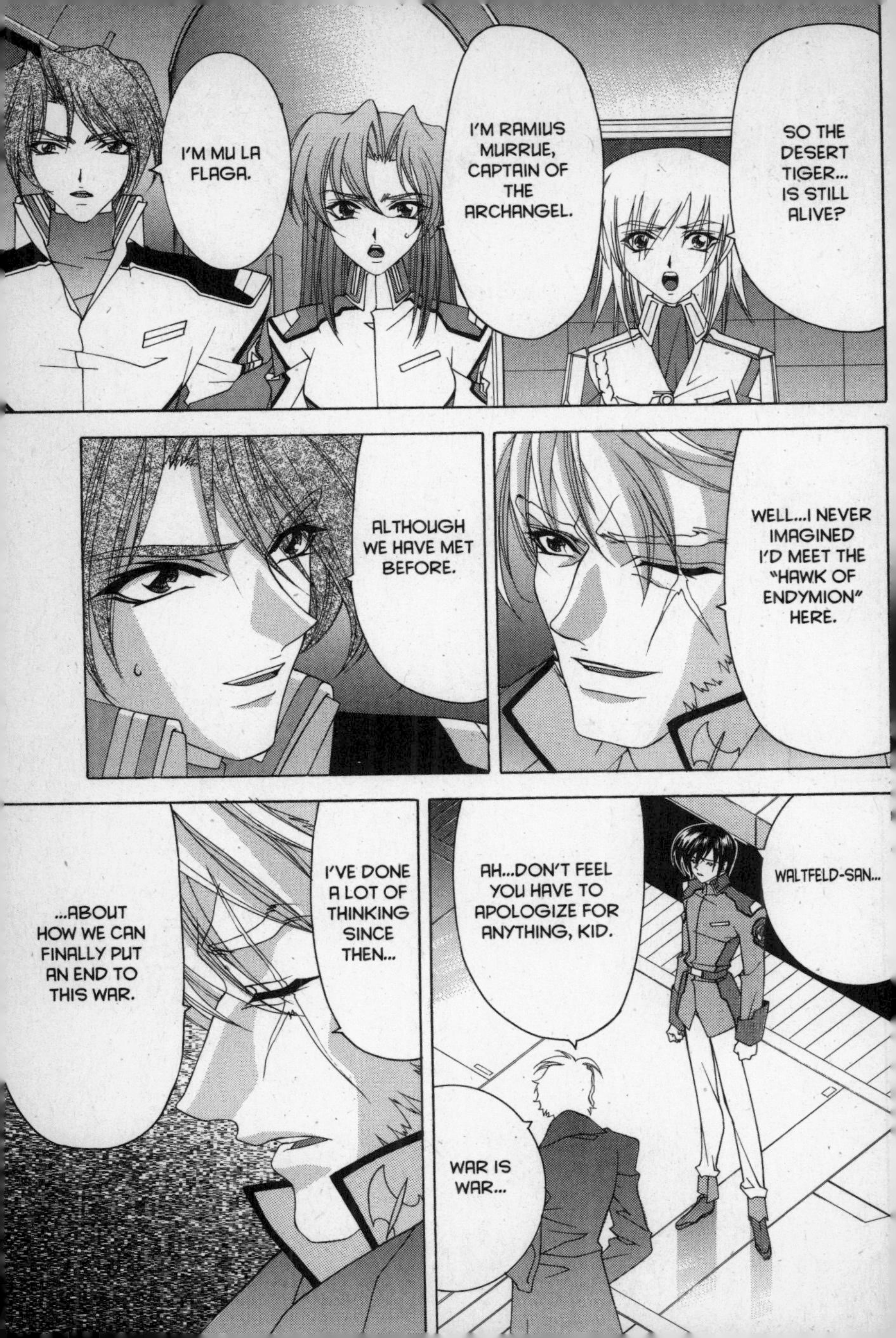
SO THE DESERT TIGER... IS STILL ALIVE?
I'M RAMIUS MURRUE, CAPTAIN OF THE ARCHANGEL.
I'M MU LA FLAGA.
WELL...I NEVER IMAGINED I'D MEET THE "HAWK OF ENDYMION" HERE.
ALTHOUGH WE HAVE MET BEFORE.
WALTFELD-SAN...
AH...DON'T FEEL YOU HAVE TO APOLOGIZE FOR ANYTHING, KID.
WAR IS WAR...
I'VE DONE A LOT OF THINKING SINCE THEN...
...ABOUT HOW WE CAN FINALLY PUT AN END TO THIS WAR.

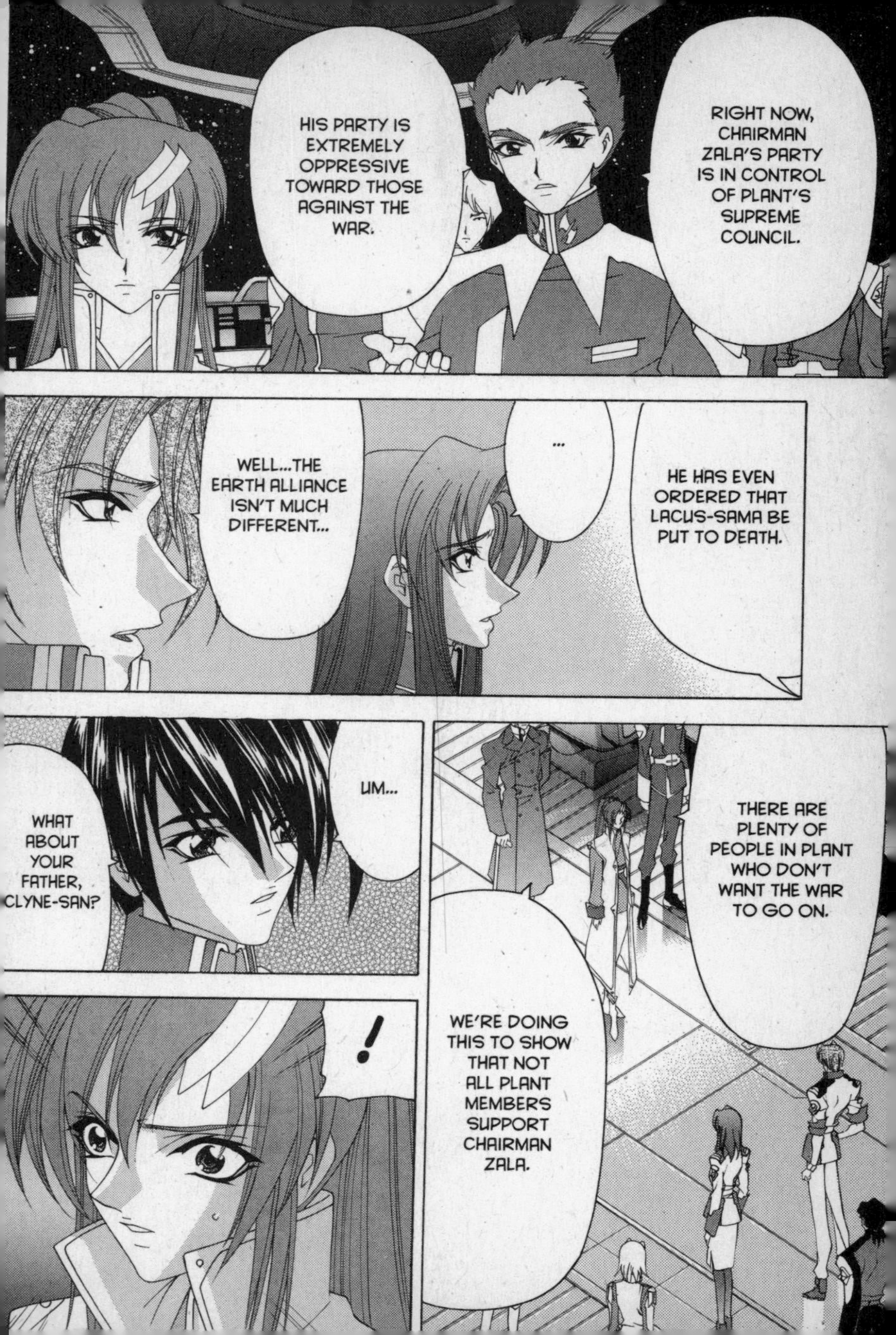
RIGHT NOW, CHAIRMAN ZALA'S PARTY IS IN CONTROL OF PLANT'S SUPREME COUNCIL.
HIS PARTY IS EXTREMELY OPPRESSIVE TOWARD THOSE AGAINST THE WAR.
HE HAS EVEN ORDERED THAT LACUS-SAMA BE PUT TO DEATH.
...
WELL...THE EARTH ALLIANCE ISN'T MUCH DIFFERENT...
THERE ARE PLENTY OF PEOPLE IN PLANT WHO DON'T WANT THE WAR TO GO ON.
WE'RE DOING THIS TO SHOW THAT NOT ALL PLANT MEMBERS SUPPORT CHAIRMAN ZALA.
UM...
WHAT ABOUT YOUR FATHER, CLYNE-SAN?
!

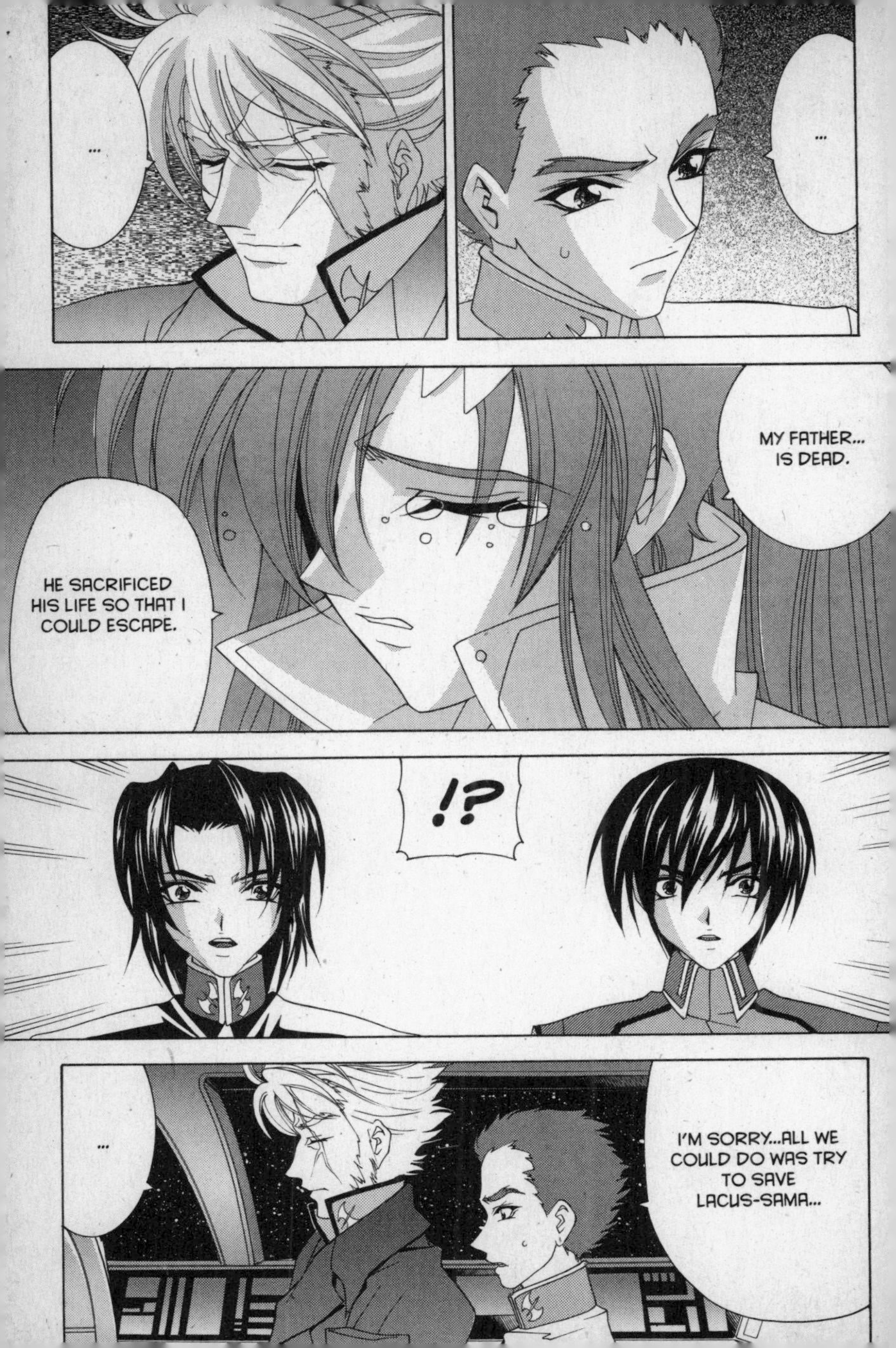
...
...
MY FATHER... IS DEAD.
HE SACRIFICED HIS LIFE SO THAT I COULD ESCAPE.
!?
I'M SORRY...ALL WE COULD DO WAS TRY TO SAVE LACUS-SAMA...
...

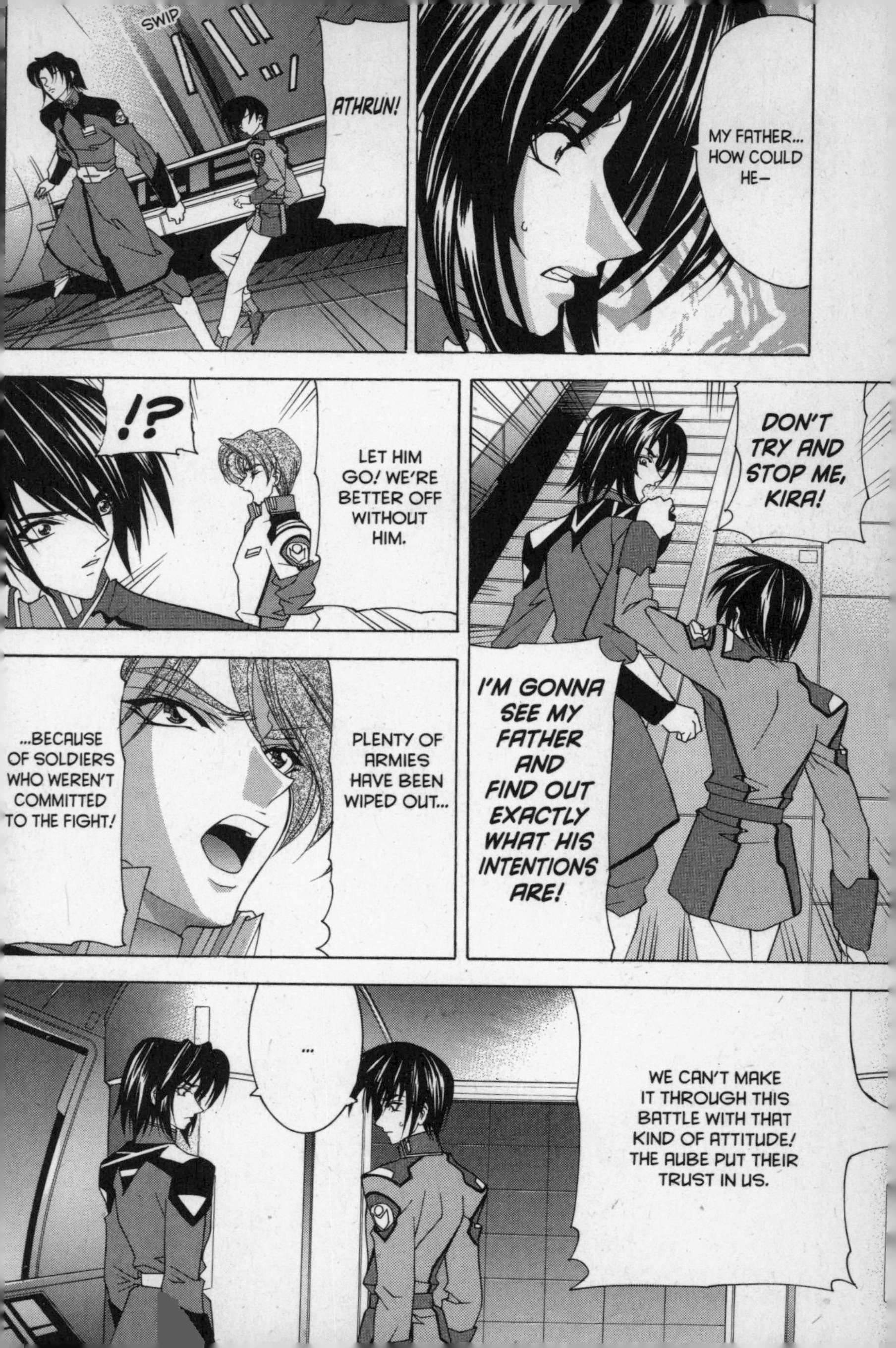
MY FATHER... HOW COULD HE—
SWIP
ATHRUN!
DON'T TRY AND STOP ME, KIRA!
I'M GONNA SEE MY FATHER AND FIND OUT EXACTLY WHAT HIS INTENTIONS ARE!
LET HIM GO! WE'RE BETTER OFF WITHOUT HIM.
!?
PLENTY OF ARMIES HAVE BEEN WIPED OUT...
...BECAUSE OF SOLDIERS WHO WEREN'T COMMITTED TO THE FIGHT!
WE CAN'T MAKE IT THROUGH THIS BATTLE WITH THAT KIND OF ATTITUDE! THE AUBE PUT THEIR TRUST IN US.
...

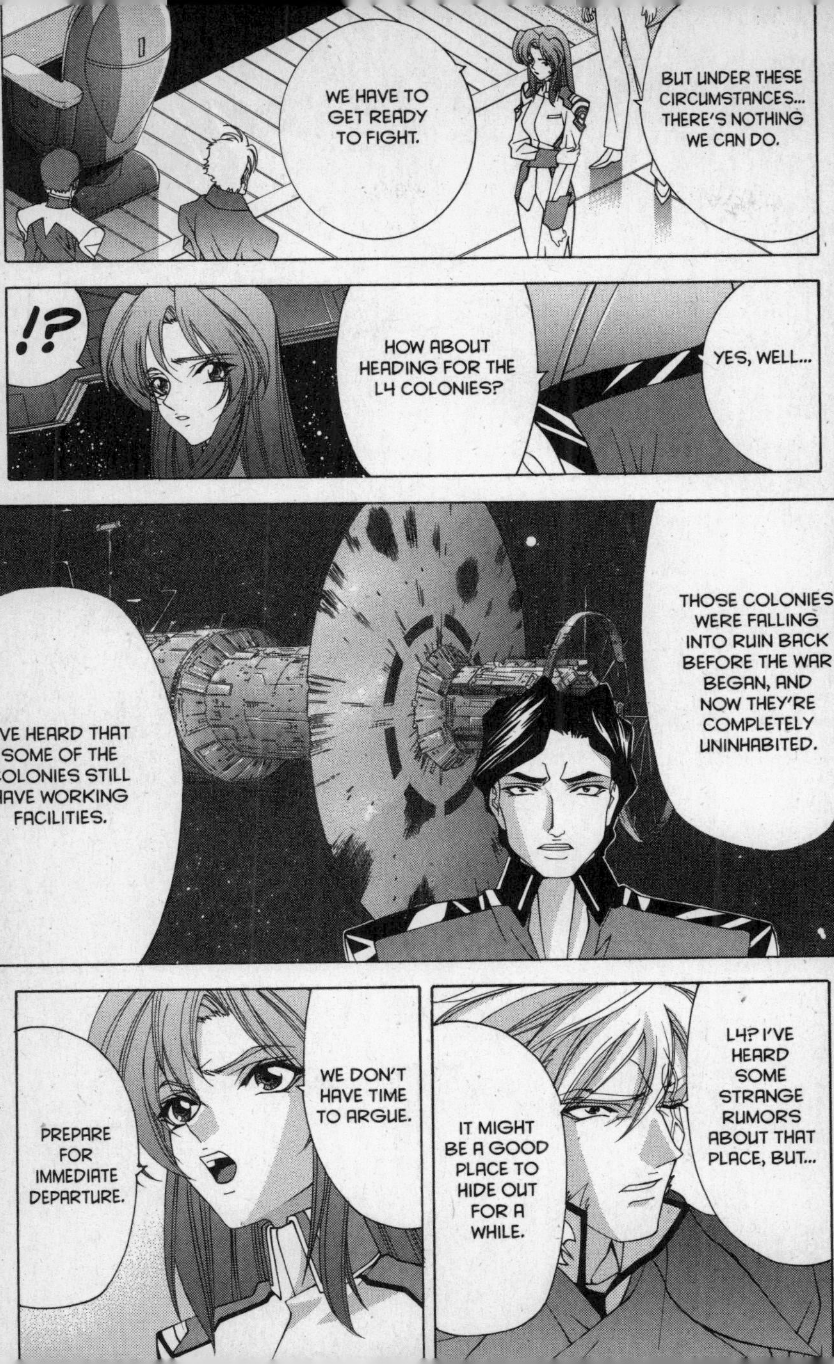
BUT UNDER THESE CIRCUMSTANCES... THERE'S NOTHING WE CAN DO.
WE HAVE TO GET READY TO FIGHT.
YES, WELL...
HOW ABOUT HEADING FOR THE L4 COLONIES?
!?
THOSE COLONIES WERE FALLING INTO RUIN BACK BEFORE THE WAR BEGAN, AND NOW THEY'RE COMPLETELY UNINHABITED.
I'VE HEARD THAT SOME OF THE COLONIES STILL HAVE WORKING FACILITIES.
L4? I'VE HEARD SOME STRANGE RUMORS ABOUT THAT PLACE, BUT...
IT MIGHT BE A GOOD PLACE TO HIDE OUT FOR A WHILE.
WE DON'T HAVE TIME TO ARGUE.
PREPARE FOR IMMEDIATE DEPARTURE.

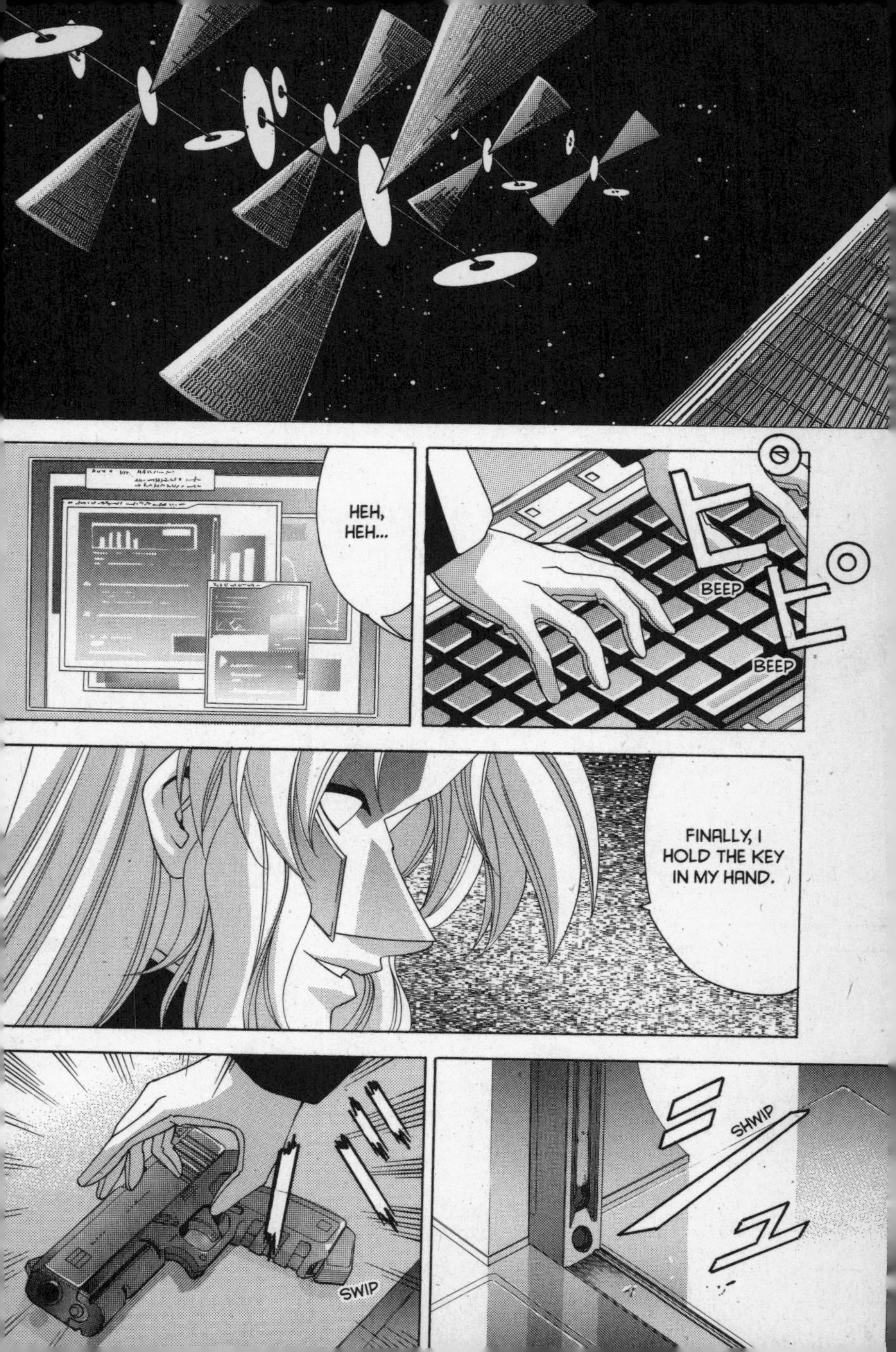
BEEP
BEEP
HEH, HEH...
FINALLY, I HOLD THE KEY IN MY HAND.
SHWIP
SWIP

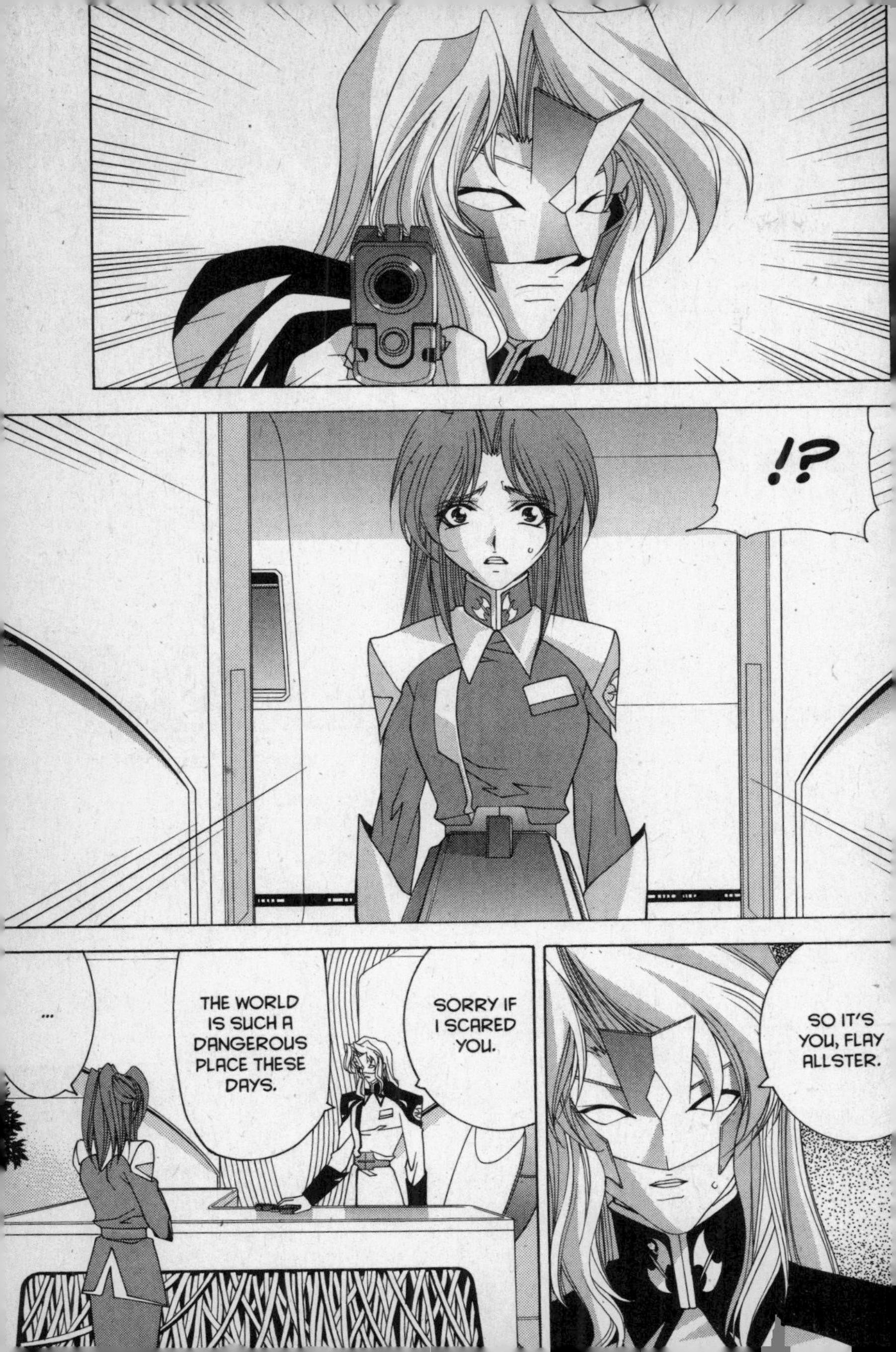
!?
SO IT'S YOU, FLAY ALLSTER.
SORRY IF I SCARED YOU.
THE WORLD IS SUCH A DANGEROUS PLACE THESE DAYS.
...

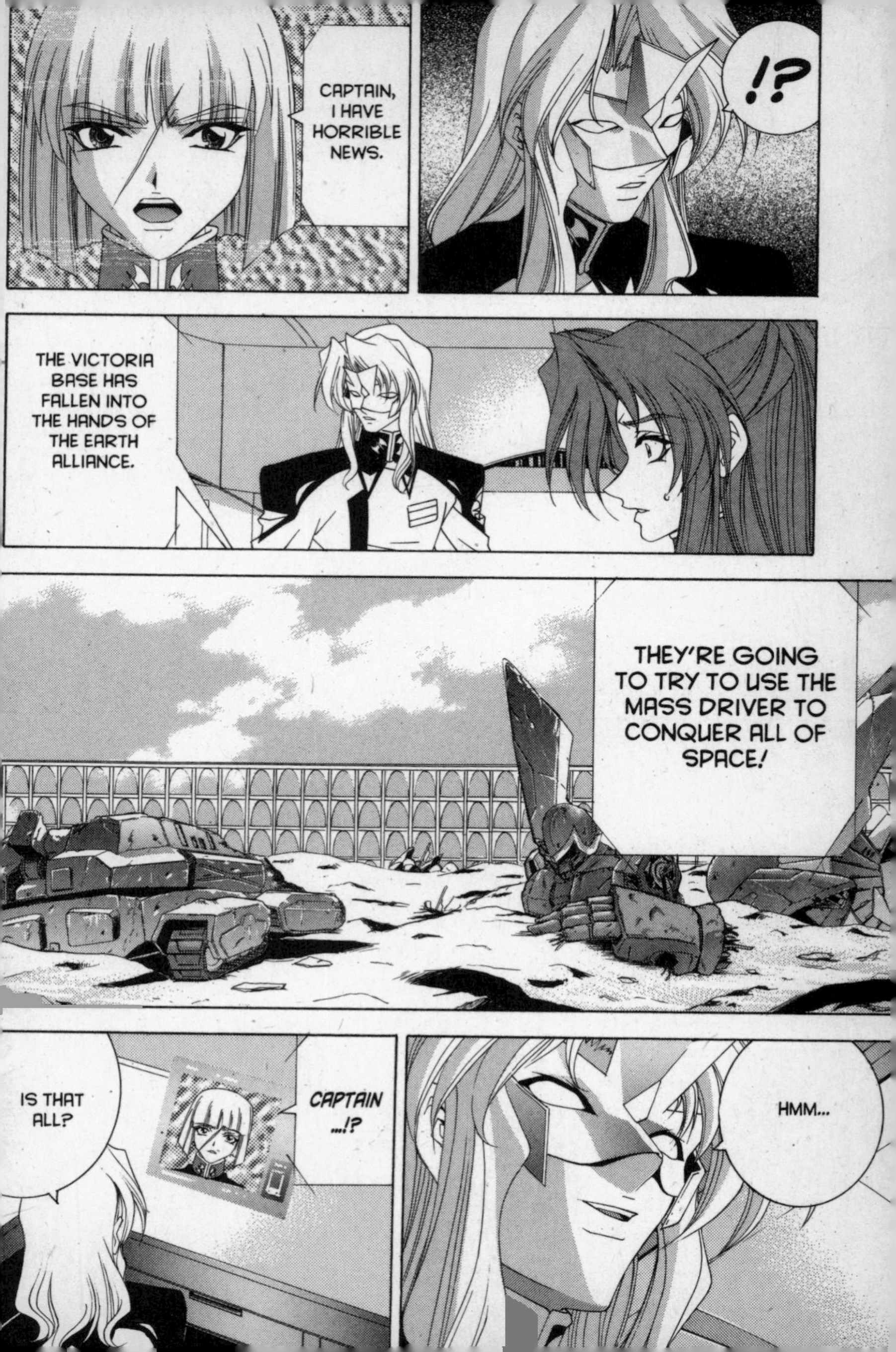
!?
CAPTAIN, I HAVE HORRIBLE NEWS.
THE VICTORIA BASE HAS FALLEN INTO THE HANDS OF THE EARTH ALLIANCE.
THEY'RE GOING TO TRY TO USE THE MASS DRIVER TO CONQUER ALL OF SPACE!
HMM...
CAPTAIN ...!?
IS THAT ALL?

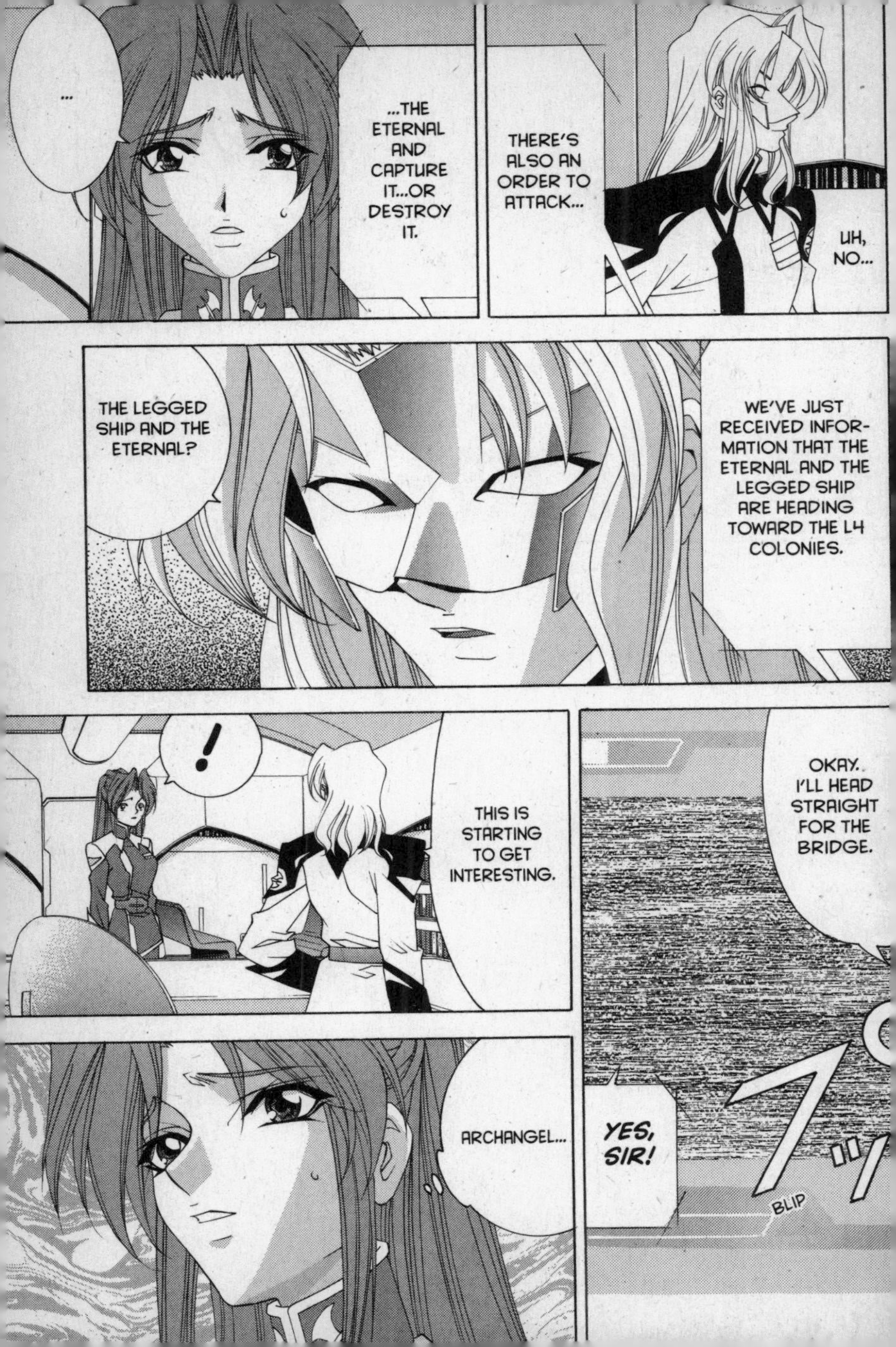
UH, NO...
THERE'S ALSO AN ORDER TO ATTACK...
...THE ETERNAL AND CAPTURE IT...OR DESTROY IT.
...
WE'VE JUST RECEIVED INFORMATION THAT THE ETERNAL AND THE LEGGED SHIP ARE HEADING TOWARD THE L4 COLONIES.
THE LEGGED SHIP AND THE ETERNAL?
OKAY. I'LL HEAD STRAIGHT FOR THE BRIDGE.
YES, SIR!
BLIP
THIS IS STARTING TO GET INTERESTING.
!
ARCHANGEL...

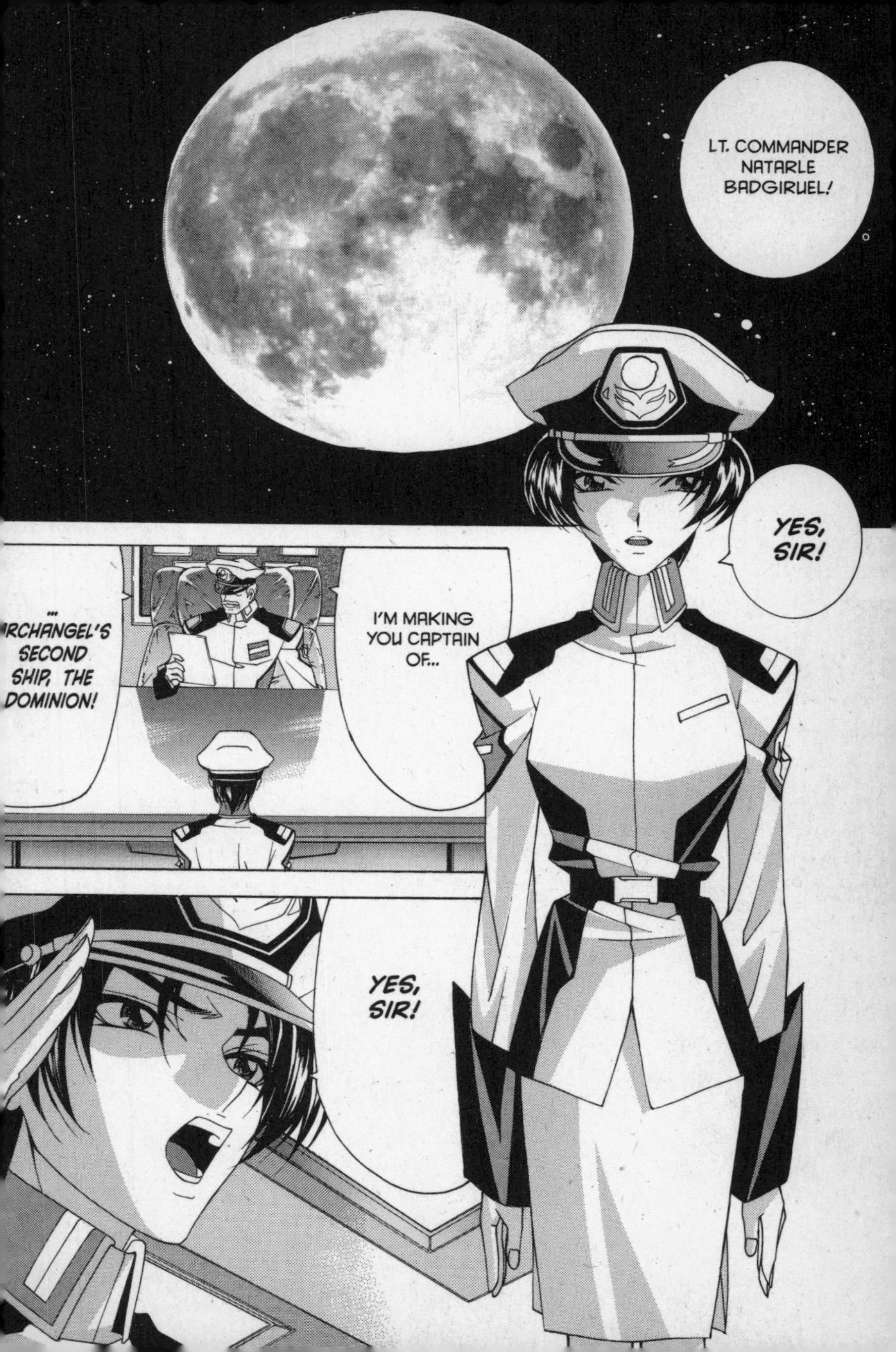
LT. COMMANDER NATARLE BADGIRUEL!
YES, SIR!
I'M MAKING YOU CAPTAIN OF...
...RCHANGEL'S SECOND SHIP, THE DOMINION!
YES, SIR!

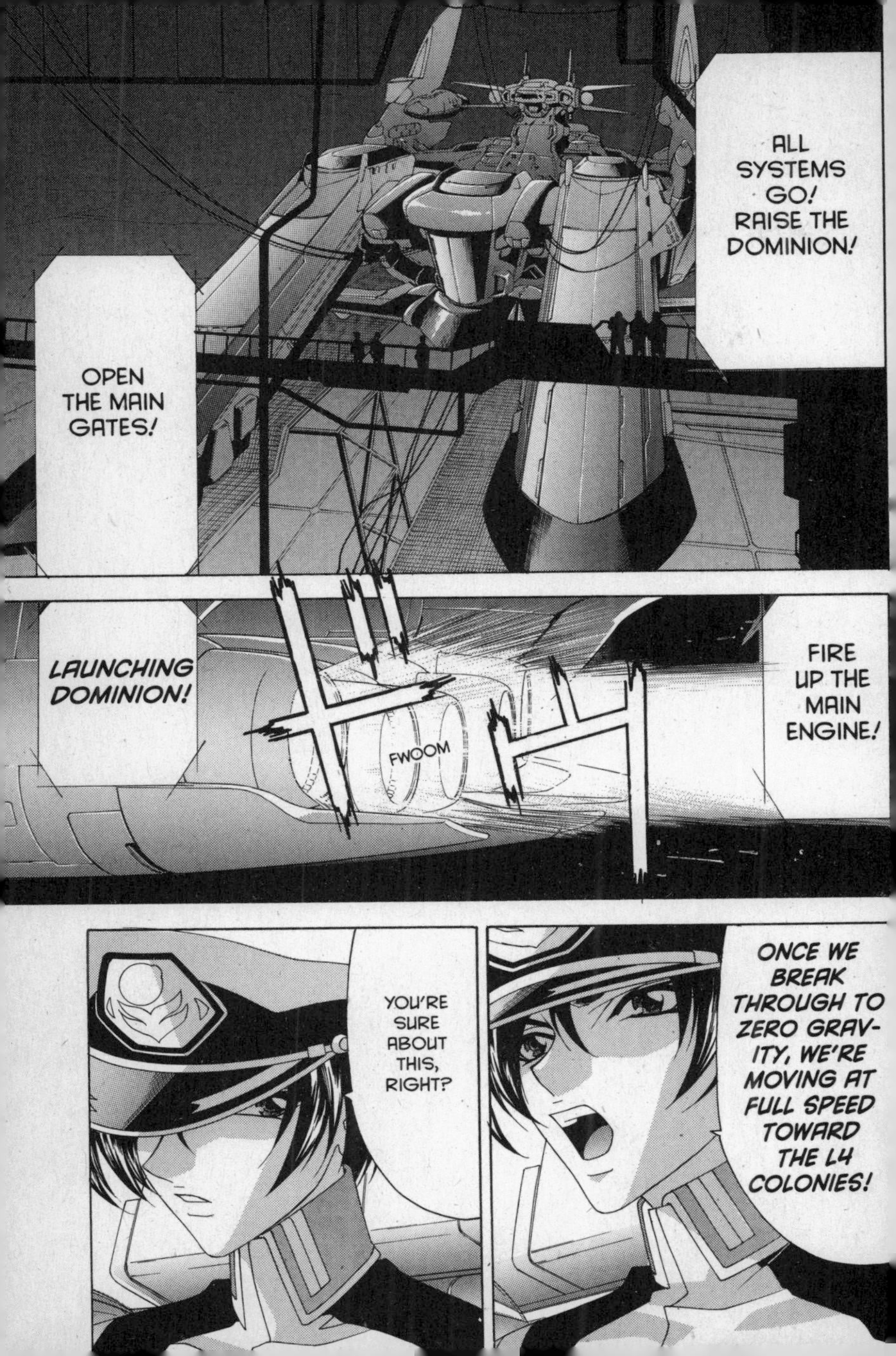
ALL SYSTEMS GO! RAISE THE DOMINION!
OPEN THE MAIN GATES!
FIRE UP THE MAIN ENGINE!
FWOOM
LAUNCHING DOMINION!
ONCE WE BREAK THROUGH TO ZERO GRAV-ITY, WE'RE MOVING AT FULL SPEED TOWARD THE L4 COLONIES!
YOU'RE SURE ABOUT THIS, RIGHT?

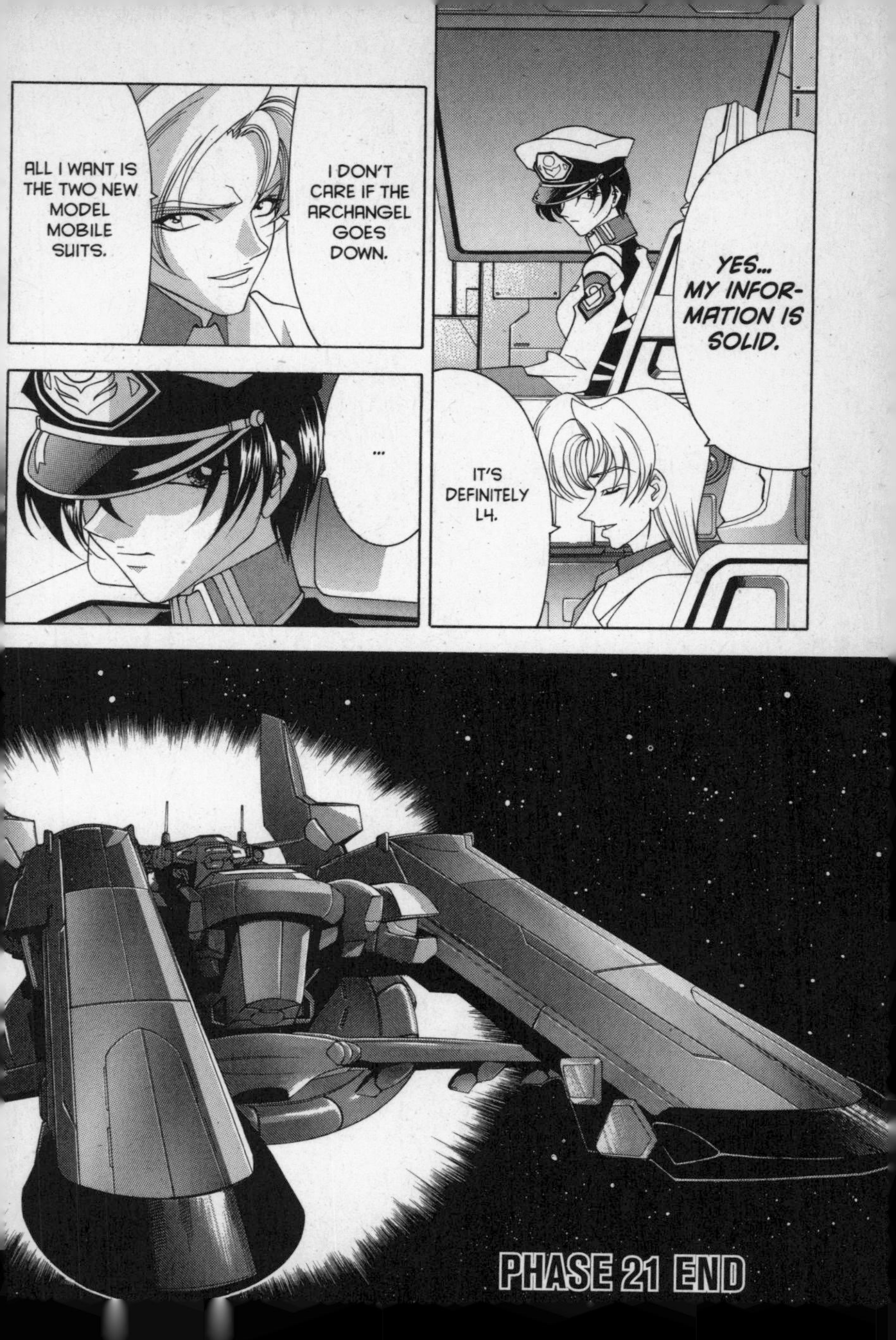
YES... MY INFORMATION IS SOLID.
IT'S DEFINITELY L4.
I DON'T CARE IF THE ARCHANGEL GOES DOWN.
ALL I WANT IS THE TWO NEW MODEL MOBILE SUITS.
...
PHASE 21 END

PHASE 22 - THE SPIRAL ENCOUNTER

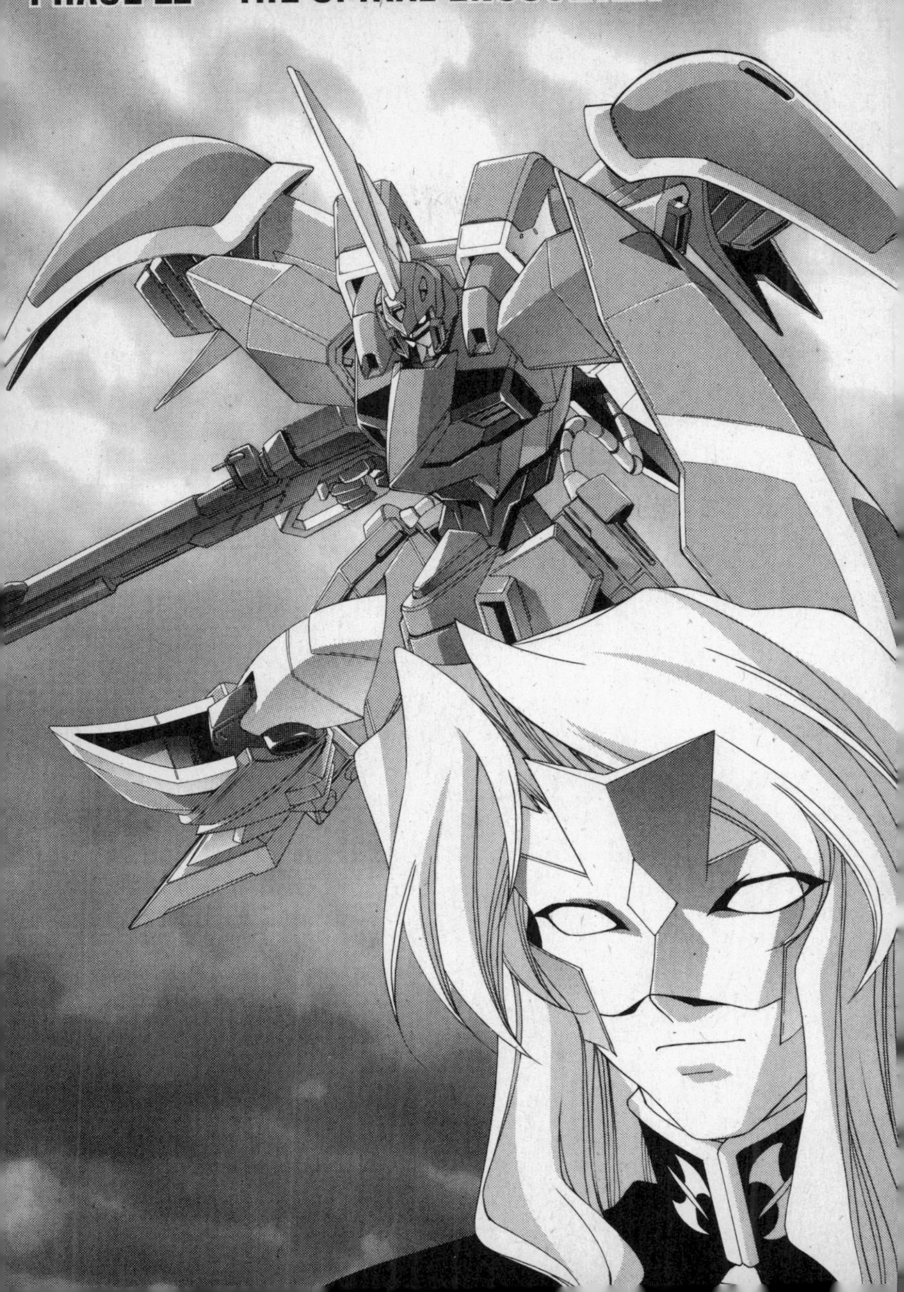

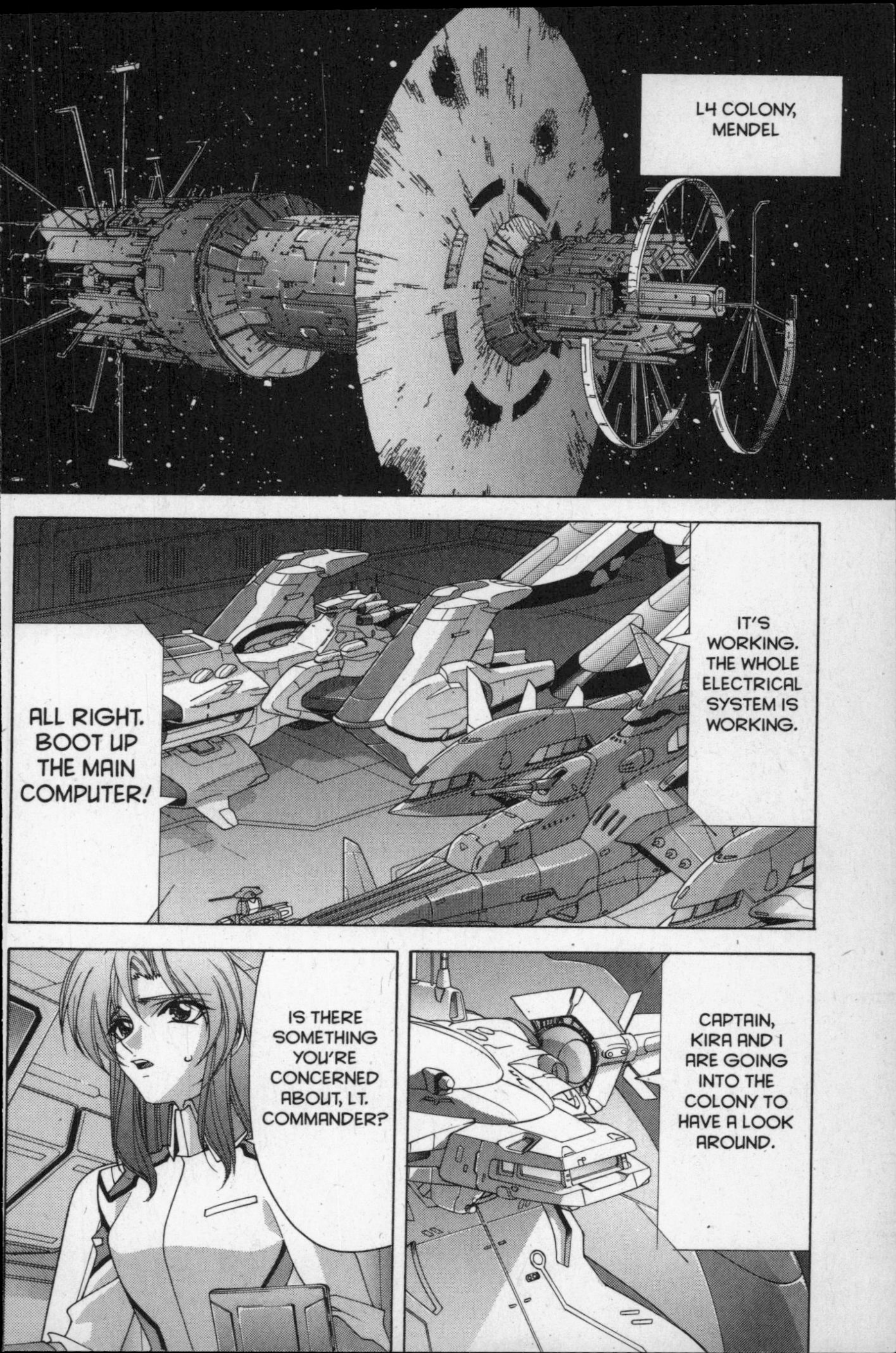
L4 COLONY, MENDEL
IT'S WORKING. THE WHOLE ELECTRICAL SYSTEM IS WORKING.
ALL RIGHT. BOOT UP THE MAIN COMPUTER!
CAPTAIN, KIRA AND I ARE GOING INTO THE COLONY TO HAVE A LOOK AROUND.
IS THERE SOMETHING YOU'RE CONCERNED ABOUT, LT. COMMANDER?

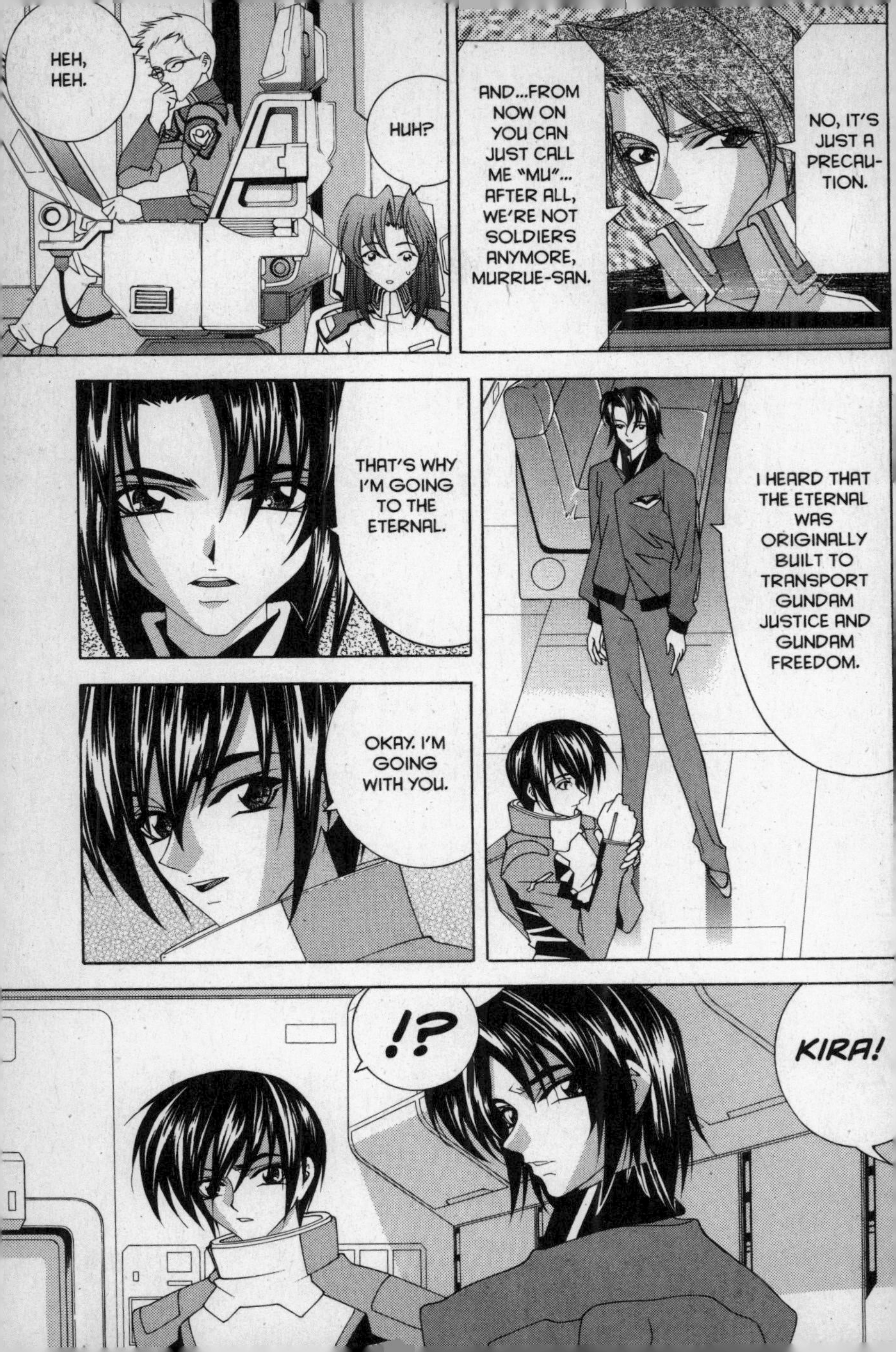
NO, IT'S JUST A PRECAUTION.
AND...FROM NOW ON YOU CAN JUST CALL ME "MU"... AFTER ALL, WE'RE NOT SOLDIERS ANYMORE, MURRUE-SAN.
HUH?
HEH, HEH.
I HEARD THAT THE ETERNAL WAS ORIGINALLY BUILT TO TRANSPORT GUNDAM JUSTICE AND GUNDAM FREEDOM.
THAT'S WHY I'M GOING TO THE ETERNAL.
OKAY. I'M GOING WITH YOU.
KIRA!
!?

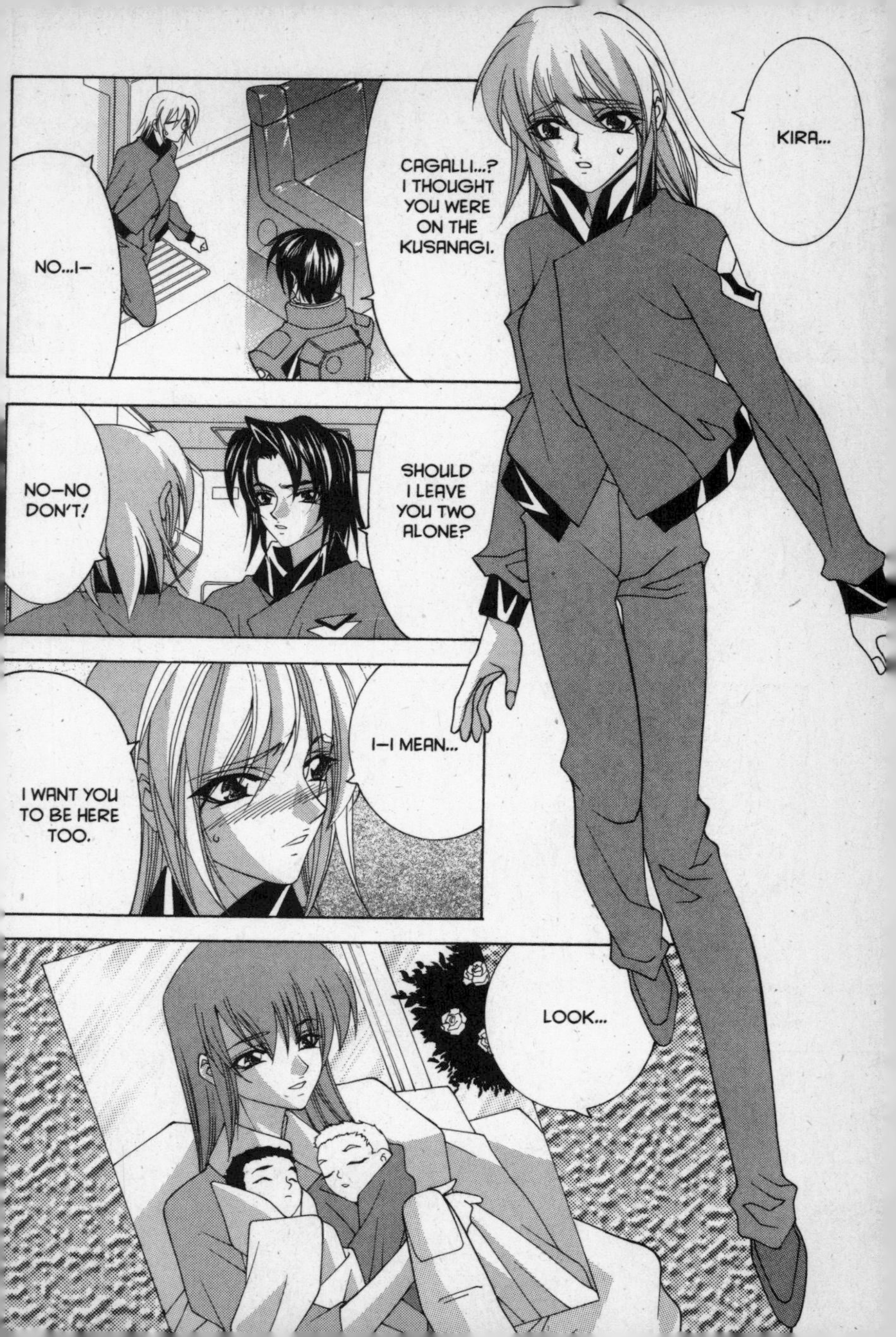
KIRA...
CAGALLI...? I THOUGHT YOU WERE ON THE KUSANAGI.
NO...I–
SHOULD I LEAVE YOU TWO ALONE?
NO–NO DON'T!
I–I MEAN...
I WANT YOU TO BE HERE TOO.
LOOK...

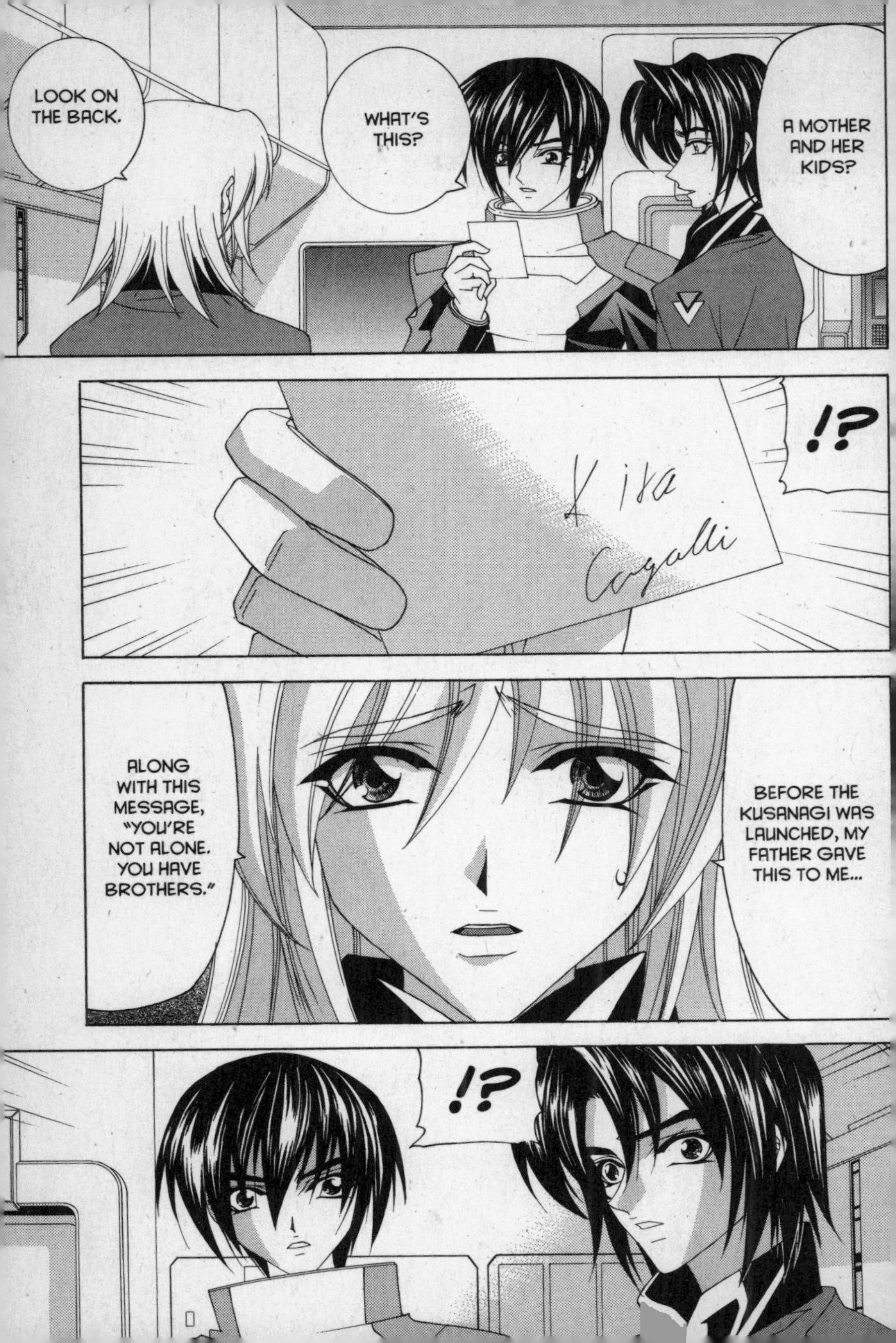
A MOTHER AND HER KIDS?
WHAT'S THIS?
LOOK ON THE BACK.
!?
Kira
Cagalli
BEFORE THE KUSANAGI WAS LAUNCHED, MY FATHER GAVE THIS TO ME...
ALONG WITH THIS MESSAGE, "YOU'RE NOT ALONE. YOU HAVE BROTHERS."
!?

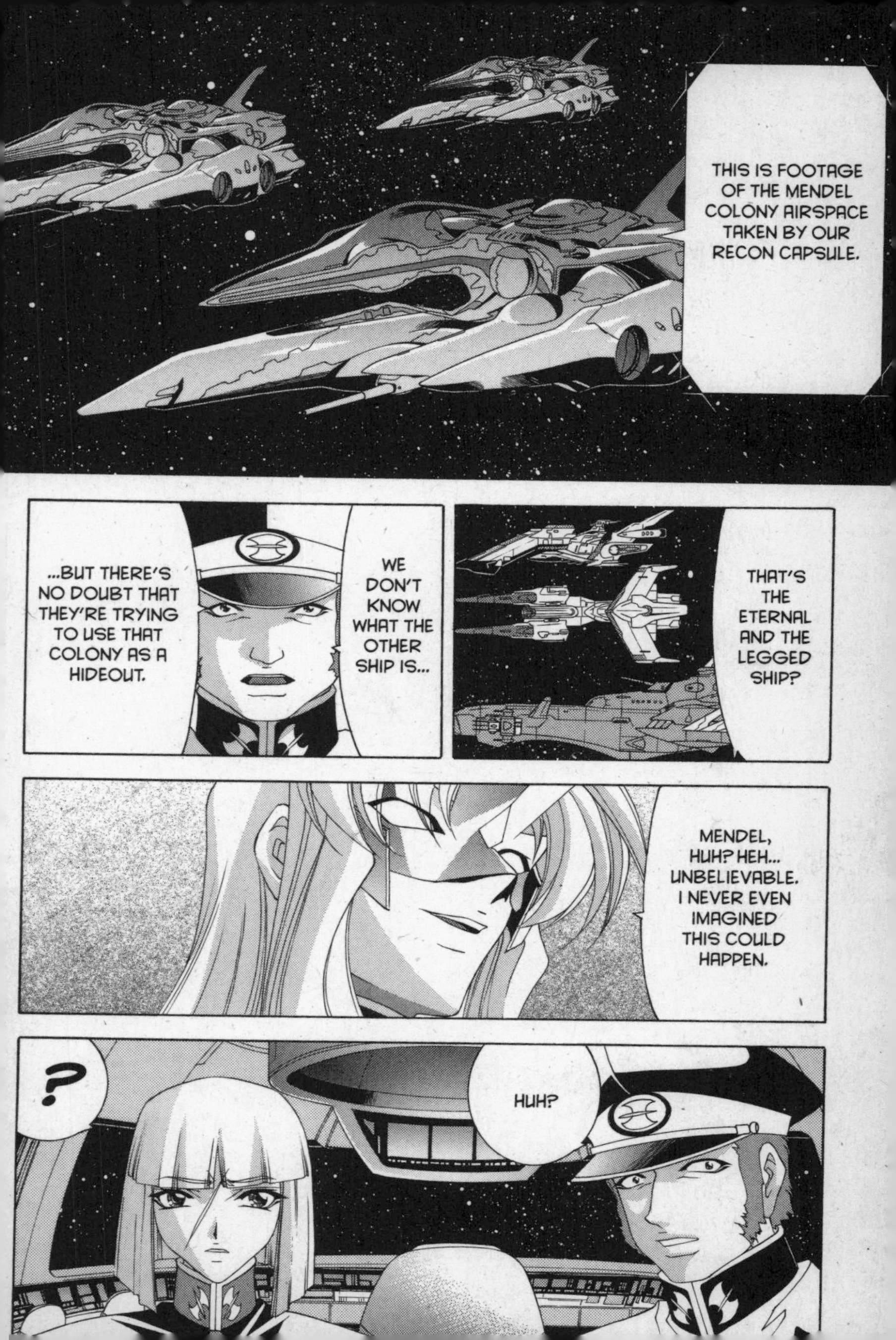
THIS IS FOOTAGE OF THE MENDEL COLONY AIRSPACE TAKEN BY OUR RECON CAPSULE.
THAT'S THE ETERNAL AND THE LEGGED SHIP?
WE DON'T KNOW WHAT THE OTHER SHIP IS...
...BUT THERE'S NO DOUBT THAT THEY'RE TRYING TO USE THAT COLONY AS A HIDEOUT.
MENDEL, HUH? HEH... UNBELIEVABLE. I NEVER EVEN IMAGINED THIS COULD HAPPEN.
HUH?
?

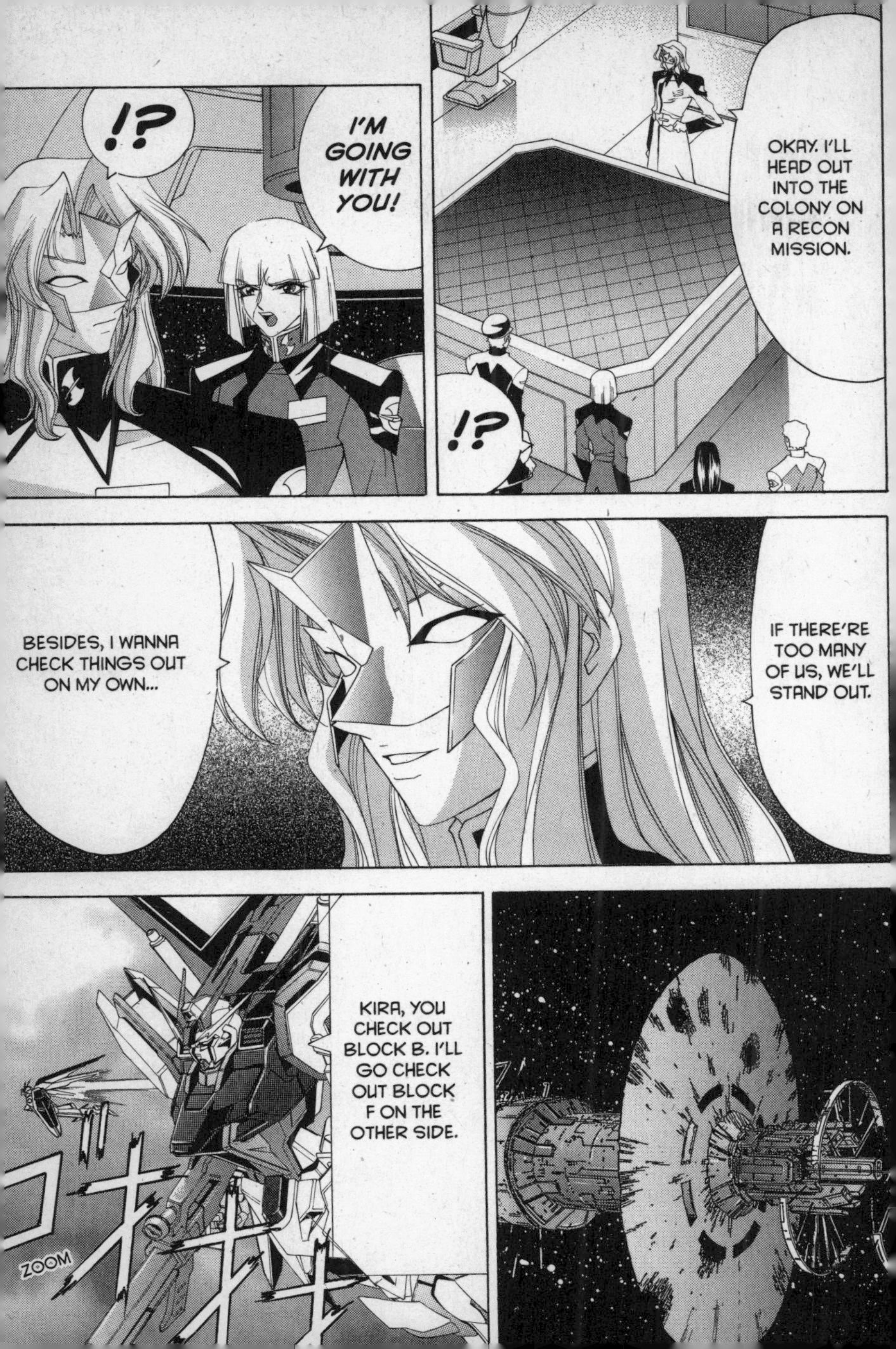
OKAY. I'LL HEAD OUT INTO THE COLONY ON A RECON MISSION.
!?
I'M GOING WITH YOU!
!?
IF THERE'RE TOO MANY OF US, WE'LL STAND OUT.
BESIDES, I WANNA CHECK THINGS OUT ON MY OWN...
KIRA, YOU CHECK OUT BLOCK B. I'LL GO CHECK OUT BLOCK F ON THE OTHER SIDE.
ZOOM

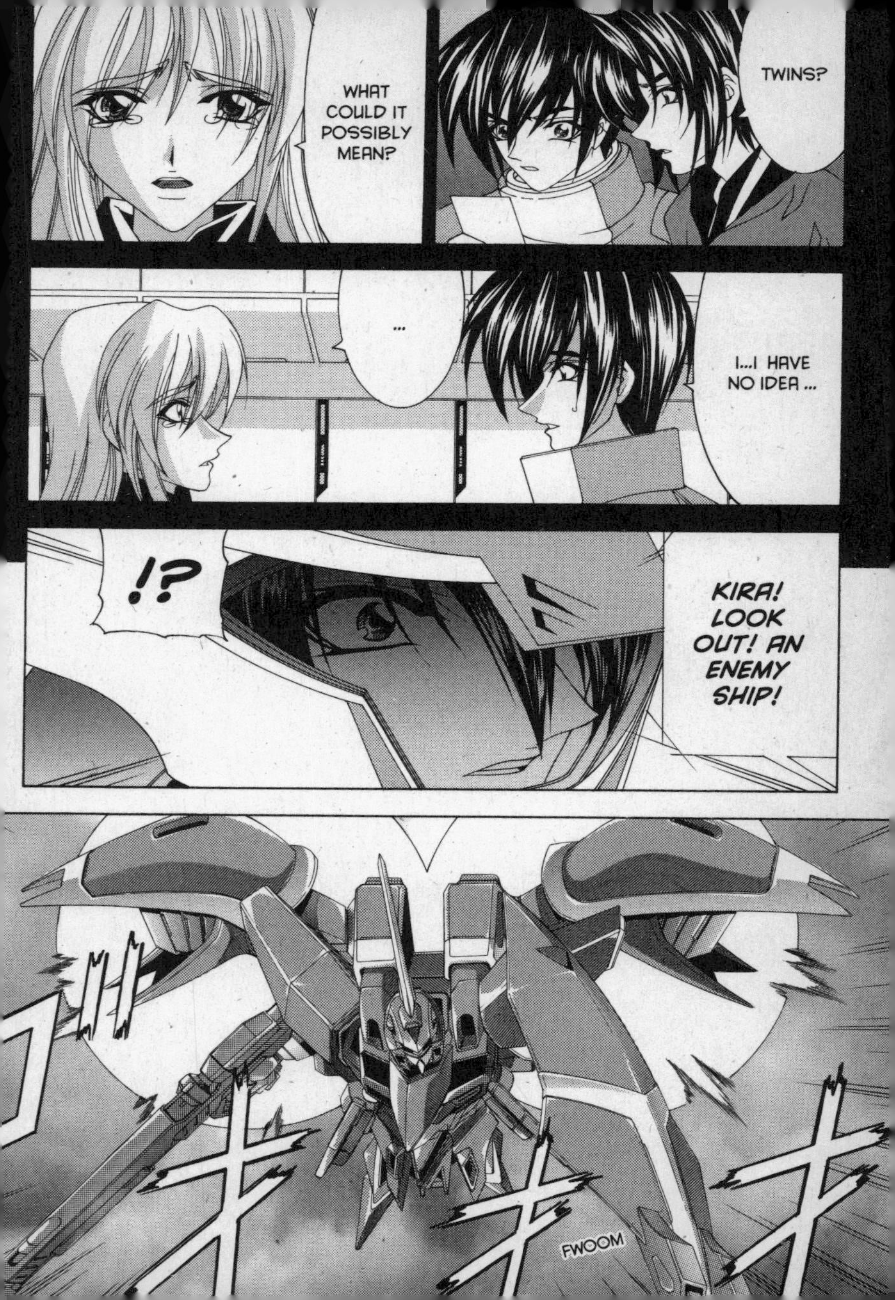
TWINS?
WHAT COULD IT POSSIBLY MEAN?
I...I HAVE NO IDEA ...
...
KIRA! LOOK OUT! AN ENEMY SHIP!
!?
FWOOM

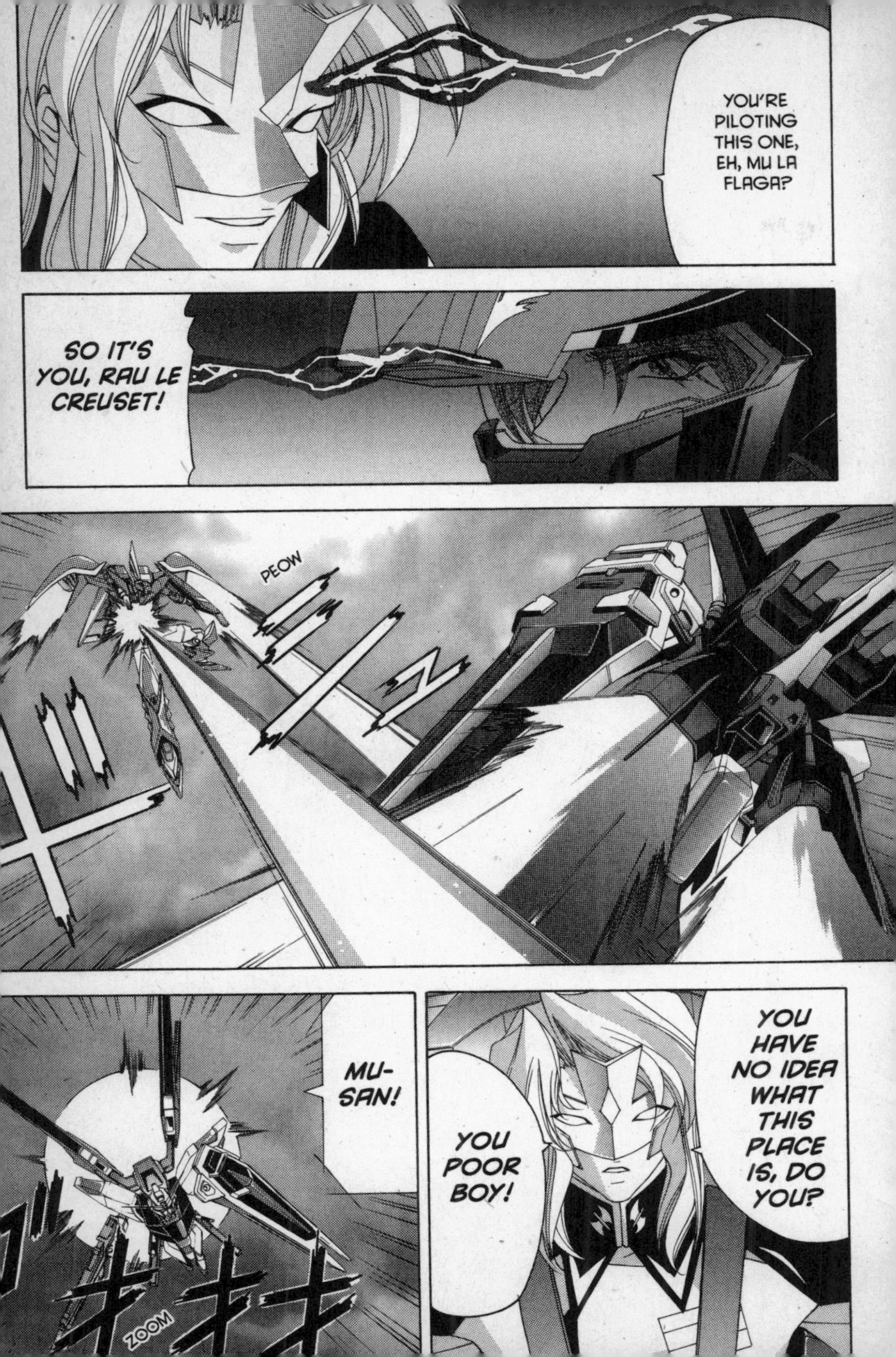
YOU'RE PILOTING THIS ONE, EH, MU LA FLAGA?
SO IT'S YOU, RAU LE CREUSET!
PEOW
YOU HAVE NO IDEA WHAT THIS PLACE IS, DO YOU?
YOU POOR BOY!
MU-SAN!
ZOOM

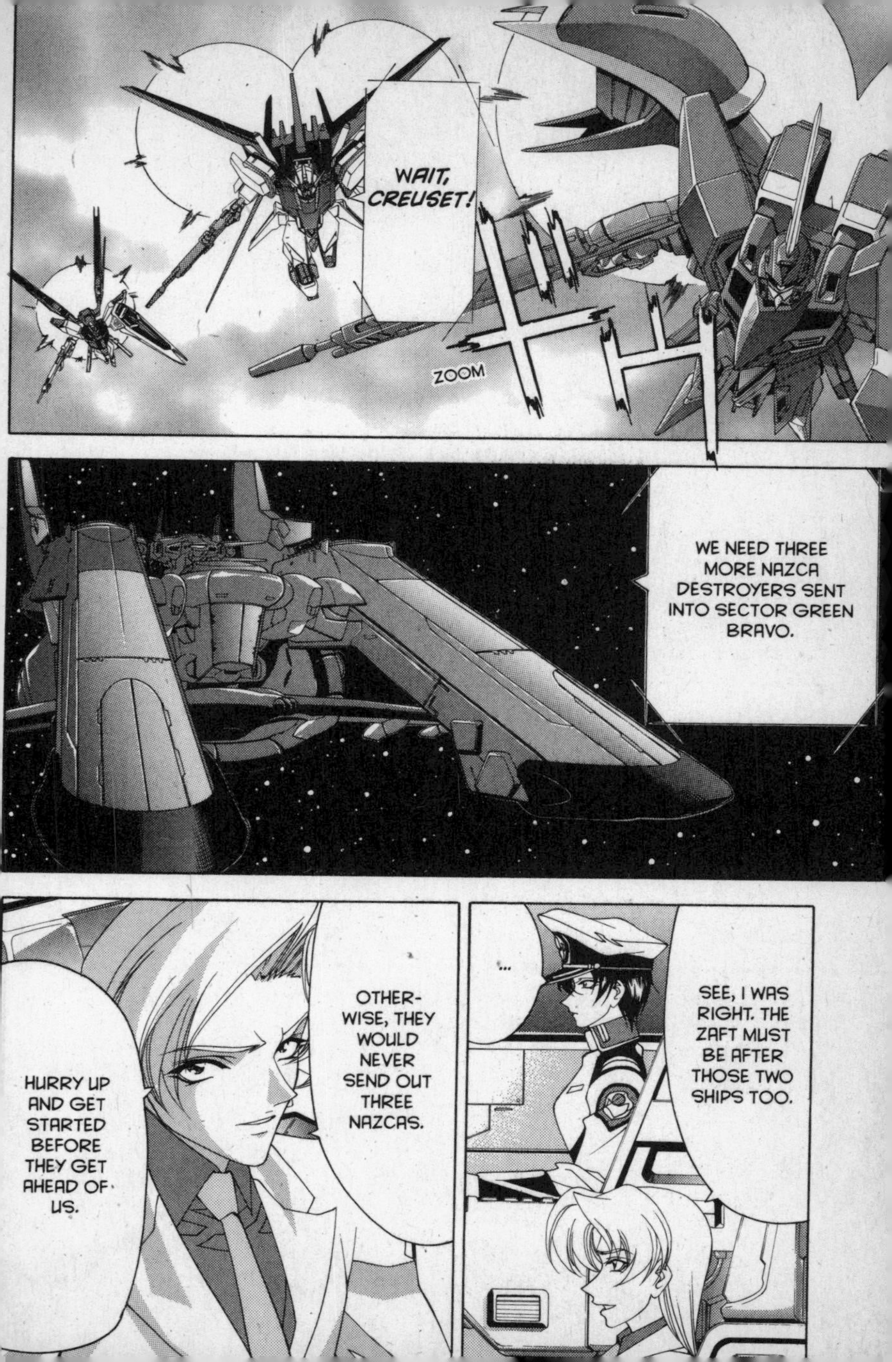
WAIT, CREUSET!
ZOOM
WE NEED THREE MORE NAZCA DESTROYERS SENT INTO SECTOR GREEN BRAVO.
SEE, I WAS RIGHT. THE ZAFT MUST BE AFTER THOSE TWO SHIPS TOO.
...
OTHER-WISE, THEY WOULD NEVER SEND OUT THREE NAZCAS.
HURRY UP AND GET STARTED BEFORE THEY GET AHEAD OF US.

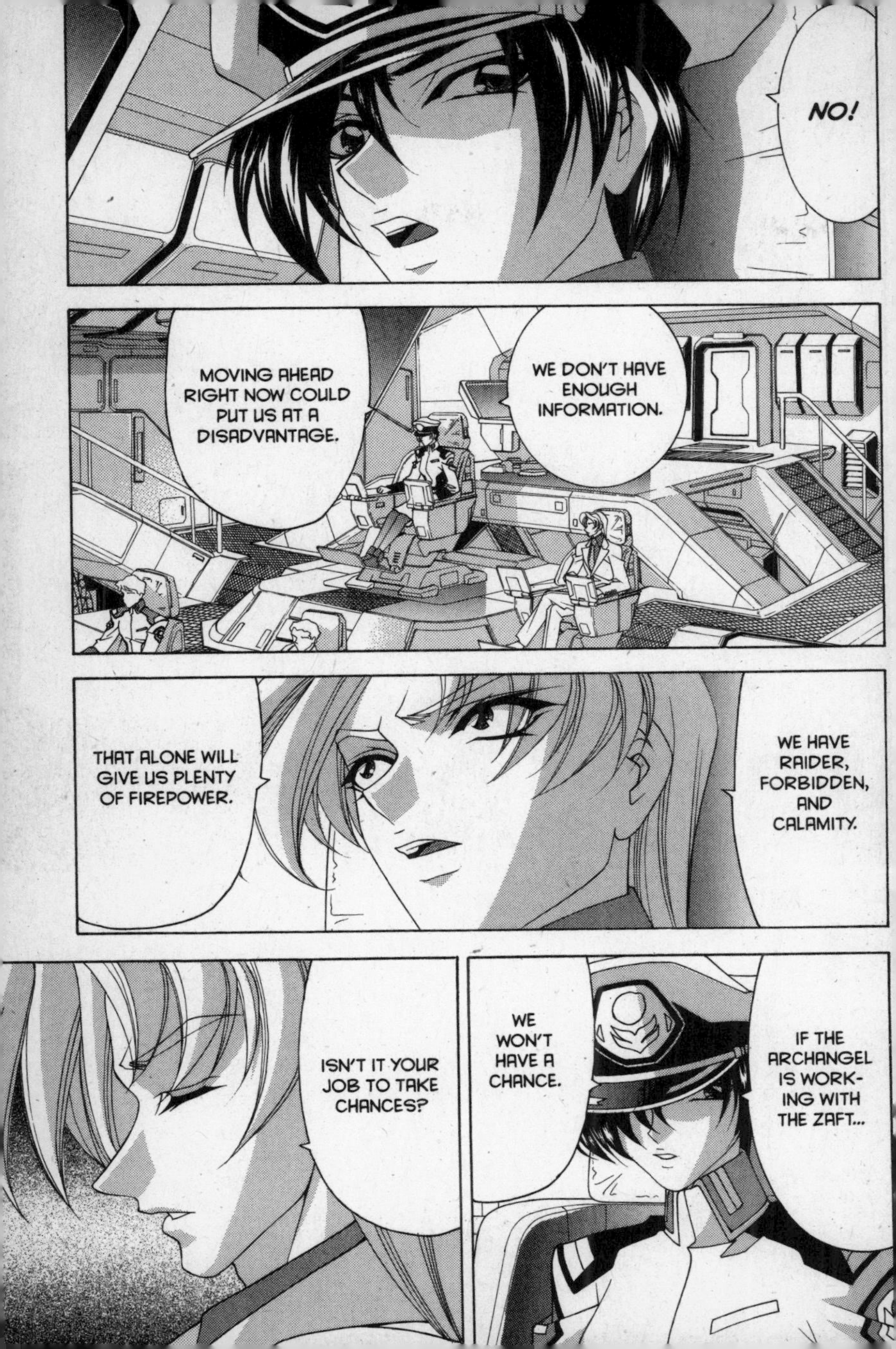
NO!
WE DON'T HAVE ENOUGH INFORMATION.
MOVING AHEAD RIGHT NOW COULD PUT US AT A DISADVANTAGE.
WE HAVE RAIDER, FORBIDDEN, AND CALAMITY.
THAT ALONE WILL GIVE US PLENTY OF FIREPOWER.
IF THE ARCHANGEL IS WORKING WITH THE ZAFT...
WE WON'T HAVE A CHANCE.
ISN'T IT YOUR JOB TO TAKE CHANCES?

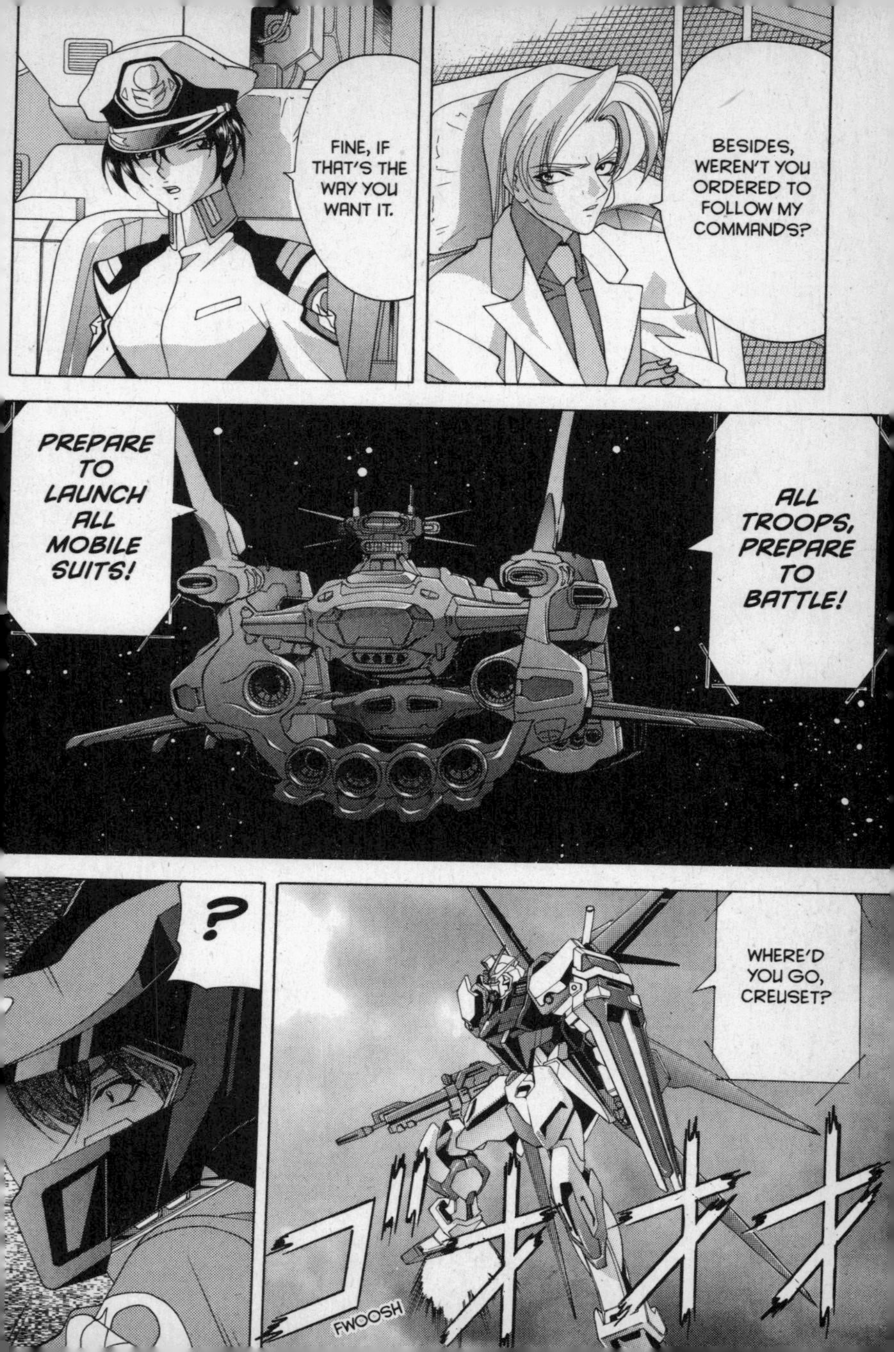

BESIDES, WEREN'T YOU ORDERED TO FOLLOW MY COMMANDS?
FINE, IF THAT'S THE WAY YOU WANT IT.
ALL TROOPS, PREPARE TO BATTLE!
PREPARE TO LAUNCH ALL MOBILE SUITS!
WHERE'D YOU GO, CREUSET?
FWOOSH
?

HE MUST'VE GONE INSIDE THE COLONY'S FACILITIES.

WHAT'S THAT?

IT'S A TRAP.

I KNOW!

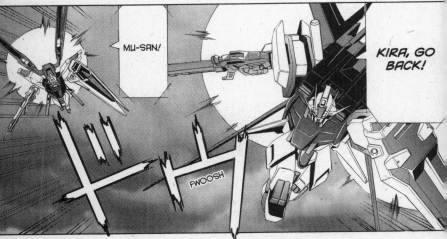

MU-SAN!

KIRA, GO BACK!

FWOOSH

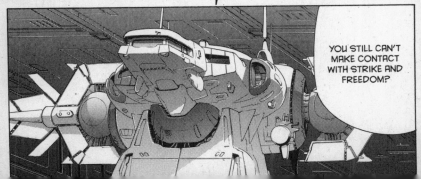

YOU STILL CAN'T MAKE CONTACT WITH STRIKE AND FREEDOM?

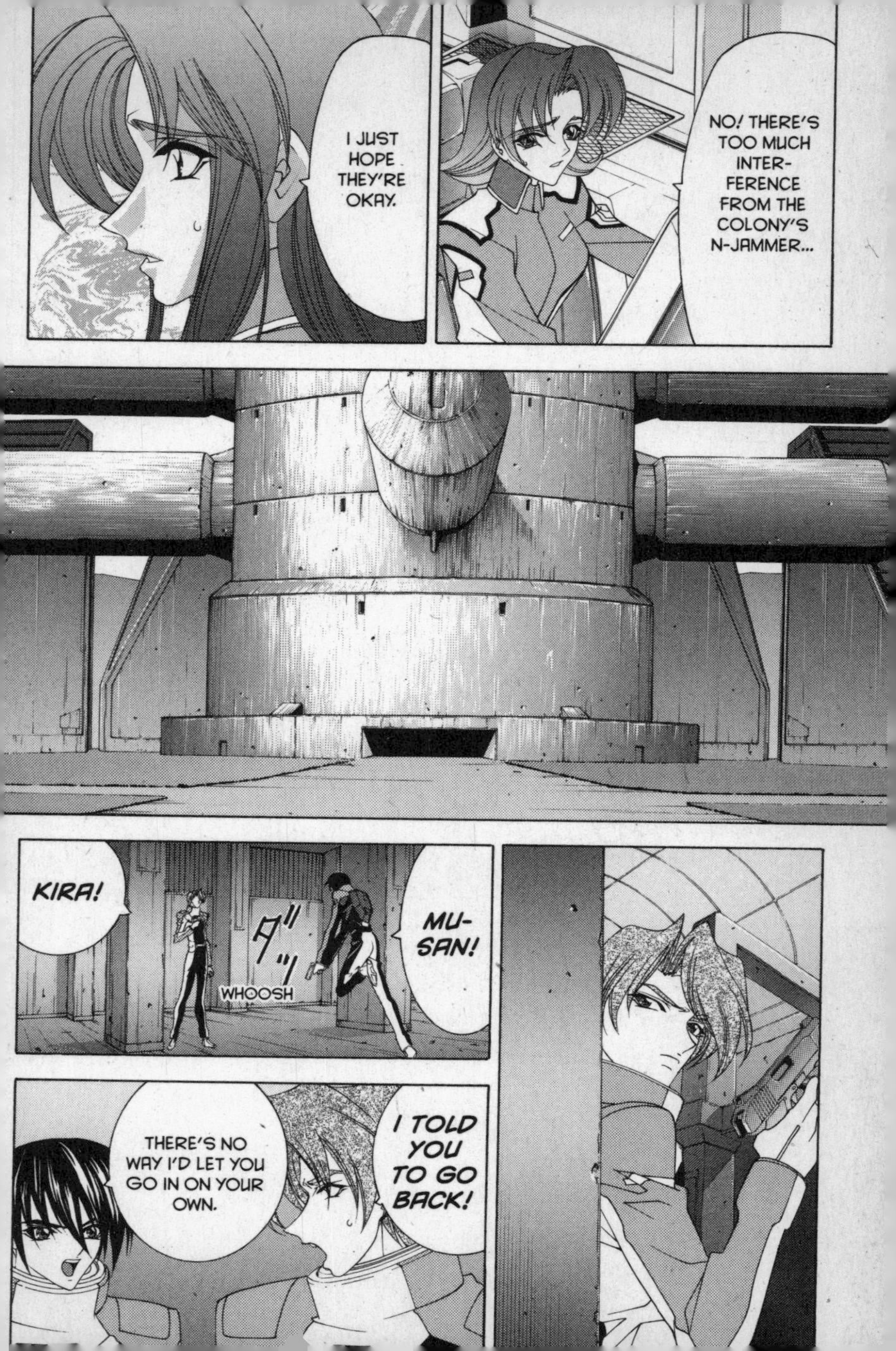
NO! THERE'S TOO MUCH INTER-FERENCE FROM THE COLONY'S N-JAMMER...
I JUST HOPE THEY'RE OKAY.
MU-SAN!
ダッ
WHOOSH
KIRA!
I TOLD YOU TO GO BACK!
THERE'S NO WAY I'D LET YOU GO IN ON YOUR OWN.

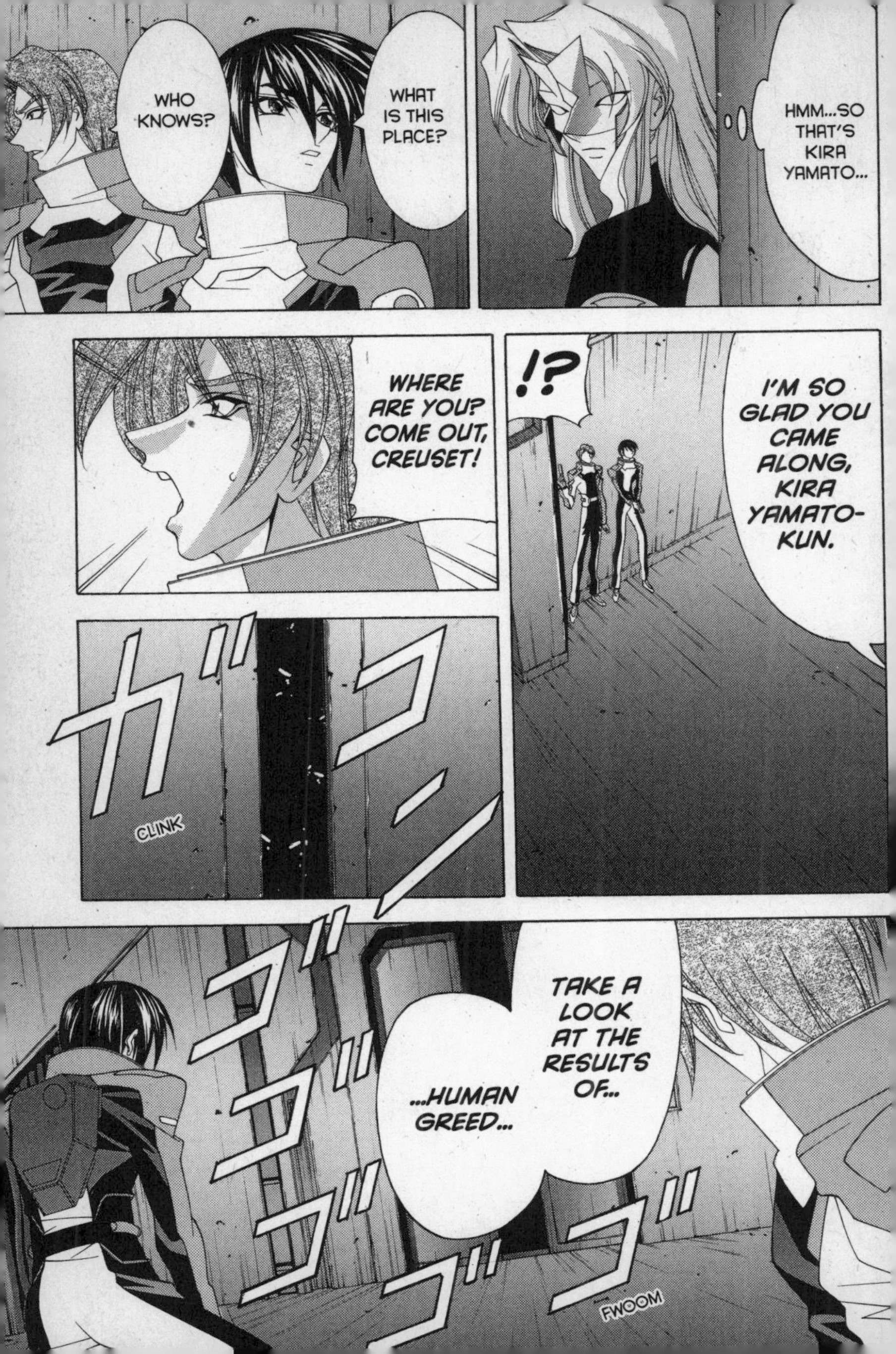
HMM...SO THAT'S KIRA YAMATO...
WHAT IS THIS PLACE?
WHO KNOWS?
I'M SO GLAD YOU CAME ALONG, KIRA YAMATO-KUN.
!?
WHERE ARE YOU? COME OUT, CREUSET!
CLINK
TAKE A LOOK AT THE RESULTS OF...
...HUMAN GREED...
FWOOM

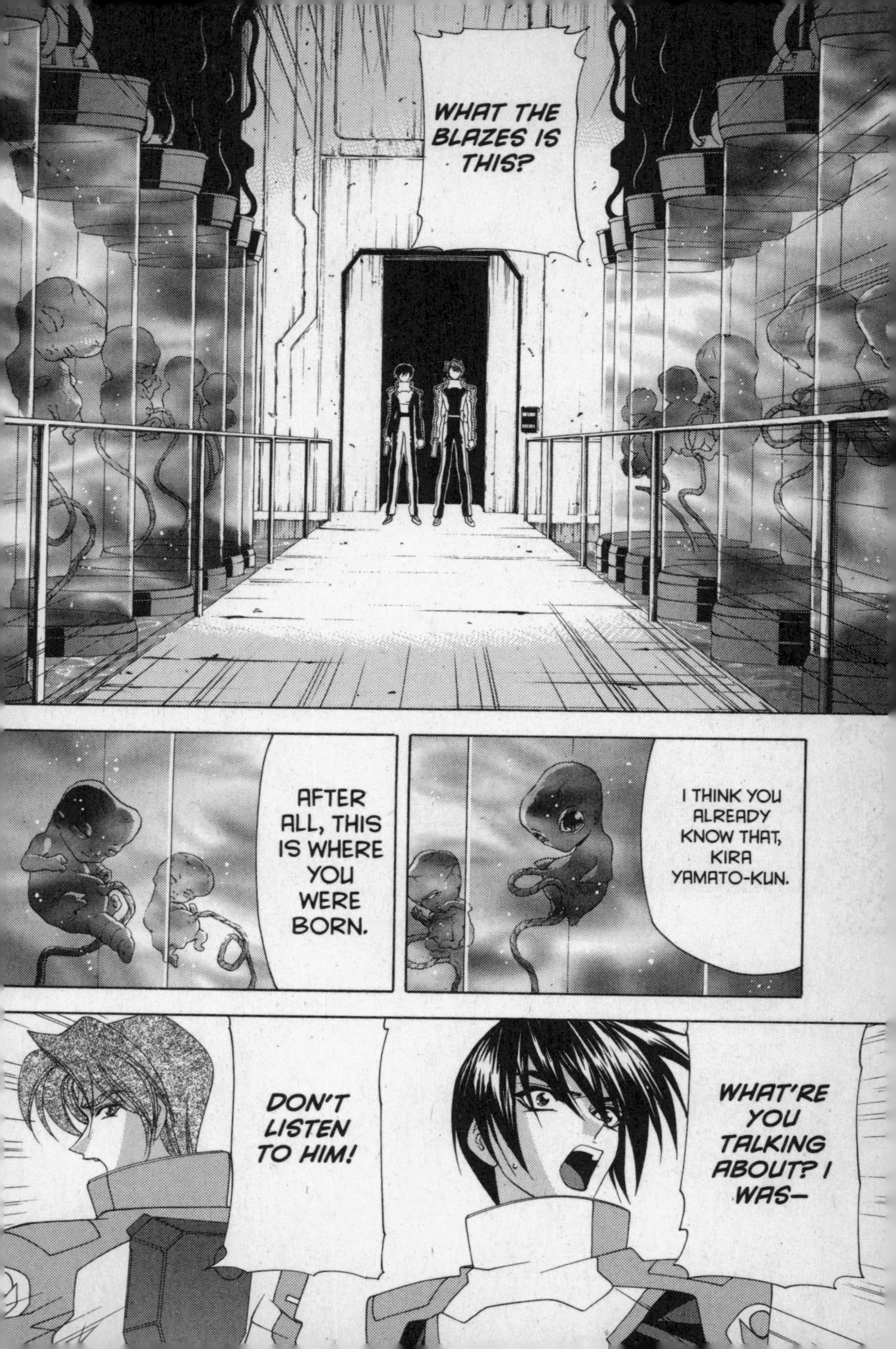
WHAT THE BLAZES IS THIS?
I THINK YOU ALREADY KNOW THAT, KIRA YAMATO-KUN.
AFTER ALL, THIS IS WHERE YOU WERE BORN.
WHAT'RE YOU TALKING ABOUT? I WAS–
DON'T LISTEN TO HIM!

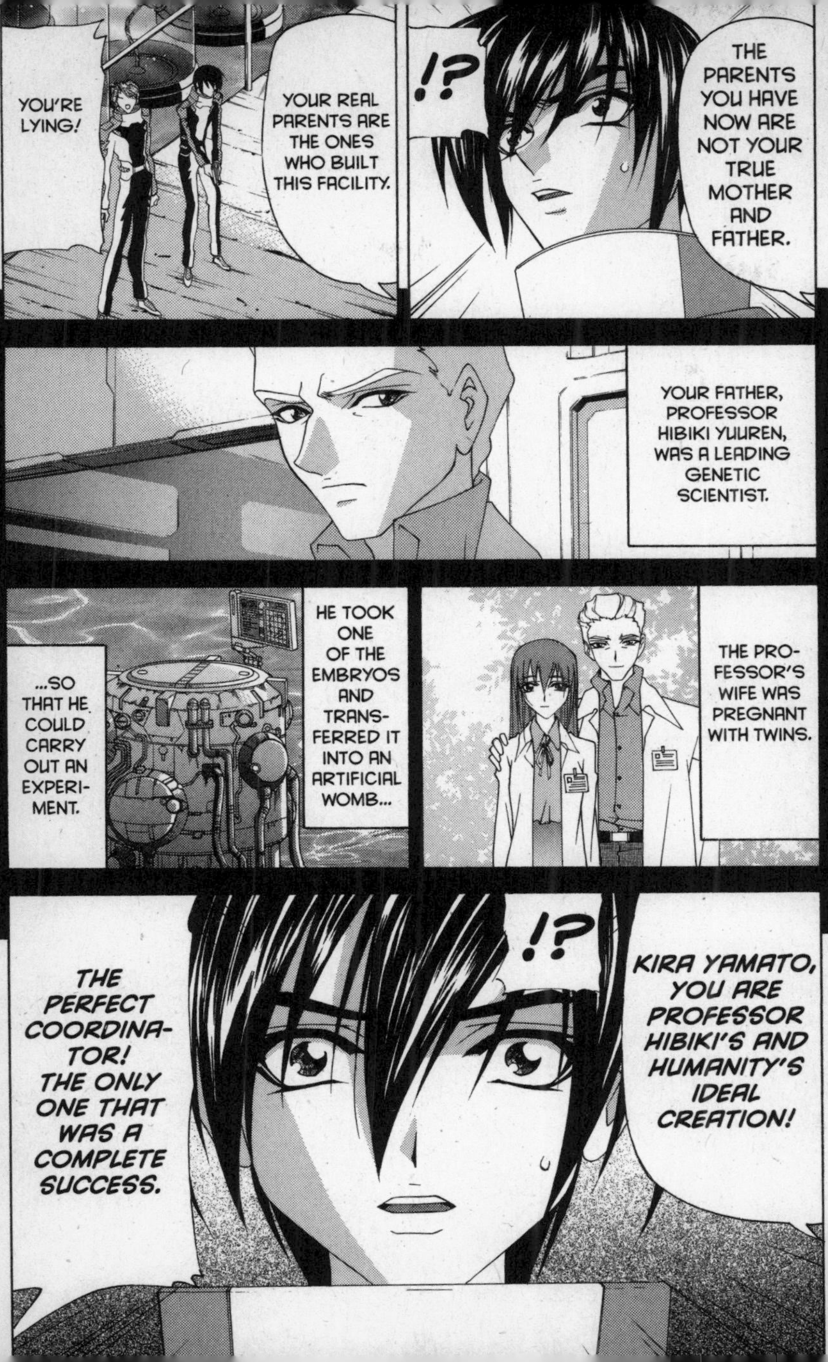
THE PARENTS YOU HAVE NOW ARE NOT YOUR TRUE MOTHER AND FATHER.
!?
YOUR REAL PARENTS ARE THE ONES WHO BUILT THIS FACILITY.
YOU'RE LYING!
YOUR FATHER, PROFESSOR HIBIKI YUUREN, WAS A LEADING GENETIC SCIENTIST.
THE PROFESSOR'S WIFE WAS PREGNANT WITH TWINS.
HE TOOK ONE OF THE EMBRYOS AND TRANSFERRED IT INTO AN ARTIFICIAL WOMB...
...SO THAT HE COULD CARRY OUT AN EXPERIMENT.
KIRA YAMATO, YOU ARE PROFESSOR HIBIKI'S AND HUMANITY'S IDEAL CREATION!
!?
THE PERFECT COORDINATOR! THE ONLY ONE THAT WAS A COMPLETE SUCCESS.

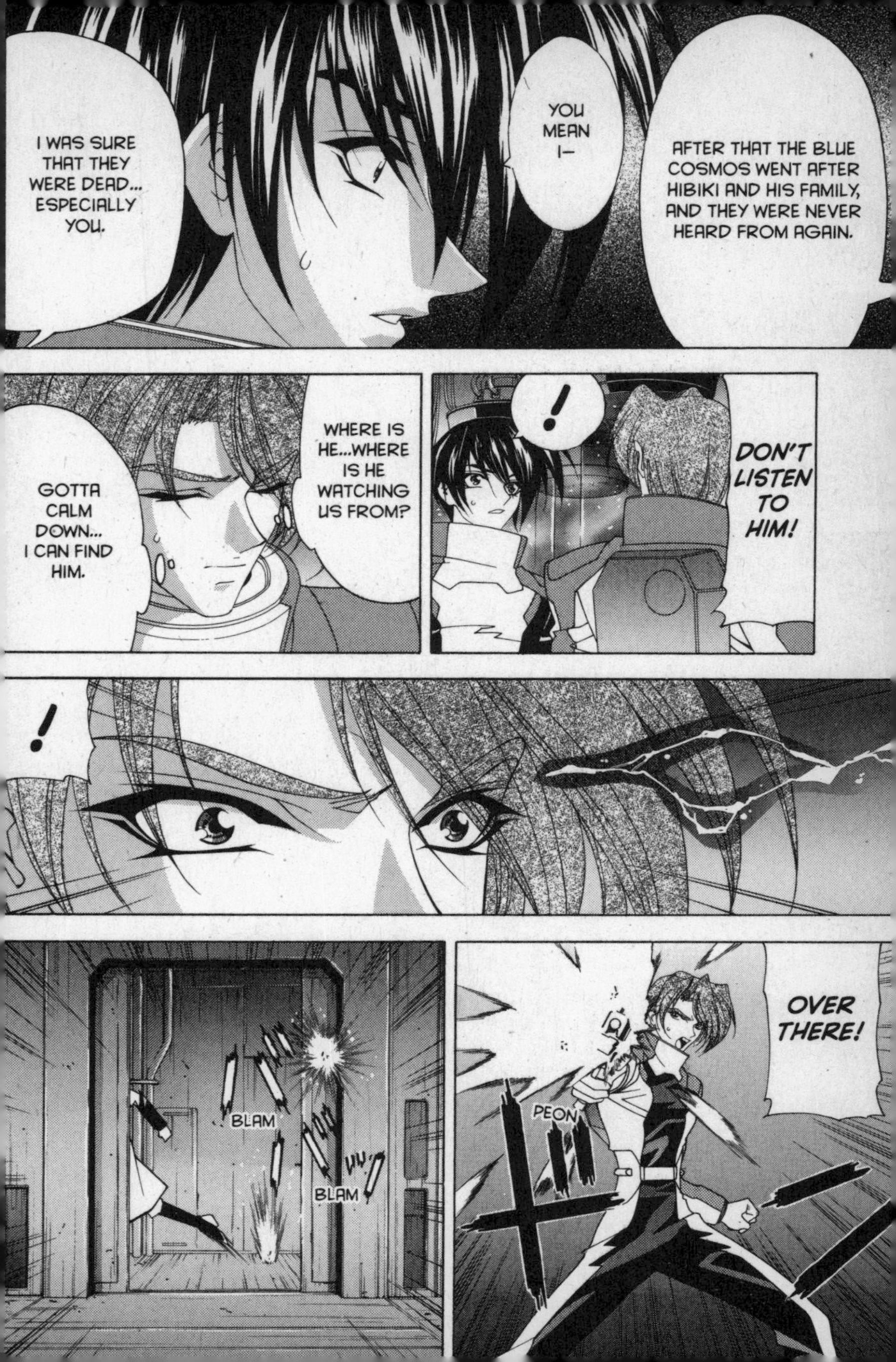
AFTER THAT THE BLUE COSMOS WENT AFTER HIBIKI AND HIS FAMILY, AND THEY WERE NEVER HEARD FROM AGAIN.
YOU MEAN I—
I WAS SURE THAT THEY WERE DEAD... ESPECIALLY YOU.
DON'T LISTEN TO HIM!
!
WHERE IS HE...WHERE IS HE WATCHING US FROM?
GOTTA CALM DOWN... I CAN FIND HIM.
!
OVER THERE!
PEON
BLAM
BLAM

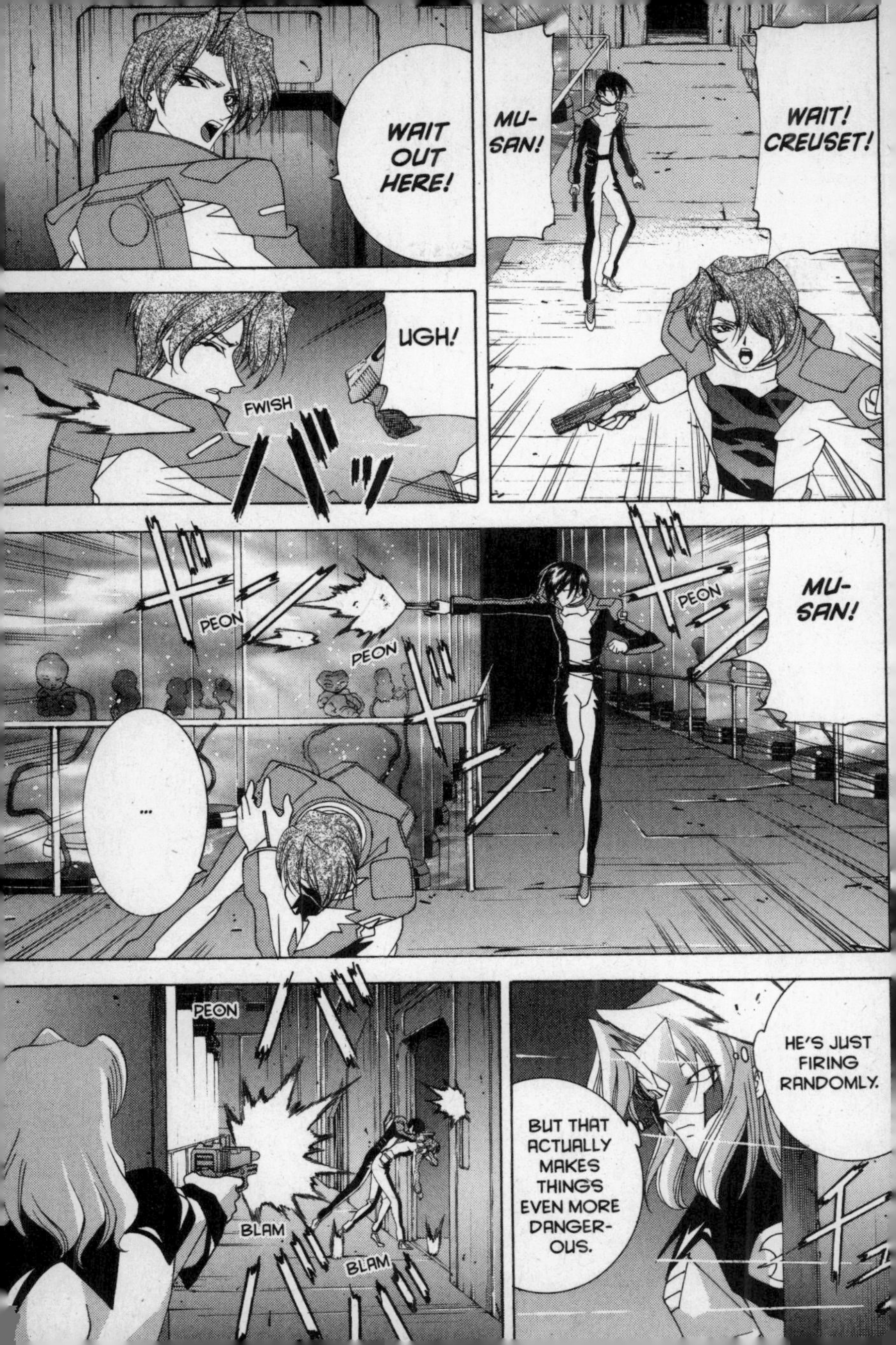
WAIT! CREUSET!
MU-SAN!
WAIT OUT HERE!
UGH!
FWISH
バッ
MU-SAN!
PEON
PEON
PEON
...
HE'S JUST FIRING RANDOMLY.
BUT THAT ACTUALLY MAKES THINGS EVEN MORE DANGEROUS.
PEON
BLAM
BLAM

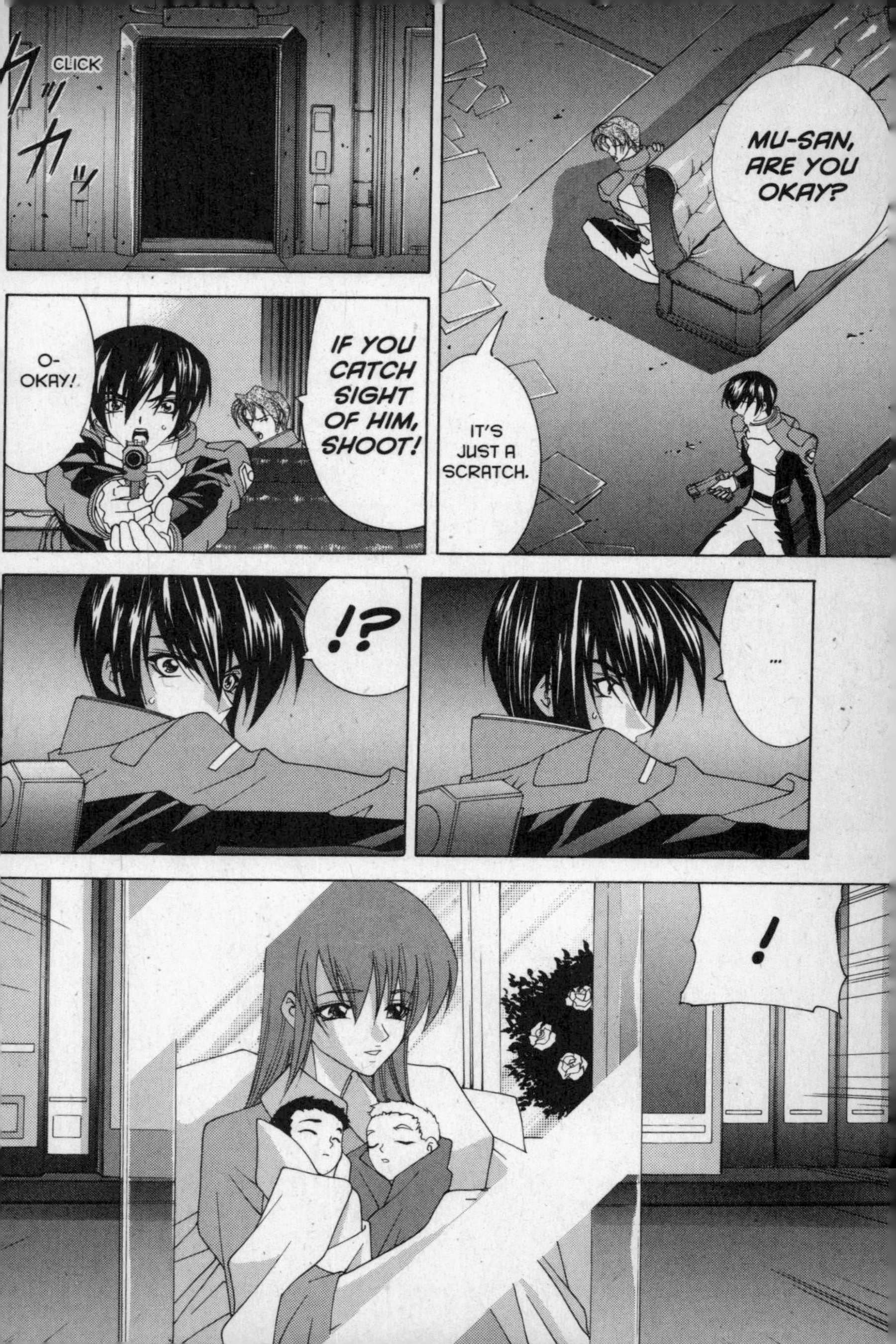
MU-SAN, ARE YOU OKAY?
IT'S JUST A SCRATCH.
CLICK
IF YOU CATCH SIGHT OF HIM, SHOOT!
O-OKAY!
...
!?
!

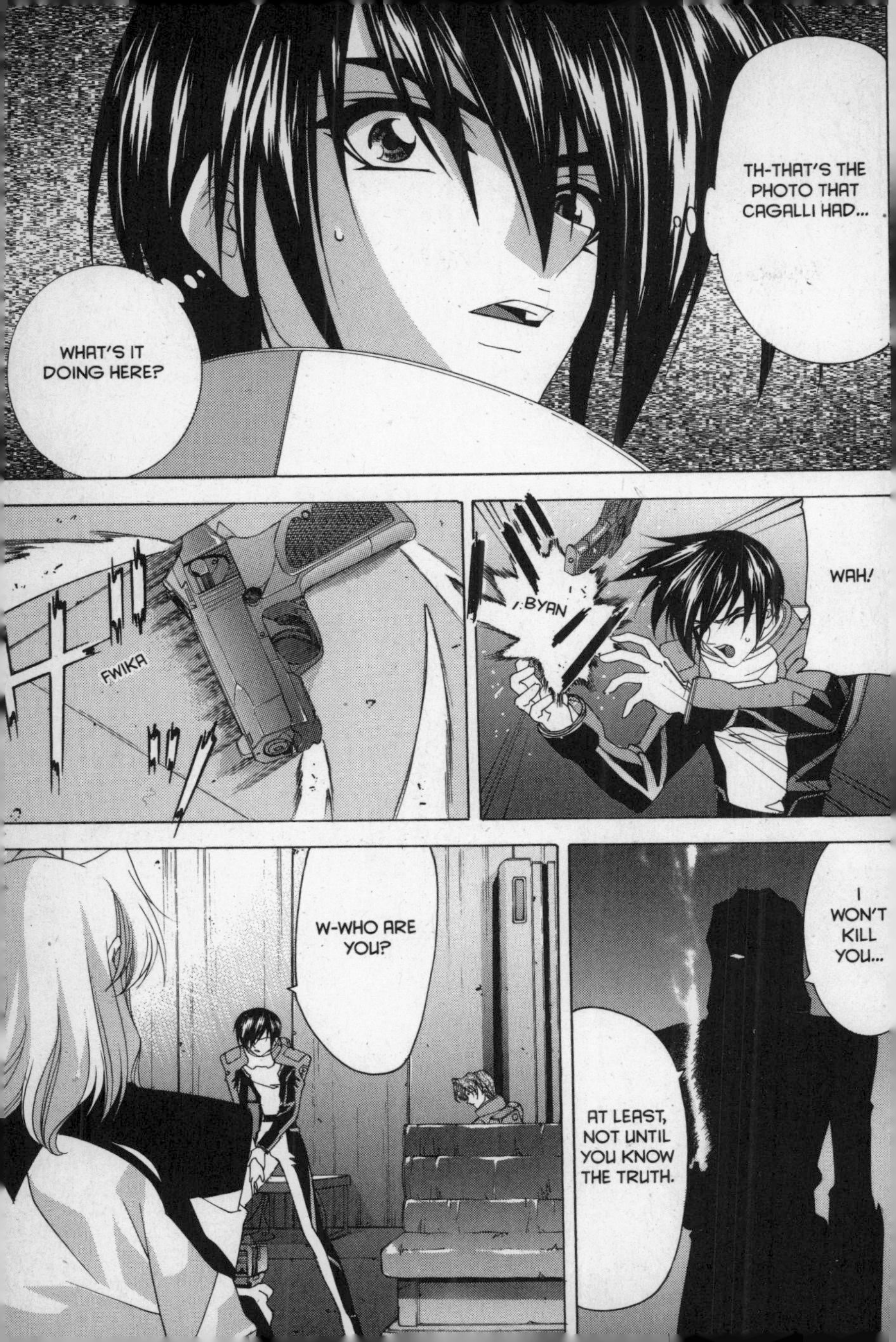
TH-THAT'S THE PHOTO THAT CAGALLI HAD...
WHAT'S IT DOING HERE?
WAH!
BYAN
FWIKA
I WON'T KILL YOU...
AT LEAST, NOT UNTIL YOU KNOW THE TRUTH.
W-WHO ARE YOU?

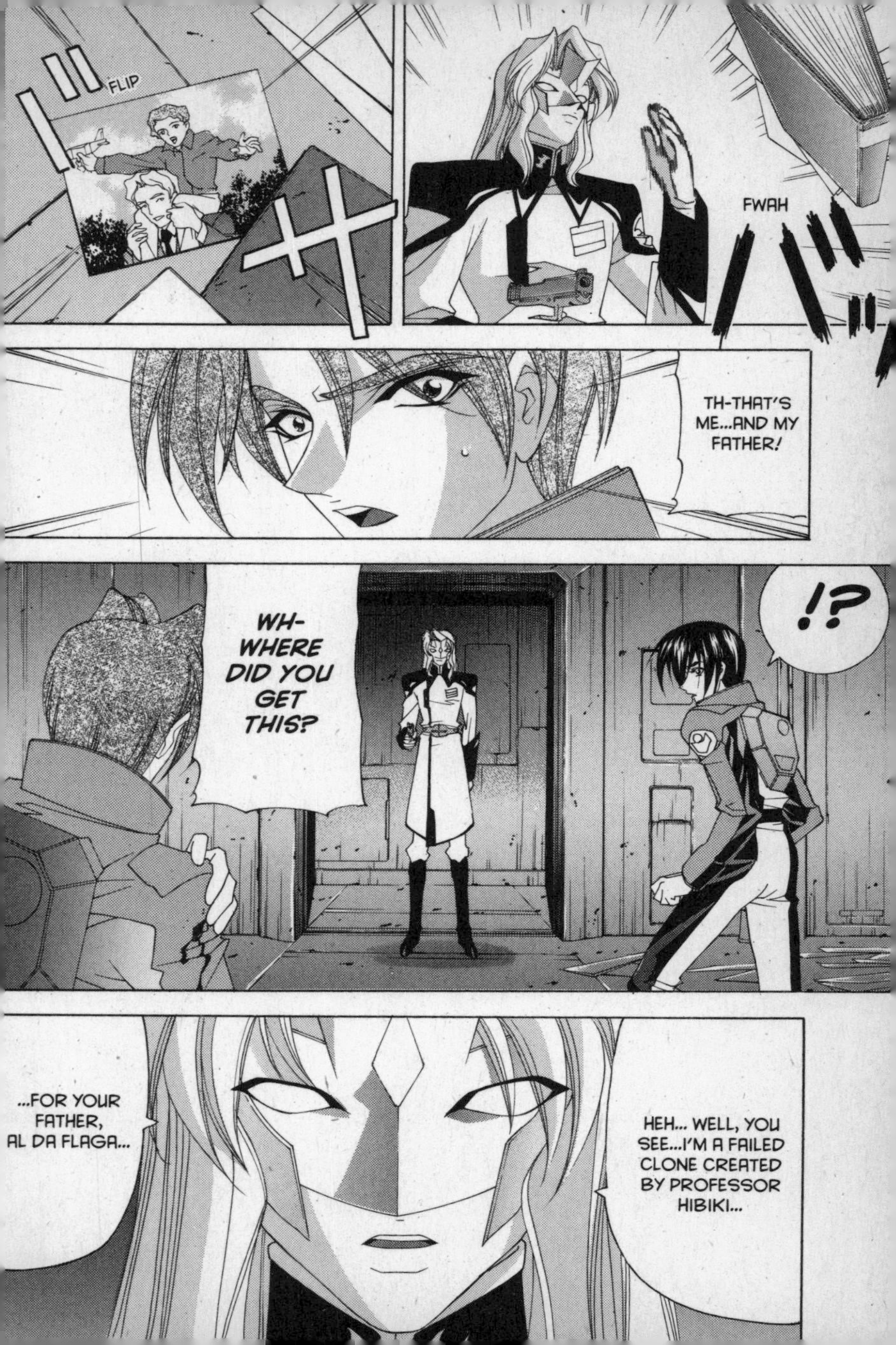
FWAH
FLIP
TH-THAT'S ME...AND MY FATHER!
!?
WH-WHERE DID YOU GET THIS?
HEH... WELL, YOU SEE...I'M A FAILED CLONE CREATED BY PROFESSOR HIBIKI...
...FOR YOUR FATHER, AL DA FLAGA...

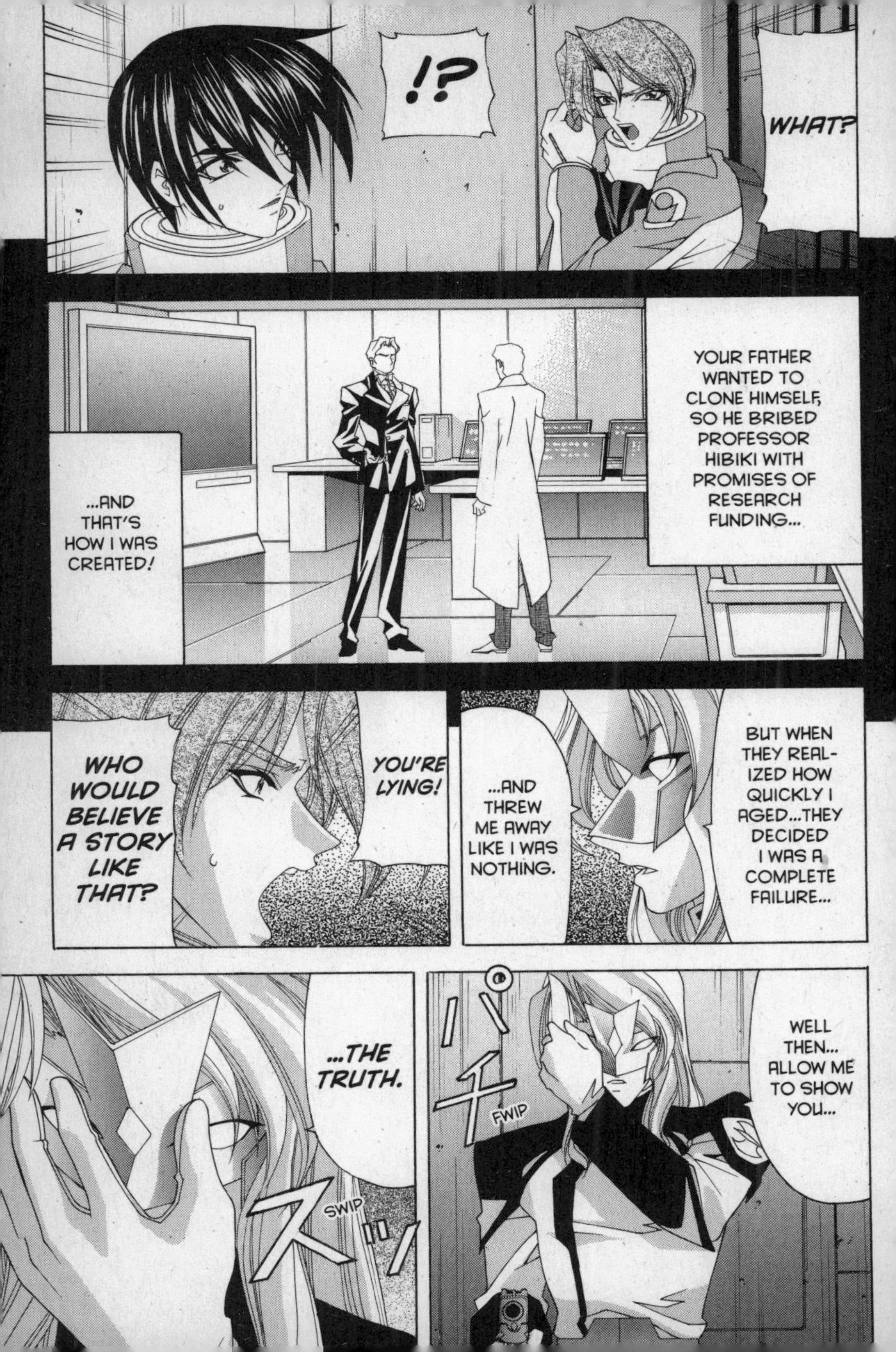
WHAT?
!?
YOUR FATHER WANTED TO CLONE HIMSELF, SO HE BRIBED PROFESSOR HIBIKI WITH PROMISES OF RESEARCH FUNDING...
...AND THAT'S HOW I WAS CREATED!
BUT WHEN THEY REAL-IZED HOW QUICKLY I AGED...THEY DECIDED I WAS A COMPLETE FAILURE...
...AND THREW ME AWAY LIKE I WAS NOTHING.
YOU'RE LYING!
WHO WOULD BELIEVE A STORY LIKE THAT?
WELL THEN... ALLOW ME TO SHOW YOU...
FWIP
...THE TRUTH.
SWIP

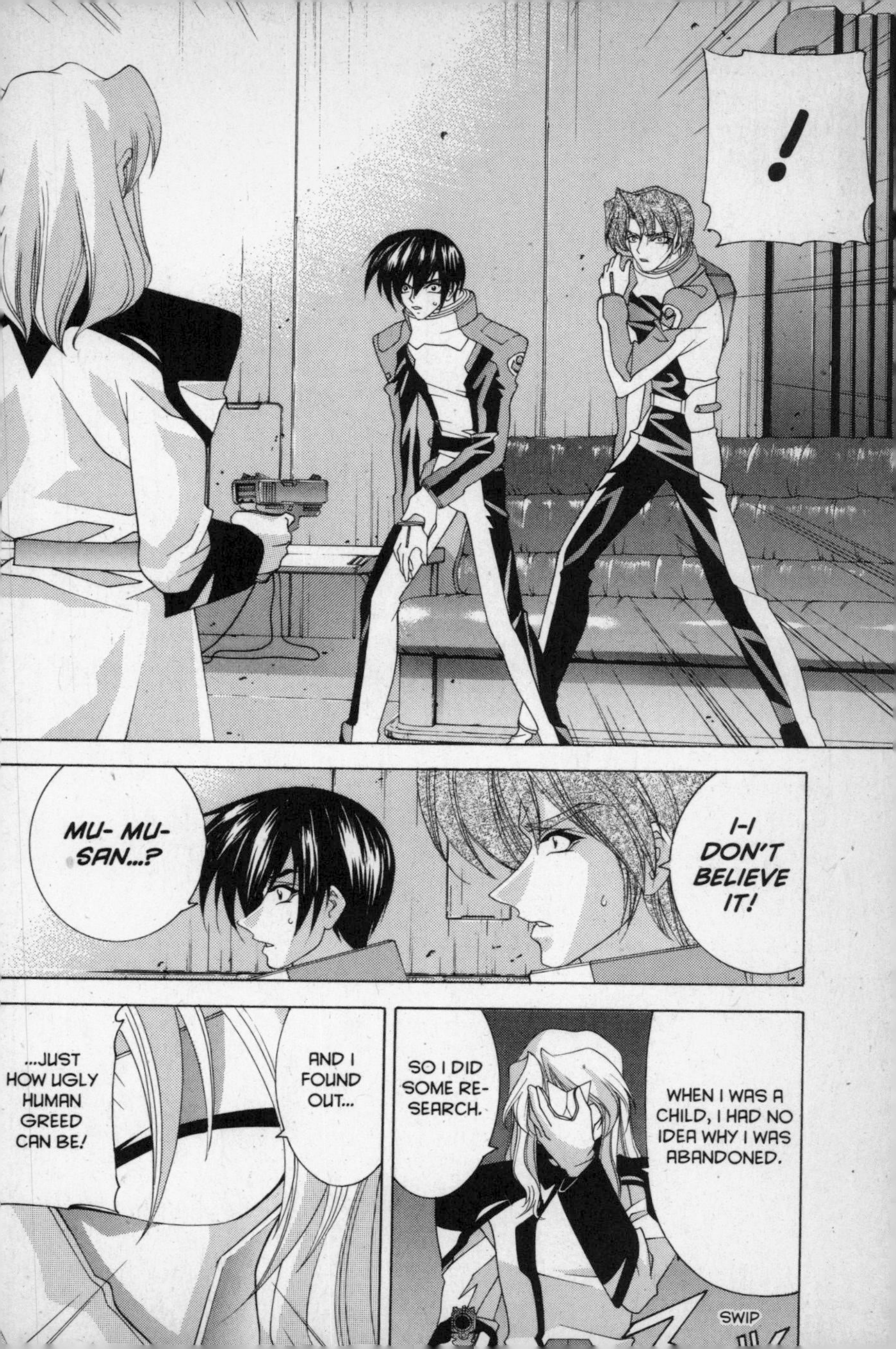
!
I-I DON'T BELIEVE IT!
MU- MU-SAN...?
WHEN I WAS A CHILD, I HAD NO IDEA WHY I WAS ABANDONED.
SO I DID SOME RE-SEARCH.
SWIP
AND I FOUND OUT...
...JUST HOW UGLY HUMAN GREED CAN BE!

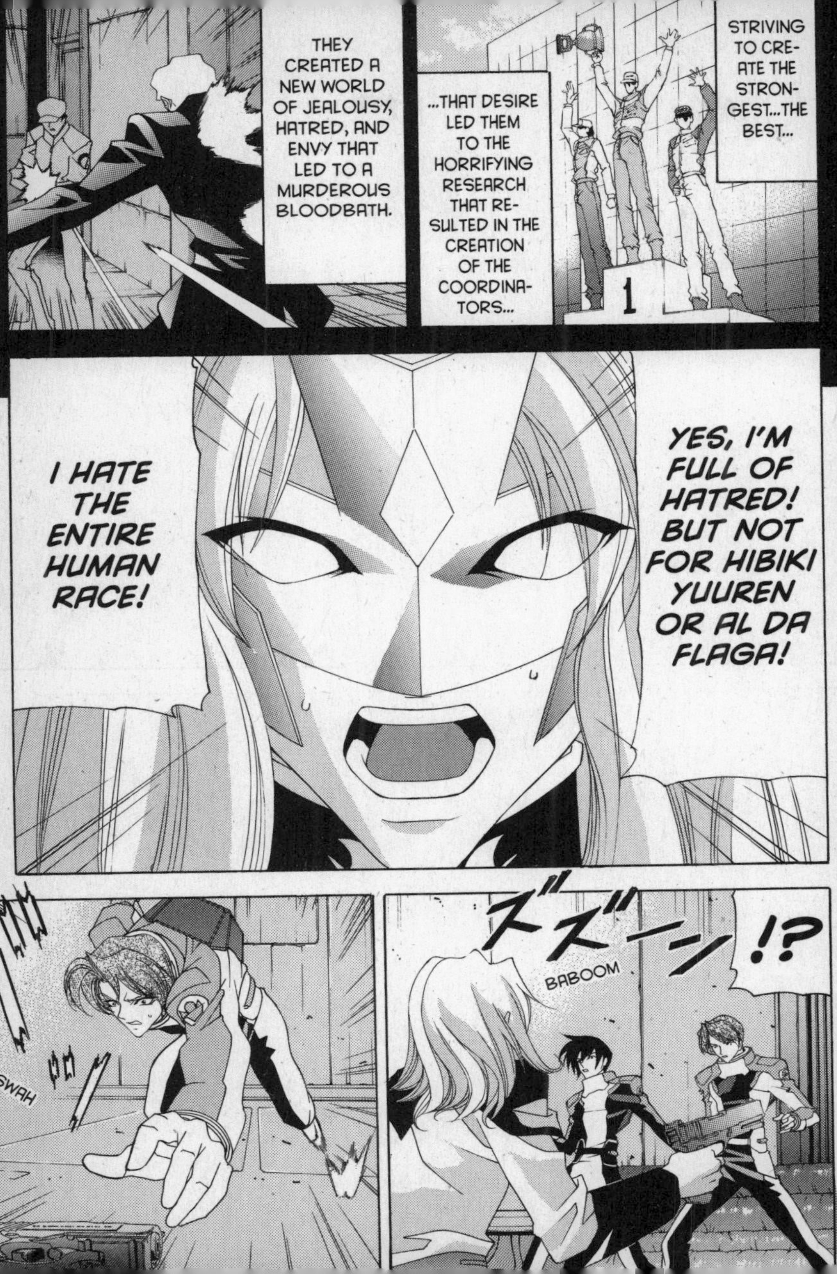
STRIVING TO CREATE THE STRONGEST...THE BEST...
1
...THAT DESIRE LED THEM TO THE HORRIFYING RESEARCH THAT RESULTED IN THE CREATION OF THE COORDINATORS...
THEY CREATED A NEW WORLD OF JEALOUSY, HATRED, AND ENVY THAT LED TO A MURDEROUS BLOODBATH.
YES, I'M FULL OF HATRED! BUT NOT FOR HIBIKI YUUREN OR AL DA FLAGA!
I HATE THE ENTIRE HUMAN RACE!
ズズーン
BABOOM
!?
SWAH

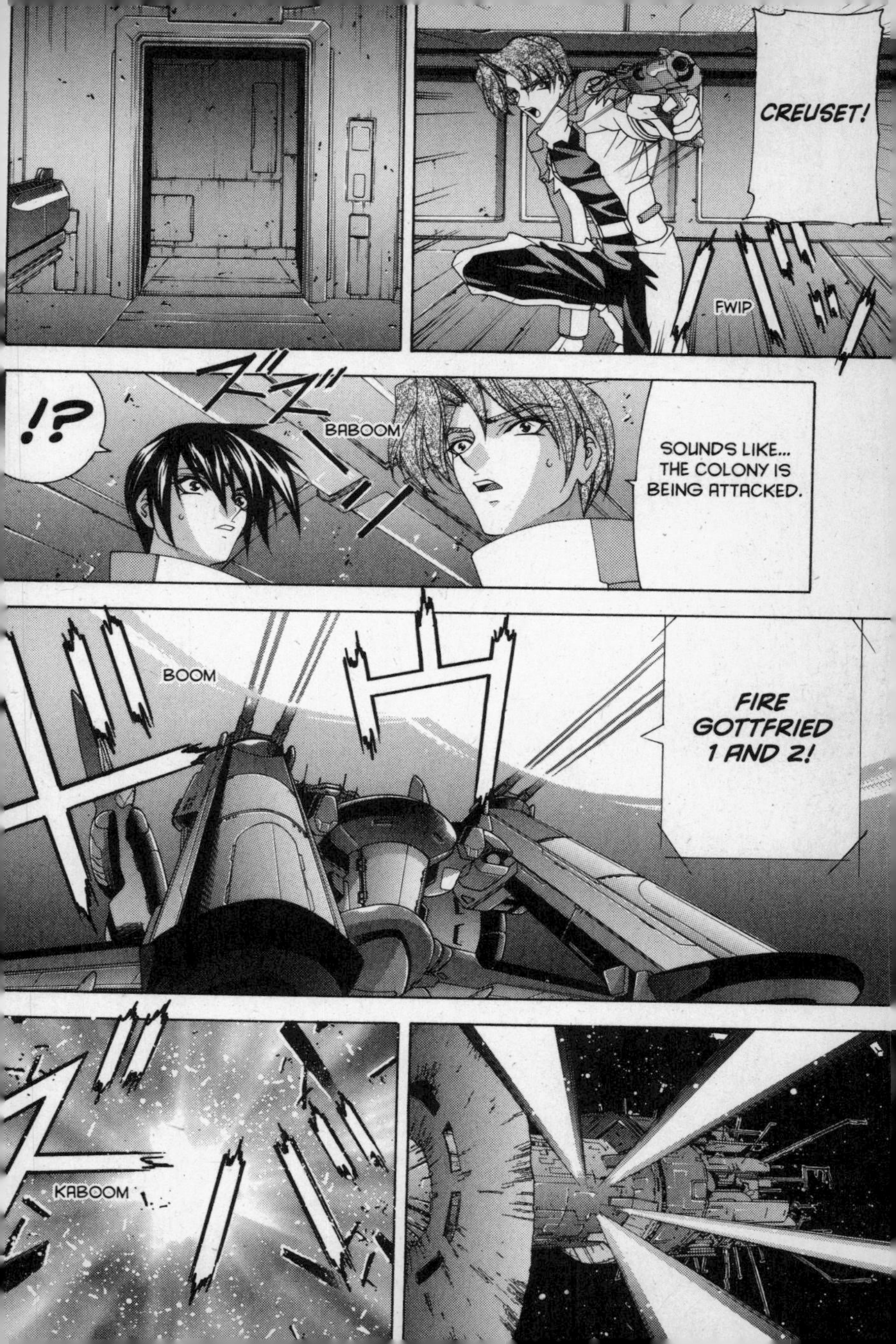
CREUSET!
FWIP
SOUNDS LIKE... THE COLONY IS BEING ATTACKED.
ズズ
BABOOM
!?
FIRE GOTTFRIED 1 AND 2!
BOOM
KABOOM

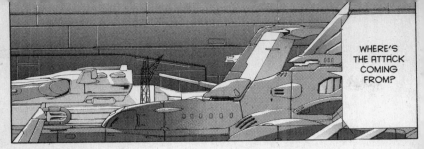

WHERE'S THE ATTACK COMING FROM?

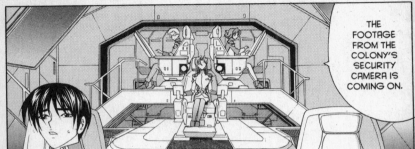

THE FOOTAGE FROM THE COLONY'S SECURITY CAMERA IS COMING ON.

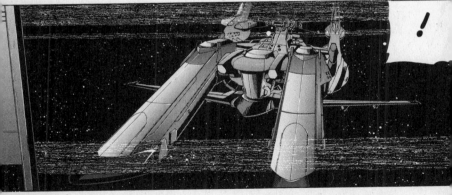

!

THE ARCHANGEL...?

WHA-WHAT THE—

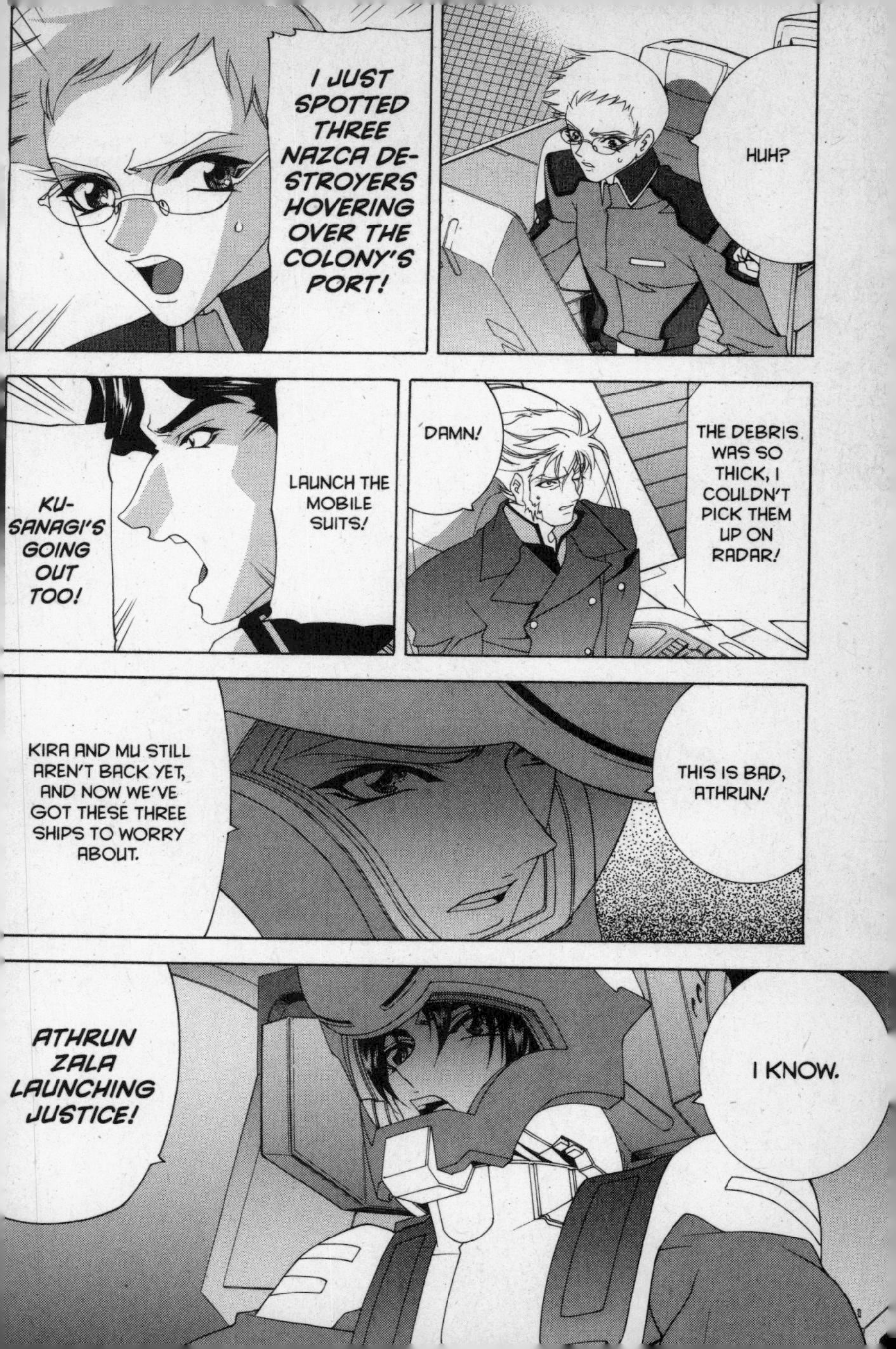
HUH?
I JUST SPOTTED THREE NAZCA DE-STROYERS HOVERING OVER THE COLONY'S PORT!
THE DEBRIS WAS SO THICK, I COULDN'T PICK THEM UP ON RADAR!
DAMN!
LAUNCH THE MOBILE SUITS!
KU-SANAGI'S GOING OUT TOO!
THIS IS BAD, ATHRUN!
KIRA AND MU STILL AREN'T BACK YET, AND NOW WE'VE GOT THESE THREE SHIPS TO WORRY ABOUT.
I KNOW.
ATHRUN ZALA LAUNCHING JUSTICE!

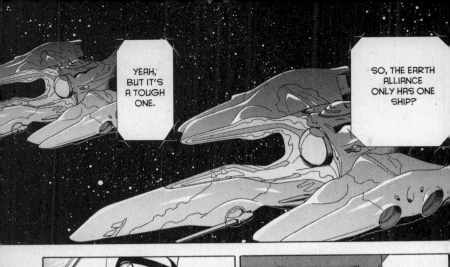

SO, THE EARTH ALLIANCE ONLY HAS ONE SHIP?
YEAH, BUT IT'S A TOUGH ONE.
DO I HAVE PERMISSION TO LAUNCH, SIR?
NO! WE STILL HAVEN'T HEARD FROM THE COM-MANDER.
ADESU!
PUT FLAY ALLSTER IN AN ESCAPE POD, AND SHOOT HER OUT...
...TOWARD THE EARTH ALLIANCE SHIP.
THAT WILL BUY US SOME TIME.
ゴオオオ
ZOOM
WHILE THEY'RE BUSY WITH THAT, WE'LL LAUNCH ALL OF OUR MOBILE SUITS!

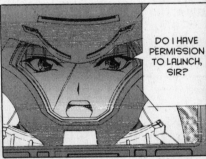

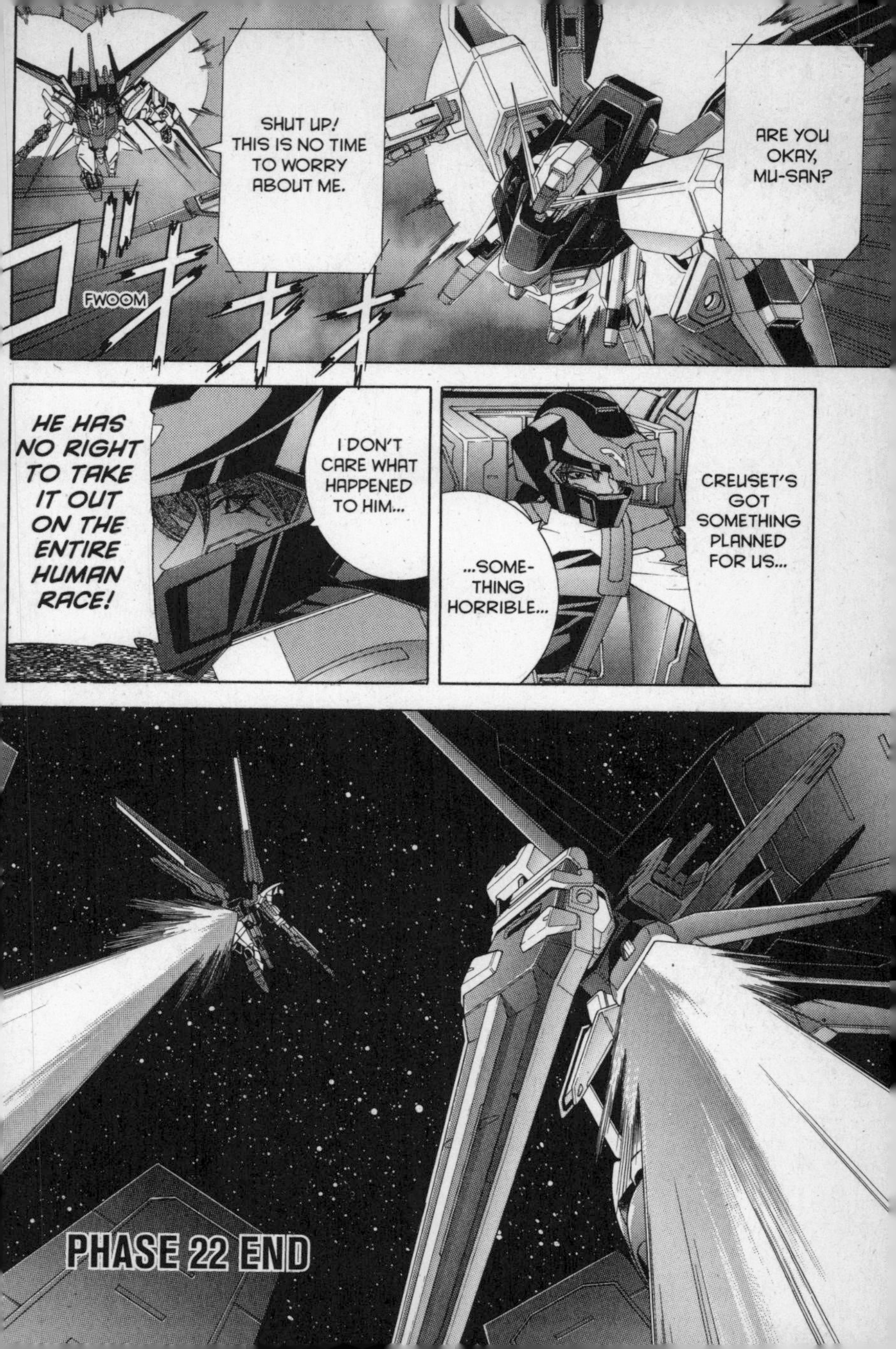
ARE YOU OKAY, MU-SAN?
SHUT UP! THIS IS NO TIME TO WORRY ABOUT ME.
FWOOM
CREUSET'S GOT SOMETHING PLANNED FOR US...
...SOME-THING HORRIBLE...
I DON'T CARE WHAT HAPPENED TO HIM...
HE HAS NO RIGHT TO TAKE IT OUT ON THE ENTIRE HUMAN RACE!
PHASE 22 END

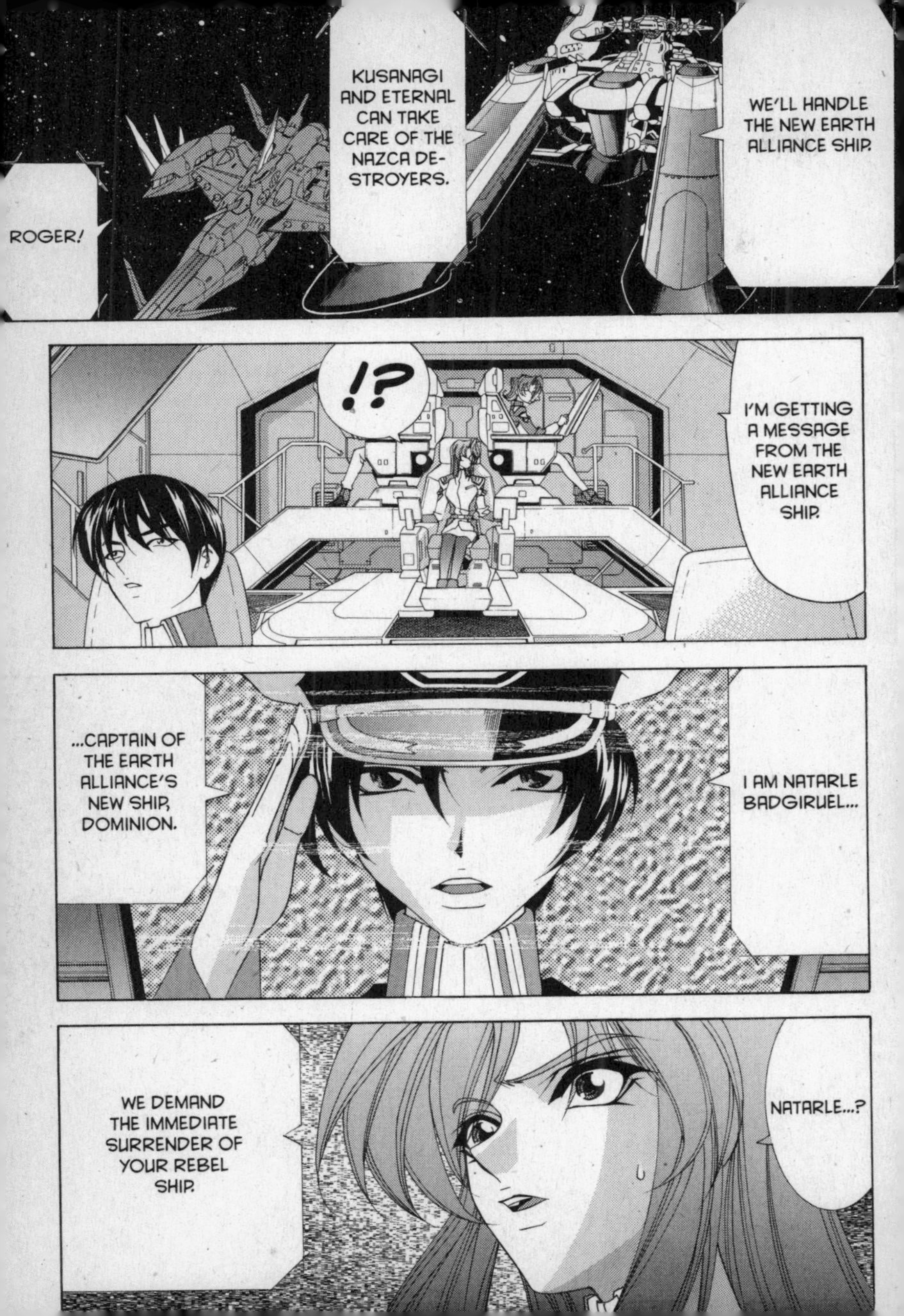
WE'LL HANDLE THE NEW EARTH ALLIANCE SHIP.
KUSANAGI AND ETERNAL CAN TAKE CARE OF THE NAZCA DE-STROYERS.
ROGER!
I'M GETTING A MESSAGE FROM THE NEW EARTH ALLIANCE SHIP.
!?
I AM NATARLE BADGIRUEL...
...CAPTAIN OF THE EARTH ALLIANCE'S NEW SHIP, DOMINION.
NATARLE...?
WE DEMAND THE IMMEDIATE SURRENDER OF YOUR REBEL SHIP.

PHASE 23 – RECURRING NIGHTMARE

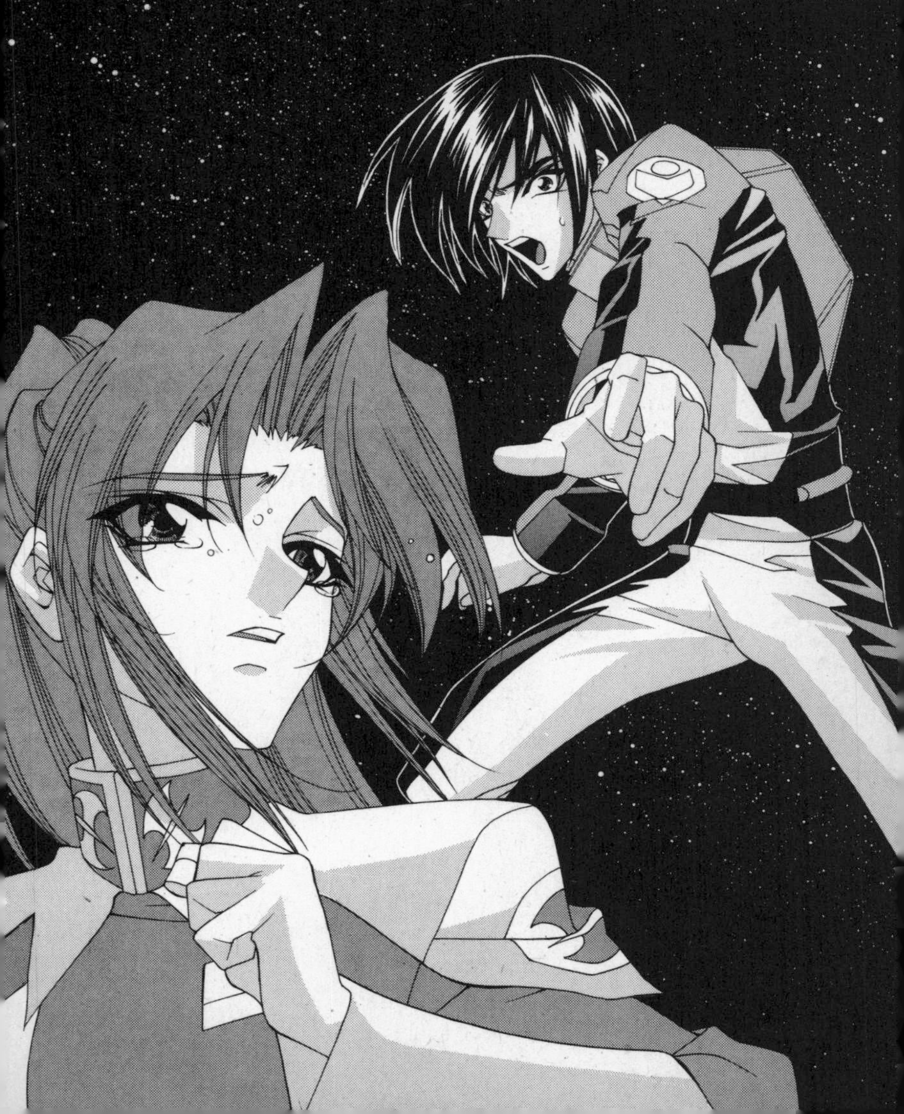

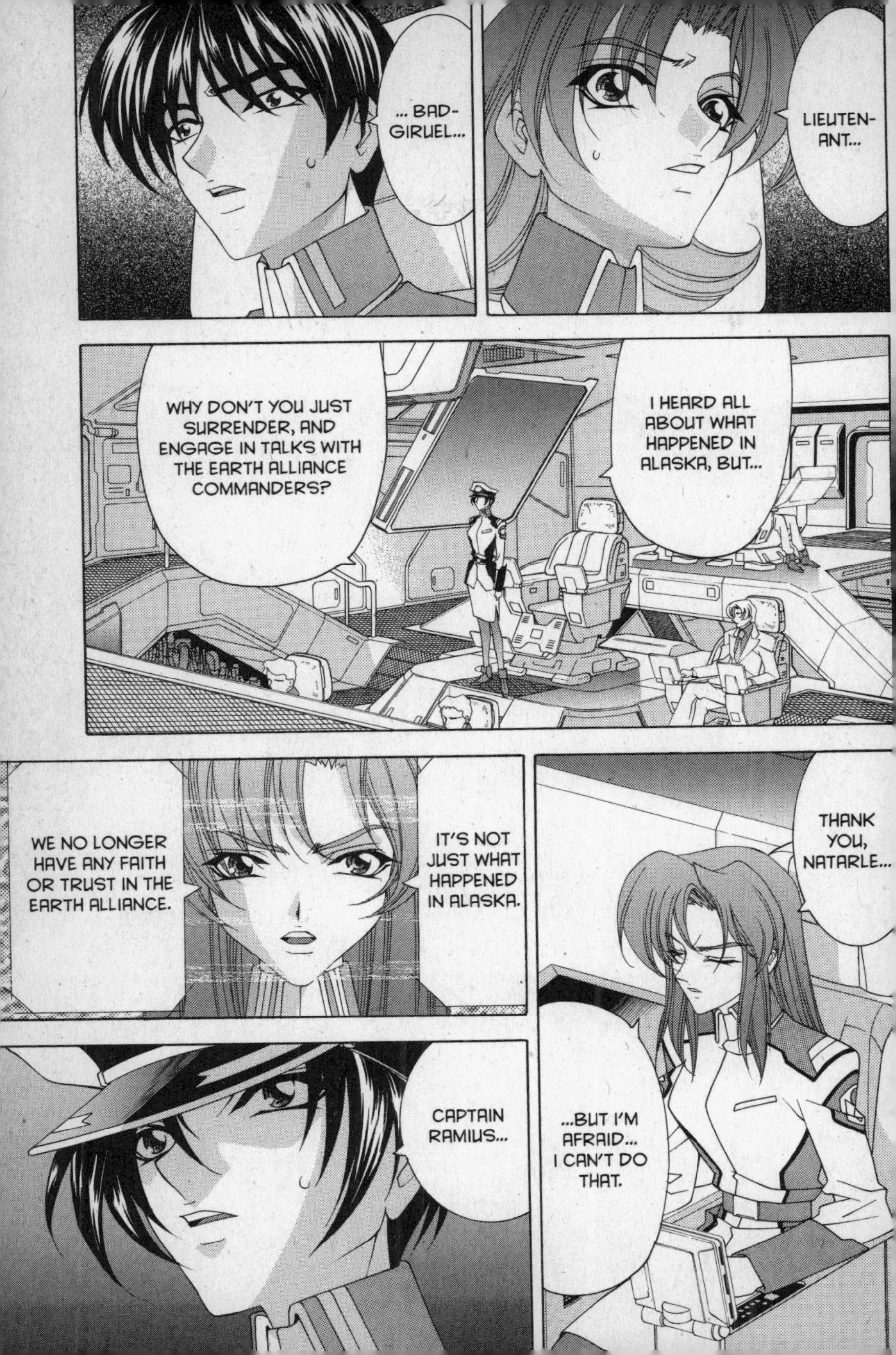
LIEUTENANT...
... BAD-GIRUEL...
I HEARD ALL ABOUT WHAT HAPPENED IN ALASKA, BUT...
WHY DON'T YOU JUST SURRENDER, AND ENGAGE IN TALKS WITH THE EARTH ALLIANCE COMMANDERS?
THANK YOU, NATARLE...
...BUT I'M AFRAID... I CAN'T DO THAT.
IT'S NOT JUST WHAT HAPPENED IN ALASKA.
WE NO LONGER HAVE ANY FAITH OR TRUST IN THE EARTH ALLIANCE.
CAPTAIN RAMIUS...

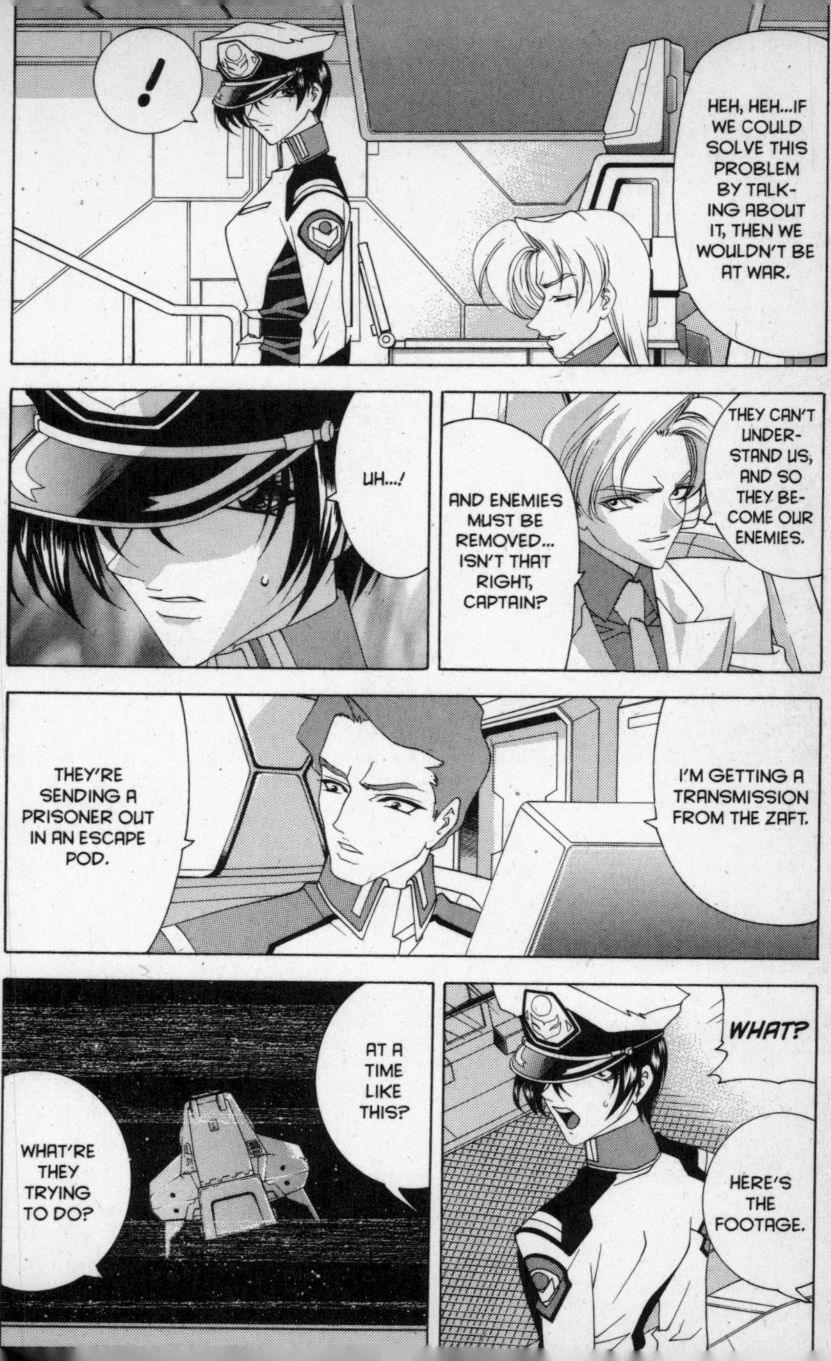
HEH, HEH...IF WE COULD SOLVE THIS PROBLEM BY TALKING ABOUT IT, THEN WE WOULDN'T BE AT WAR.
!
THEY CAN'T UNDERSTAND US, AND SO THEY BECOME OUR ENEMIES.
AND ENEMIES MUST BE REMOVED... ISN'T THAT RIGHT, CAPTAIN?
UH...!
I'M GETTING A TRANSMISSION FROM THE ZAFT.
THEY'RE SENDING A PRISONER OUT IN AN ESCAPE POD.
WHAT?
HERE'S THE FOOTAGE.
AT A TIME LIKE THIS?
WHAT'RE THEY TRYING TO DO?

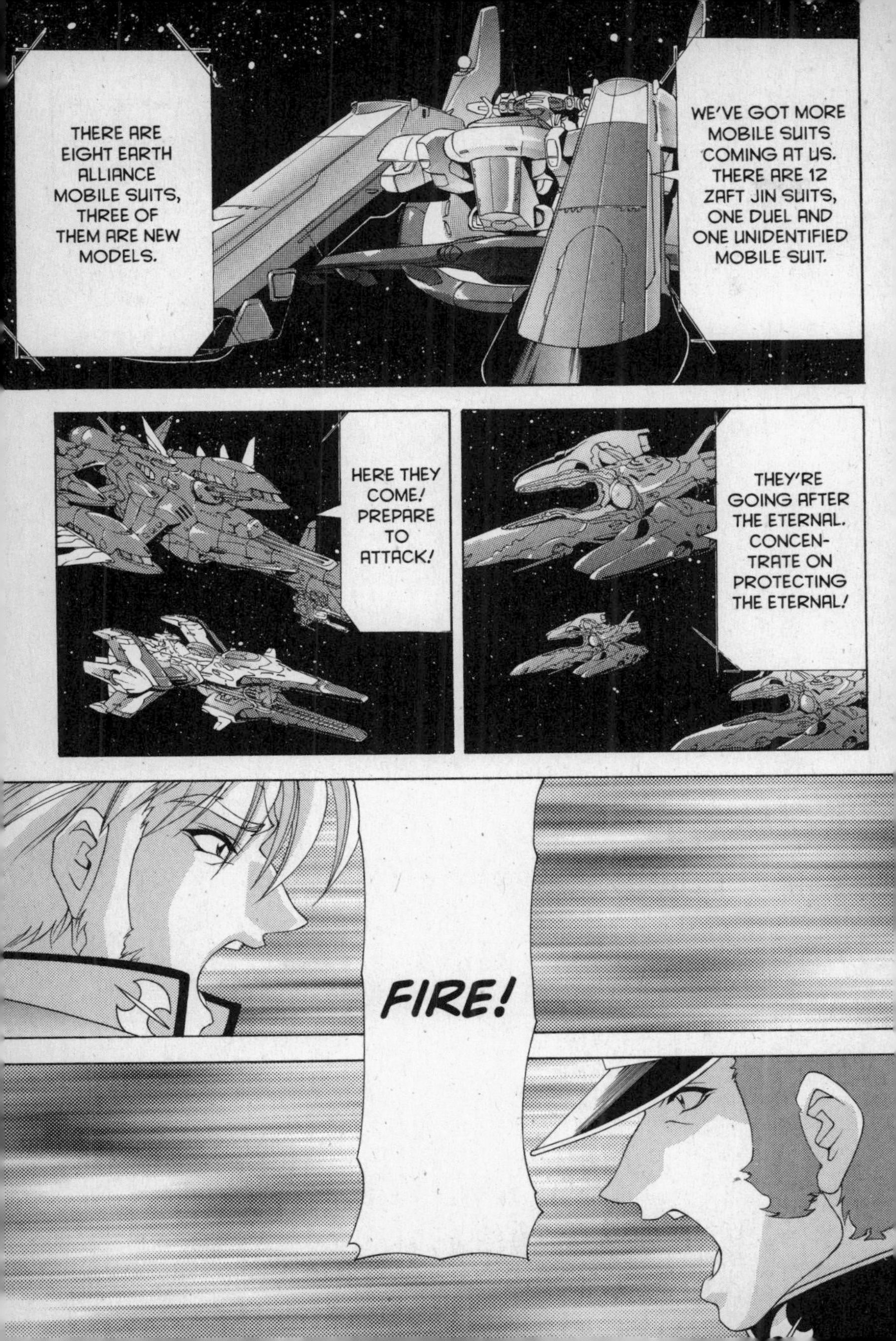
WE'VE GOT MORE MOBILE SUITS COMING AT US. THERE ARE 12 ZAFT JIN SUITS, ONE DUEL AND ONE UNIDENTIFIED MOBILE SUIT.
THERE ARE EIGHT EARTH ALLIANCE MOBILE SUITS, THREE OF THEM ARE NEW MODELS.
THEY'RE GOING AFTER THE ETERNAL. CONCEN-TRATE ON PROTECTING THE ETERNAL!
HERE THEY COME! PREPARE TO ATTACK!
FIRE!

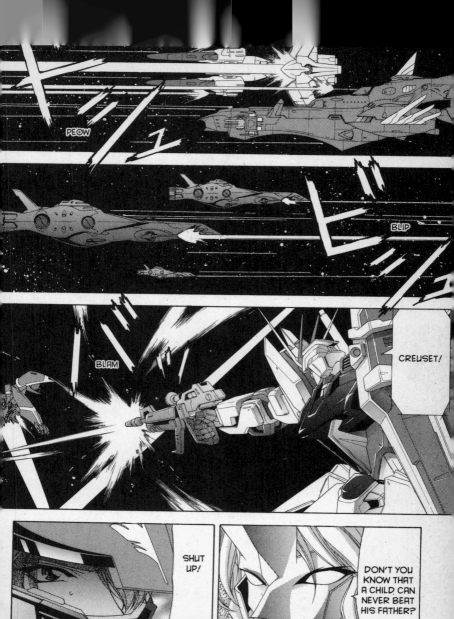

PEOW

BLIP

BLAM

CREUSET!

SHUT UP!

DON'T YOU KNOW THAT A CHILD CAN NEVER BEAT HIS FATHER?

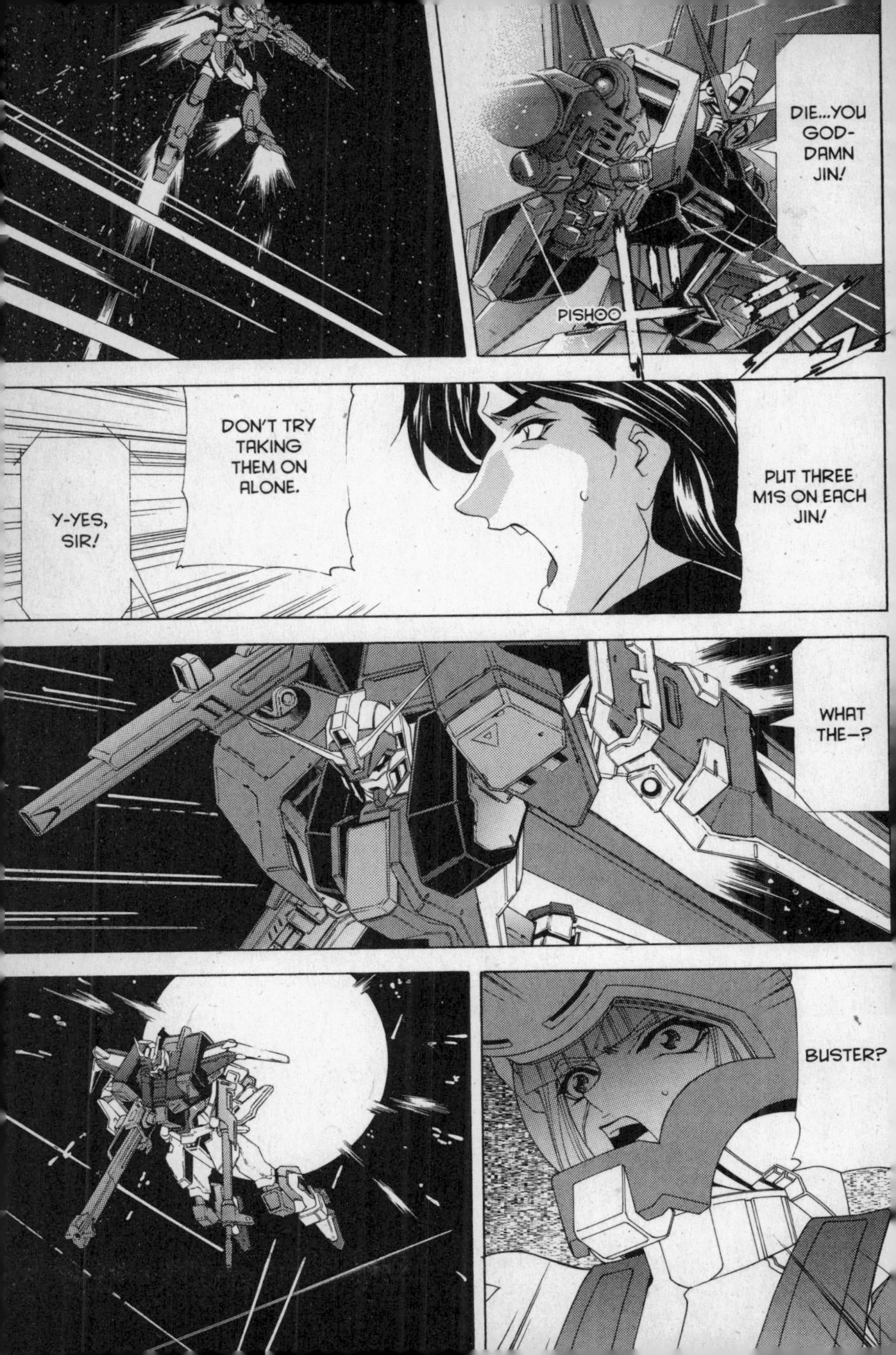
DIE...YOU GOD-DAMN JIN!
PISHOO
PUT THREE M1S ON EACH JIN!
DON'T TRY TAKING THEM ON ALONE.
Y-YES, SIR!
WHAT THE–?
BUSTER?

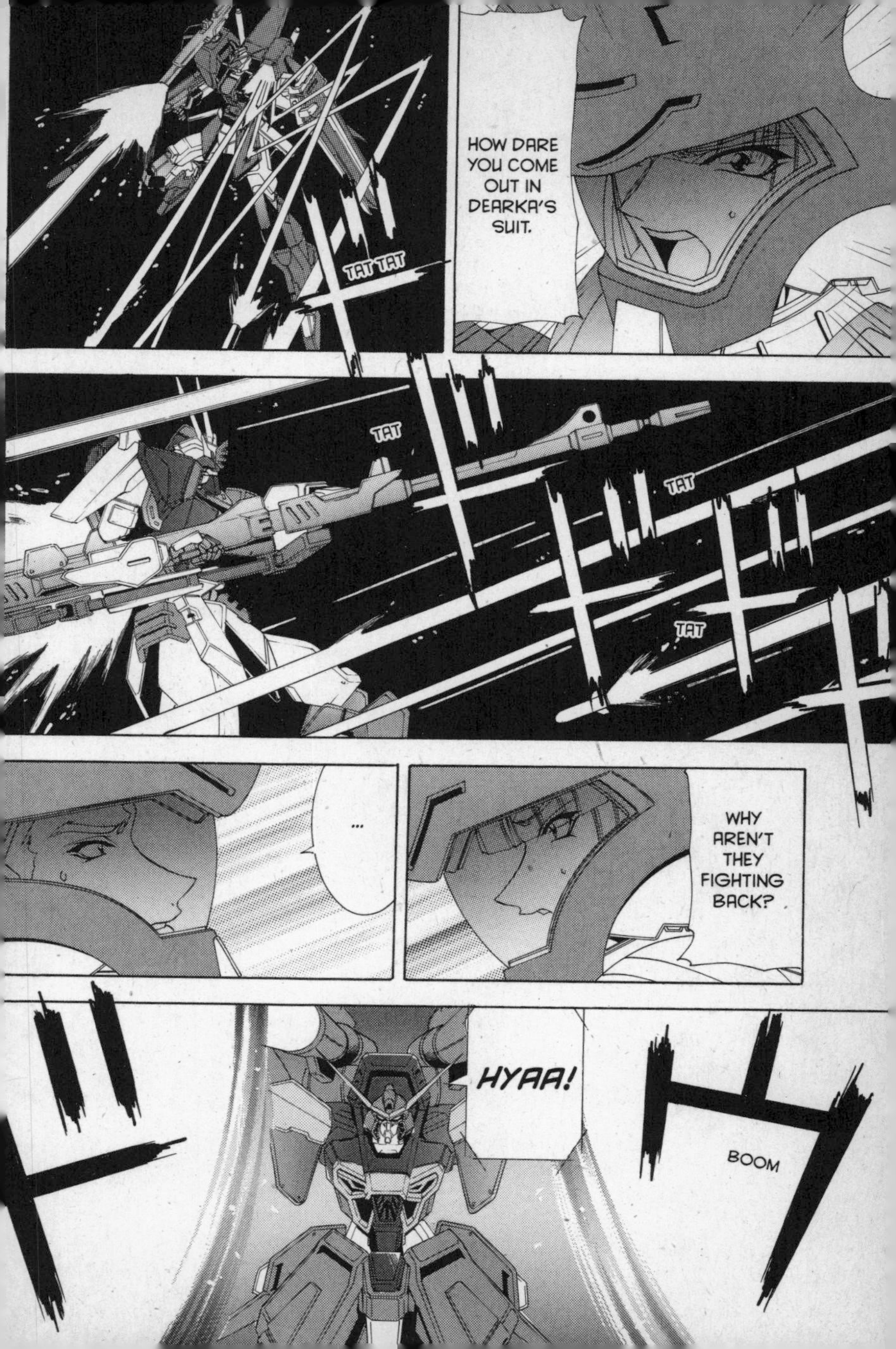
HOW DARE YOU COME OUT IN DEARKA'S SUIT.
TAT TAT
TAT
TAT
TAT
WHY AREN'T THEY FIGHTING BACK?
...
HYAA!
BOOM

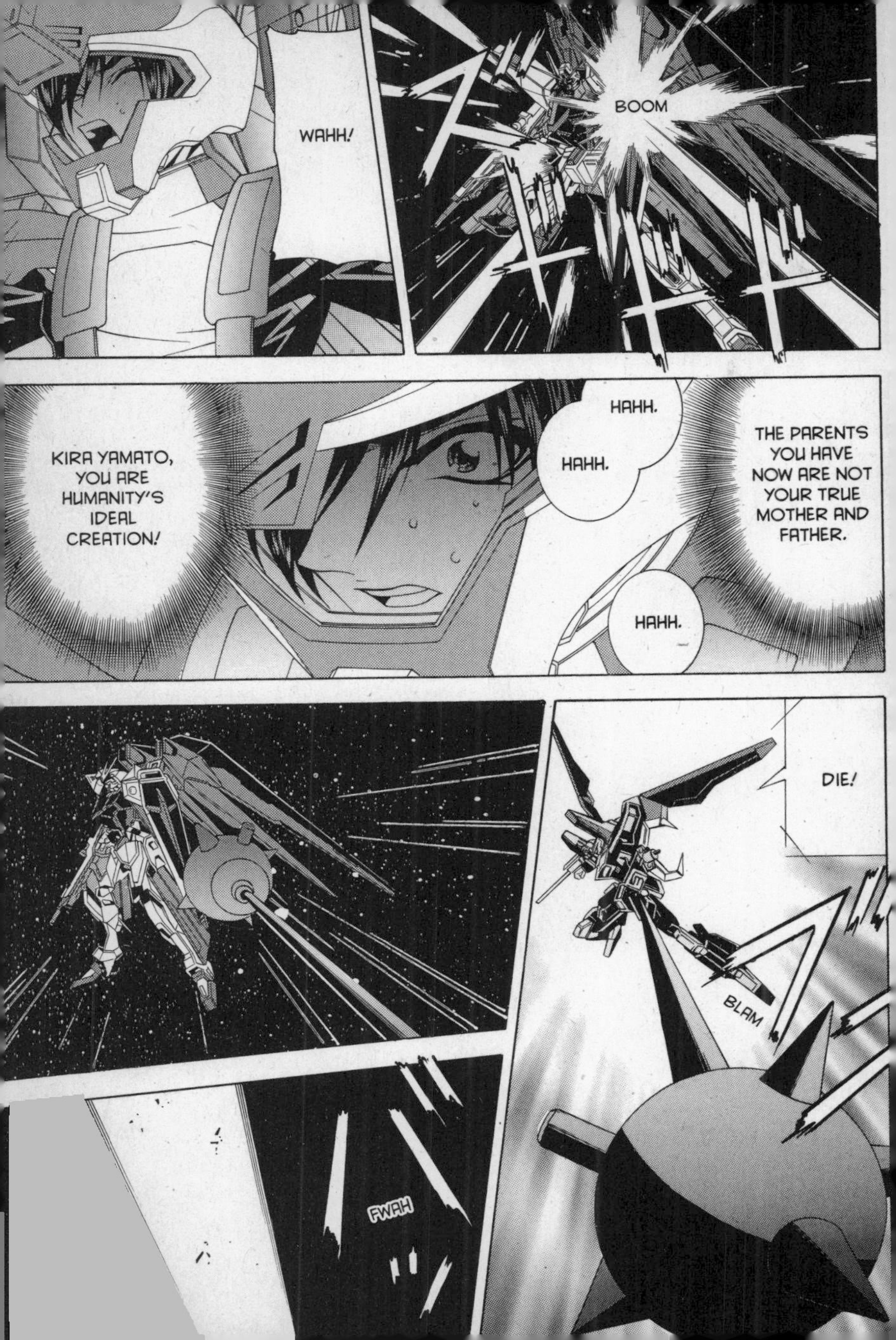
BOOM
WAHH!
THE PARENTS YOU HAVE NOW ARE NOT YOUR TRUE MOTHER AND FATHER.
HAHH.
HAHH.
HAHH.
KIRA YAMATO, YOU ARE HUMANITY'S IDEAL CREATION!
DIE!
BLAM
FWAH

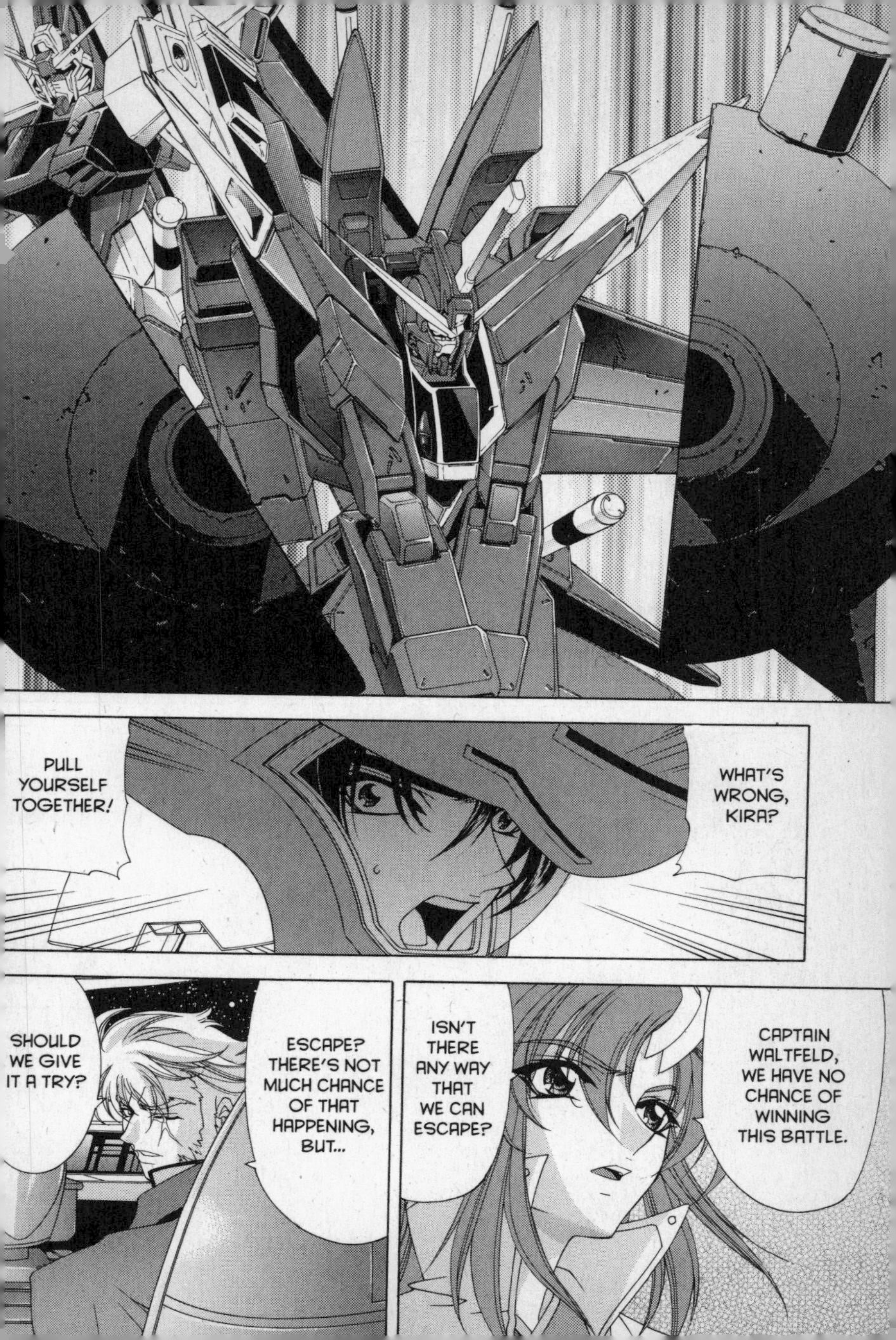
WHAT'S WRONG, KIRA?
PULL YOURSELF TOGETHER!
CAPTAIN WALTFELD, WE HAVE NO CHANCE OF WINNING THIS BATTLE.
ISN'T THERE ANY WAY THAT WE CAN ESCAPE?
ESCAPE? THERE'S NOT MUCH CHANCE OF THAT HAPPENING, BUT...
SHOULD WE GIVE IT A TRY?

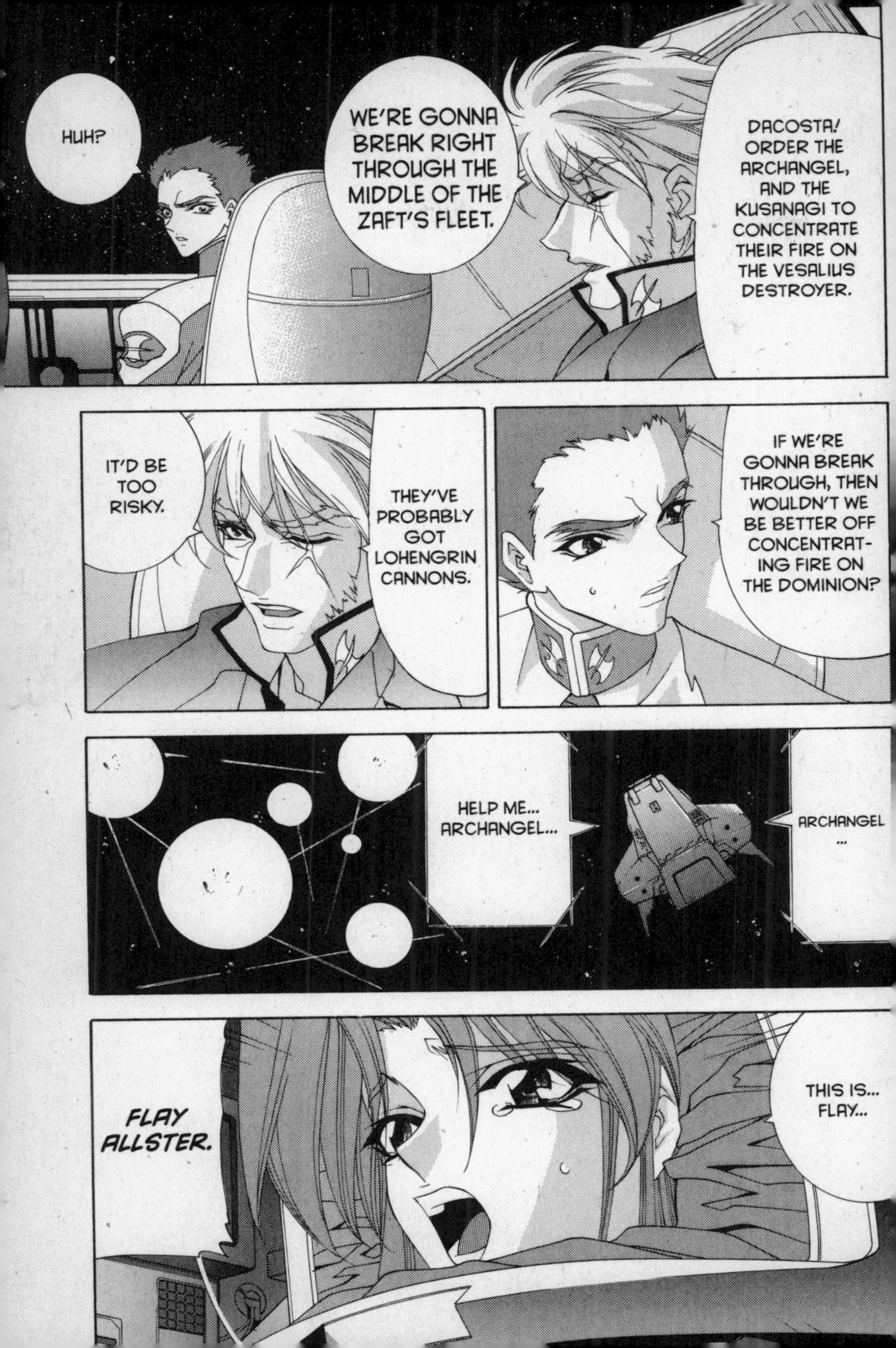
DACOSTA! ORDER THE ARCHANGEL, AND THE KUSANAGI TO CONCENTRATE THEIR FIRE ON THE VESALIUS DESTROYER.
WE'RE GONNA BREAK RIGHT THROUGH THE MIDDLE OF THE ZAFT'S FLEET.
HUH?
IF WE'RE GONNA BREAK THROUGH, THEN WOULDN'T WE BE BETTER OFF CONCENTRAT-ING FIRE ON THE DOMINION?
THEY'VE PROBABLY GOT LOHENGRIN CANNONS.
IT'D BE TOO RISKY.
ARCHANGEL ...
HELP ME... ARCHANGEL...
THIS IS... FLAY...
FLAY ALLSTER.

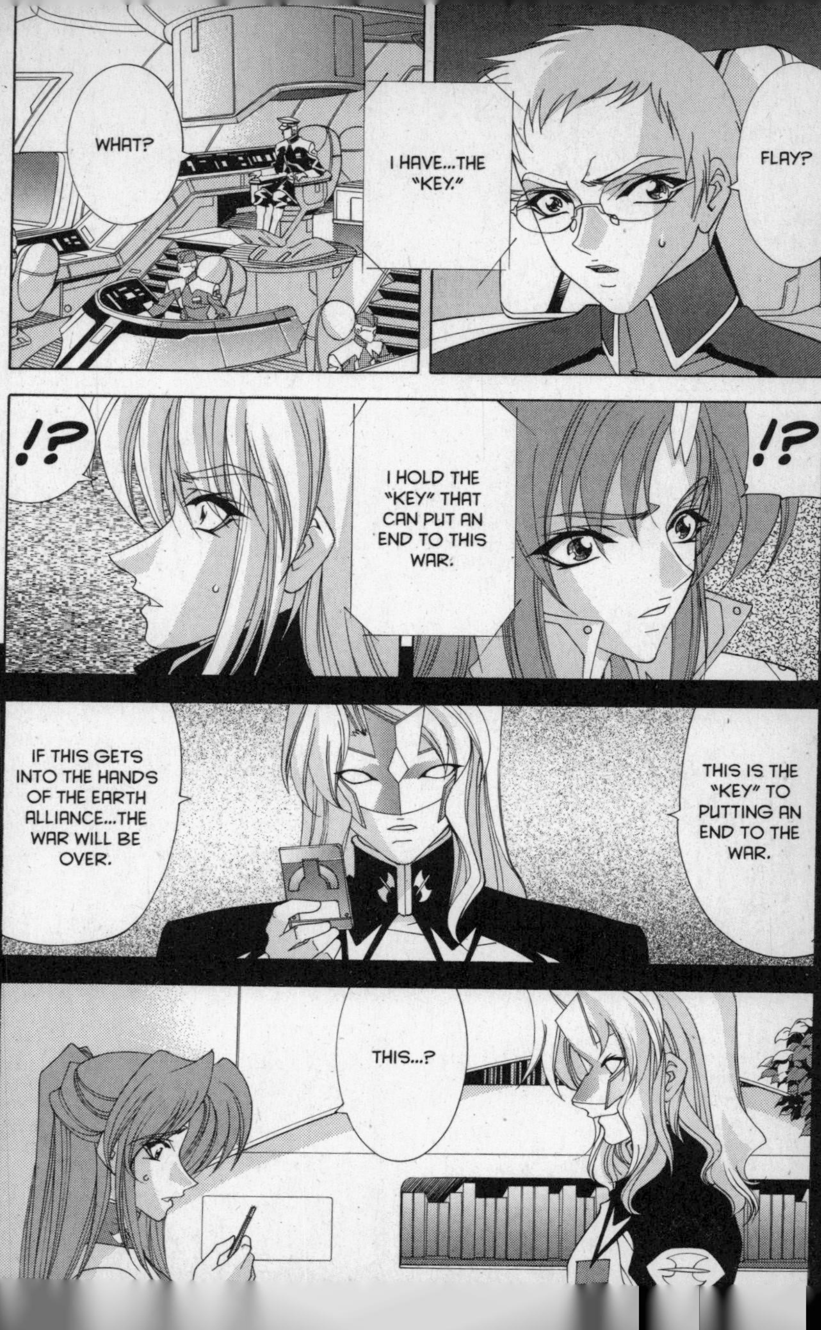
FLAY?
I HAVE...THE "KEY."
WHAT?
!?
I HOLD THE "KEY" THAT CAN PUT AN END TO THIS WAR.
!?
THIS IS THE "KEY" TO PUTTING AN END TO THE WAR.
IF THIS GETS INTO THE HANDS OF THE EARTH ALLIANCE...THE WAR WILL BE OVER.
THIS...?

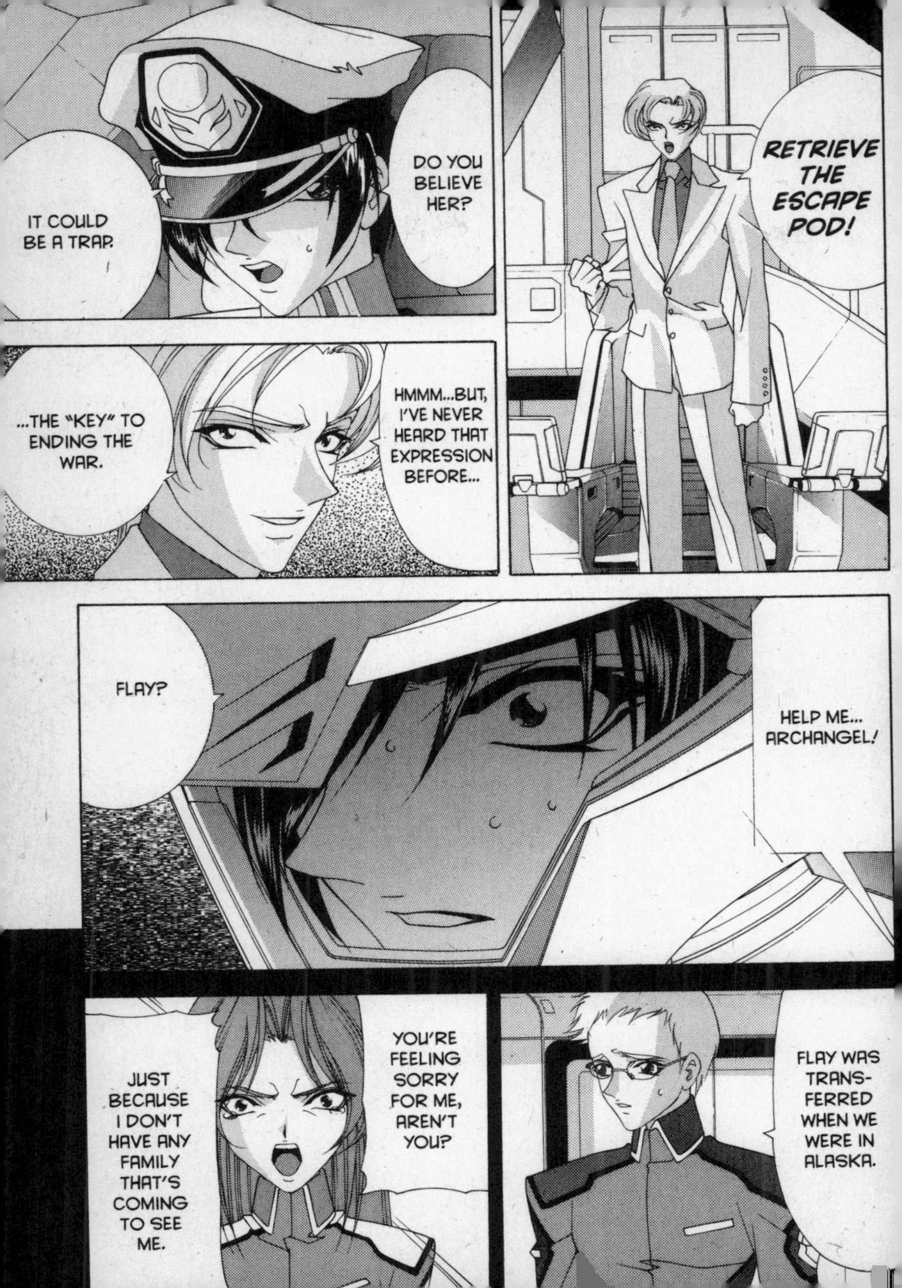
RETRIEVE THE ESCAPE POD!
DO YOU BELIEVE HER?
IT COULD BE A TRAP.
HMMM...BUT, I'VE NEVER HEARD THAT EXPRESSION BEFORE...
...THE "KEY" TO ENDING THE WAR.
HELP ME... ARCHANGEL!
FLAY?
FLAY WAS TRANS-FERRED WHEN WE WERE IN ALASKA.
YOU'RE FEELING SORRY FOR ME, AREN'T YOU?
JUST BECAUSE I DON'T HAVE ANY FAMILY THAT'S COMING TO SEE ME.

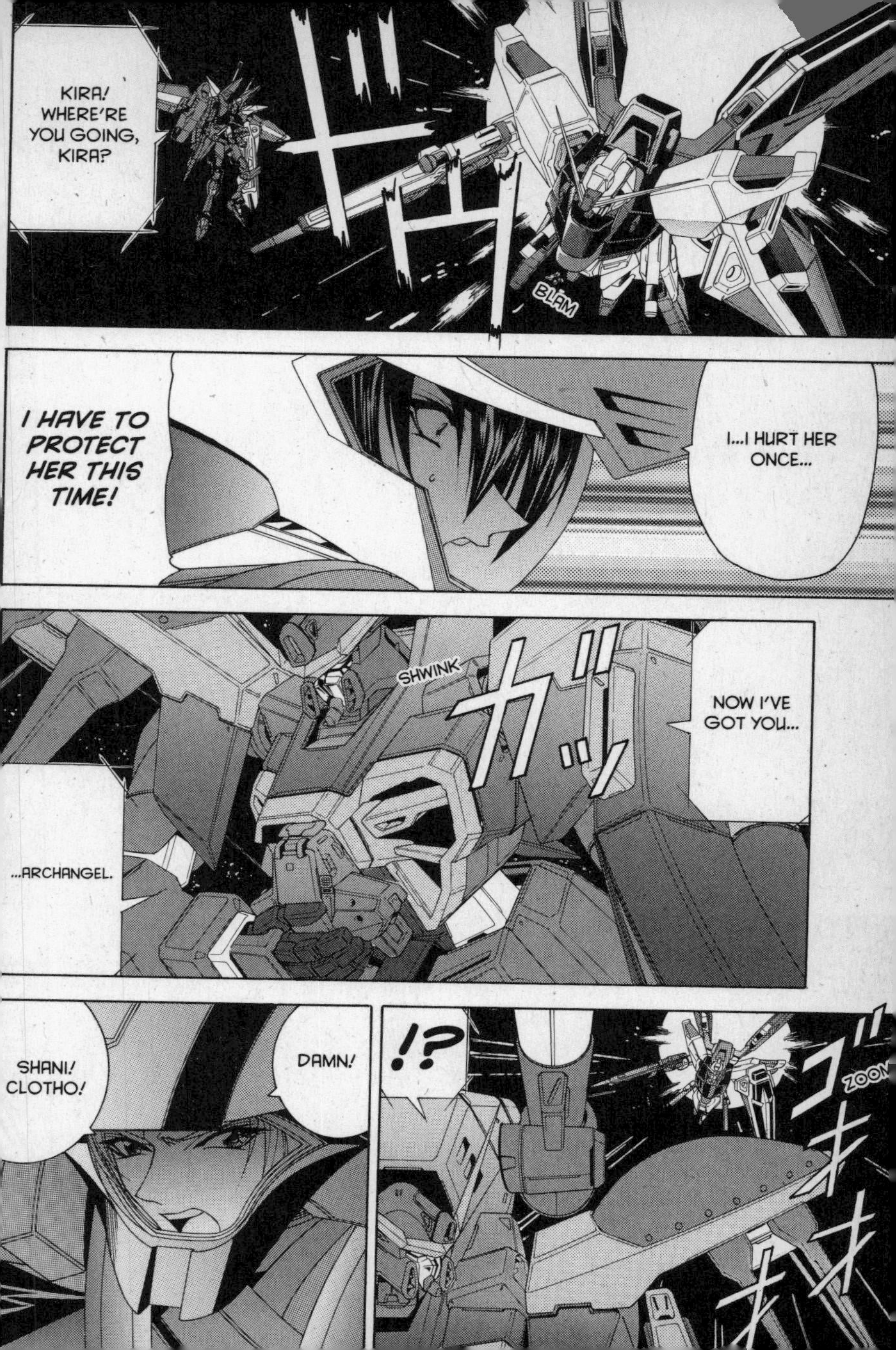
KIRA! WHERE'RE YOU GOING, KIRA?
BLAM
I...I HURT HER ONCE...
I HAVE TO PROTECT HER THIS TIME!
NOW I'VE GOT YOU...
SHWINK
...ARCHANGEL.
ZOOM
!?
DAMN!
SHANI! CLOTHO!

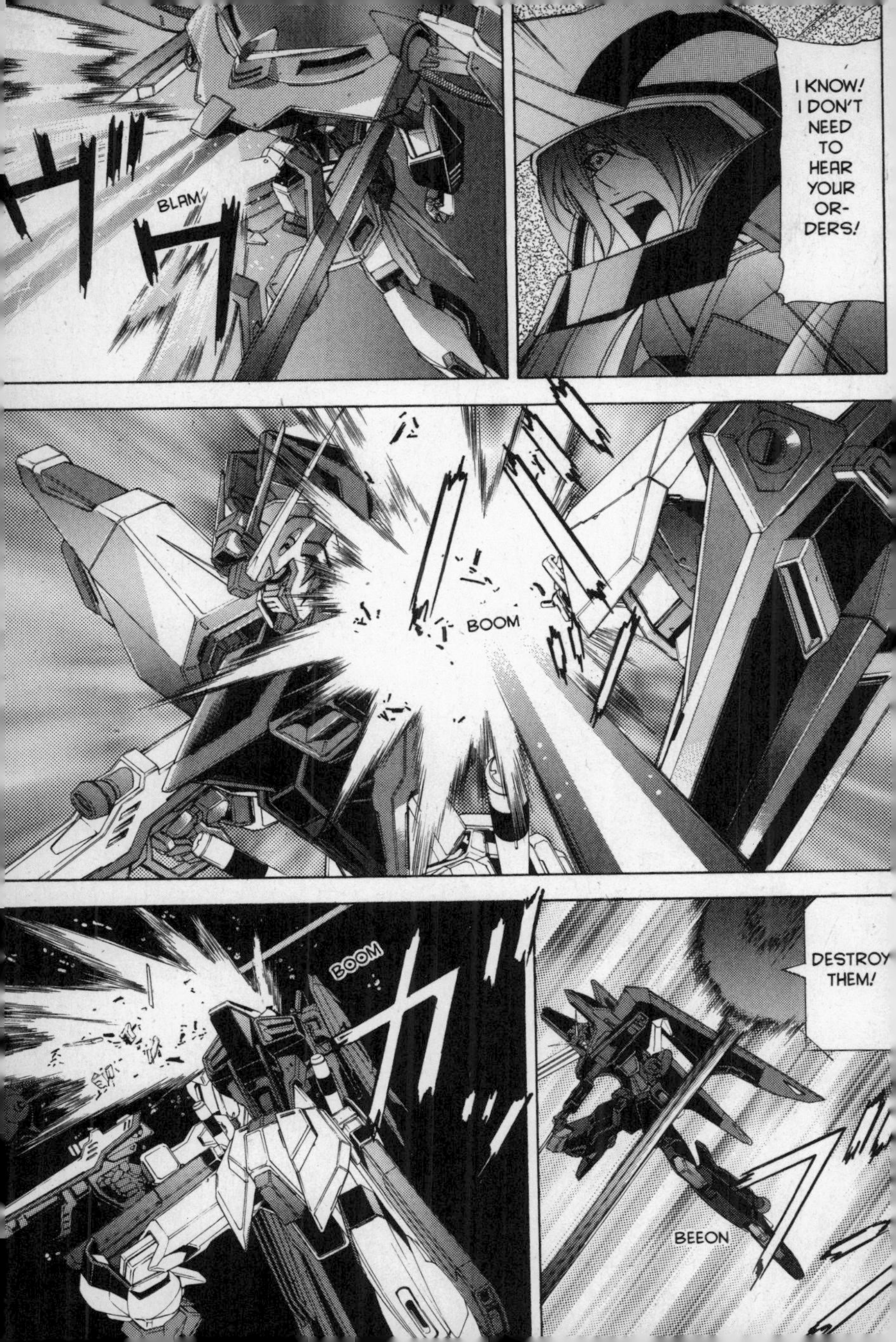
I KNOW! I DON'T NEED TO HEAR YOUR ORDERS!
BLAM
BOOM
DESTROY THEM!
BEEON
BOOM

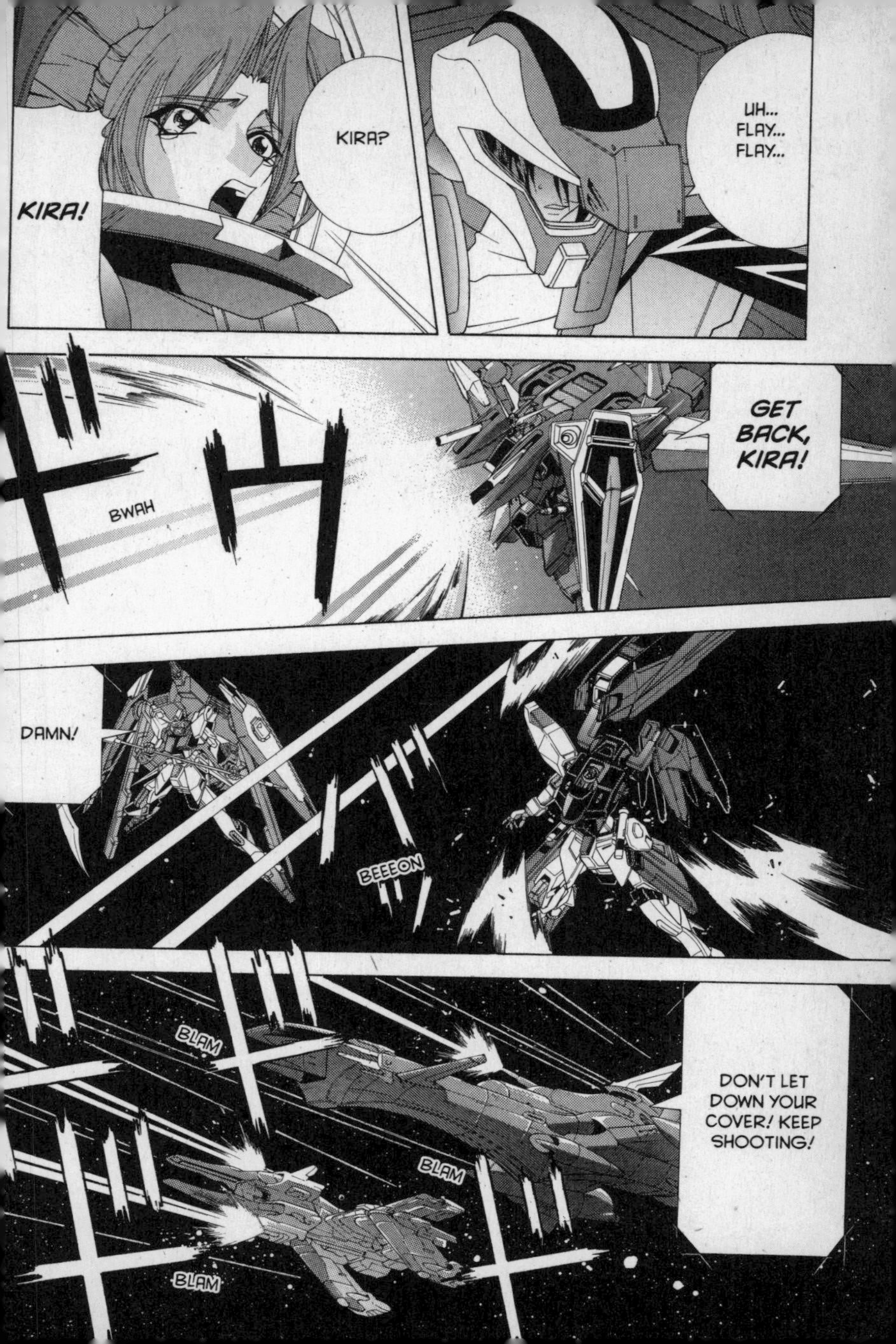
UH... FLAY... FLAY...
KIRA?
KIRA!
GET BACK, KIRA!
BWAH
DAMN!
BEEEON
DON'T LET DOWN YOUR COVER! KEEP SHOOTING!
BLAM
BLAM
BLAM

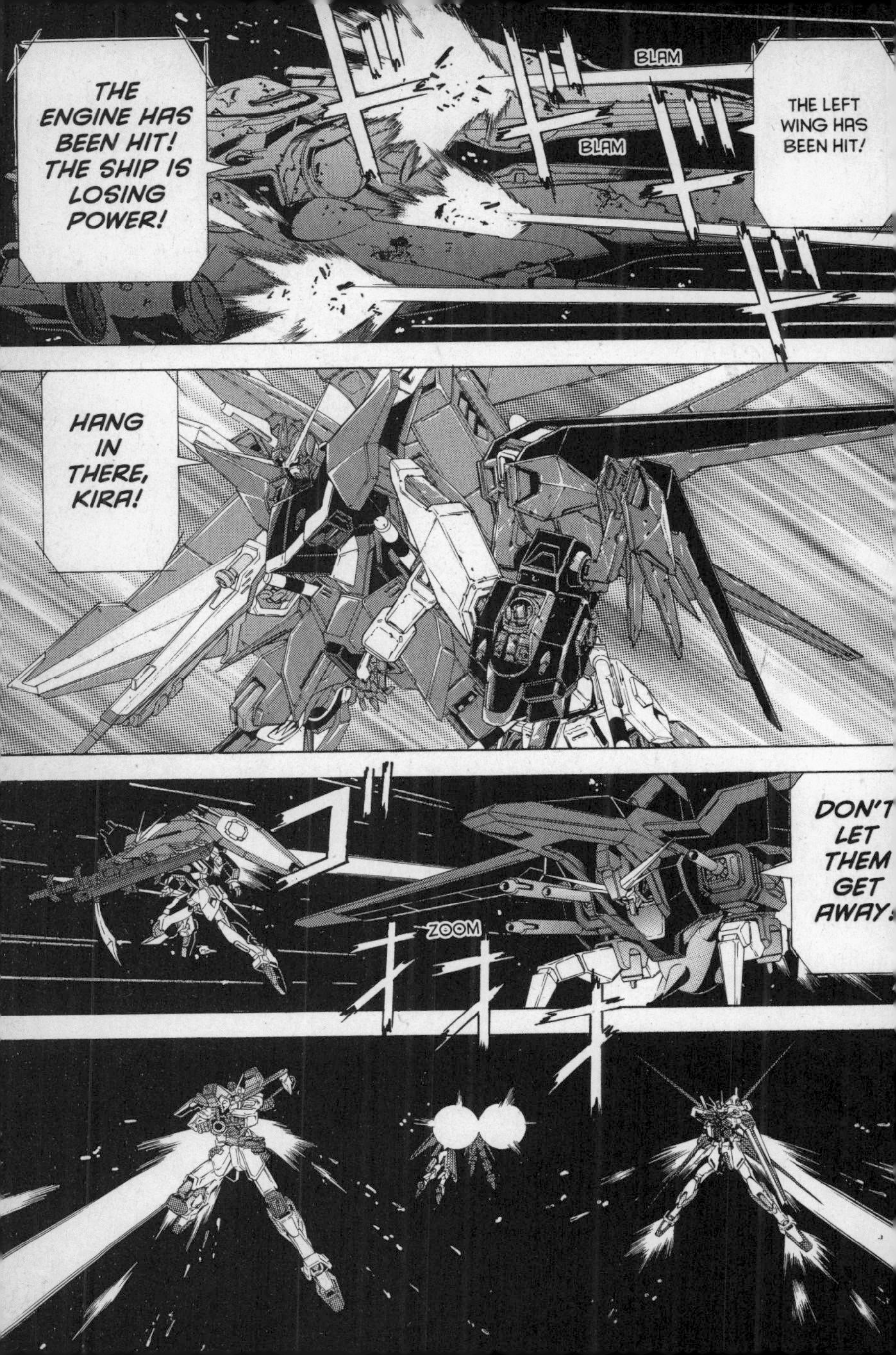
THE LEFT WING HAS BEEN HIT!
BLAM
BLAM
THE ENGINE HAS BEEN HIT! THE SHIP IS LOSING POWER!
HANG IN THERE, KIRA!
DON'T LET THEM GET AWAY!
ZOOM

PEON

DON'T CHASE THEM TOO FAR. YOUR POWER WON'T LAST.

DAMN!

BLAM

DAMN!

PRIMARY

SECONDARY

HYPER CAPA

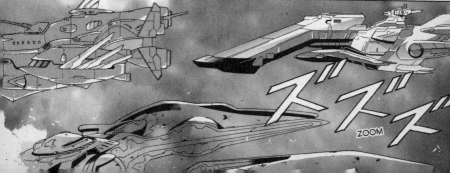

ZOOM

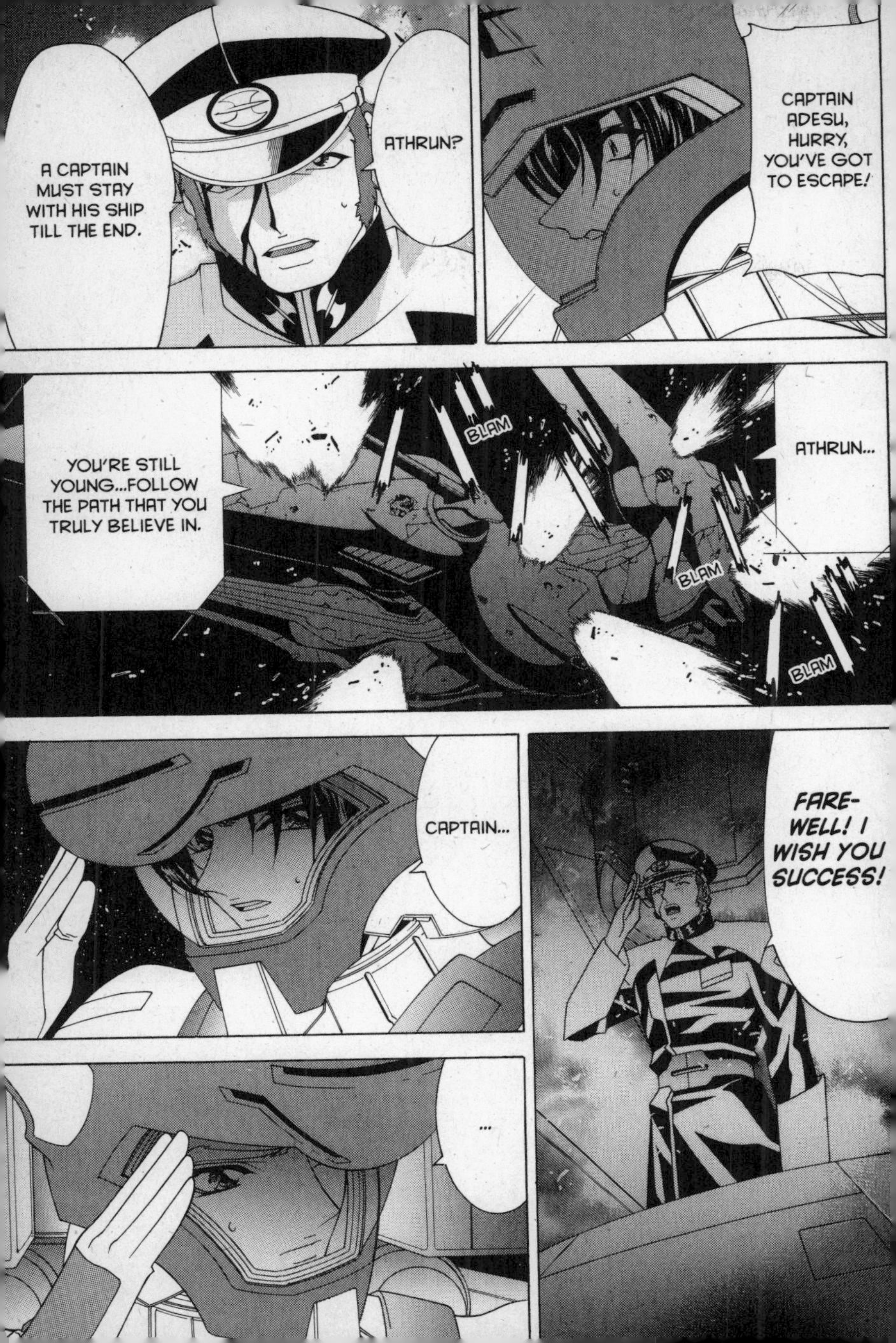
CAPTAIN ADESU, HURRY, YOU'VE GOT TO ESCAPE!
ATHRUN?
A CAPTAIN MUST STAY WITH HIS SHIP TILL THE END.
ATHRUN...
BLAM
BLAM
BLAM
YOU'RE STILL YOUNG...FOLLOW THE PATH THAT YOU TRULY BELIEVE IN.
FARE-WELL! I WISH YOU SUCCESS!
CAPTAIN...
...

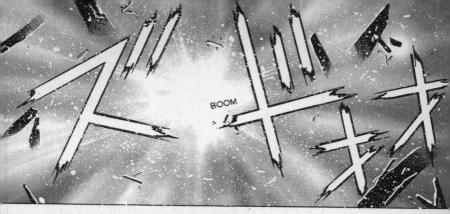

BOOM

YZAK, WE'RE PULLING OUT.

THE VESA-LIUS—

UH...

YES, SIR.

THERE'S NO POINT IN FIGHTING THE EARTH ALLIANCE LIKE THIS.

SEND FREEDOM'S PILOT TO THE MEDICAL ROOM IM-MEDIATELY.

FREEDOM, JUSTICE, COME BACK TO BASE.

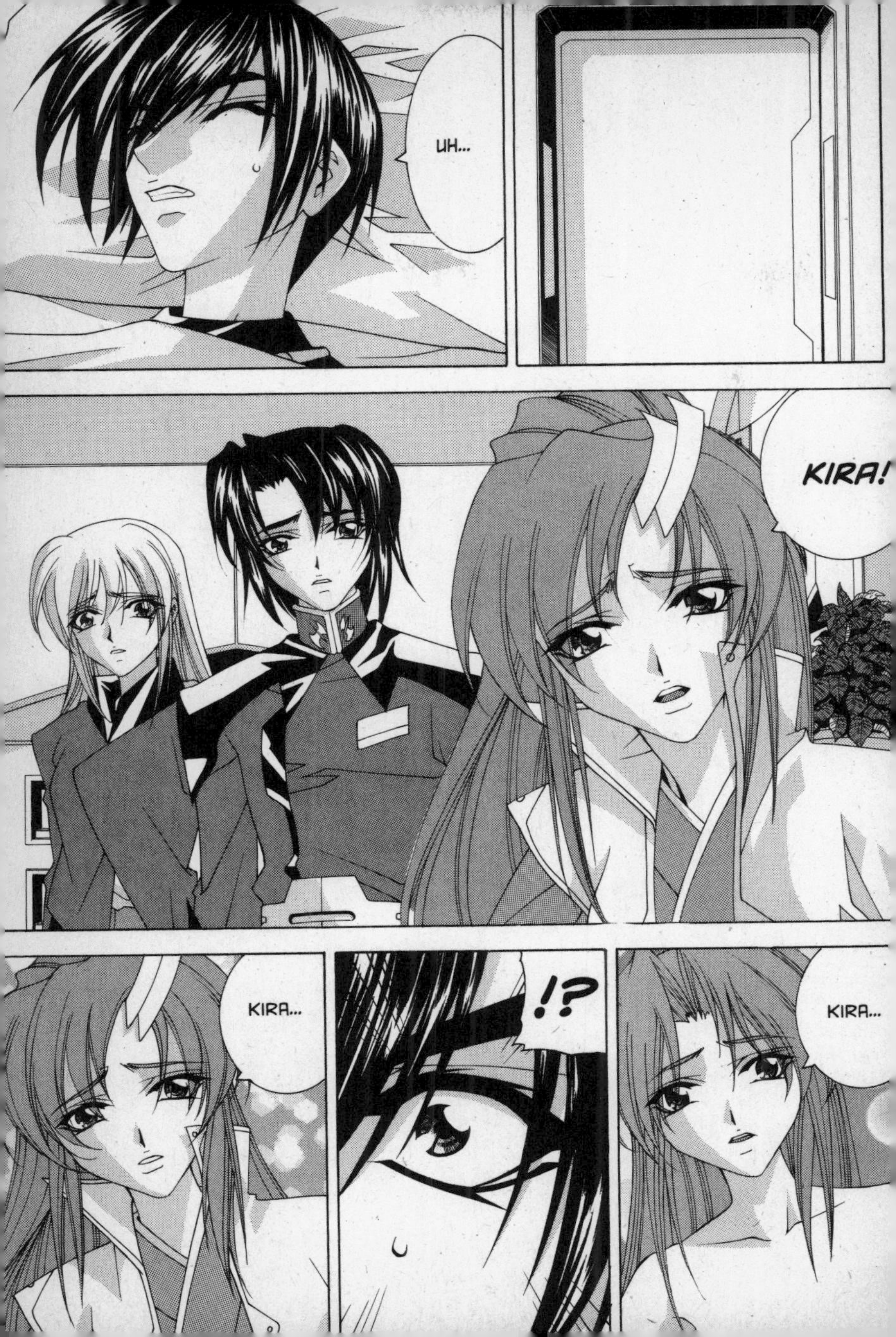
UH...
KIRA!
KIRA...
!?
KIRA...

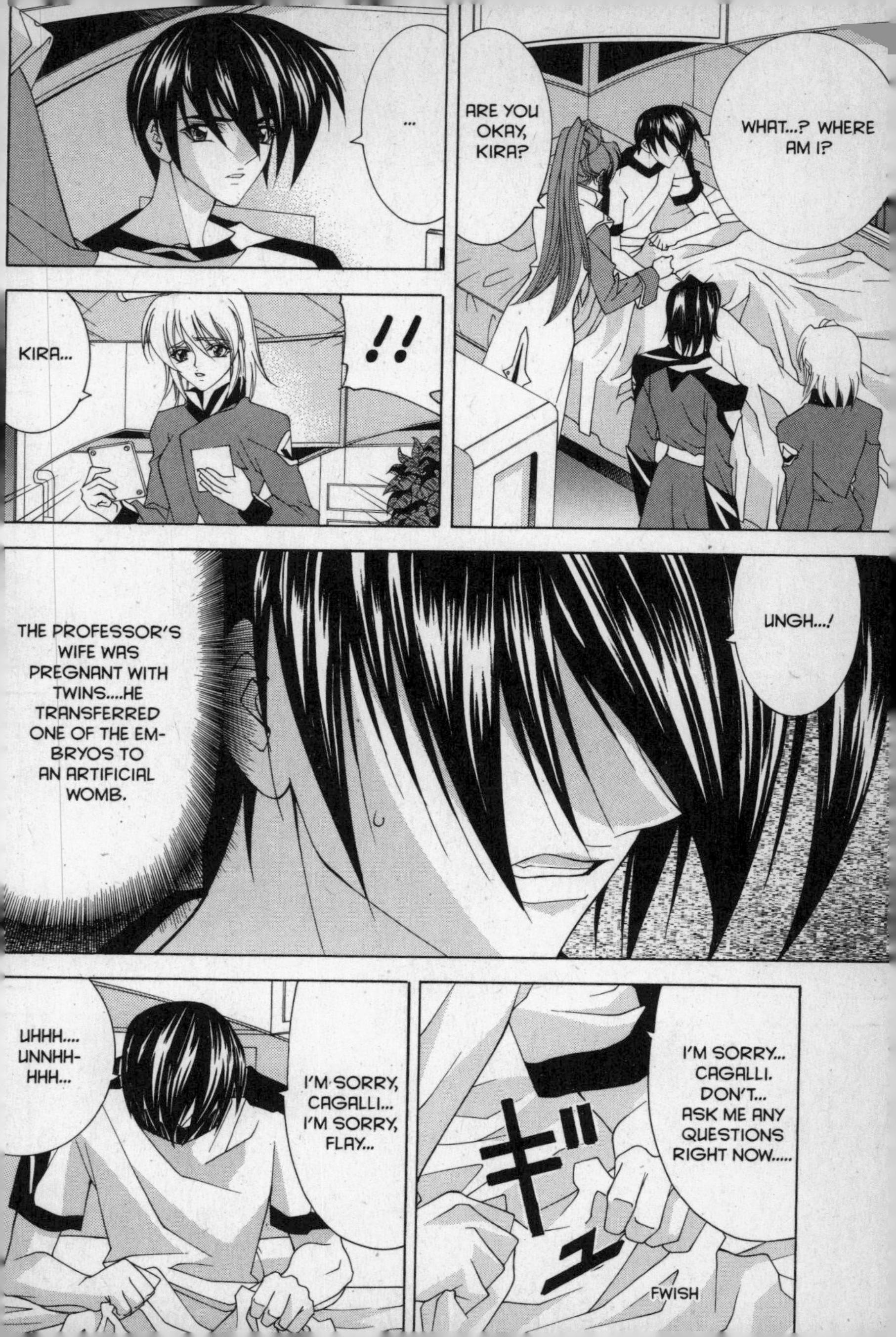
WHAT...? WHERE AM I?
ARE YOU OKAY, KIRA?
...
!!
KIRA...
UNGH...!
THE PROFESSOR'S WIFE WAS PREGNANT WITH TWINS....HE TRANSFERRED ONE OF THE EM-BRYOS TO AN ARTIFICIAL WOMB.
I'M SORRY... CAGALLI. DON'T... ASK ME ANY QUESTIONS RIGHT NOW.....
ギュ
FWISH
I'M SORRY, CAGALLI... I'M SORRY, FLAY...
UHHH.... UNNHH-HHH...

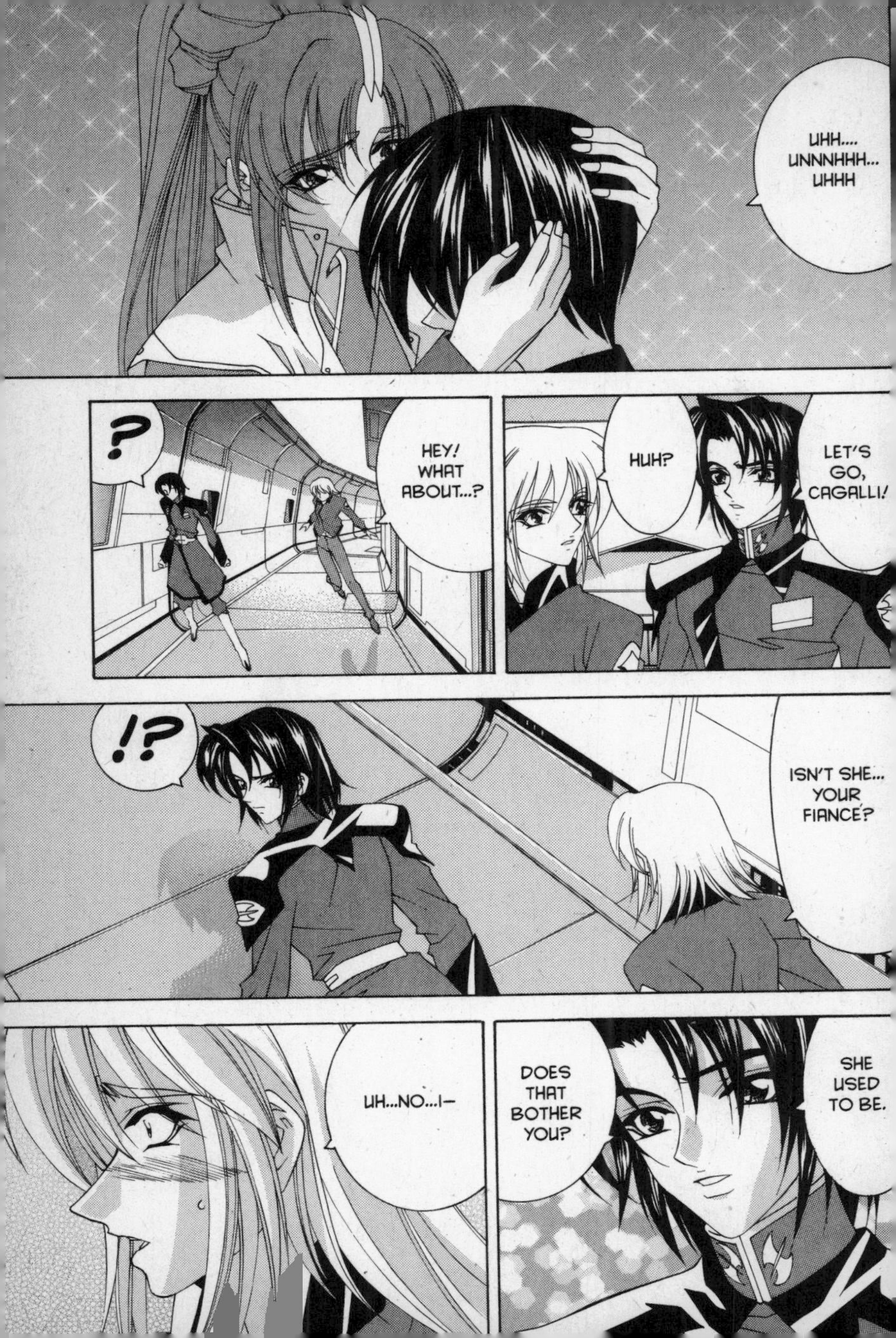
UHH.... UNNNHHH... UHHH
LET'S GO, CAGALLI!
HUH?
HEY! WHAT ABOUT...?
?
ISN'T SHE... YOUR FIANCE?
!?
SHE USED TO BE.
DOES THAT BOTHER YOU?
UH...NO...I–

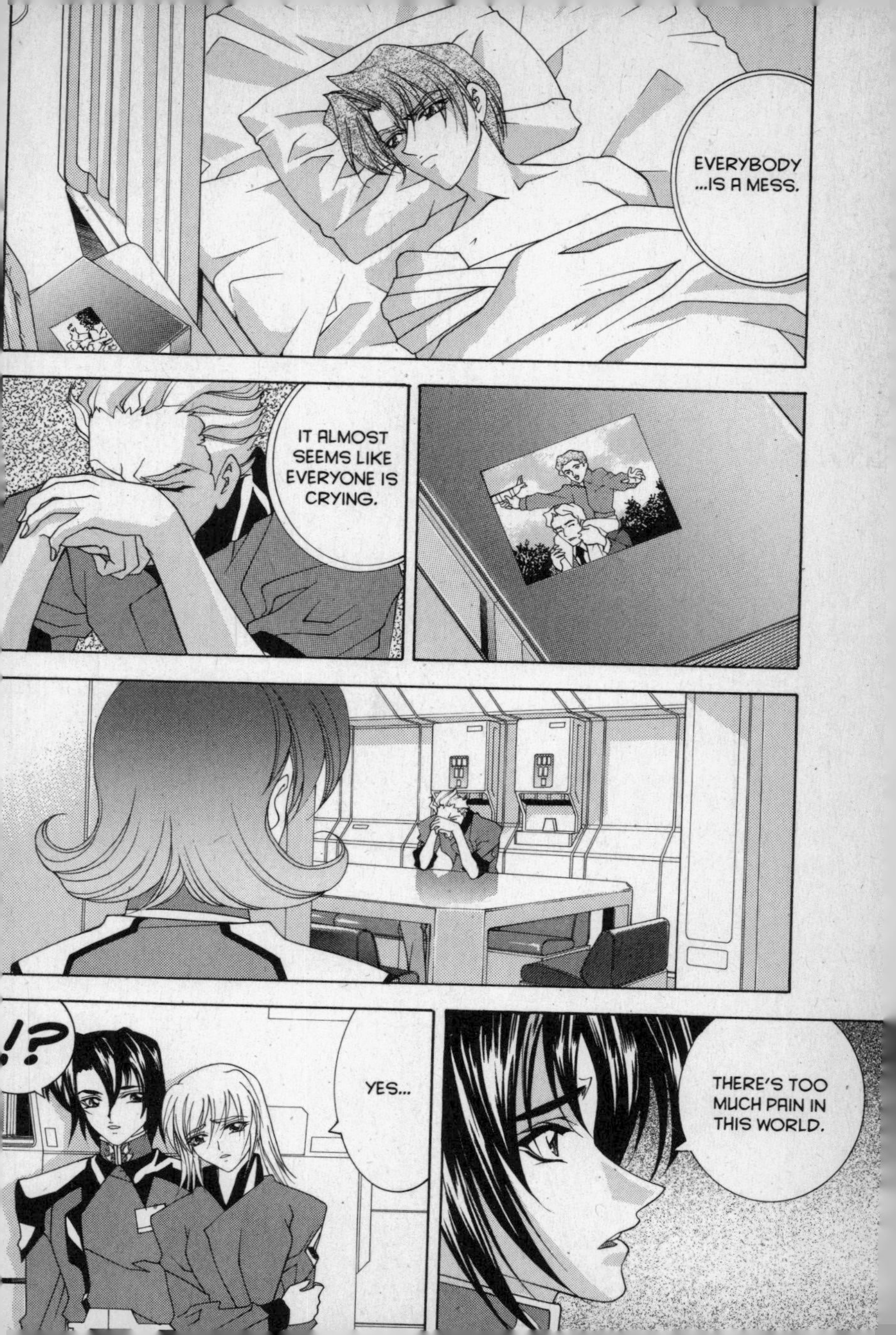
EVERYBODY ...IS A MESS.
IT ALMOST SEEMS LIKE EVERYONE IS CRYING.
THERE'S TOO MUCH PAIN IN THIS WORLD.
YES...
!?

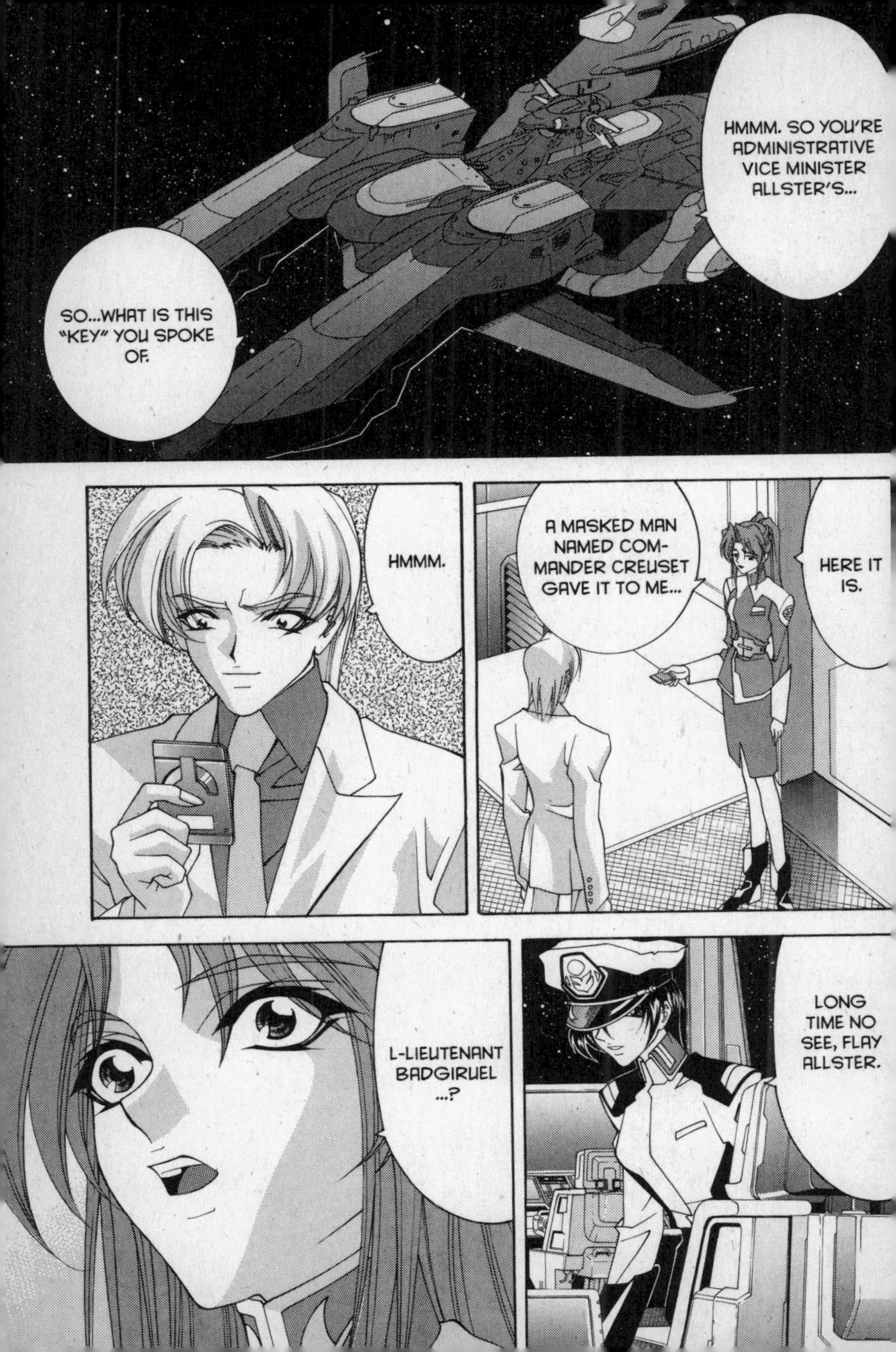
HMMM. SO YOU'RE ADMINISTRATIVE VICE MINISTER ALLSTER'S...
SO...WHAT IS THIS "KEY" YOU SPOKE OF.
HERE IT IS.
A MASKED MAN NAMED COM-MANDER CREUSET GAVE IT TO ME...
HMMM.
LONG TIME NO SEE, FLAY ALLSTER.
L-LIEUTENANT BADGIRUEL ...?

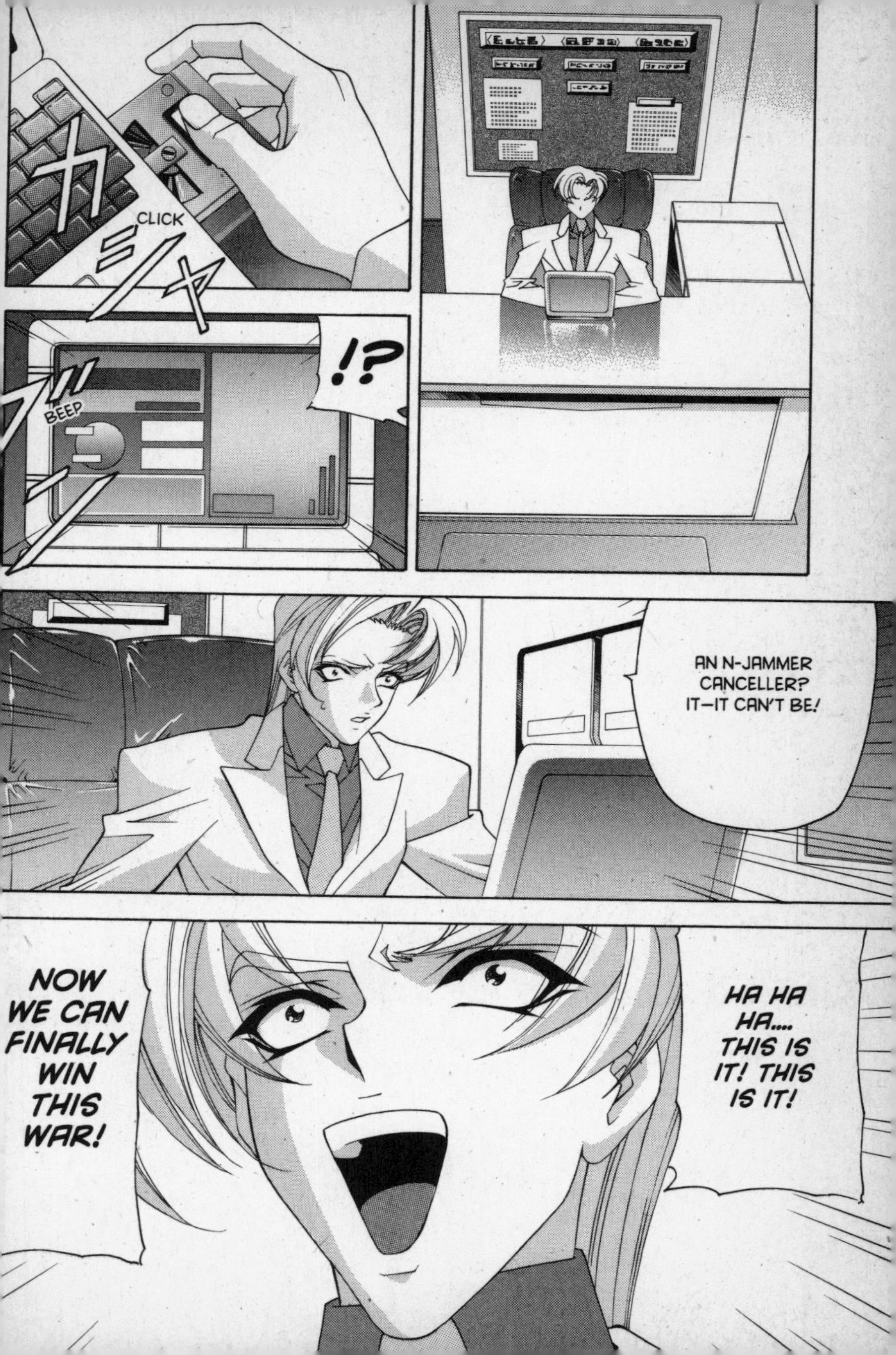
CLICK
BEEP
!?
AN N-JAMMER CANCELLER? IT—IT CAN'T BE!
HA HA HA.... THIS IS IT! THIS IS IT!
NOW WE CAN FINALLY WIN THIS WAR!

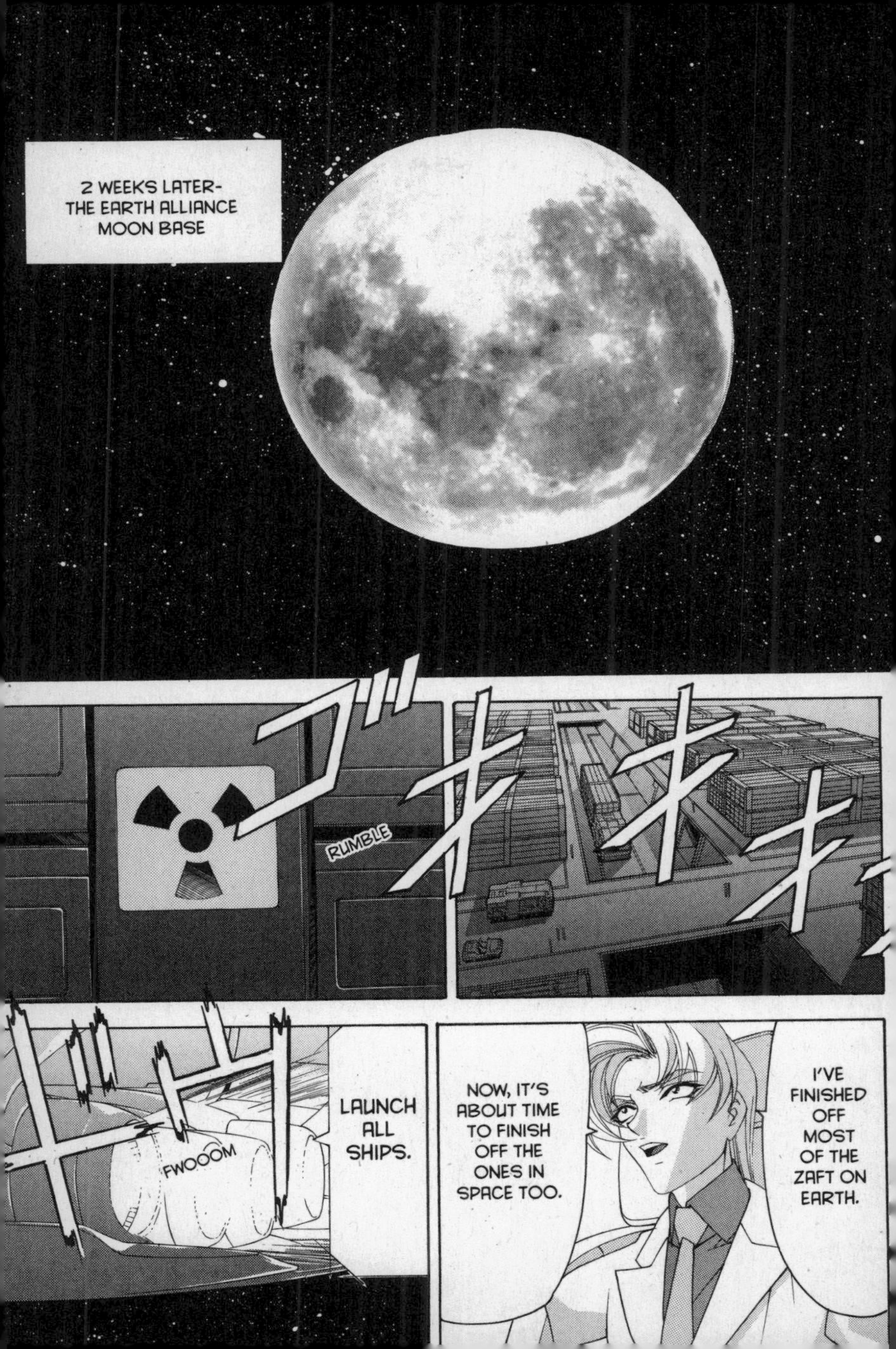
2 WEEKS LATER-
THE EARTH ALLIANCE
MOON BASE
RUMBLE
I'VE FINISHED OFF MOST OF THE ZAFT ON EARTH.
NOW, IT'S ABOUT TIME TO FINISH OFF THE ONES IN SPACE TOO.
LAUNCH ALL SHIPS.
FWOOOM

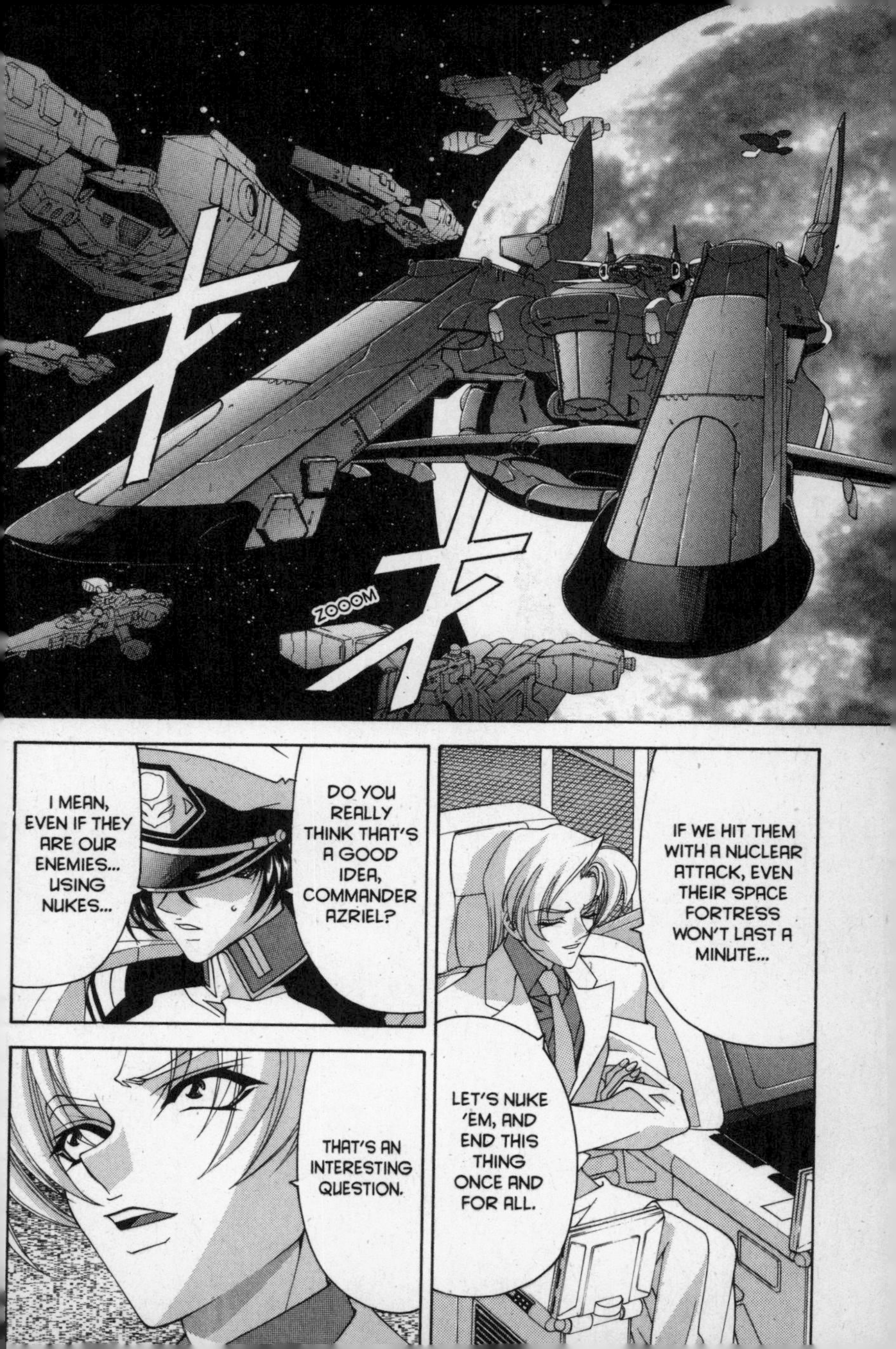
ZOOOM
IF WE HIT THEM WITH A NUCLEAR ATTACK, EVEN THEIR SPACE FORTRESS WON'T LAST A MINUTE...
LET'S NUKE 'EM, AND END THIS THING ONCE AND FOR ALL.
DO YOU REALLY THINK THAT'S A GOOD IDEA, COMMANDER AZRIEL?
I MEAN, EVEN IF THEY ARE OUR ENEMIES... USING NUKES...
THAT'S AN INTERESTING QUESTION.

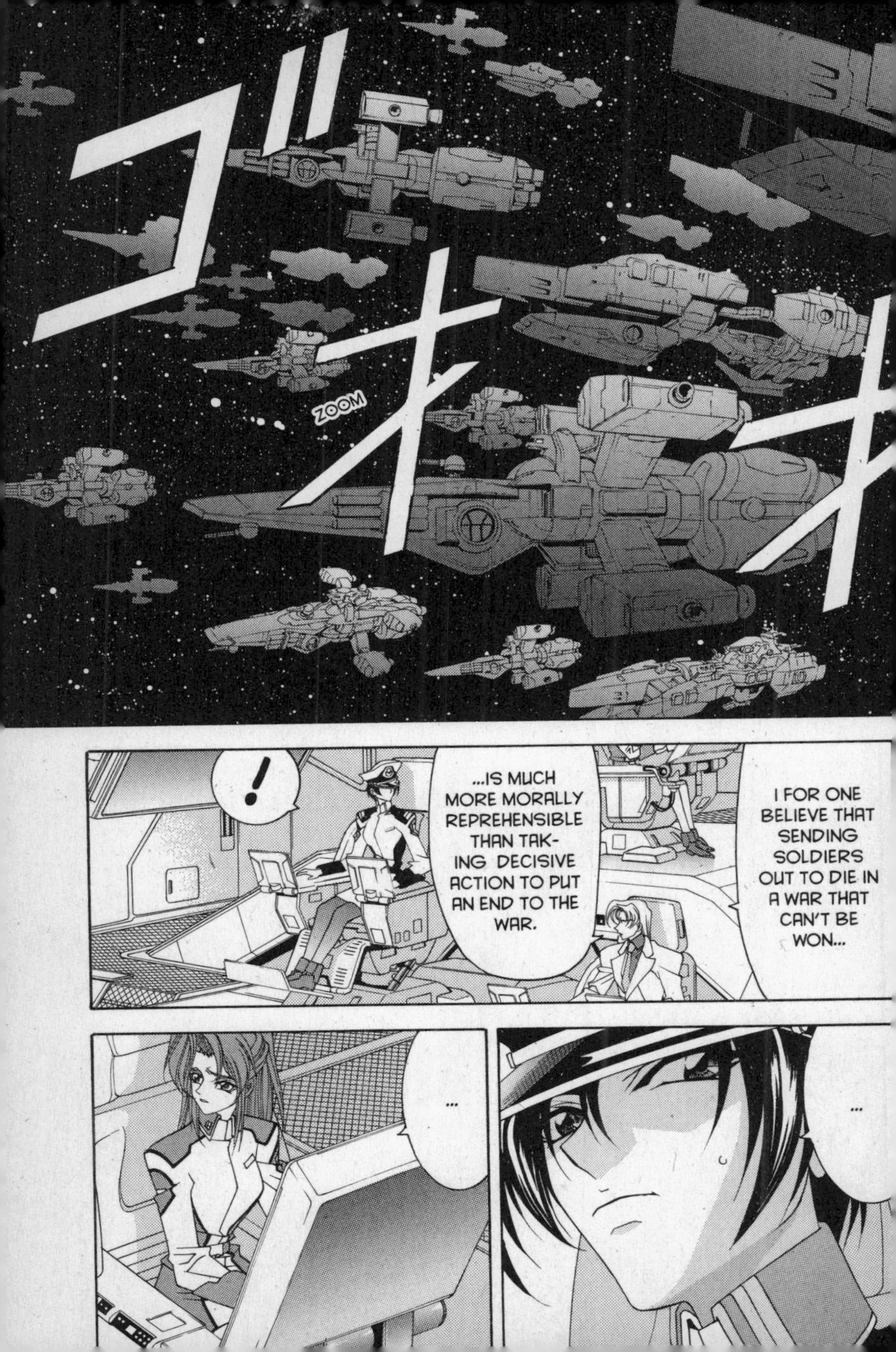
ゴオオオ
ZOOM
I FOR ONE BELIEVE THAT SENDING SOLDIERS OUT TO DIE IN A WAR THAT CAN'T BE WON...
...IS MUCH MORE MORALLY REPREHENSIBLE THAN TAK-ING DECISIVE ACTION TO PUT AN END TO THE WAR.
!
...
...

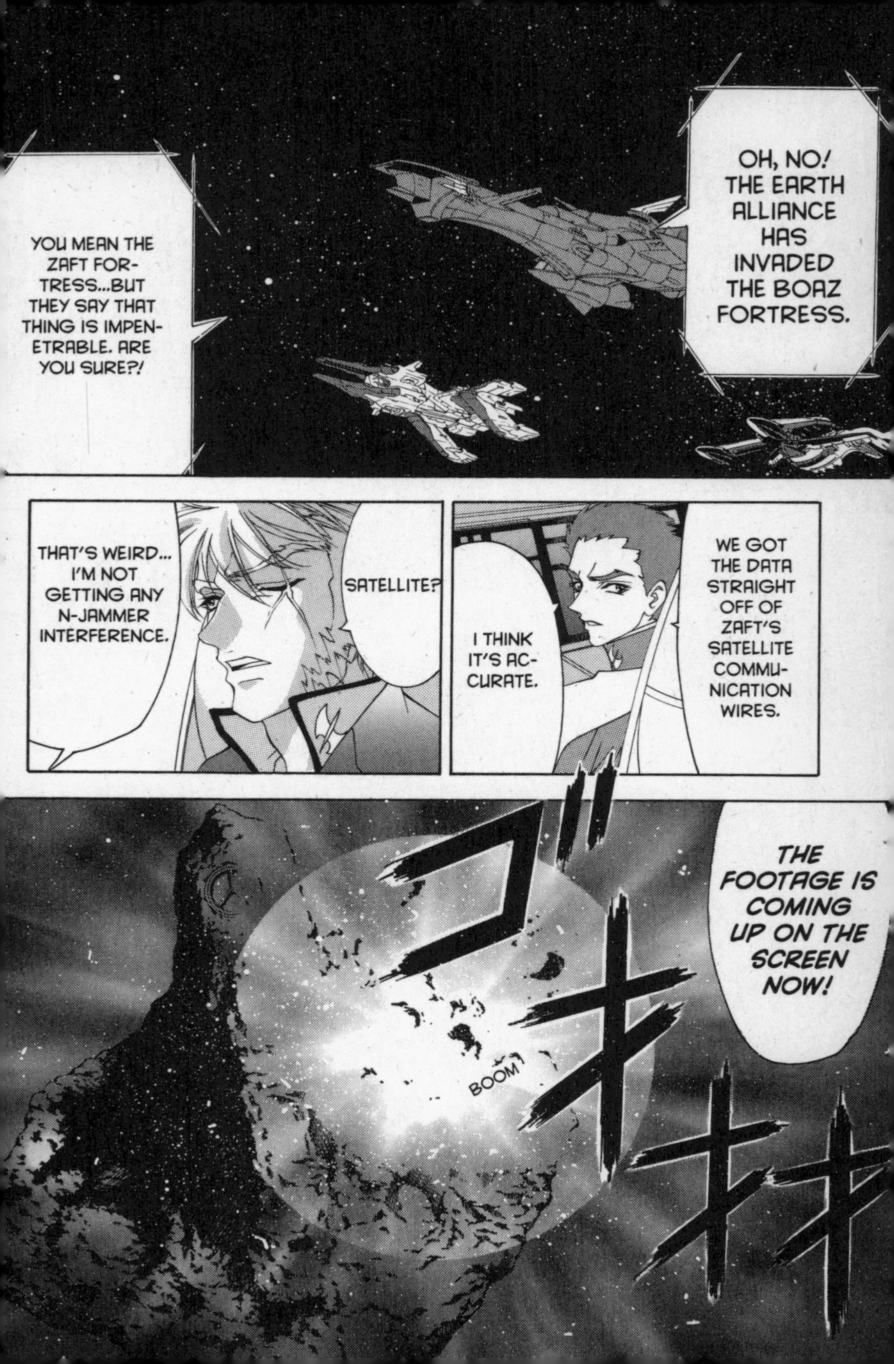
OH, NO! THE EARTH ALLIANCE HAS INVADED THE BOAZ FORTRESS.
YOU MEAN THE ZAFT FOR-TRESS...BUT THEY SAY THAT THING IS IMPEN-ETRABLE. ARE YOU SURE?!
WE GOT THE DATA STRAIGHT OFF OF ZAFT'S SATELLITE COMMU-NICATION WIRES.
I THINK IT'S AC-CURATE.
SATELLITE?
THAT'S WEIRD... I'M NOT GETTING ANY N-JAMMER INTERFERENCE.
THE FOOTAGE IS COMING UP ON THE SCREEN NOW!
BOOM

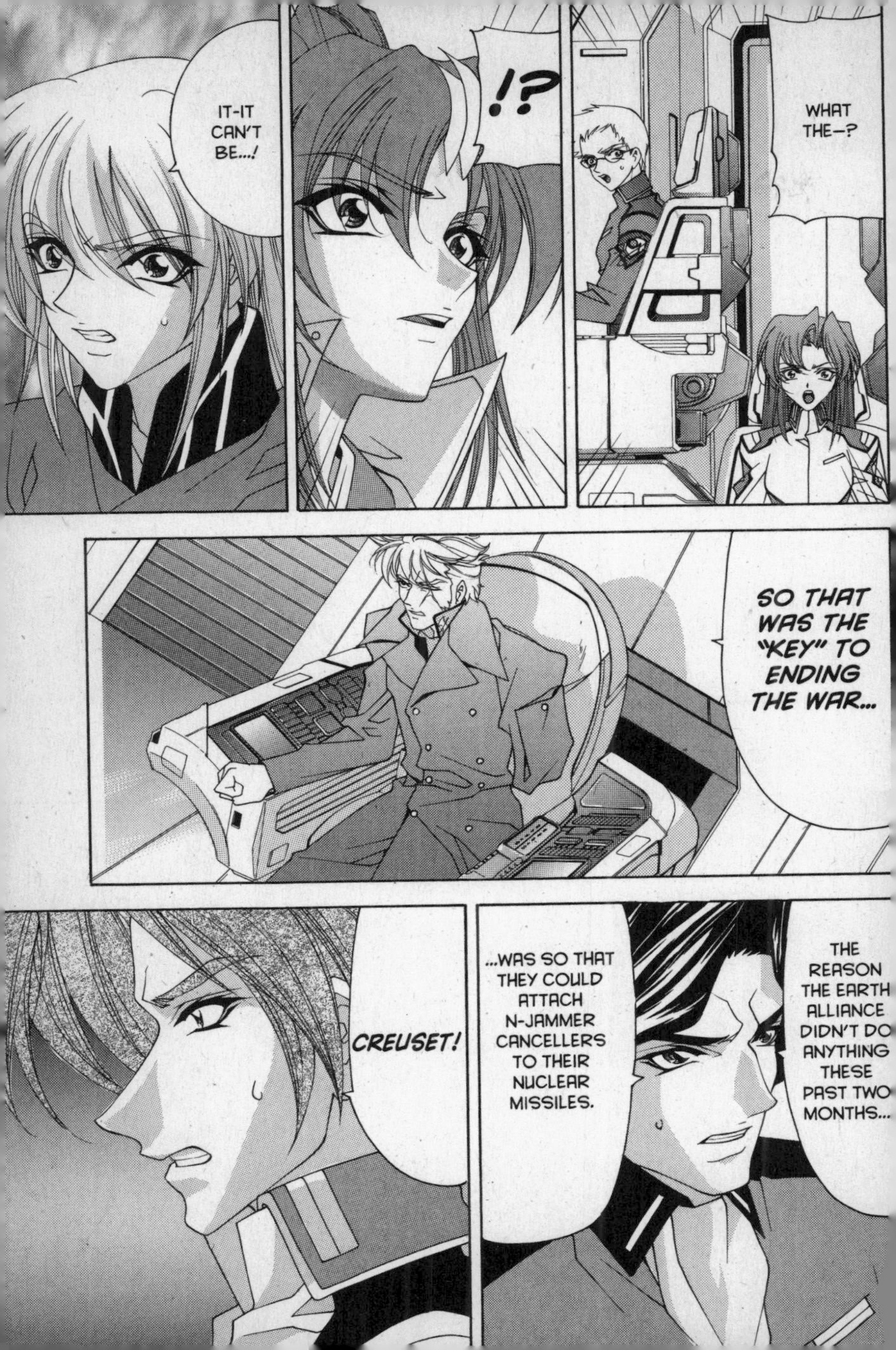
WHAT THE—?
!?
IT-IT CAN'T BE...!
SO THAT WAS THE "KEY" TO ENDING THE WAR...
THE REASON THE EARTH ALLIANCE DIDN'T DO ANYTHING THESE PAST TWO MONTHS...
...WAS SO THAT THEY COULD ATTACH N-JAMMER CANCELLERS TO THEIR NUCLEAR MISSILES.
CREUSET!

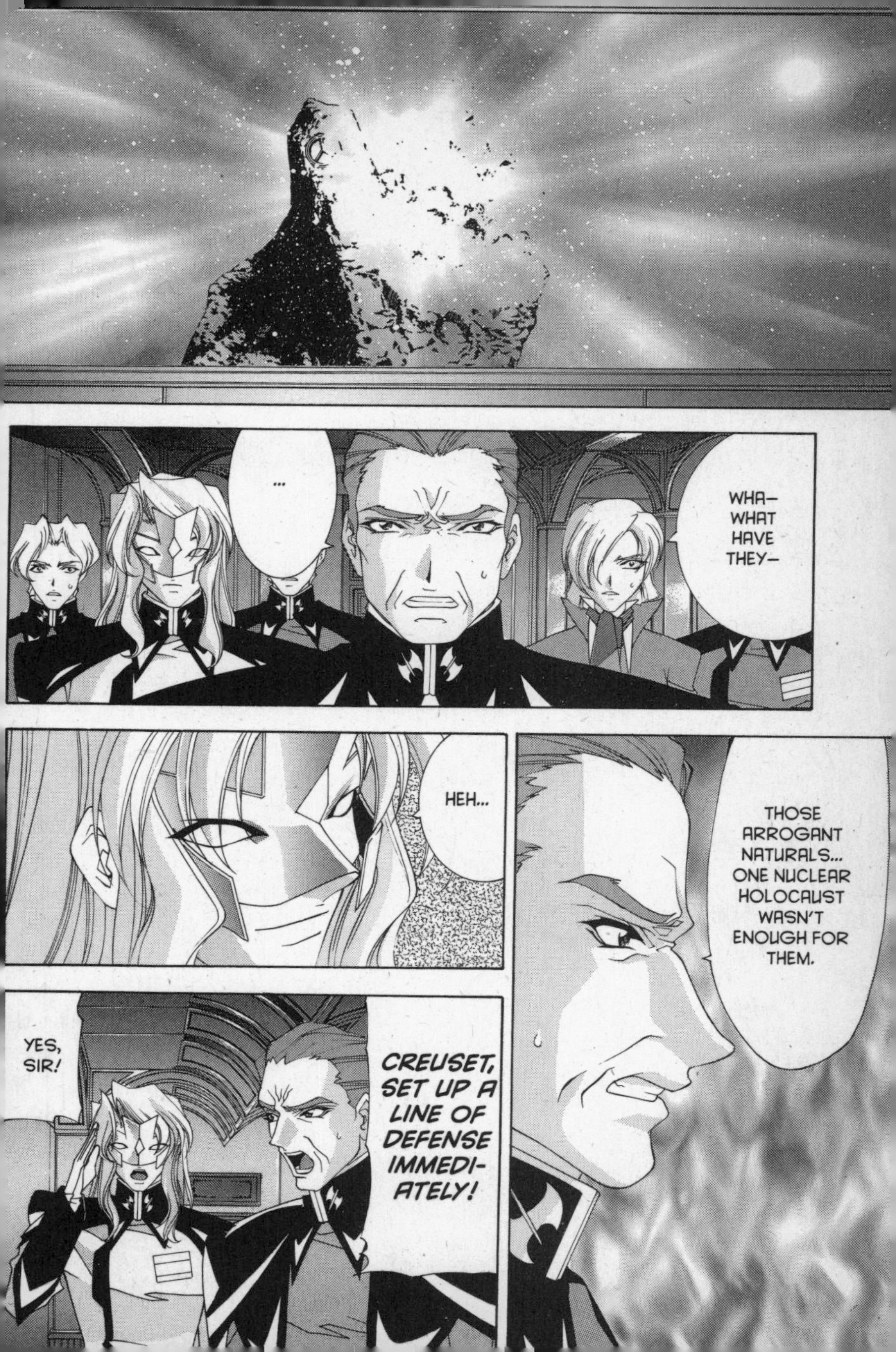
WHA— WHAT HAVE THEY—
...
THOSE ARROGANT NATURALS... ONE NUCLEAR HOLOCAUST WASN'T ENOUGH FOR THEM.
HEH...
CREUSET, SET UP A LINE OF DEFENSE IMMEDI-ATELY!
YES, SIR!

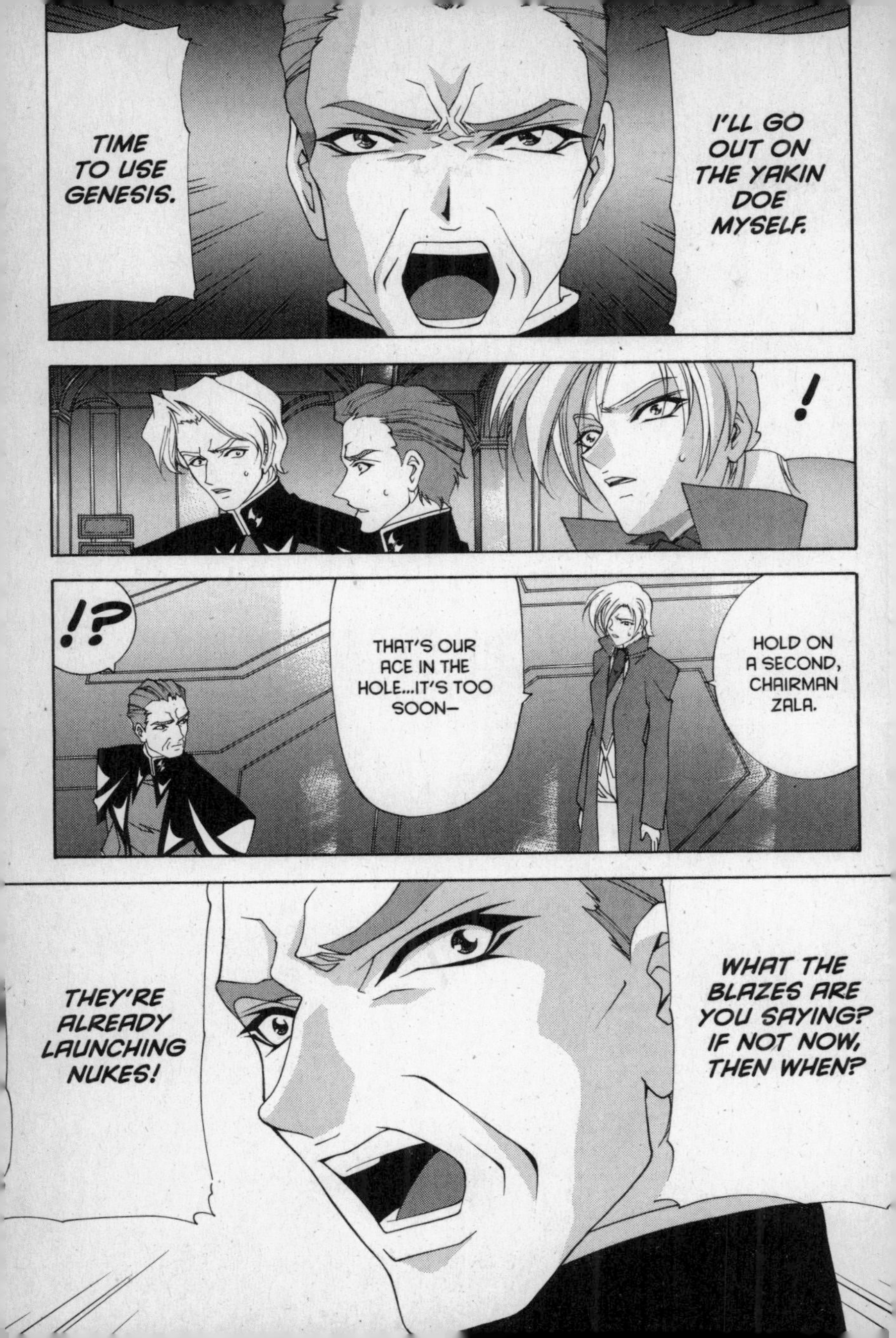
I'LL GO OUT ON THE YAKIN DOE MYSELF.
TIME TO USE GENESIS.
!
HOLD ON A SECOND, CHAIRMAN ZALA.
THAT'S OUR ACE IN THE HOLE...IT'S TOO SOON–
!?
WHAT THE BLAZES ARE YOU SAYING? IF NOT NOW, THEN WHEN?
THEY'RE ALREADY LAUNCHING NUKES!

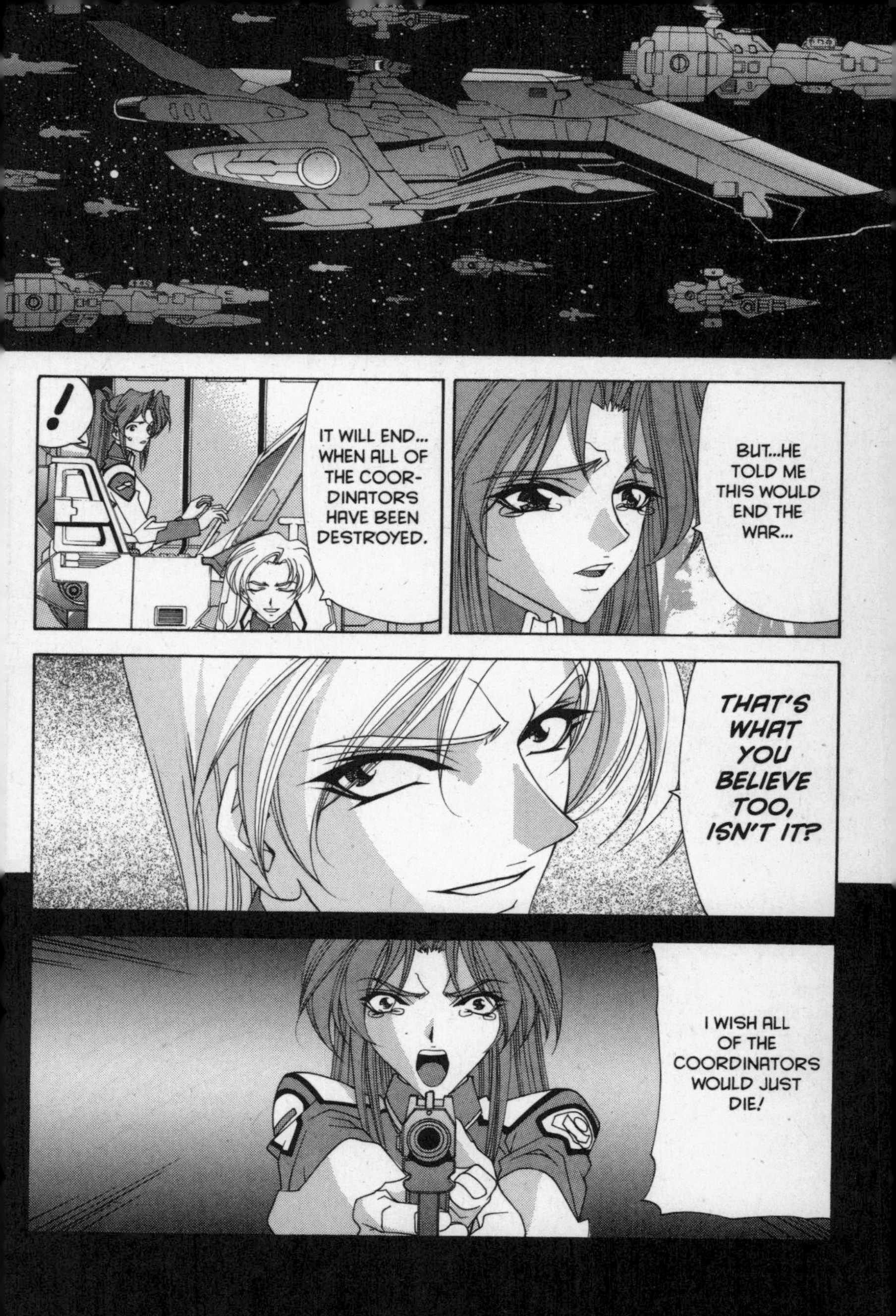
BUT...HE TOLD ME THIS WOULD END THE WAR...
!
IT WILL END... WHEN ALL OF THE COOR-DINATORS HAVE BEEN DESTROYED.
THAT'S WHAT YOU BELIEVE TOO, ISN'T IT?
I WISH ALL OF THE COORDINATORS WOULD JUST DIE!

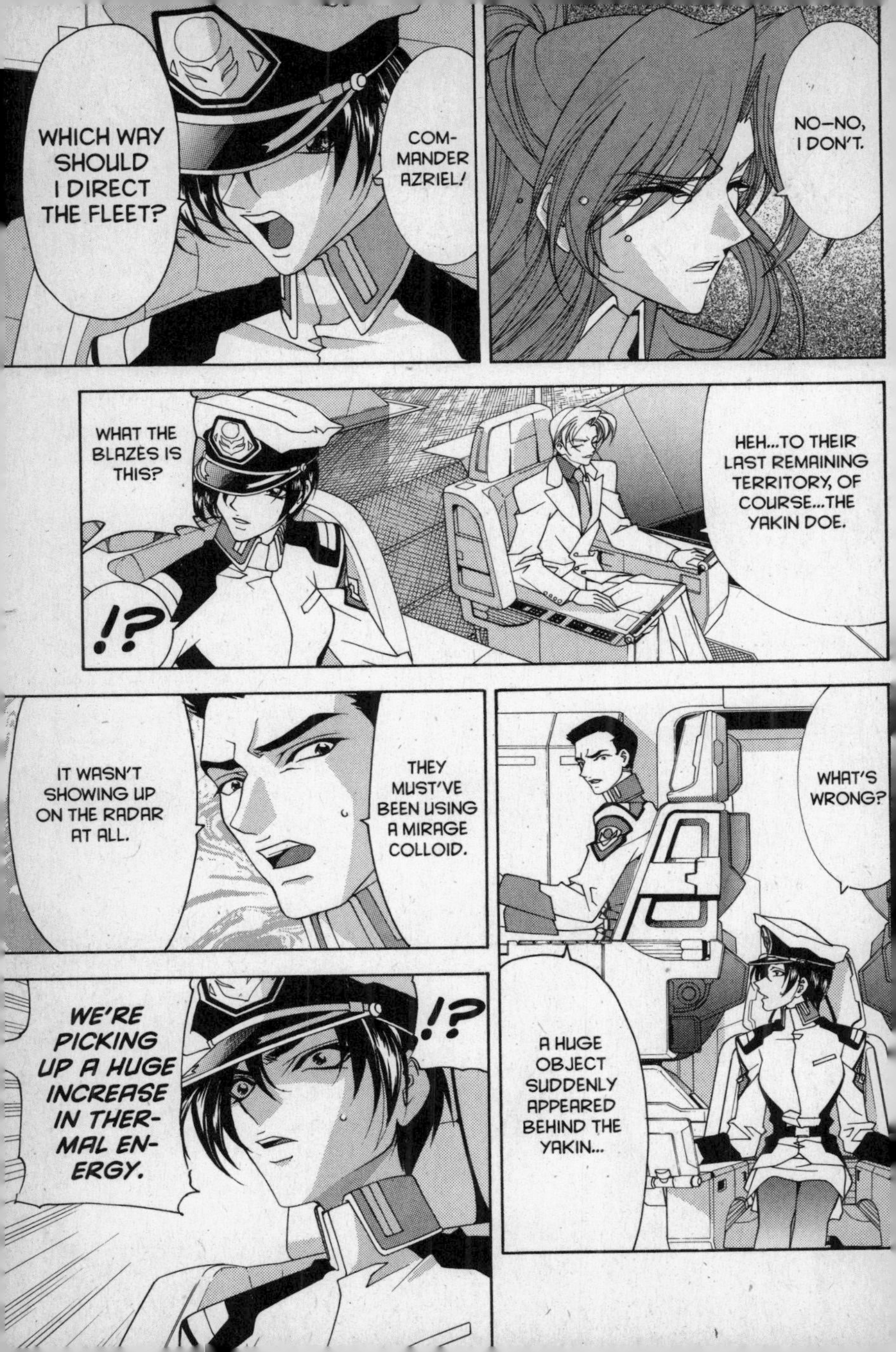

NO—NO, I DON'T.
COMMANDER AZRIEL!
WHICH WAY SHOULD I DIRECT THE FLEET?
HEH...TO THEIR LAST REMAINING TERRITORY, OF COURSE...THE YAKIN DOE.
WHAT THE BLAZES IS THIS?
!?
WHAT'S WRONG?
A HUGE OBJECT SUDDENLY APPEARED BEHIND THE YAKIN...
THEY MUST'VE BEEN USING A MIRAGE COLLOID.
IT WASN'T SHOWING UP ON THE RADAR AT ALL.
!?
WE'RE PICKING UP A HUGE INCREASE IN THERMAL ENERGY.

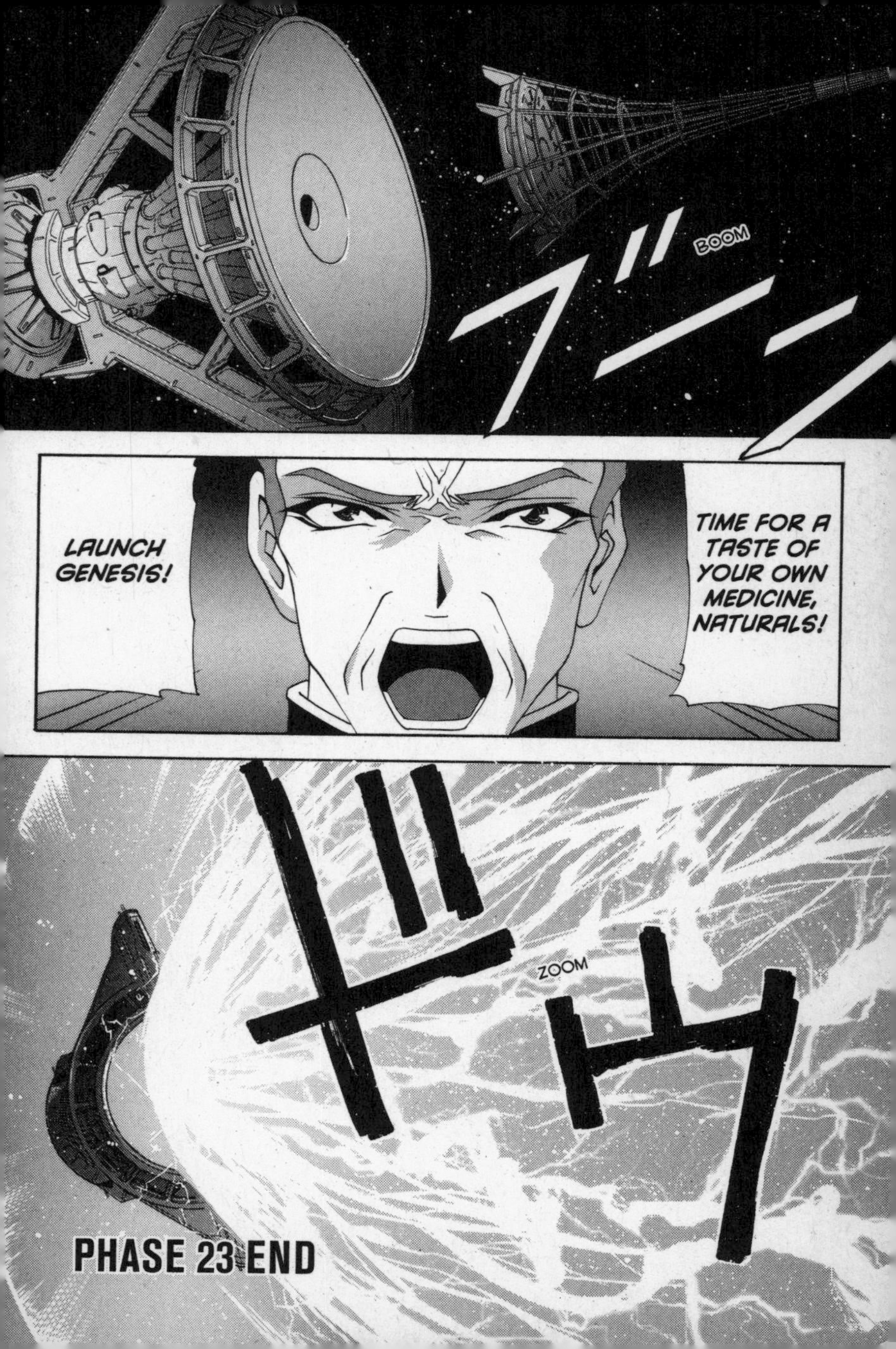
BOOM
TIME FOR A TASTE OF YOUR OWN MEDICINE, NATURALS!
LAUNCH GENESIS!
ZOOM
PHASE 23 END

PHASE 24 – A GLIMMER OF HOPE

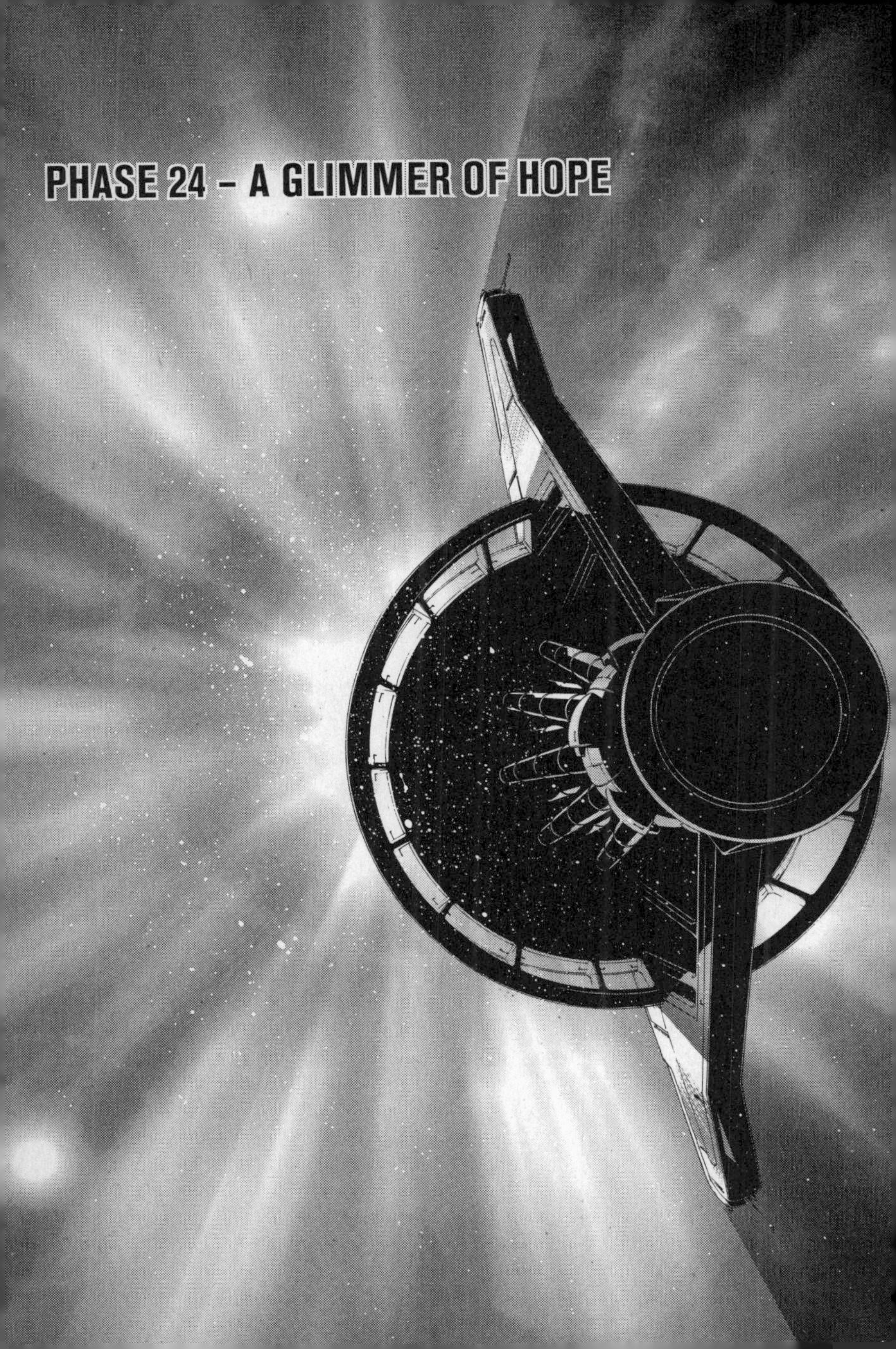

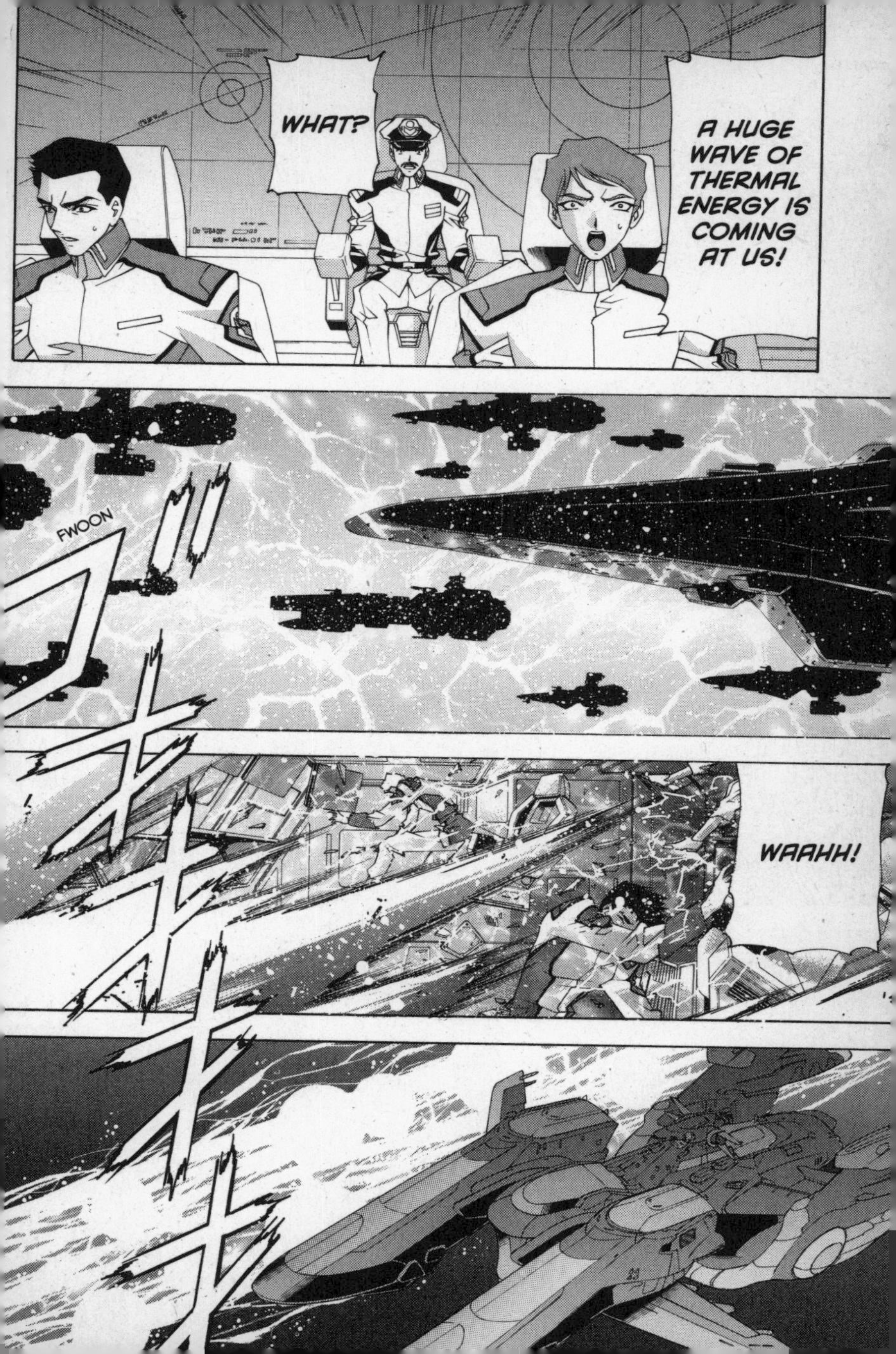
A HUGE WAVE OF THERMAL ENERGY IS COMING AT US!
WHAT?
FWOON
WAAHH!

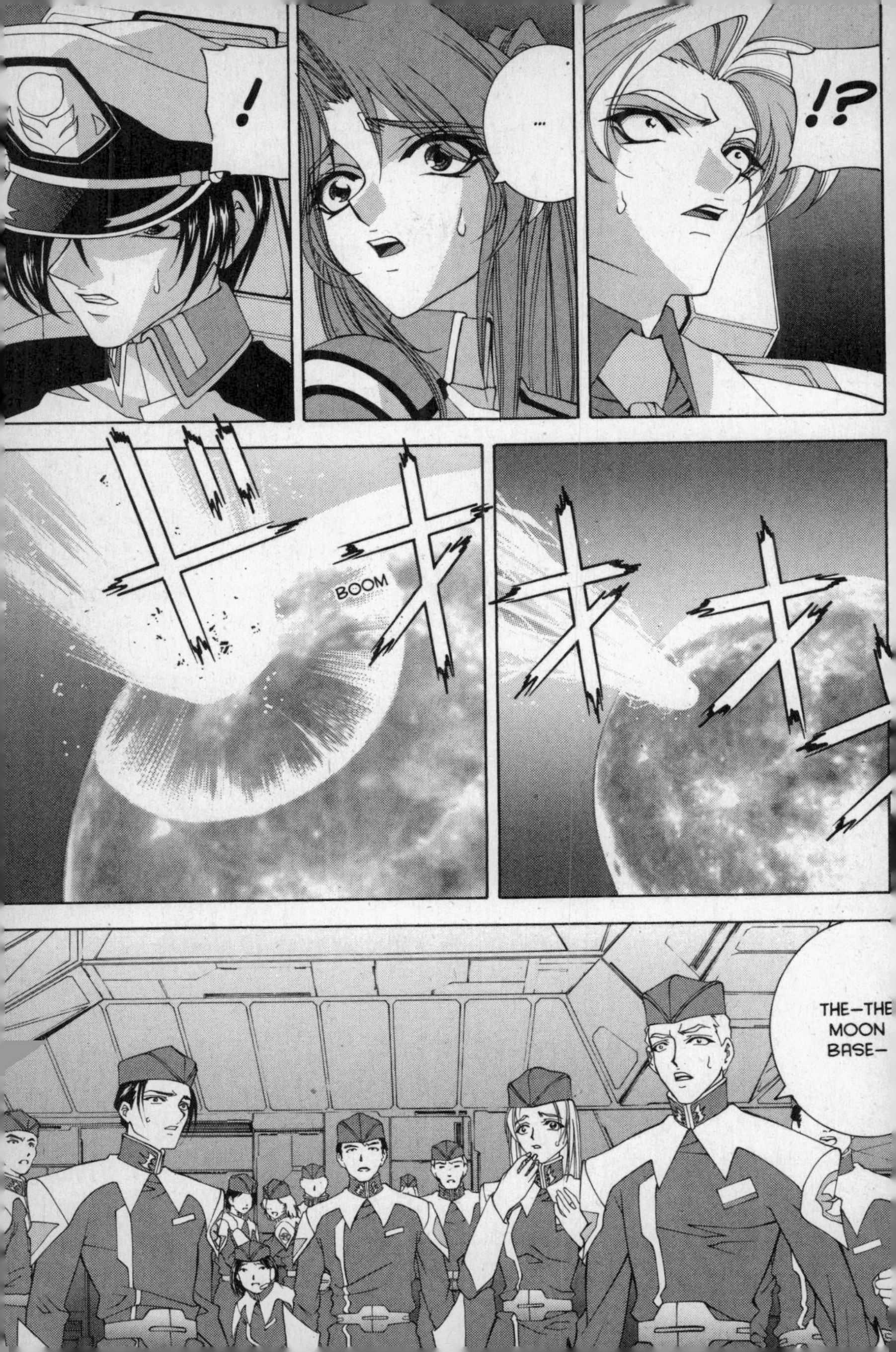
!?
...
!
BOOM
THE—THE MOON BASE—

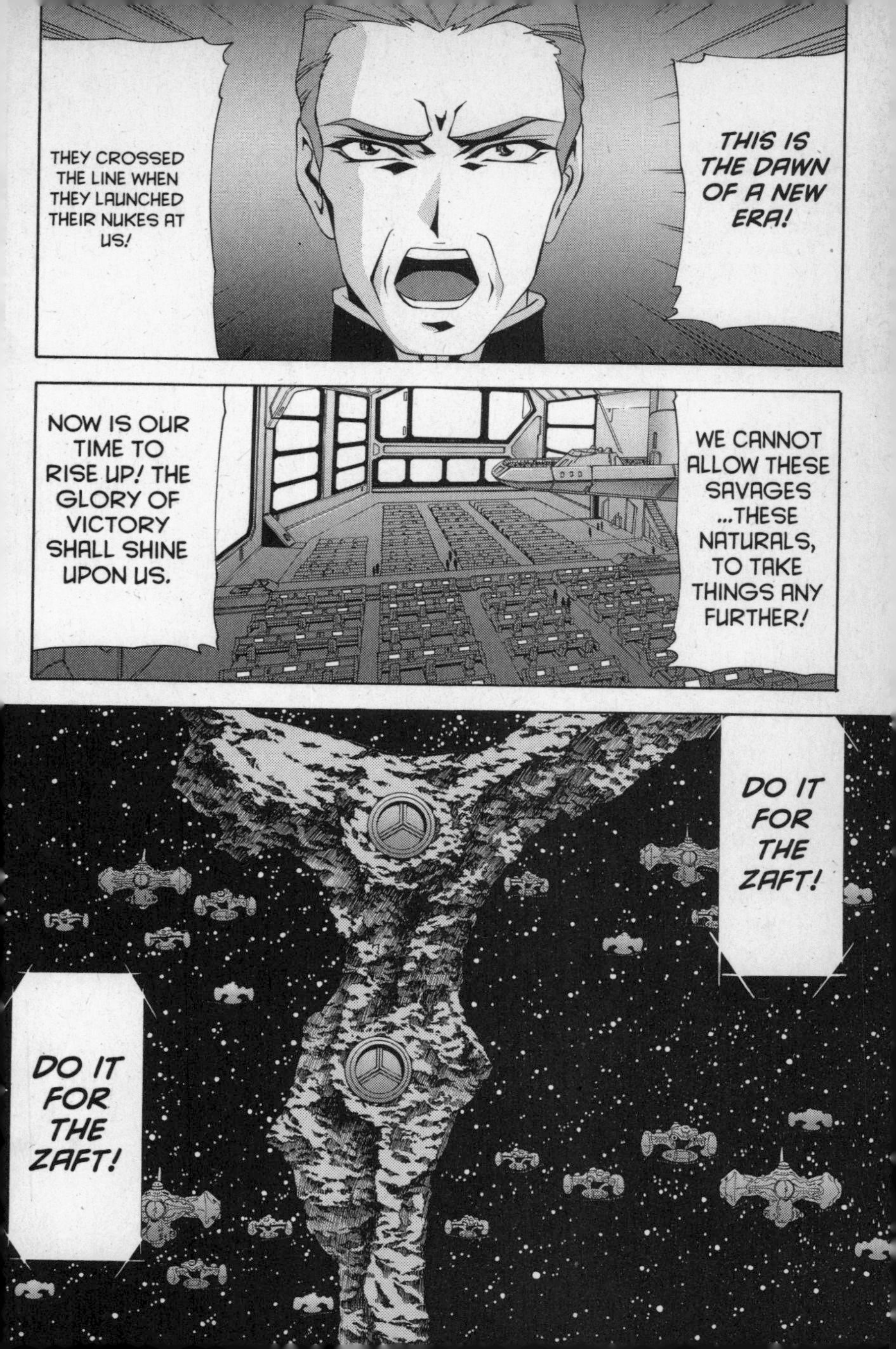
THIS IS THE DAWN OF A NEW ERA!
THEY CROSSED THE LINE WHEN THEY LAUNCHED THEIR NUKES AT US!
WE CANNOT ALLOW THESE SAVAGES ...THESE NATURALS, TO TAKE THINGS ANY FURTHER!
NOW IS OUR TIME TO RISE UP! THE GLORY OF VICTORY SHALL SHINE UPON US.
DO IT FOR THE ZAFT!
DO IT FOR THE ZAFT!

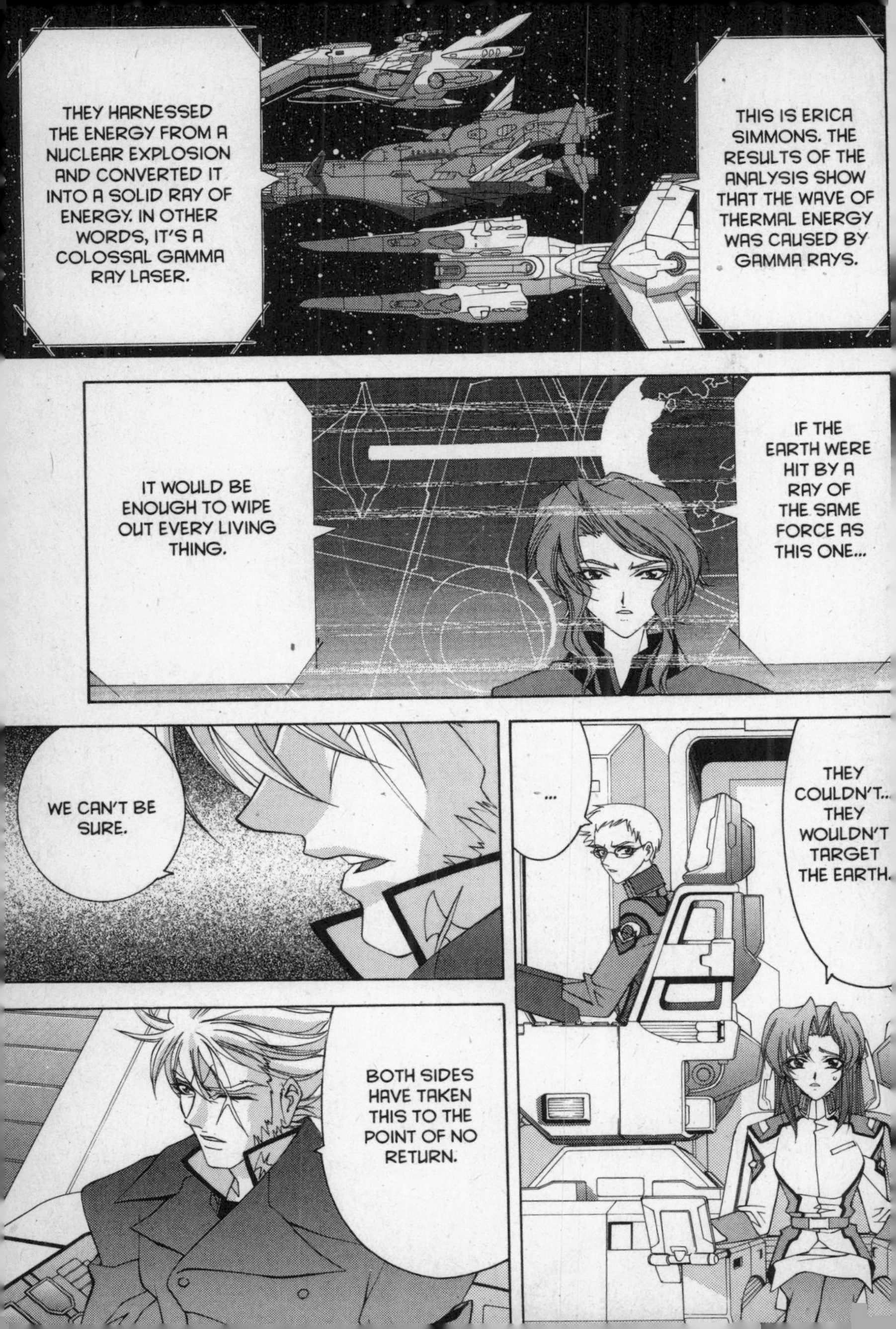
THIS IS ERICA SIMMONS. THE RESULTS OF THE ANALYSIS SHOW THAT THE WAVE OF THERMAL ENERGY WAS CAUSED BY GAMMA RAYS.
THEY HARNESSED THE ENERGY FROM A NUCLEAR EXPLOSION AND CONVERTED IT INTO A SOLID RAY OF ENERGY. IN OTHER WORDS, IT'S A COLOSSAL GAMMA RAY LASER.
IF THE EARTH WERE HIT BY A RAY OF THE SAME FORCE AS THIS ONE...
IT WOULD BE ENOUGH TO WIPE OUT EVERY LIVING THING.
THEY COULDN'T... THEY WOULDN'T TARGET THE EARTH.
...
WE CAN'T BE SURE.
BOTH SIDES HAVE TAKEN THIS TO THE POINT OF NO RETURN.

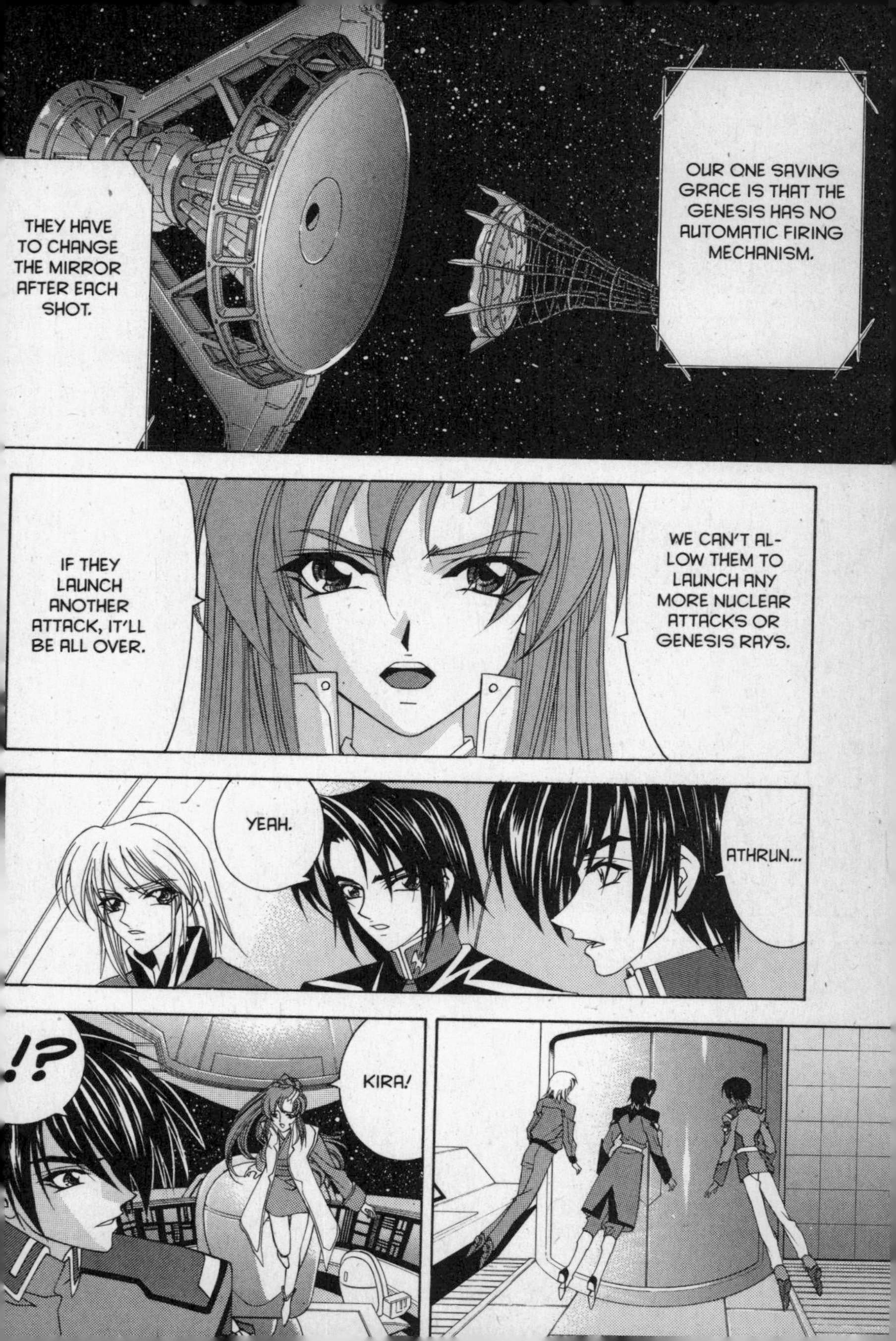
OUR ONE SAVING GRACE IS THAT THE GENESIS HAS NO AUTOMATIC FIRING MECHANISM.
THEY HAVE TO CHANGE THE MIRROR AFTER EACH SHOT.
WE CAN'T AL-LOW THEM TO LAUNCH ANY MORE NUCLEAR ATTACKS OR GENESIS RAYS.
IF THEY LAUNCH ANOTHER ATTACK, IT'LL BE ALL OVER.
ATHRUN...
YEAH.
KIRA!
!?

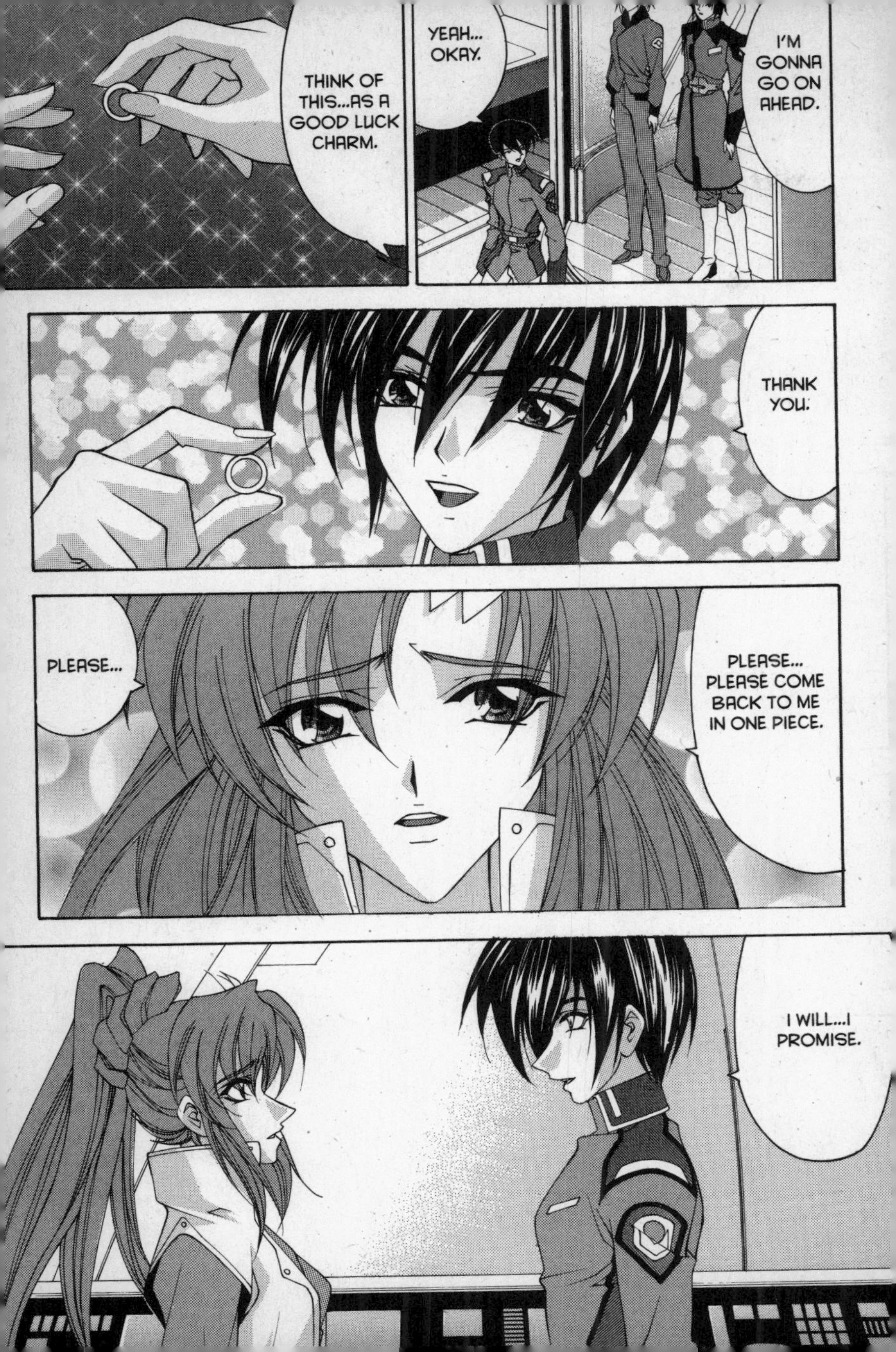
I'M GONNA GO ON AHEAD.
YEAH... OKAY.
THINK OF THIS...AS A GOOD LUCK CHARM.
THANK YOU.
PLEASE... PLEASE COME BACK TO ME IN ONE PIECE.
PLEASE...
I WILL...I PROMISE.

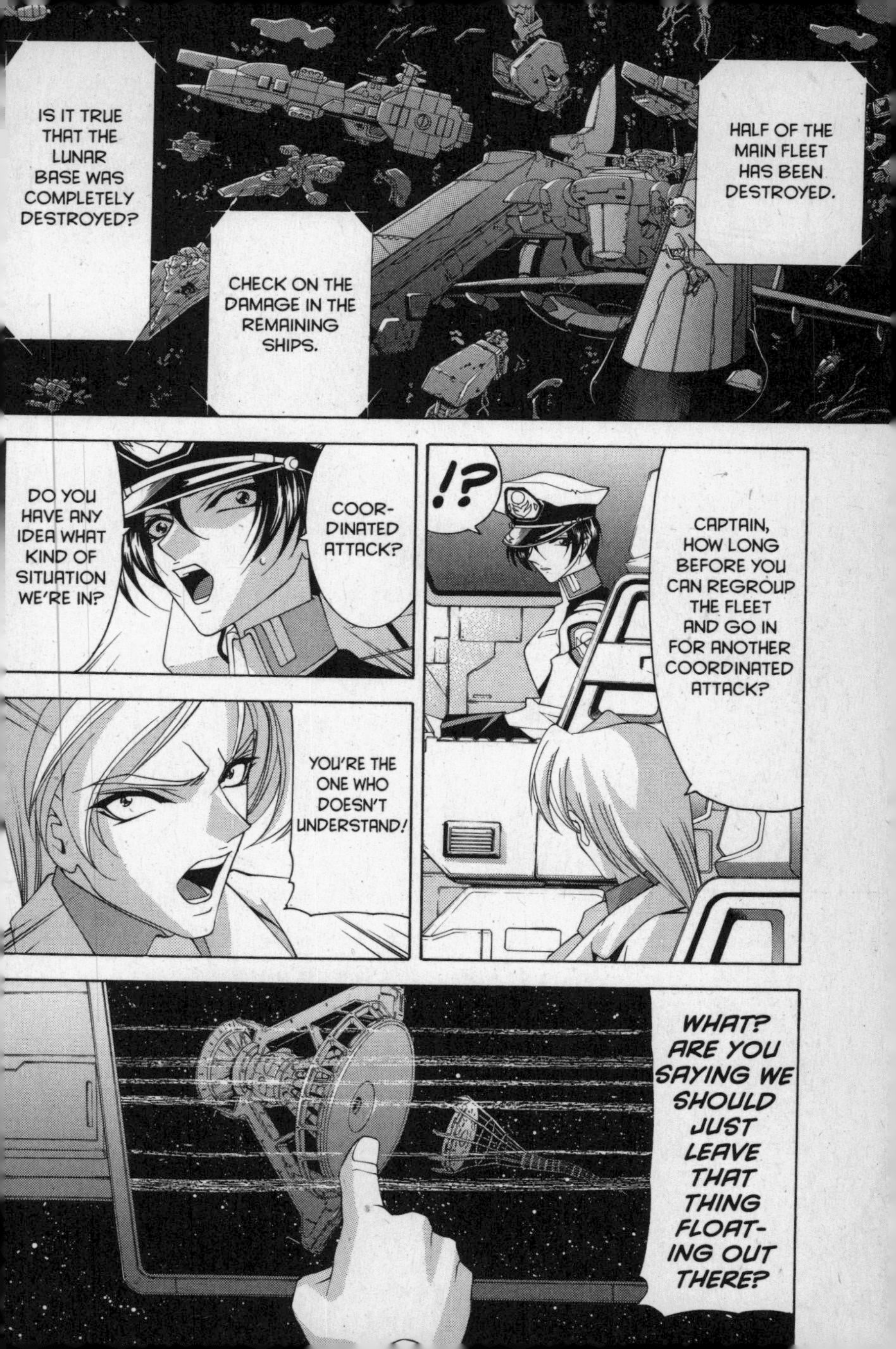
HALF OF THE MAIN FLEET HAS BEEN DESTROYED.
IS IT TRUE THAT THE LUNAR BASE WAS COMPLETELY DESTROYED?
CHECK ON THE DAMAGE IN THE REMAINING SHIPS.
CAPTAIN, HOW LONG BEFORE YOU CAN REGROUP THE FLEET AND GO IN FOR ANOTHER COORDINATED ATTACK?
!?
COOR-DINATED ATTACK?
DO YOU HAVE ANY IDEA WHAT KIND OF SITUATION WE'RE IN?
YOU'RE THE ONE WHO DOESN'T UNDERSTAND!
WHAT? ARE YOU SAYING WE SHOULD JUST LEAVE THAT THING FLOAT-ING OUT THERE?

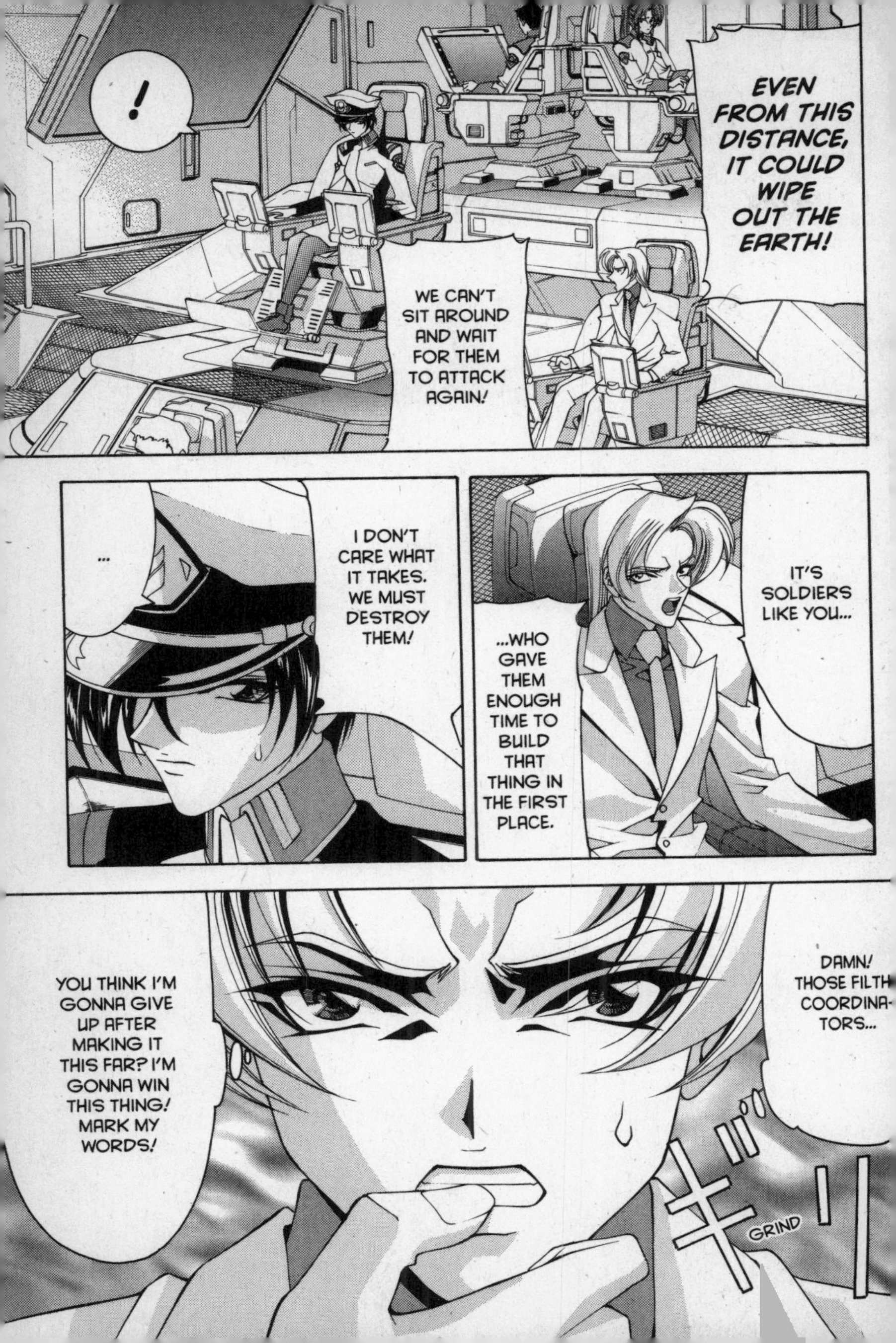
EVEN FROM THIS DISTANCE, IT COULD WIPE OUT THE EARTH!
WE CAN'T SIT AROUND AND WAIT FOR THEM TO ATTACK AGAIN!
!
IT'S SOLDIERS LIKE YOU...
...WHO GAVE THEM ENOUGH TIME TO BUILD THAT THING IN THE FIRST PLACE.
I DON'T CARE WHAT IT TAKES. WE MUST DESTROY THEM!
...
DAMN! THOSE FILTH COORDINA-TORS...
GRIND
YOU THINK I'M GONNA GIVE UP AFTER MAKING IT THIS FAR? I'M GONNA WIN THIS THING! MARK MY WORDS!

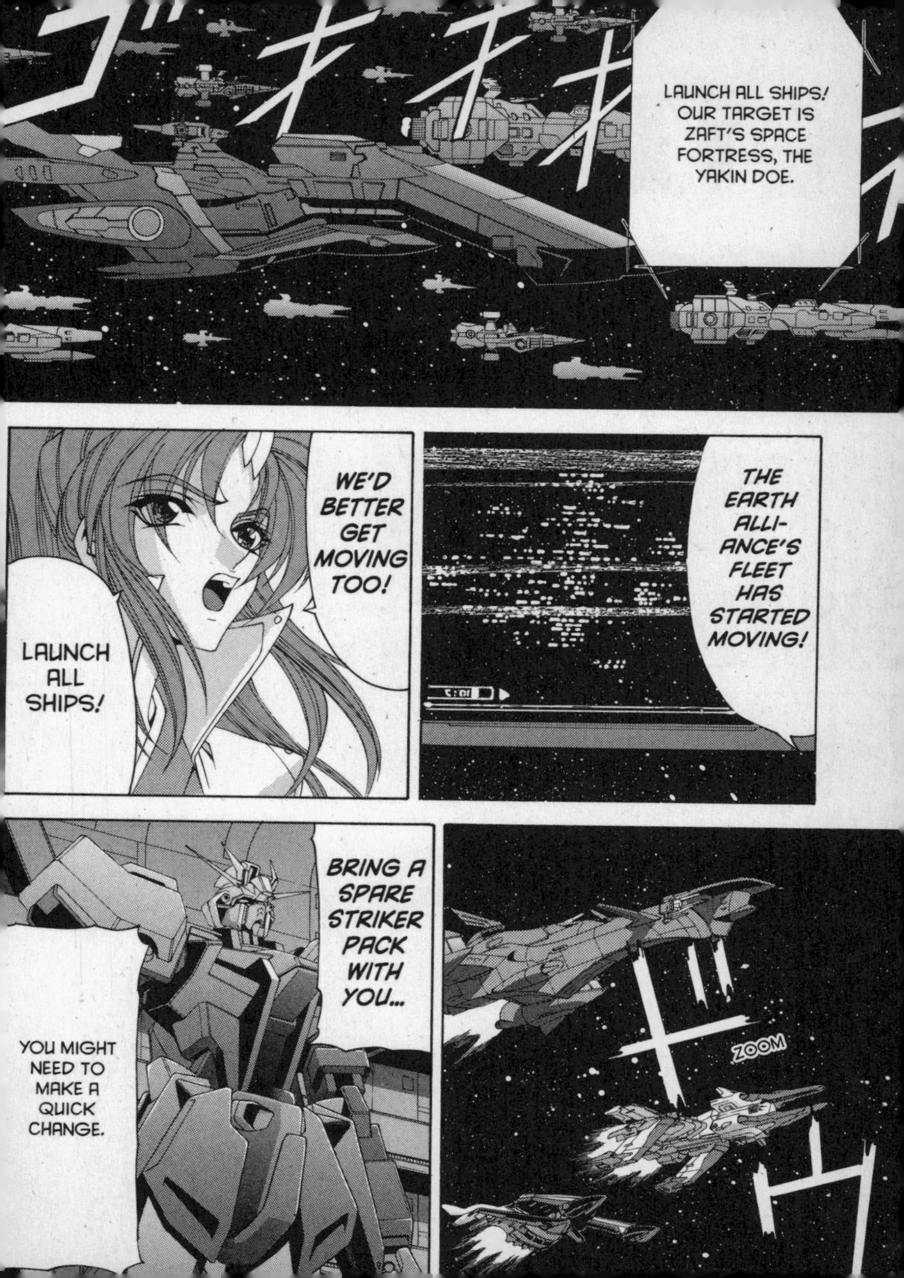
LAUNCH ALL SHIPS! OUR TARGET IS ZAFT'S SPACE FORTRESS, THE YAKIN DOE.
THE EARTH ALLI-ANCE'S FLEET HAS STARTED MOVING!
WE'D BETTER GET MOVING TOO!
LAUNCH ALL SHIPS!
ZOOM
BRING A SPARE STRIKER PACK WITH YOU...
YOU MIGHT NEED TO MAKE A QUICK CHANGE.

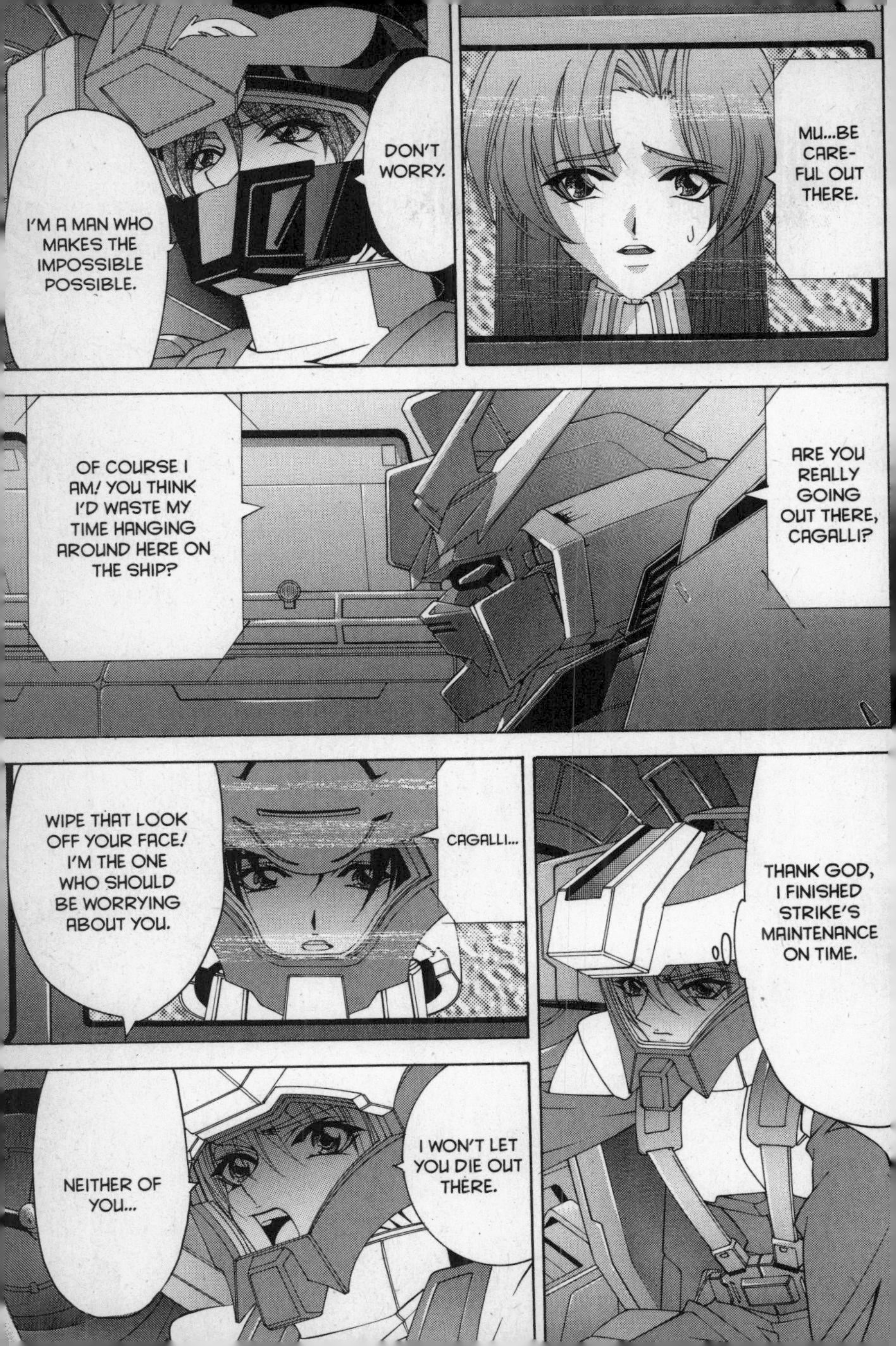
MU...BE CARE-FUL OUT THERE.
DON'T WORRY.
I'M A MAN WHO MAKES THE IMPOSSIBLE POSSIBLE.
ARE YOU REALLY GOING OUT THERE, CAGALLI?
OF COURSE I AM! YOU THINK I'D WASTE MY TIME HANGING AROUND HERE ON THE SHIP?
THANK GOD, I FINISHED STRIKE'S MAINTENANCE ON TIME.
CAGALLI...
WIPE THAT LOOK OFF YOUR FACE! I'M THE ONE WHO SHOULD BE WORRYING ABOUT YOU.
I WON'T LET YOU DIE OUT THERE.
NEITHER OF YOU...

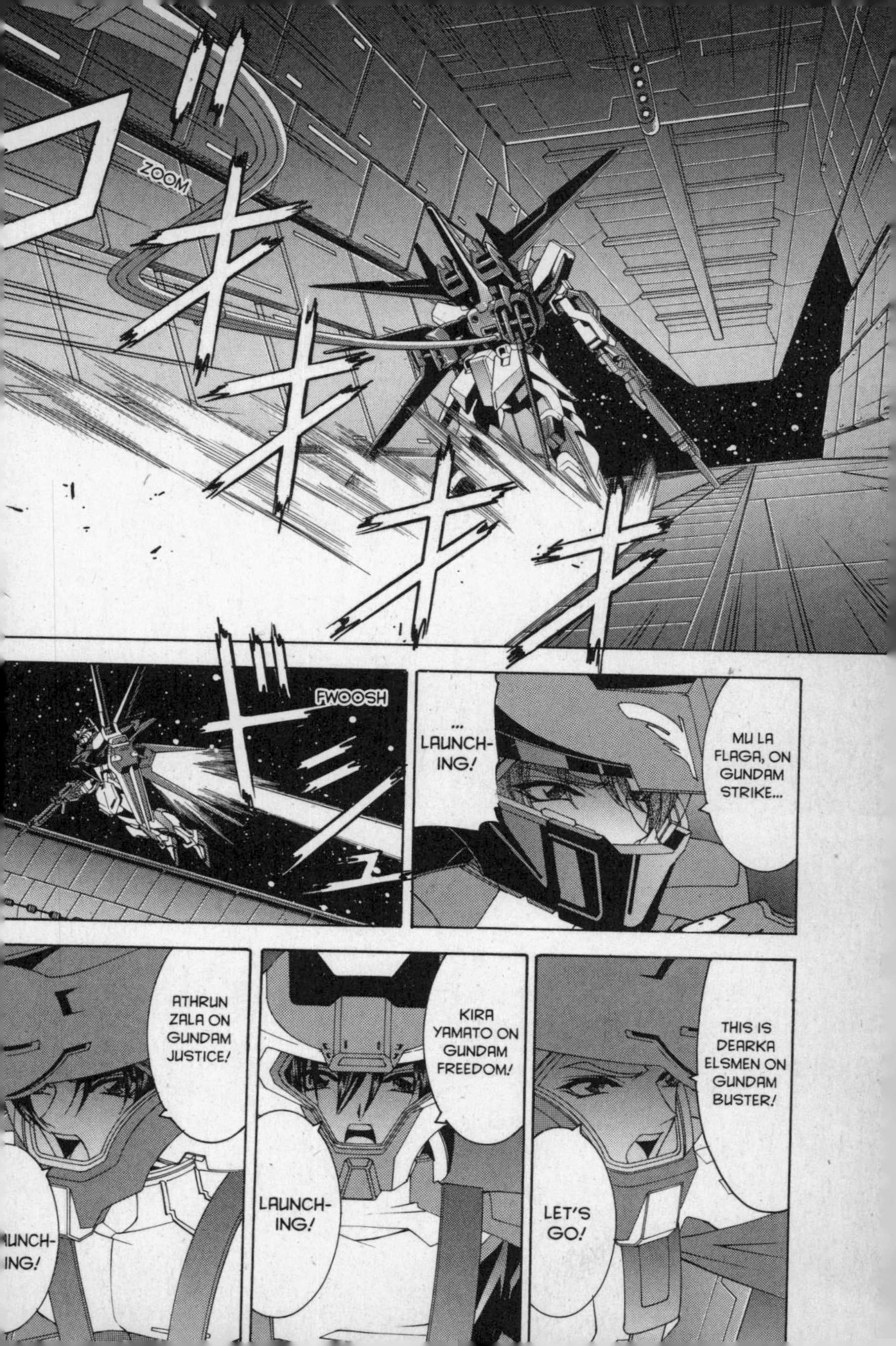
ZOOM
MU LA FLAGA, ON GUNDAM STRIKE...
...LAUNCHING!
FWOOSH
THIS IS DEARKA ELSMEN ON GUNDAM BUSTER!
LET'S GO!
KIRA YAMATO ON GUNDAM FREEDOM!
LAUNCHING!
ATHRUN ZALA ON GUNDAM JUSTICE!
AUNCH-ING!

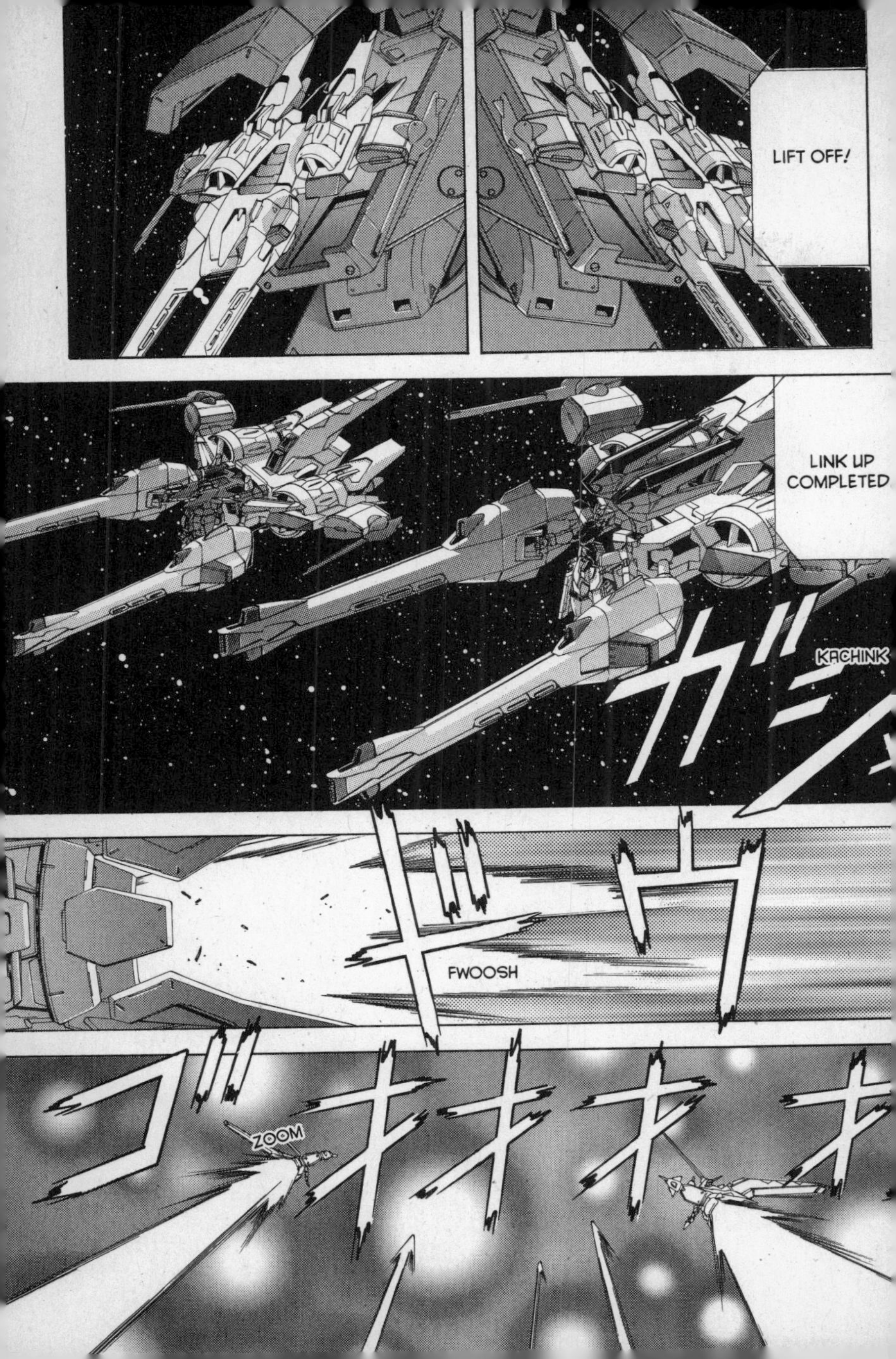
LIFT OFF!
LINK UP COMPLETED
KACHINK
FWOOSH
ZOOM

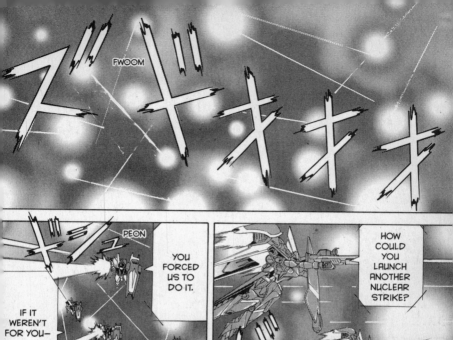

FWOOM
HOW COULD YOU LAUNCH ANOTHER NUCLEAR STRIKE?
FWAH
PEON
YOU FORCED US TO DO IT.
IF IT WEREN'T FOR YOU—

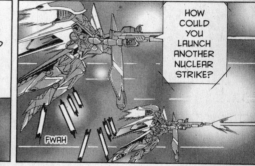

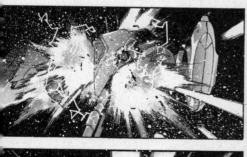

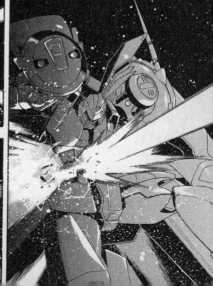

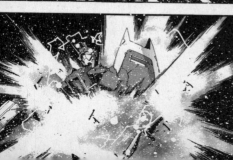

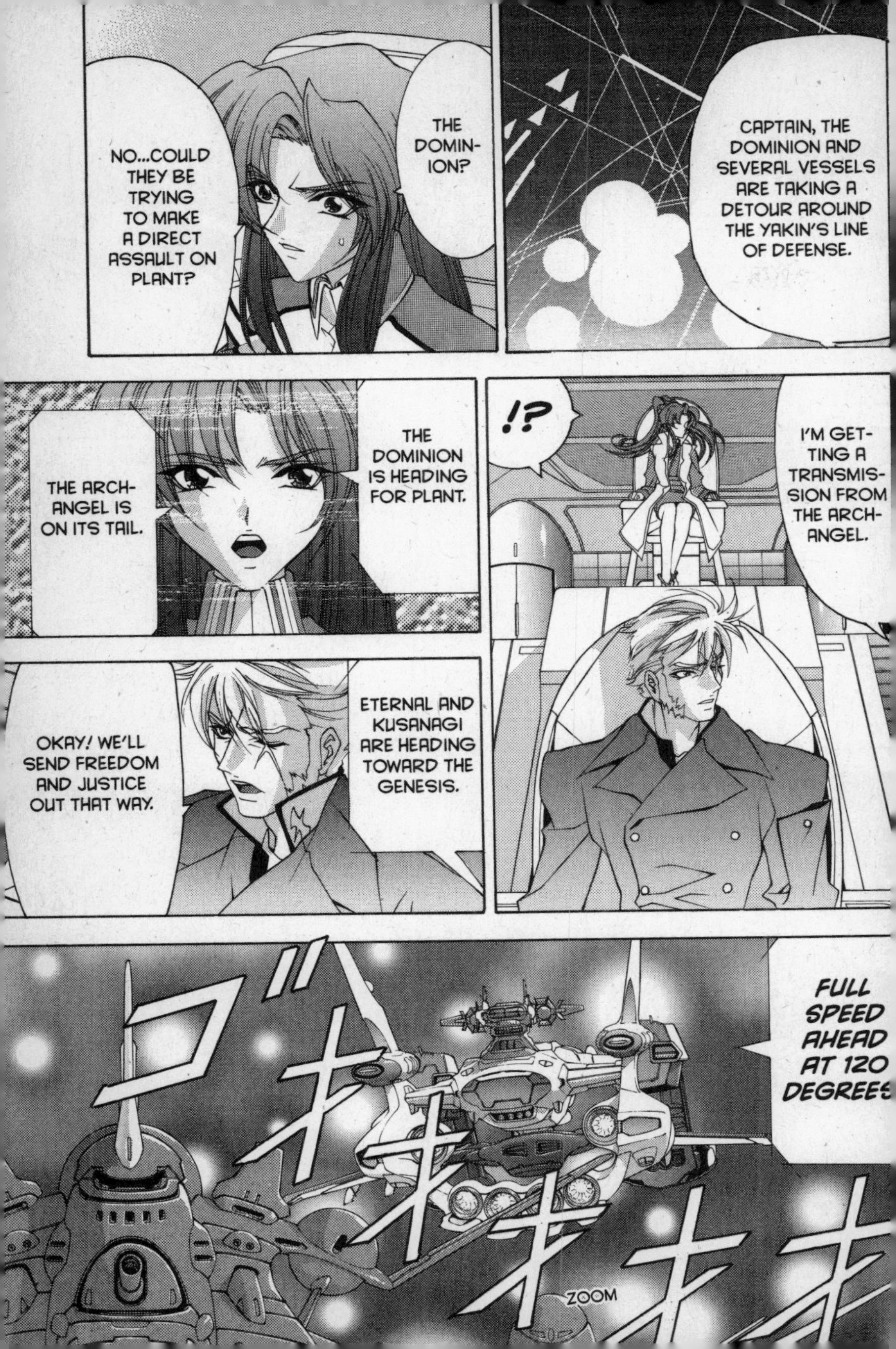
CAPTAIN, THE DOMINION AND SEVERAL VESSELS ARE TAKING A DETOUR AROUND THE YAKIN'S LINE OF DEFENSE.
THE DOMINION?
NO...COULD THEY BE TRYING TO MAKE A DIRECT ASSAULT ON PLANT?
I'M GETTING A TRANSMISSION FROM THE ARCHANGEL.
!?
THE DOMINION IS HEADING FOR PLANT.
THE ARCHANGEL IS ON ITS TAIL.
ETERNAL AND KUSANAGI ARE HEADING TOWARD THE GENESIS.
OKAY! WE'LL SEND FREEDOM AND JUSTICE OUT THAT WAY.
FULL SPEED AHEAD AT 120 DEGREES
ZOOM

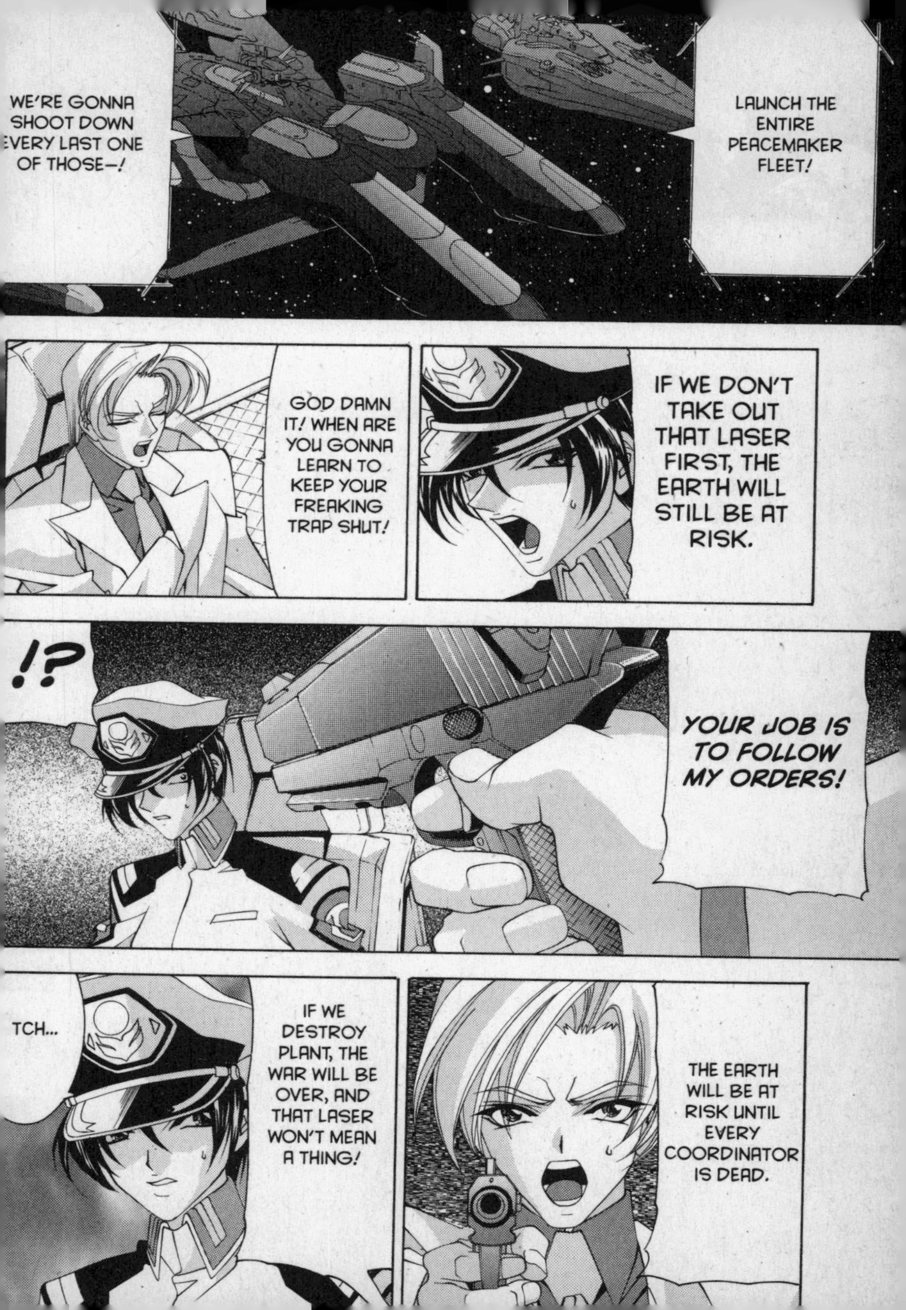
LAUNCH THE ENTIRE PEACEMAKER FLEET!
WE'RE GONNA SHOOT DOWN EVERY LAST ONE OF THOSE—!
IF WE DON'T TAKE OUT THAT LASER FIRST, THE EARTH WILL STILL BE AT RISK.
GOD DAMN IT! WHEN ARE YOU GONNA LEARN TO KEEP YOUR FREAKING TRAP SHUT!
YOUR JOB IS TO FOLLOW MY ORDERS!
!?
THE EARTH WILL BE AT RISK UNTIL EVERY COORDINATOR IS DEAD.
IF WE DESTROY PLANT, THE WAR WILL BE OVER, AND THAT LASER WON'T MEAN A THING!
TCH...

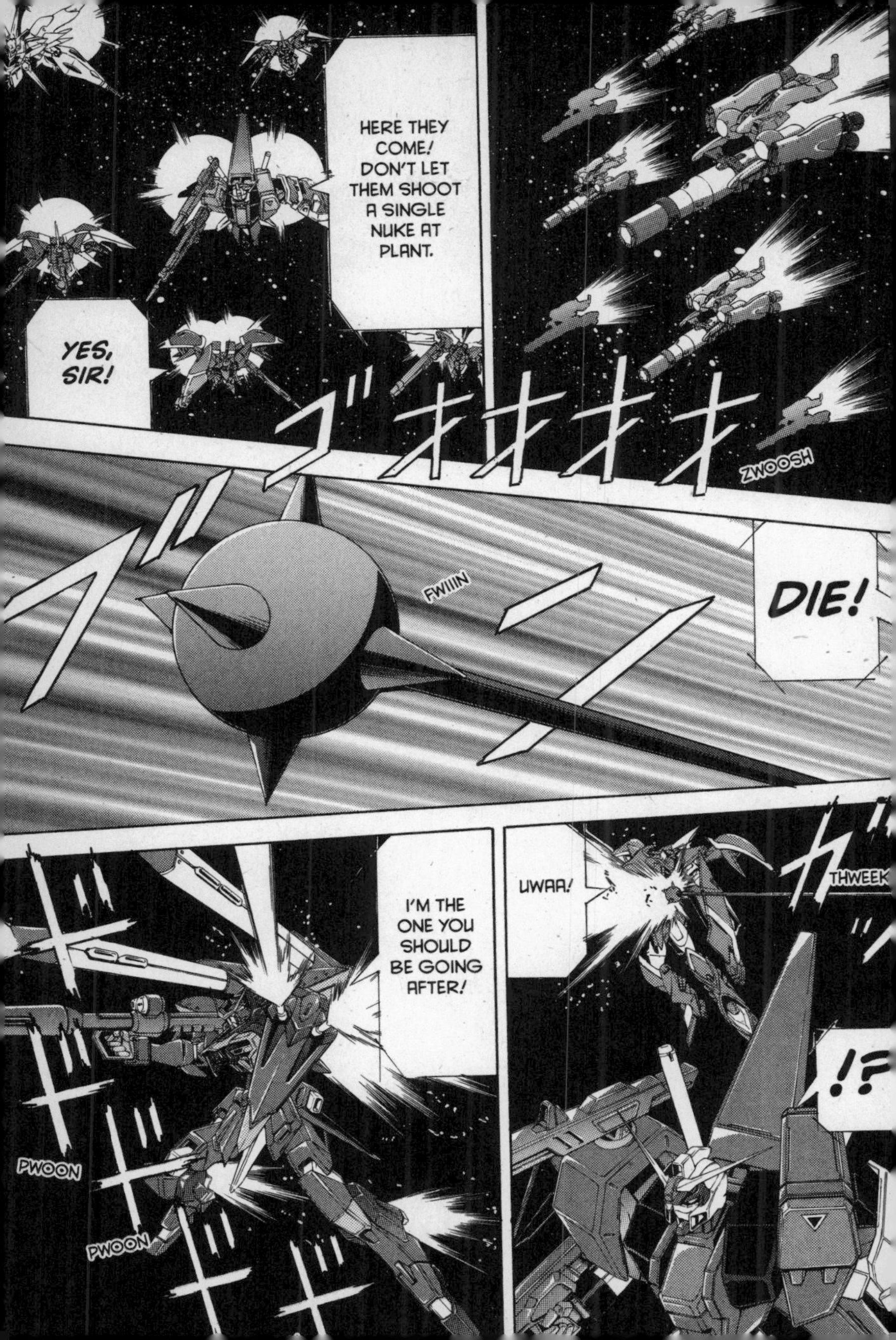
ゴオオオオ
ZWOOSH
HERE THEY COME! DON'T LET THEM SHOOT A SINGLE NUKE AT PLANT.
YES, SIR!
DIE!
FWIIIN
UWAA!
THWEEK
!?
I'M THE ONE YOU SHOULD BE GOING AFTER!
PWOON
PWOON

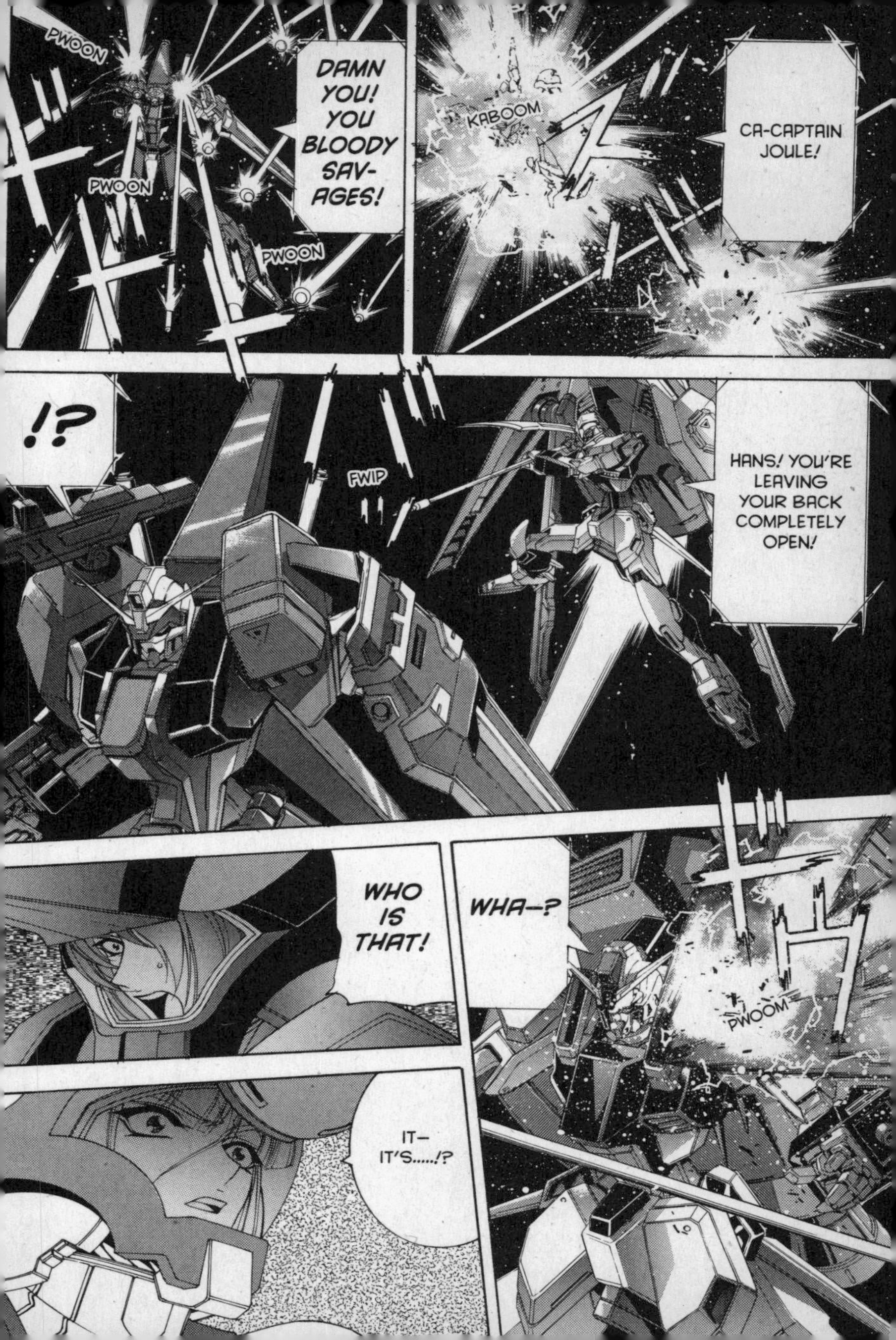
CA-CAPTAIN JOULE!
KABOOM
DAMN YOU! YOU BLOODY SAV-AGES!
PWOON
PWOON
PWOON
HANS! YOU'RE LEAVING YOUR BACK COMPLETELY OPEN!
FWIP
!?
WHA--?
PWOOM
WHO IS THAT!
IT-- IT'S......!?

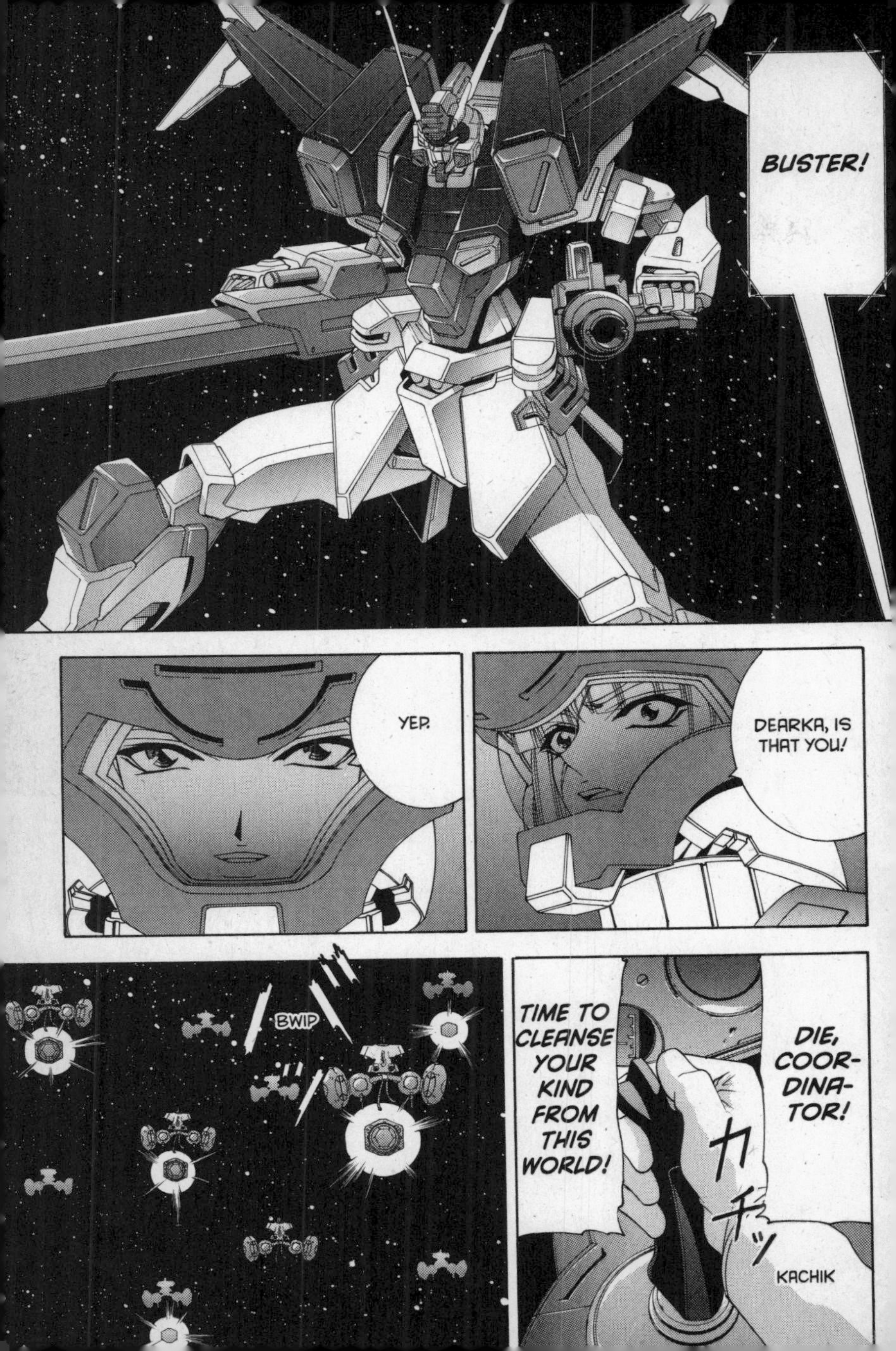
BUSTER!
DEARKA, IS THAT YOU!
YEP.
DIE, COORDINATOR!
TIME TO CLEANSE YOUR KIND FROM THIS WORLD!
カチッ
KACHIK
BWIP

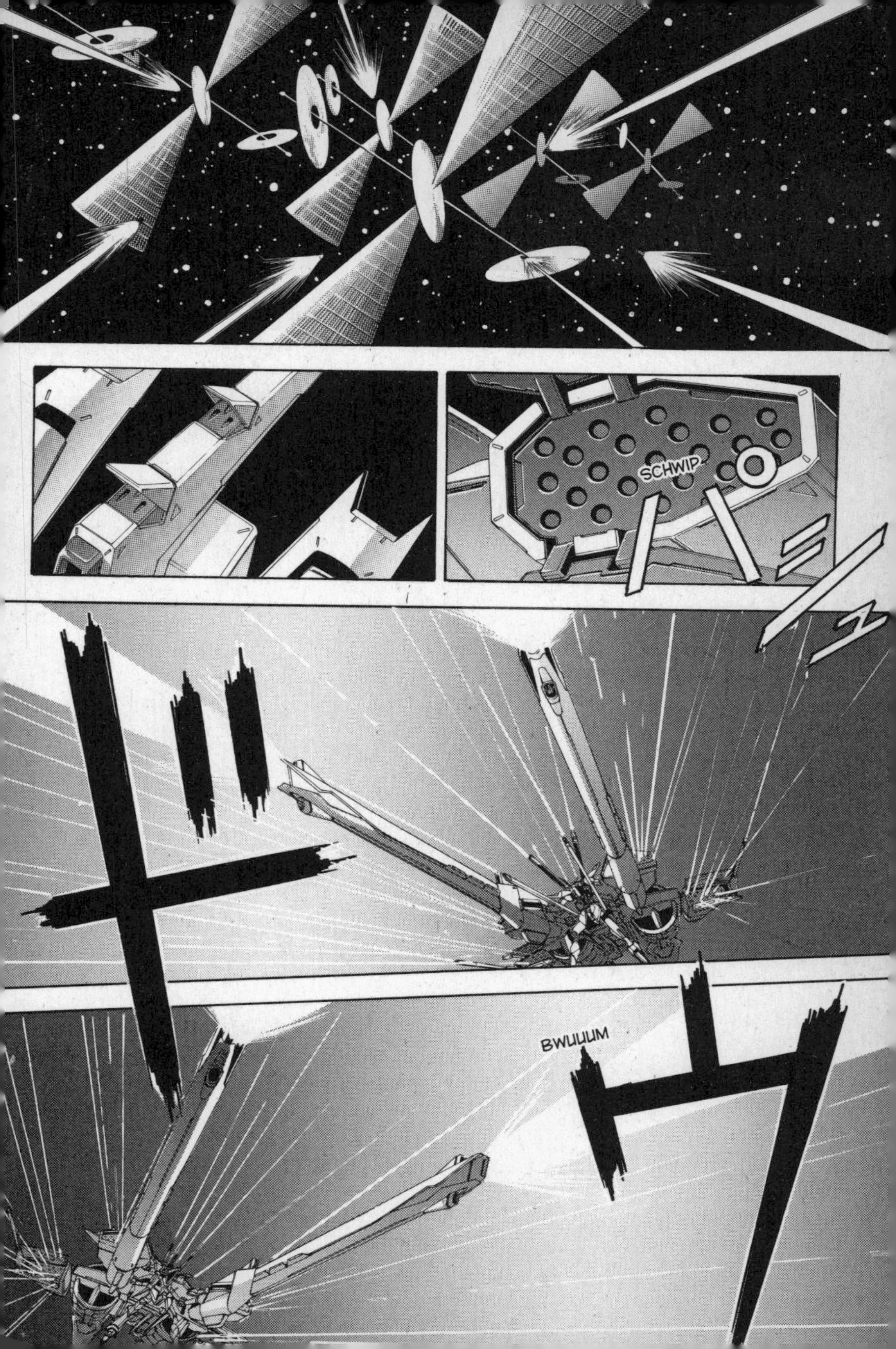
SCHWIP
BWUUUM

TAT

TAT

TAT

TAT

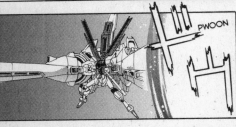

PWOON

HOW CAN THEY DO THAT?

BACHAK

IT MUST BE HIM... CREUSET...!

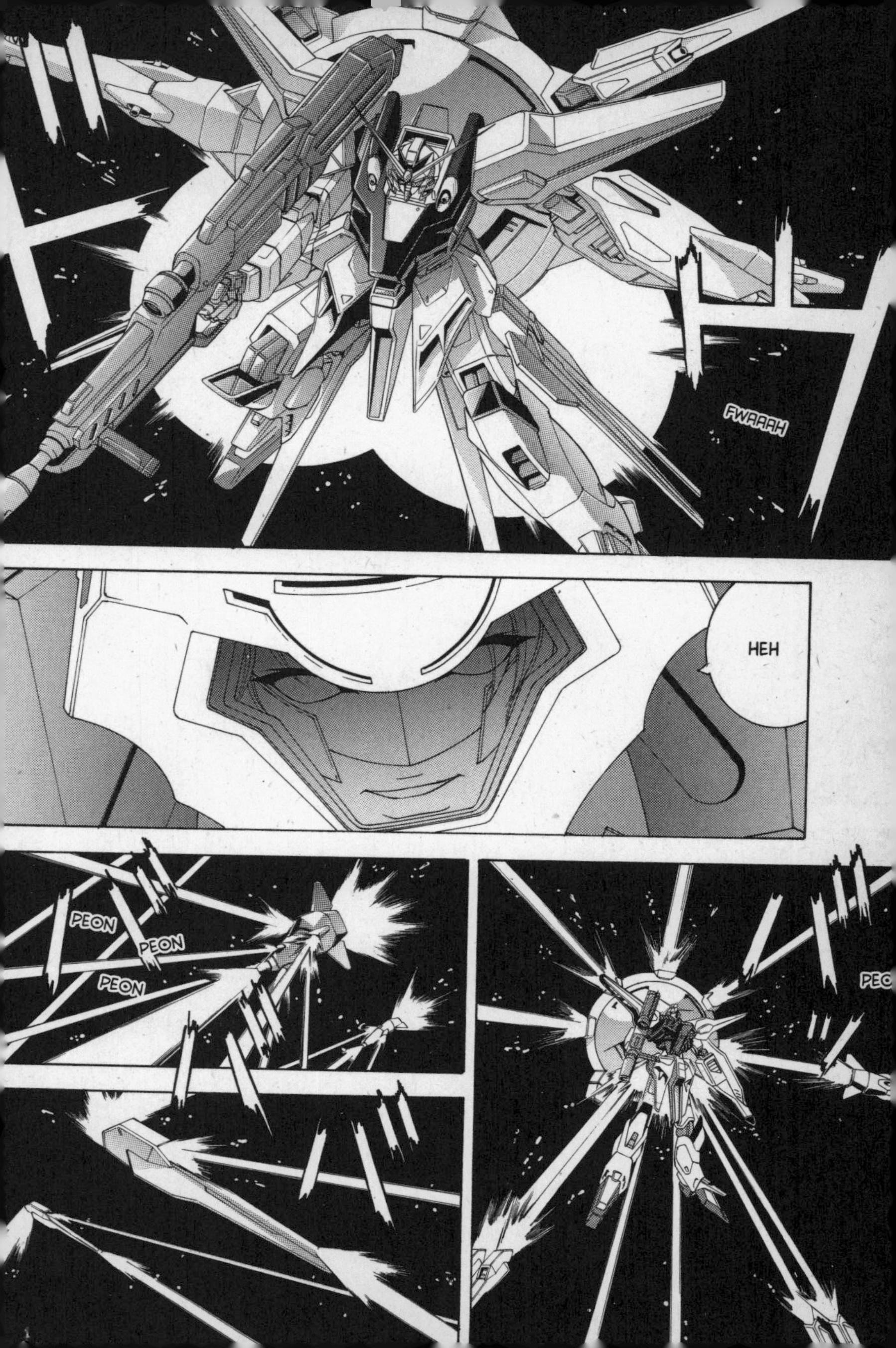
FWAAAH
HEH
PEO
PEON
PEON
PEON

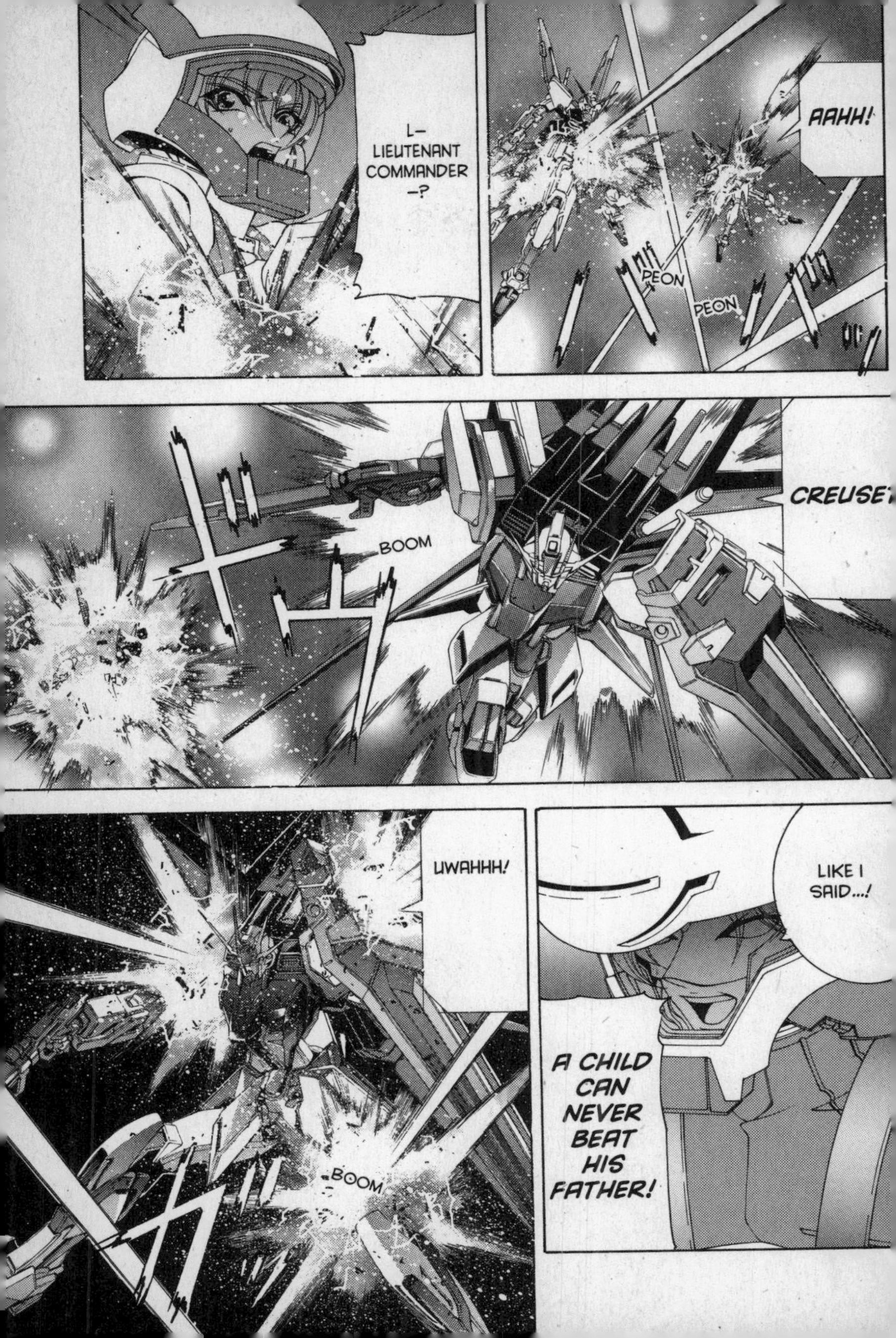
AAHH!
PEON
PEON
L—
LIEUTENANT
COMMANDER
—?
CREUSE
BOOM
LIKE I
SAID...!
A CHILD
CAN
NEVER
BEAT
HIS
FATHER!
UWAHHH!
BOOM

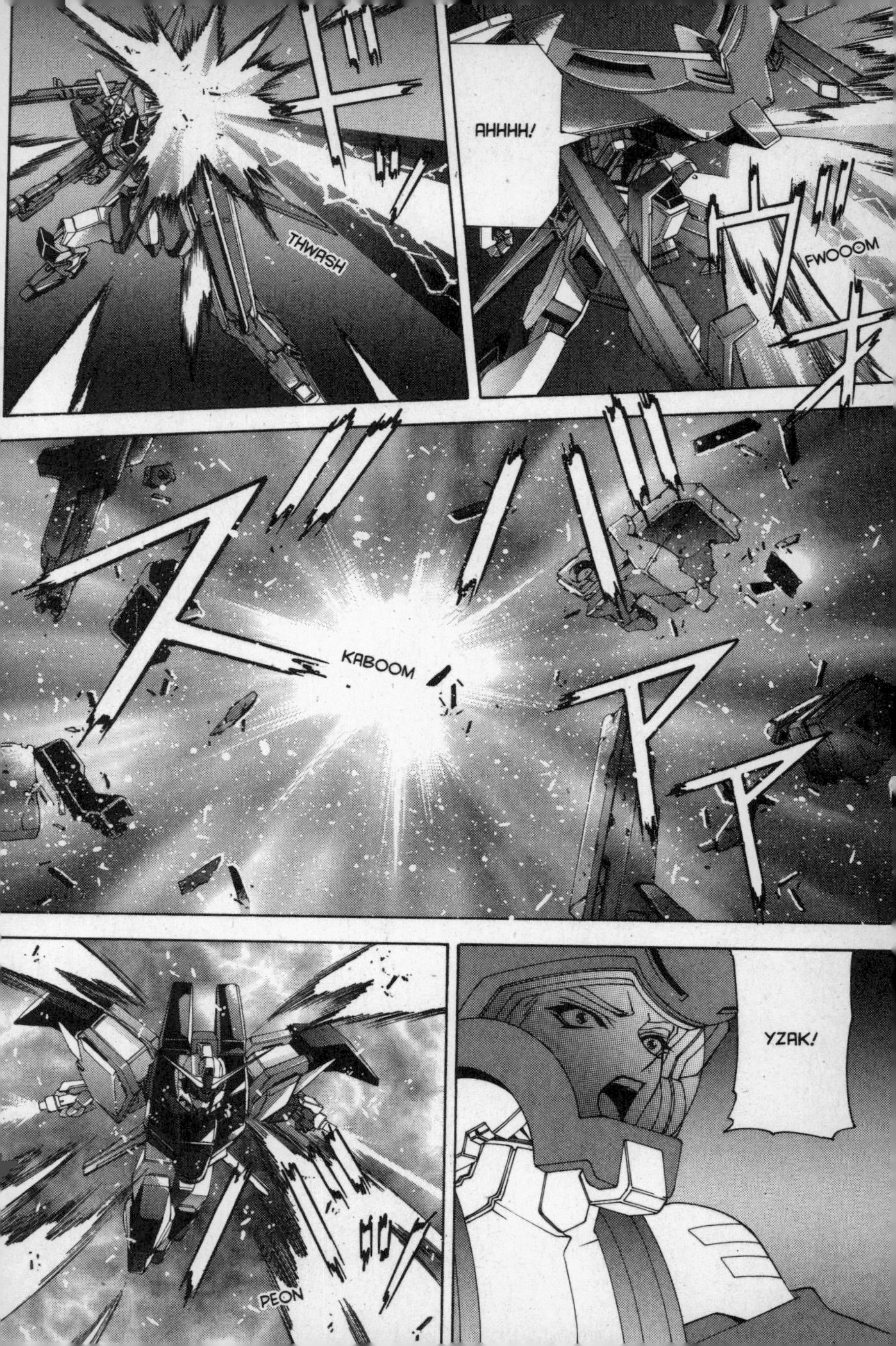
AHHHH!
FWOOOM
THWASH
KABOOM
YZAK!
PEON

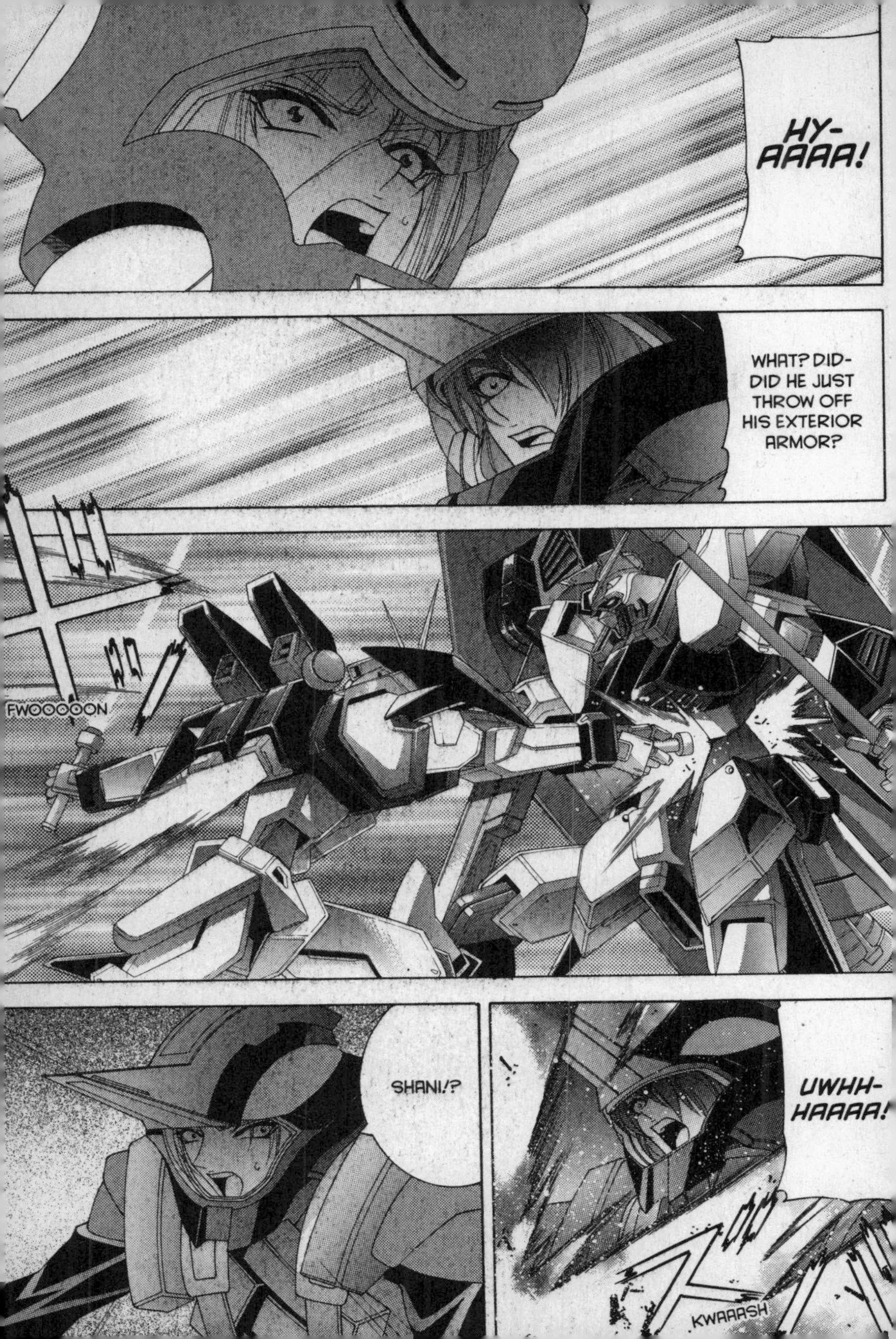
HY-AAAA!
WHAT? DID-DID HE JUST THROW OFF HIS EXTERIOR ARMOR?
FWOOOOON
UWHH-HAAAA!
KWAAASH
SHANI!?

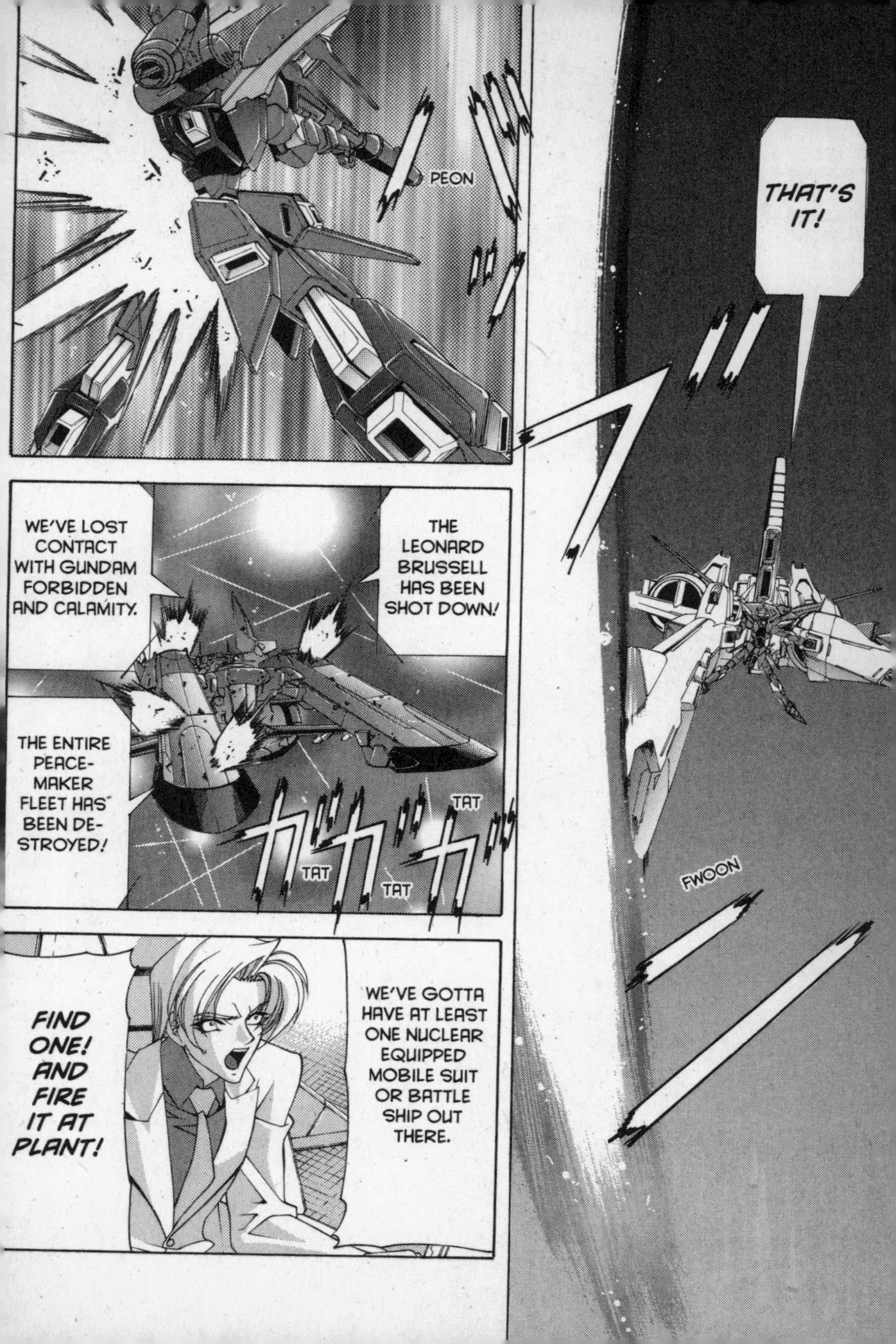
THAT'S IT!
FWOON
PEON
THE LEONARD BRUSSELL HAS BEEN SHOT DOWN!
WE'VE LOST CONTACT WITH GUNDAM FORBIDDEN AND CALAMITY.
THE ENTIRE PEACE-MAKER FLEET HAS BEEN DE-STROYED!
TAT
TAT
TAT
WE'VE GOTTA HAVE AT LEAST ONE NUCLEAR EQUIPPED MOBILE SUIT OR BATTLE SHIP OUT THERE.
FIND ONE! AND FIRE IT AT PLANT!

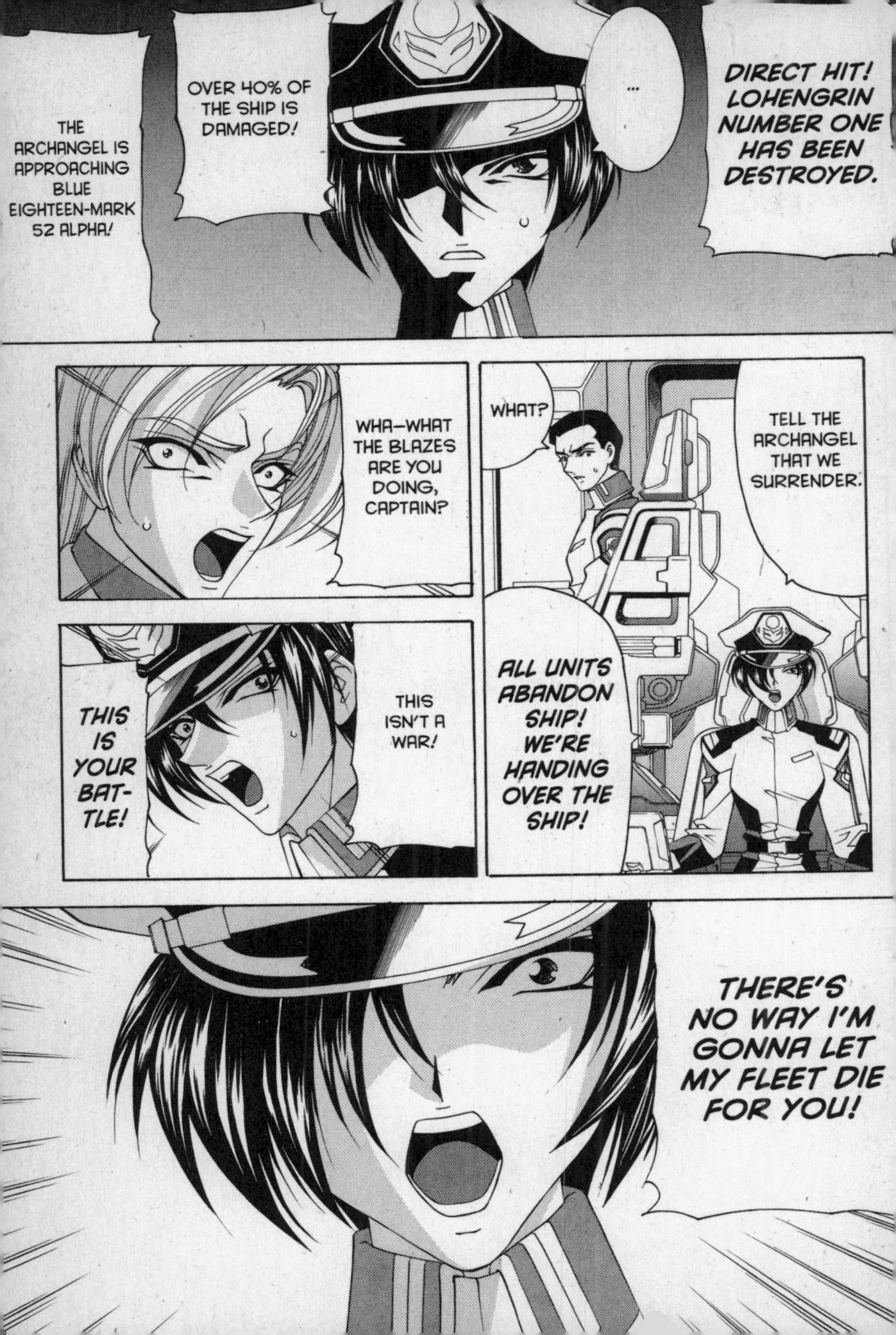

DIRECT HIT! LOHENGRIN NUMBER ONE HAS BEEN DESTROYED.
...
OVER 40% OF THE SHIP IS DAMAGED!
THE ARCHANGEL IS APPROACHING BLUE EIGHTEEN-MARK 52 ALPHA!
TELL THE ARCHANGEL THAT WE SURRENDER.
WHAT?
ALL UNITS ABANDON SHIP! WE'RE HANDING OVER THE SHIP!
WHA—WHAT THE BLAZES ARE YOU DOING, CAPTAIN?
THIS ISN'T A WAR!
THIS IS YOUR BAT-TLE!
THERE'S NO WAY I'M GONNA LET MY FLEET DIE FOR YOU!

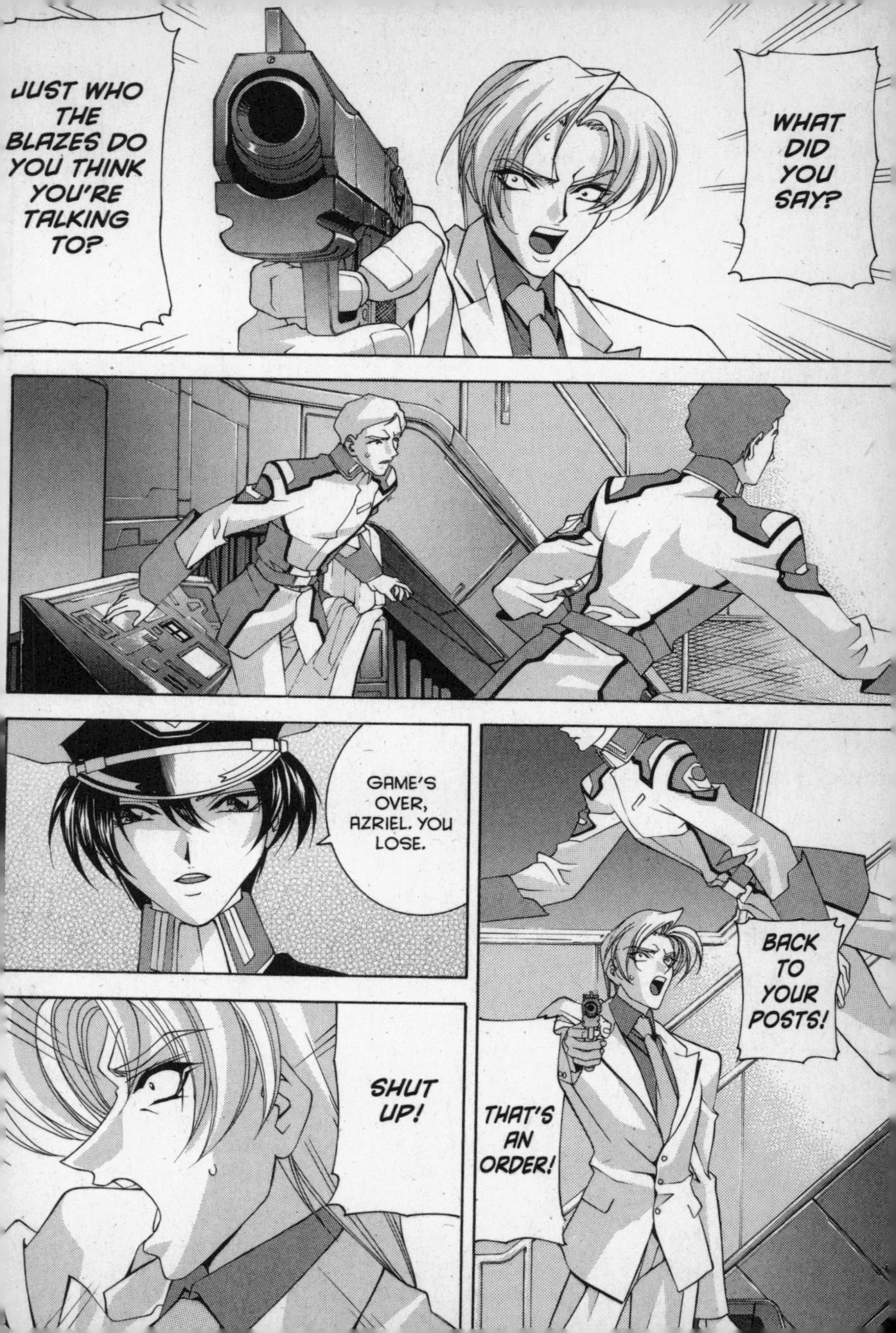
WHAT DID YOU SAY?
JUST WHO THE BLAZES DO YOU THINK YOU'RE TALKING TO?
BACK TO YOUR POSTS!
THAT'S AN ORDER!
GAME'S OVER, AZRIEL. YOU LOSE.
SHUT UP!

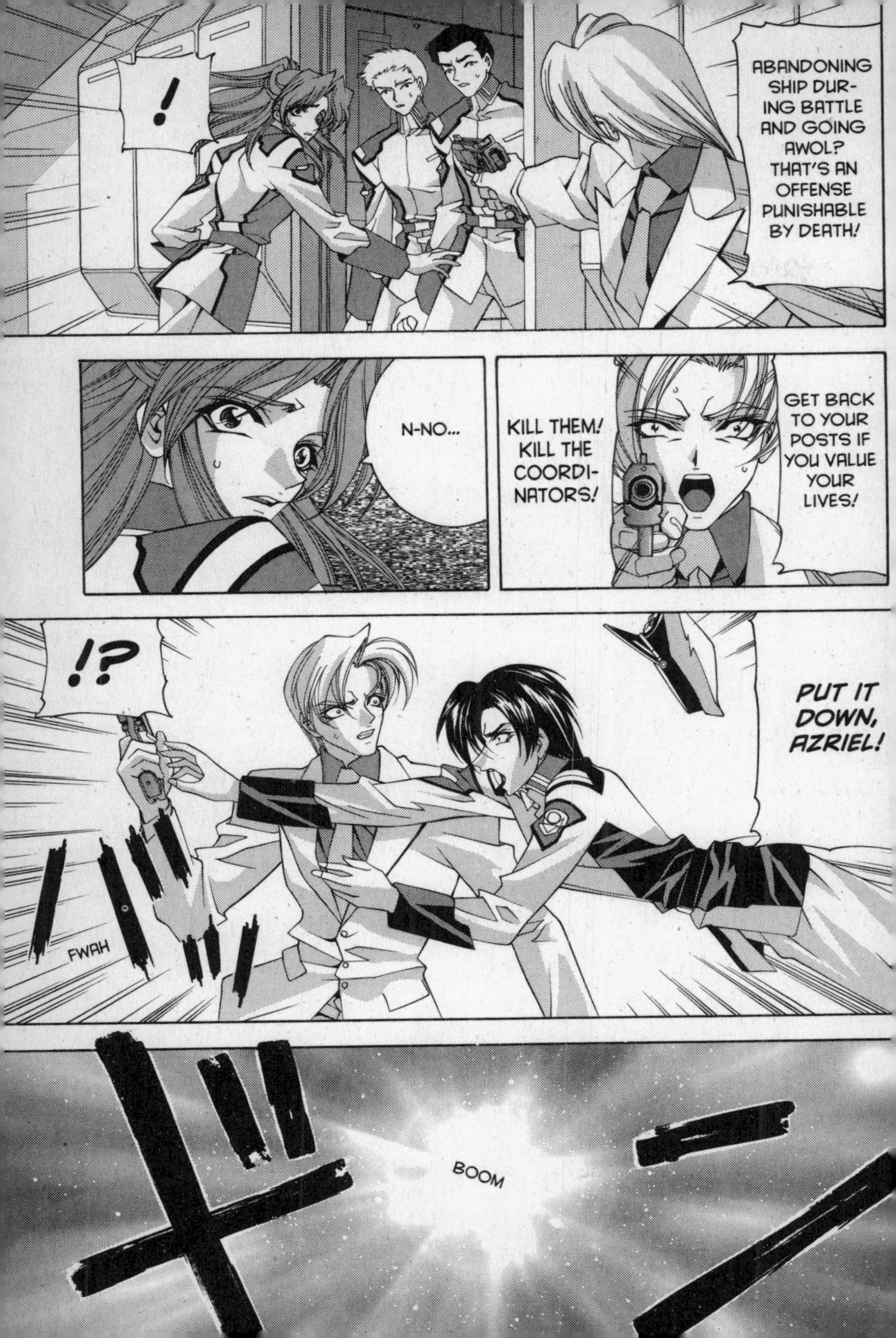
ABANDONING SHIP DURING BATTLE AND GOING AWOL? THAT'S AN OFFENSE PUNISHABLE BY DEATH!
!
GET BACK TO YOUR POSTS IF YOU VALUE YOUR LIVES!
KILL THEM! KILL THE COORDINATORS!
N-NO...
PUT IT DOWN, AZRIEL!
!?
FWAH
BOOM

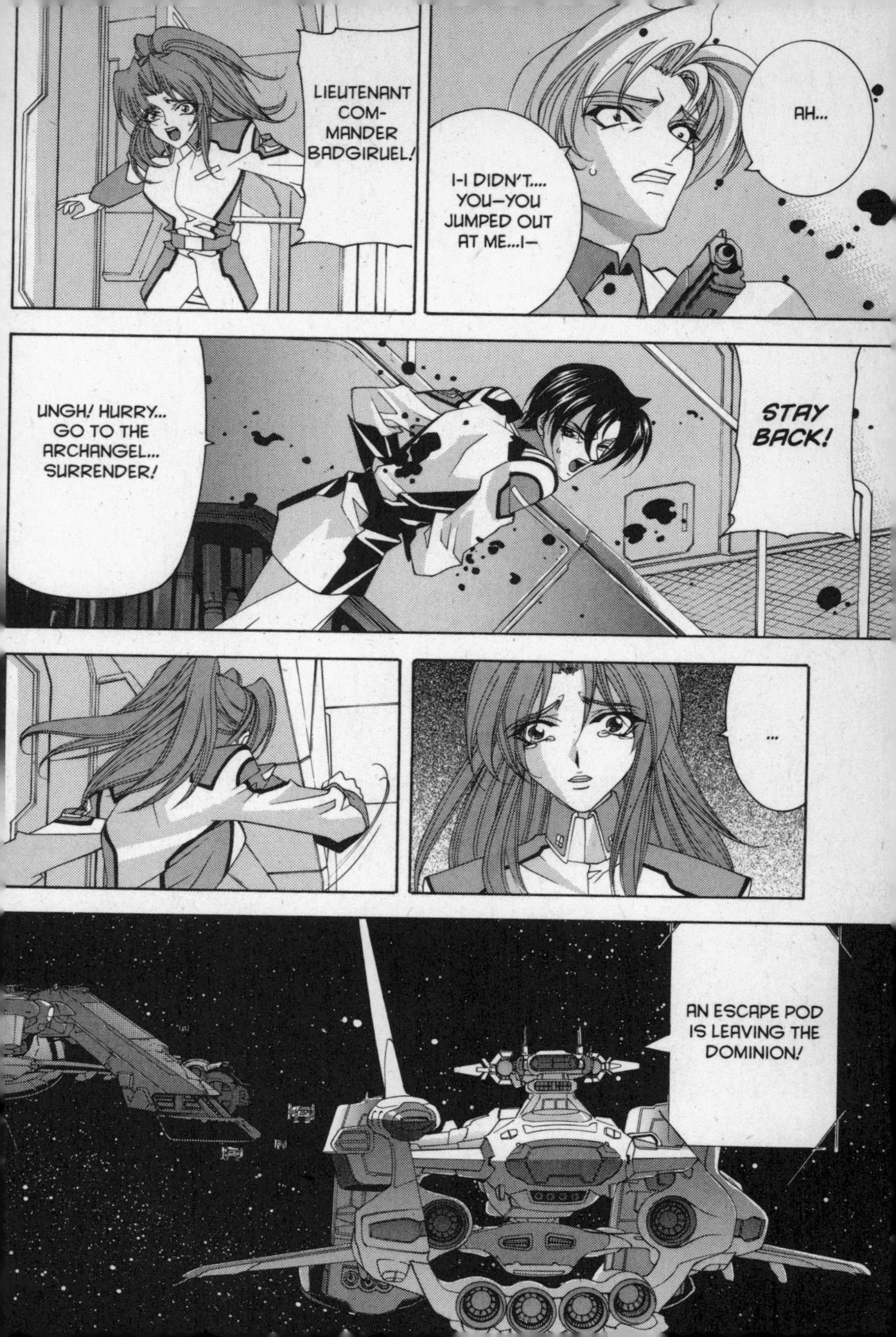
AH...
I-I DIDN'T.... YOU—YOU JUMPED OUT AT ME...I—
LIEUTENANT COM-MANDER BADGIRUEL!
STAY BACK!
UNGH! HURRY... GO TO THE ARCHANGEL... SURRENDER!
...
AN ESCAPE POD IS LEAVING THE DOMINION!

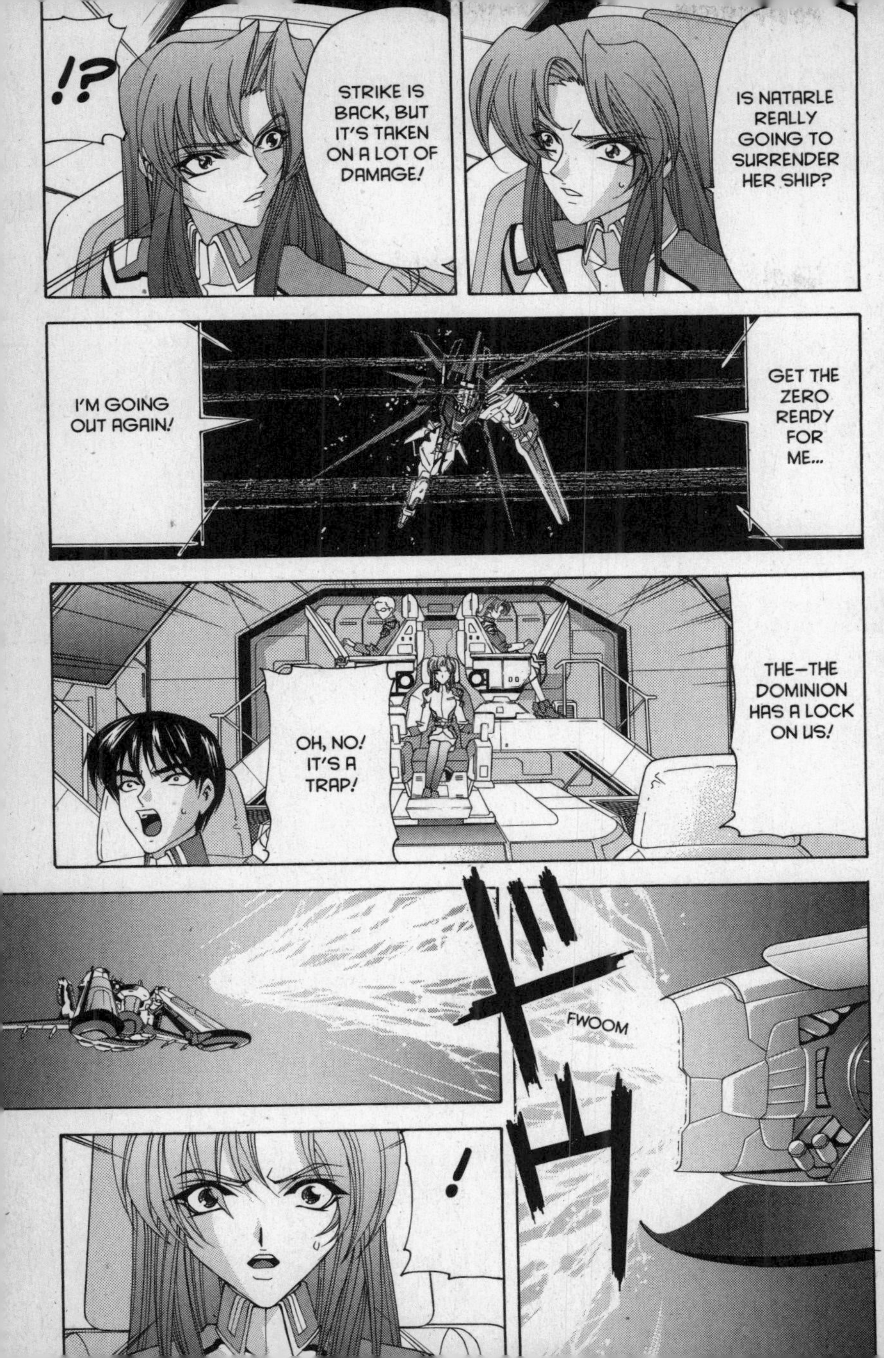
IS NATARLE REALLY GOING TO SURRENDER HER SHIP?
STRIKE IS BACK, BUT IT'S TAKEN ON A LOT OF DAMAGE!
!?
GET THE ZERO READY FOR ME...
I'M GOING OUT AGAIN!
THE—THE DOMINION HAS A LOCK ON US!
OH, NO! IT'S A TRAP!
FWOOM
!

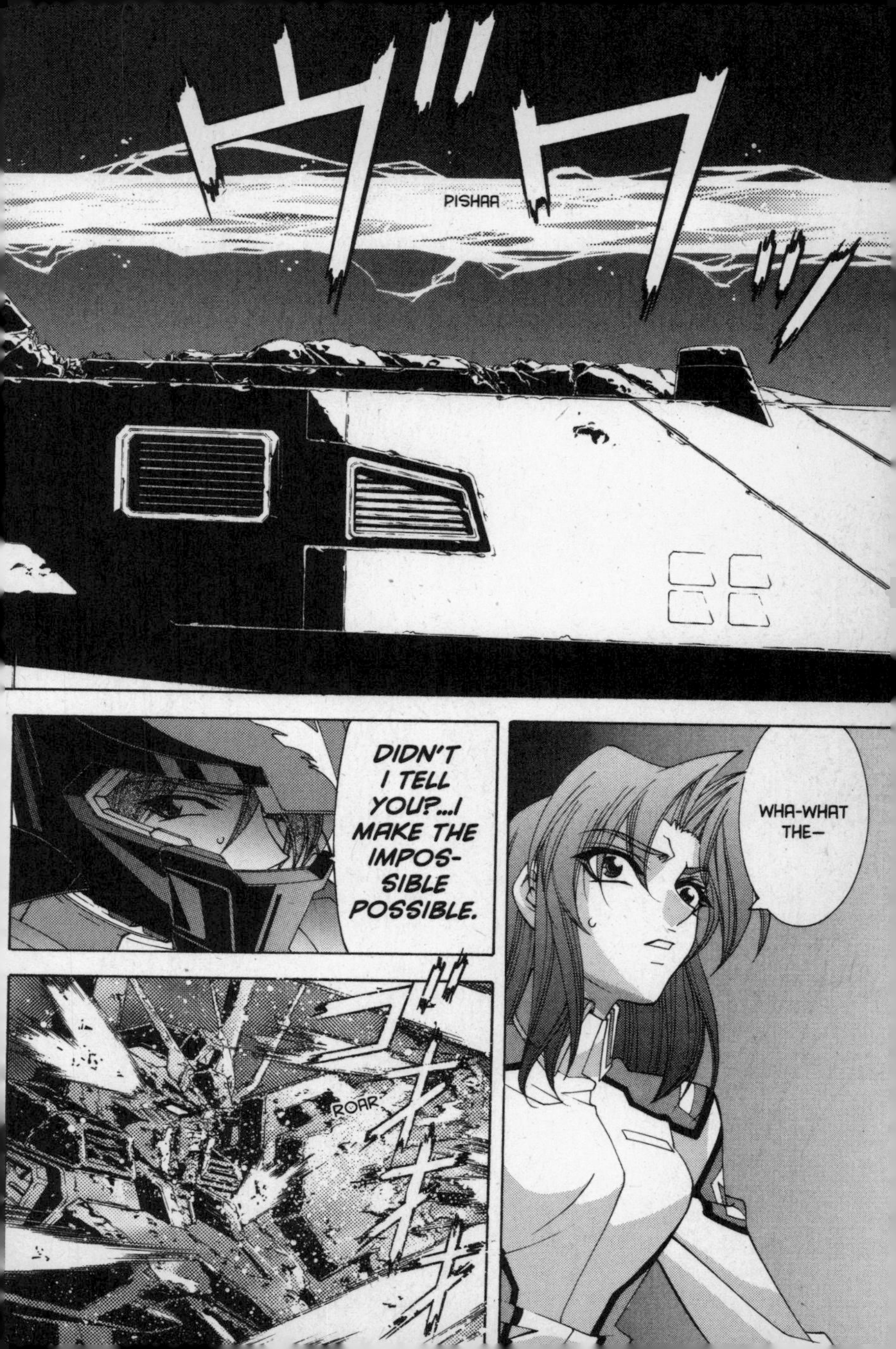
PISHAA
WHA-WHAT THE—
DIDN'T I TELL YOU?...I MAKE THE IMPOSSIBLE POSSIBLE.
ROAR

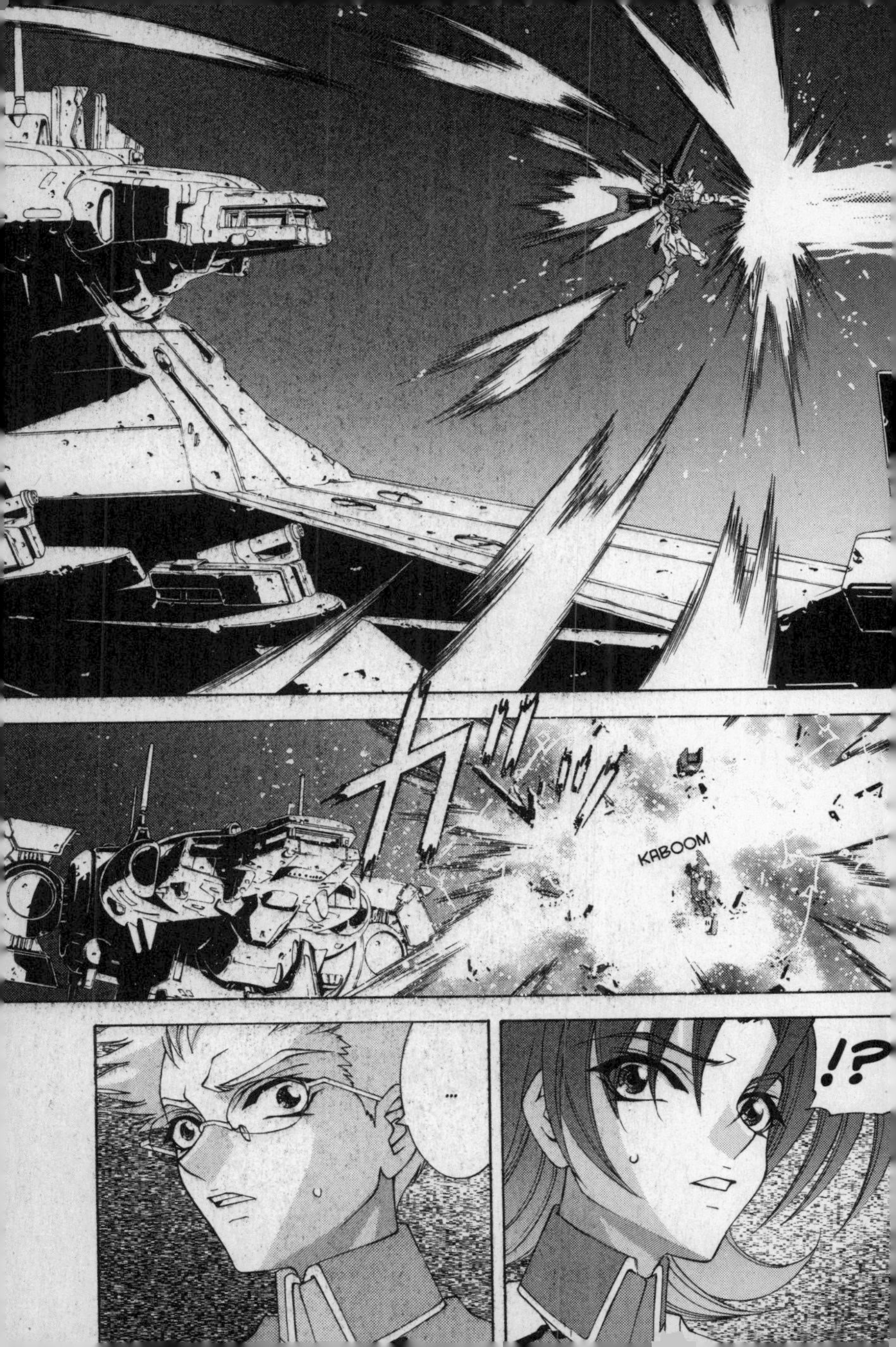
KABOOM
!?
...

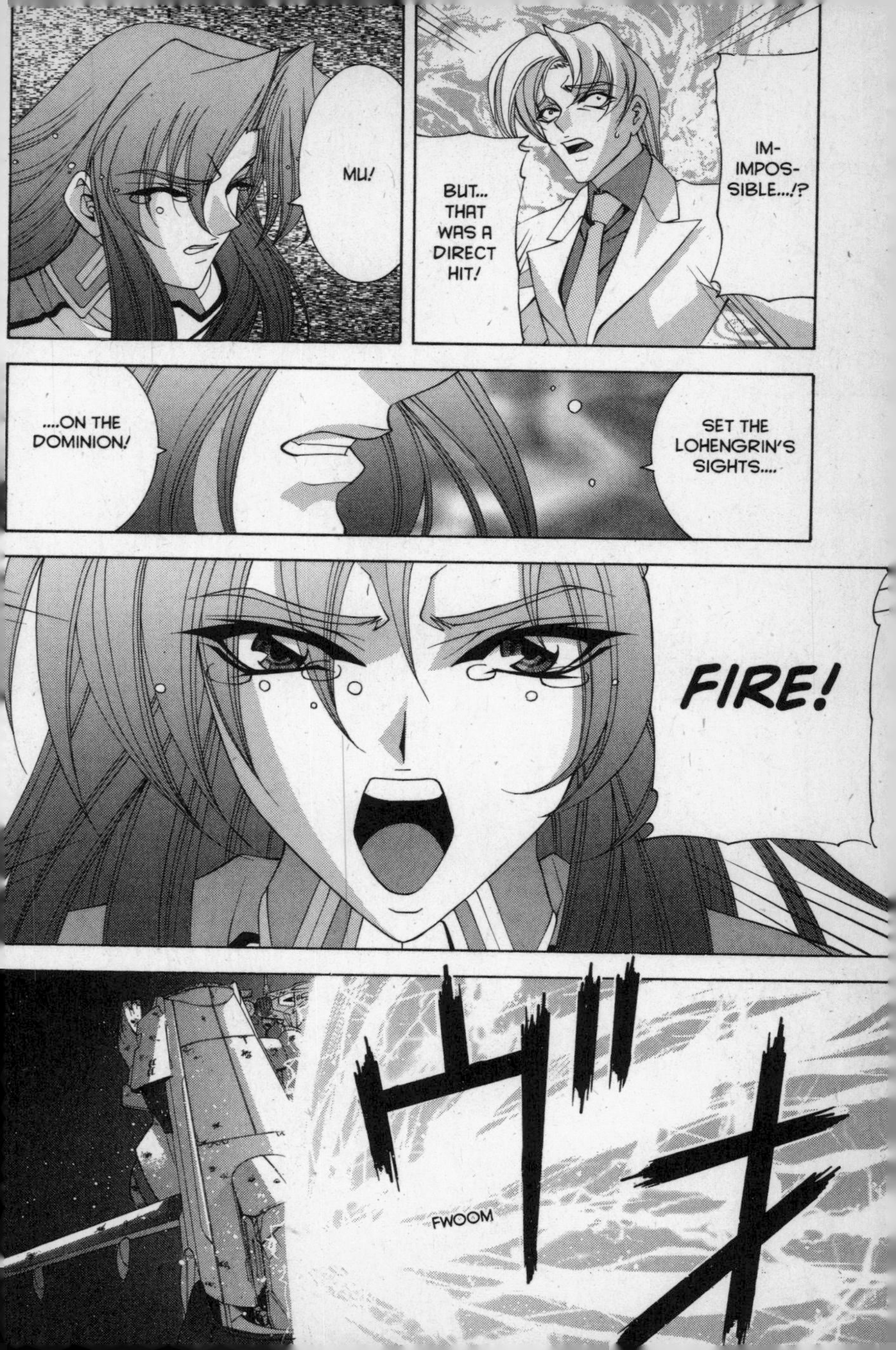
IM-IMPOSSIBLE...!?
BUT... THAT WAS A DIRECT HIT!
MU!
SET THE LOHENGRIN'S SIGHTS....
....ON THE DOMINION!
FIRE!
FWOOM

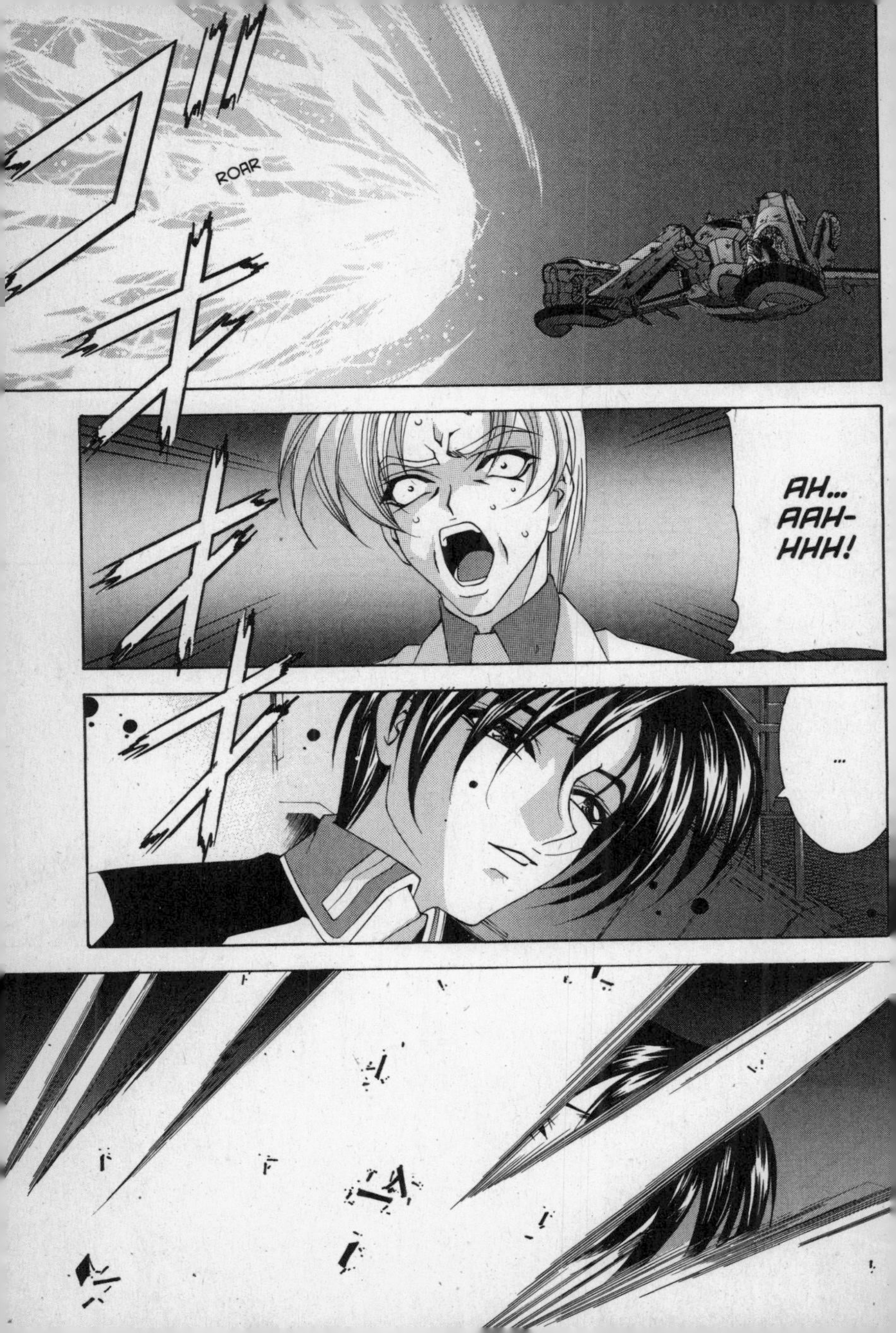
ROAR
AH... AAH-HHH!
...

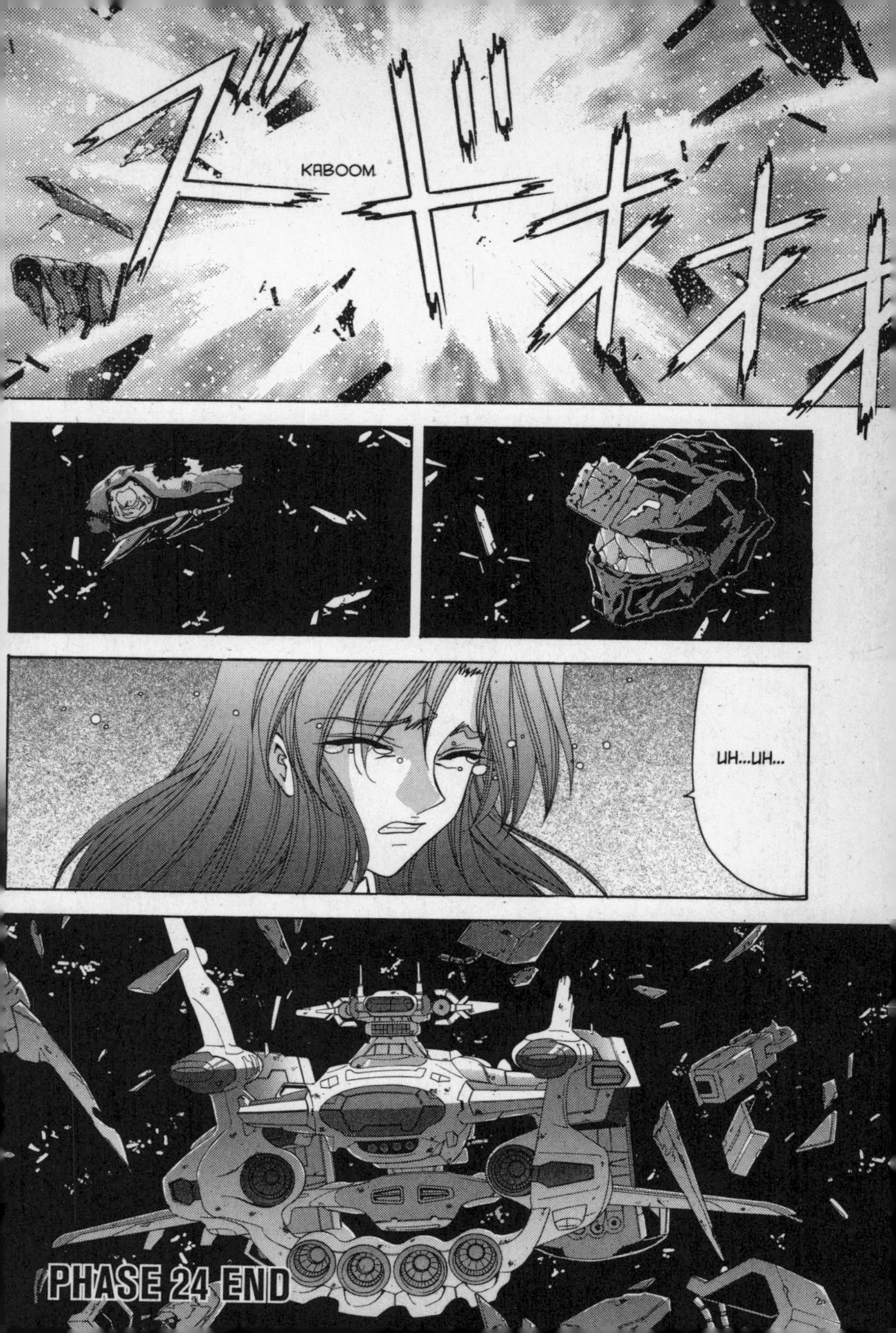
KABOOM
UH...UH...
PHASE 24 END

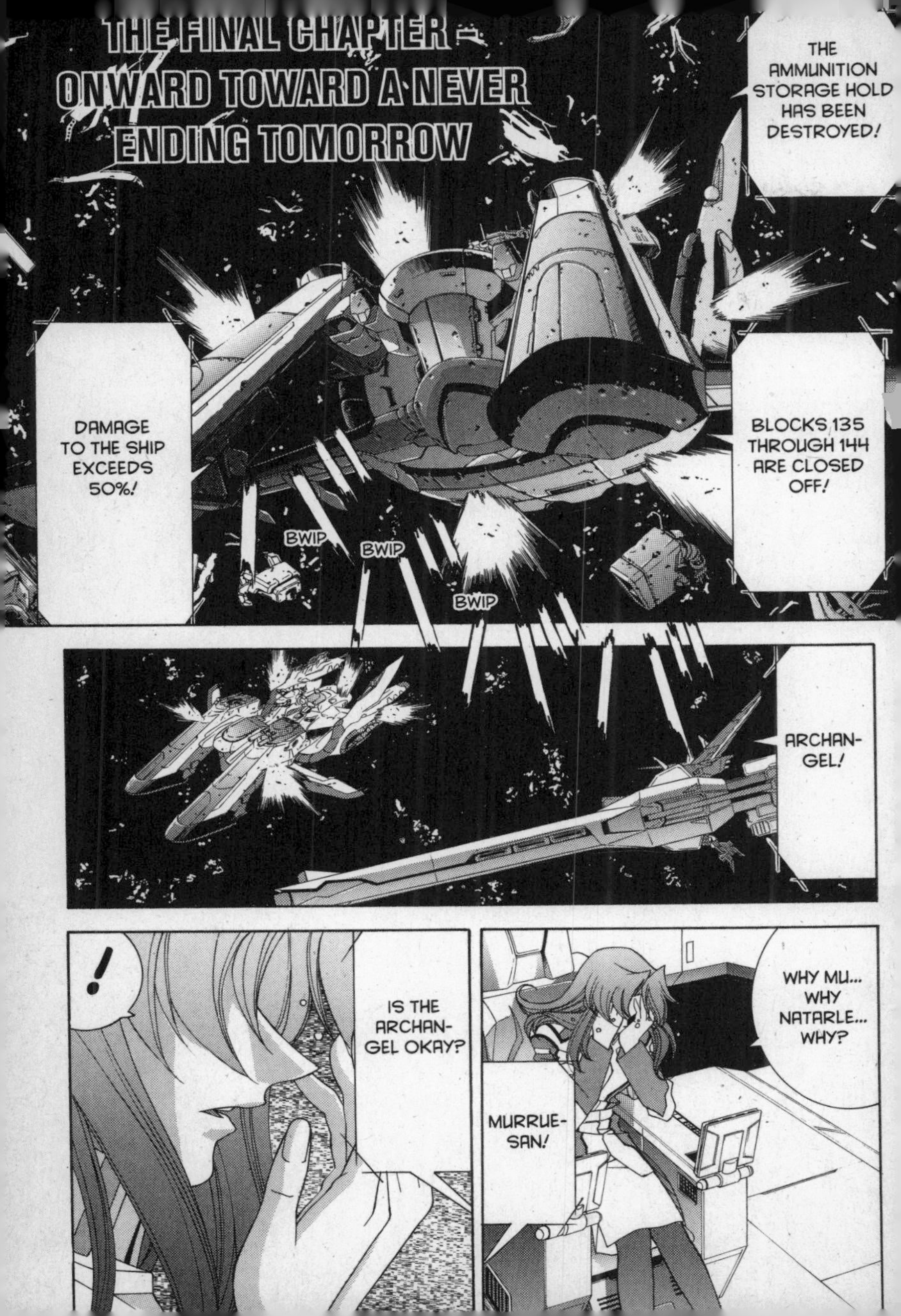
THE FINAL CHAPTER – ONWARD TOWARD A NEVER ENDING TOMORROW
THE AMMUNITION STORAGE HOLD HAS BEEN DESTROYED!
BLOCKS 135 THROUGH 144 ARE CLOSED OFF!
DAMAGE TO THE SHIP EXCEEDS 50%!
BWIP
BWIP
BWIP
ARCHAN-GEL!
WHY MU... WHY NATARLE... WHY?
MURRUE-SAN!
IS THE ARCHAN-GEL OKAY?
!

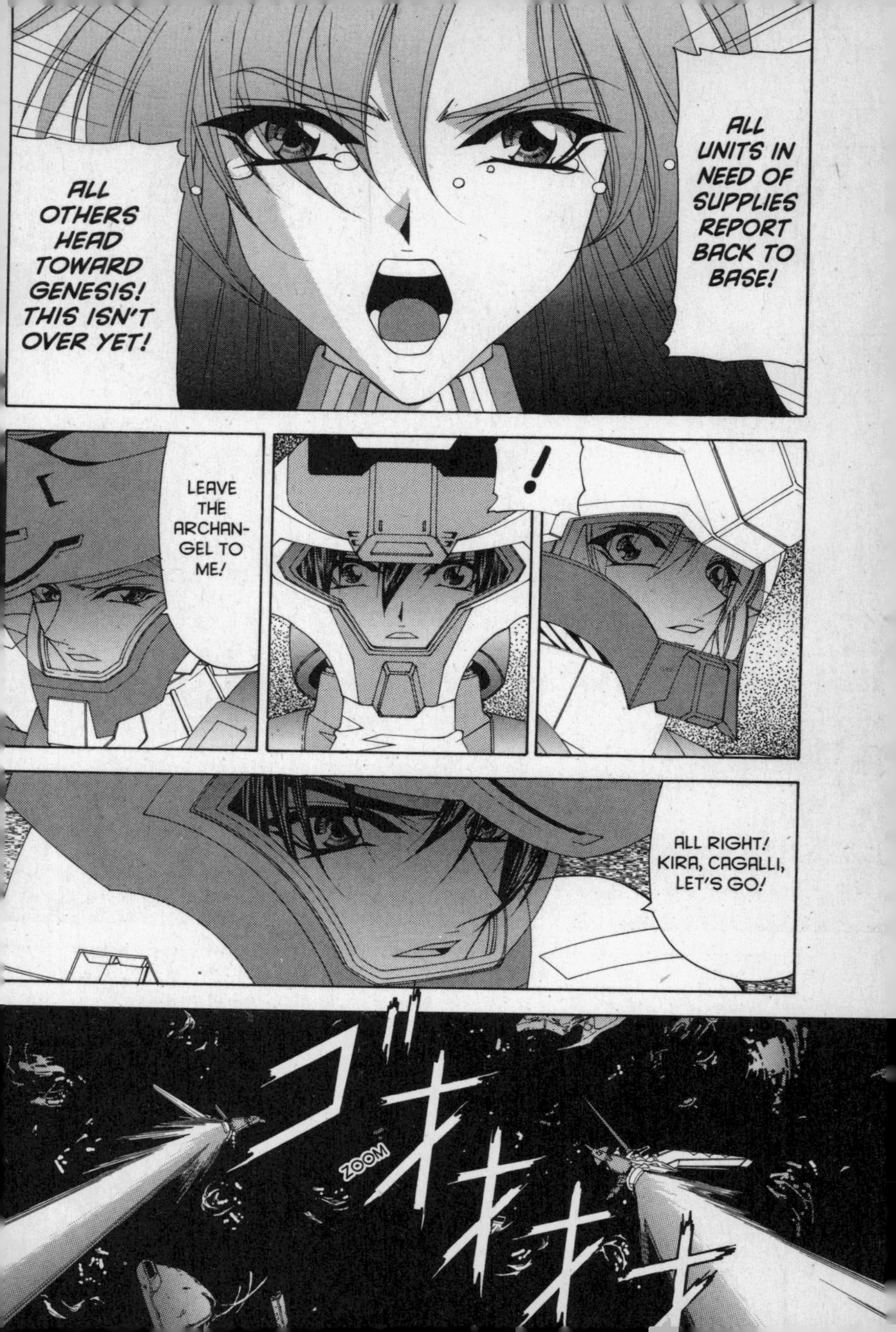
ALL UNITS IN NEED OF SUPPLIES REPORT BACK TO BASE!
ALL OTHERS HEAD TOWARD GENESIS! THIS ISN'T OVER YET!
!
LEAVE THE ARCHAN-GEL TO ME!
ALL RIGHT! KIRA, CAGALLI, LET'S GO!
ゴオオオ
ZOOM

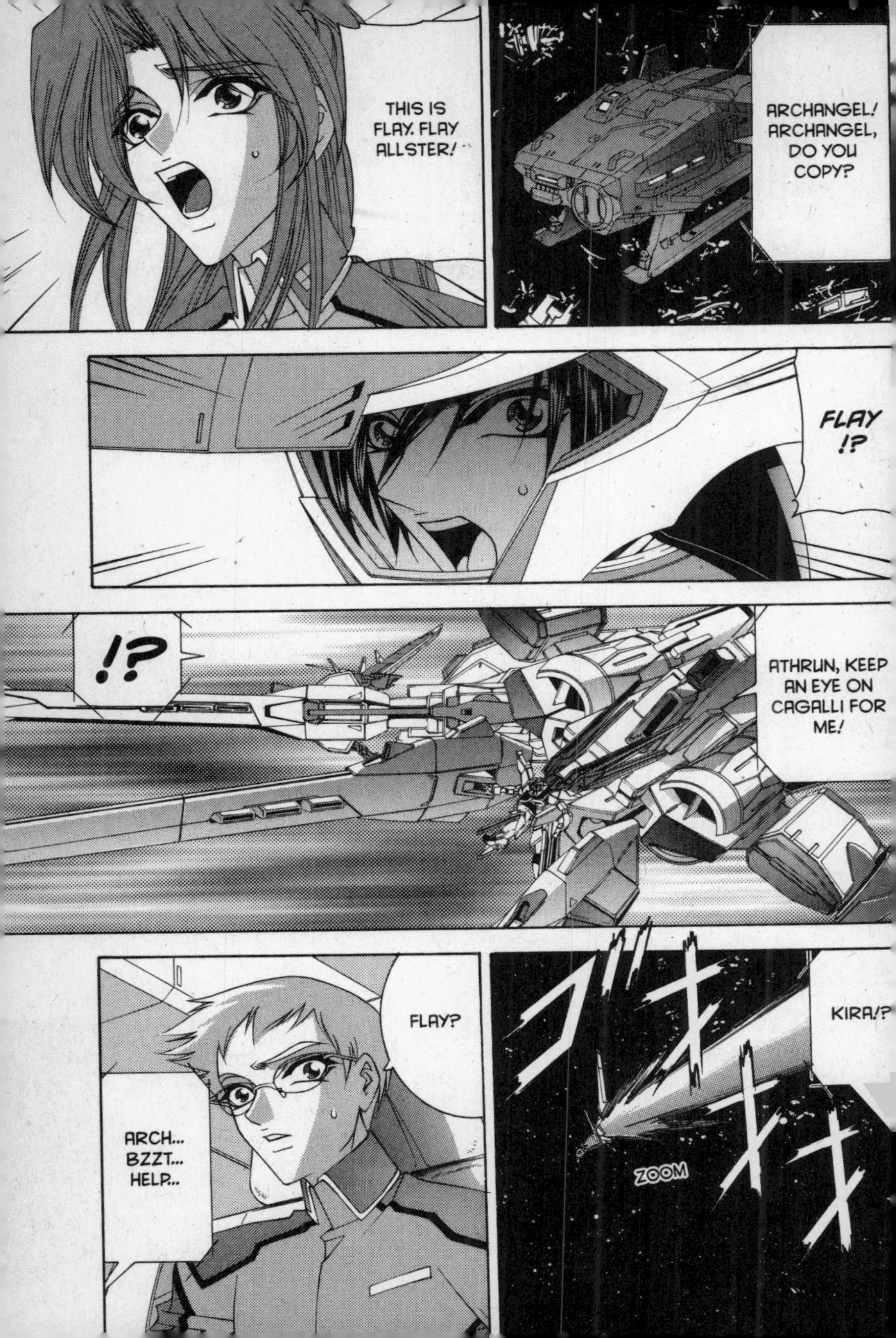
ARCHANGEL! ARCHANGEL, DO YOU COPY?
THIS IS FLAY. FLAY ALLSTER!
FLAY !?
ATHRUN, KEEP AN EYE ON CAGALLI FOR ME!
!?
KIRA!?
ZOOM
FLAY?
ARCH... BZZT... HELP...

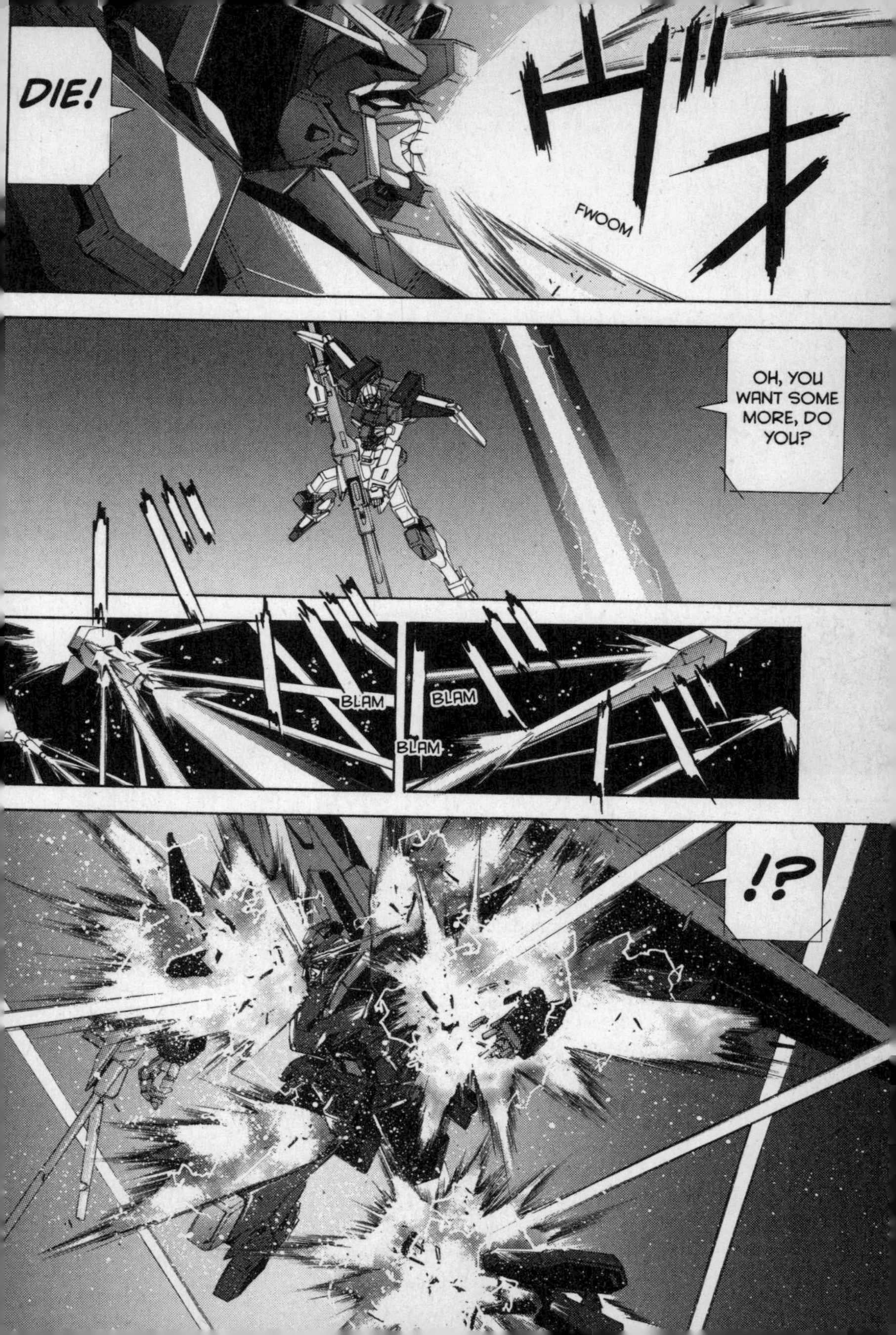
DIE!
FWOOM
OH, YOU WANT SOME MORE, DO YOU?
BLAM
BLAM
BLAM
!?

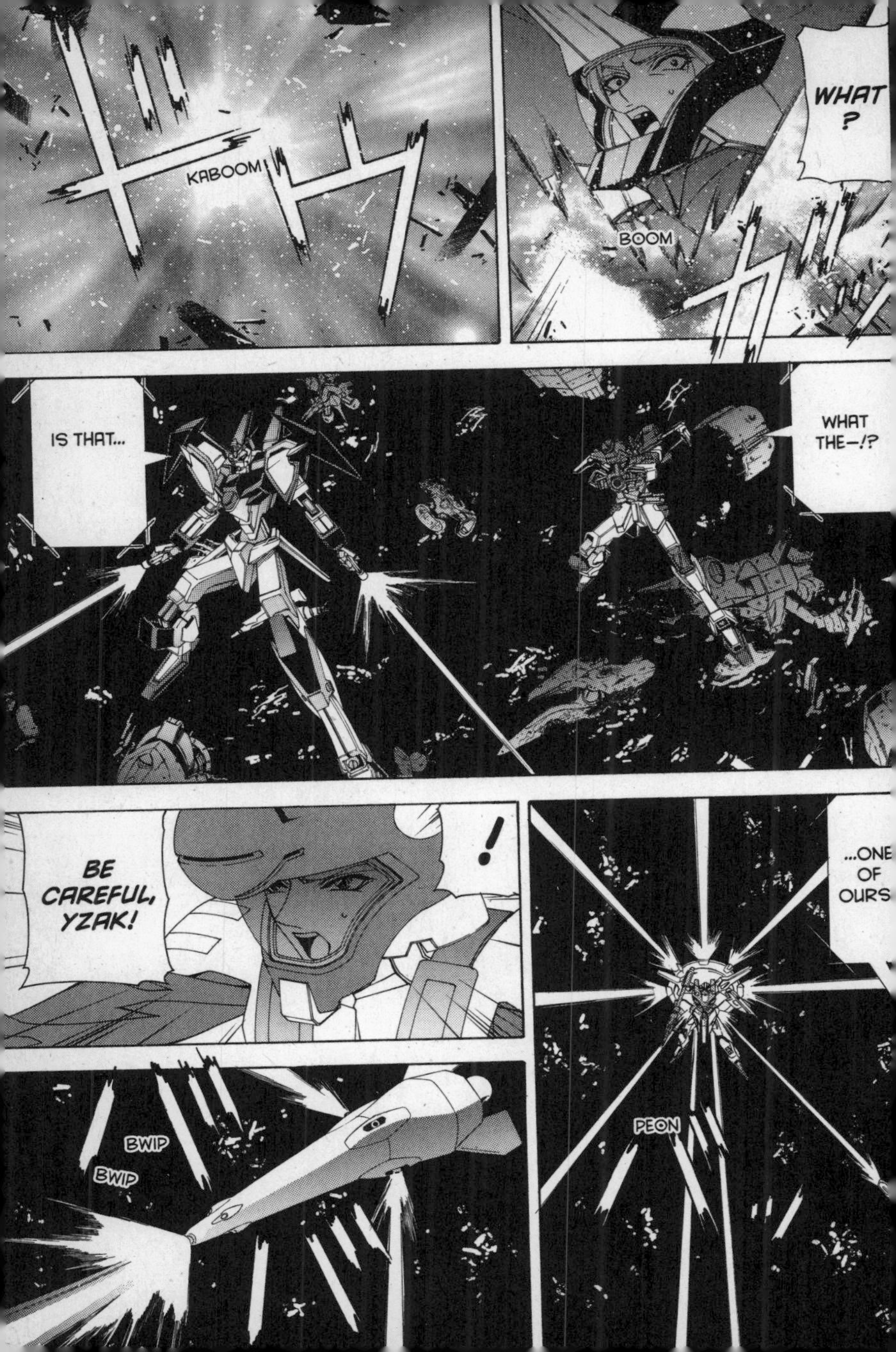
WHAT ?
BOOM
KABOOM
WHAT THE—!?
IS THAT...
...ONE OF OURS
PEON
BE CAREFUL, YZAK!
!
BWIP
BWIP

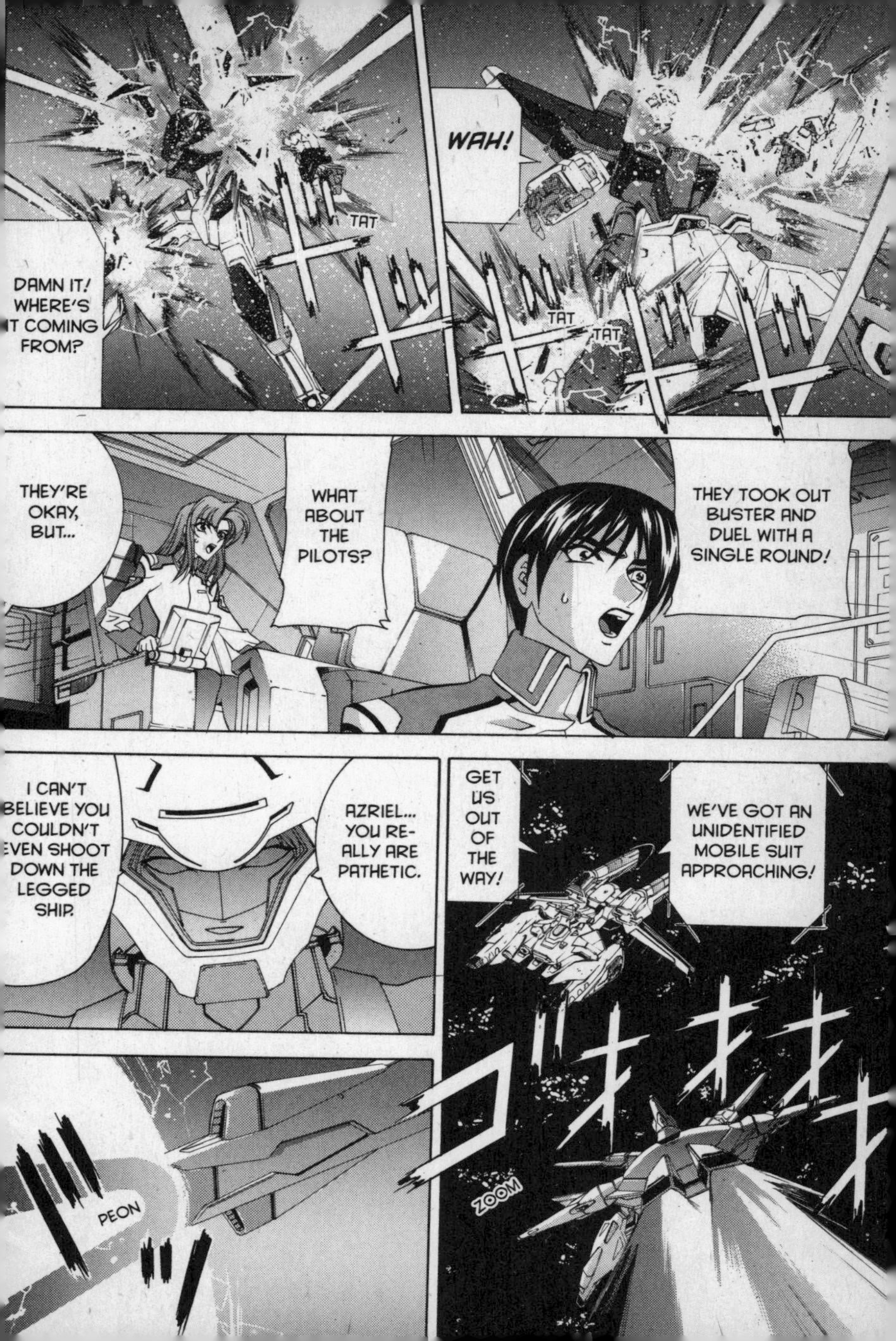
WAH!
TAT
TAT
TAT
DAMN IT! WHERE'S IT COMING FROM?
THEY TOOK OUT BUSTER AND DUEL WITH A SINGLE ROUND!
WHAT ABOUT THE PILOTS?
THEY'RE OKAY, BUT...
WE'VE GOT AN UNIDENTIFIED MOBILE SUIT APPROACHING!
GET US OUT OF THE WAY!
ZOOM
AZRIEL... YOU RE-ALLY ARE PATHETIC.
I CAN'T BELIEVE YOU COULDN'T EVEN SHOOT DOWN THE LEGGED SHIP.
PEON

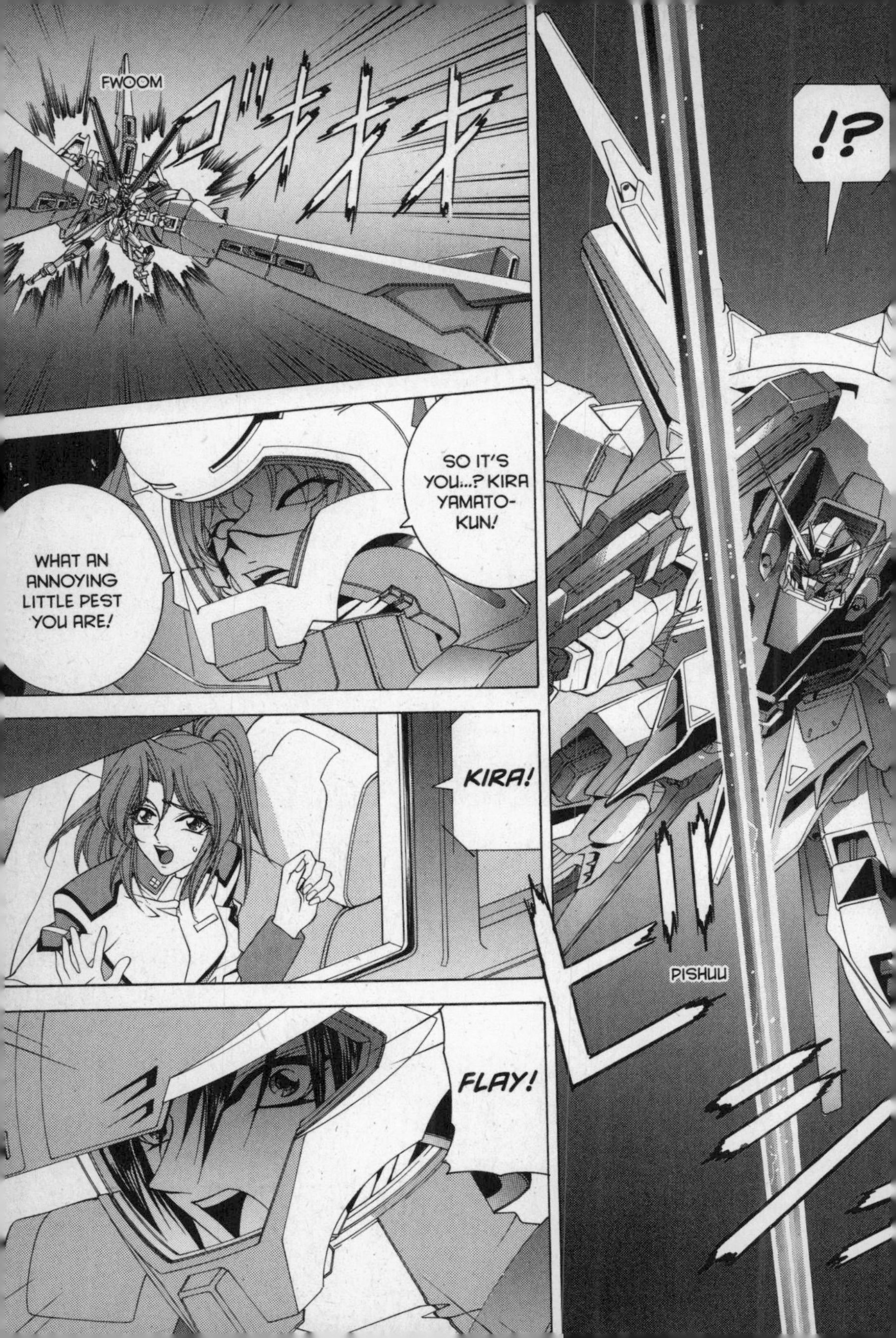
!?
PISHUU
FWOOM
ゴオオオ
SO IT'S YOU...? KIRA YAMATO-KUN!
WHAT AN ANNOYING LITTLE PEST YOU ARE!
KIRA!
FLAY!

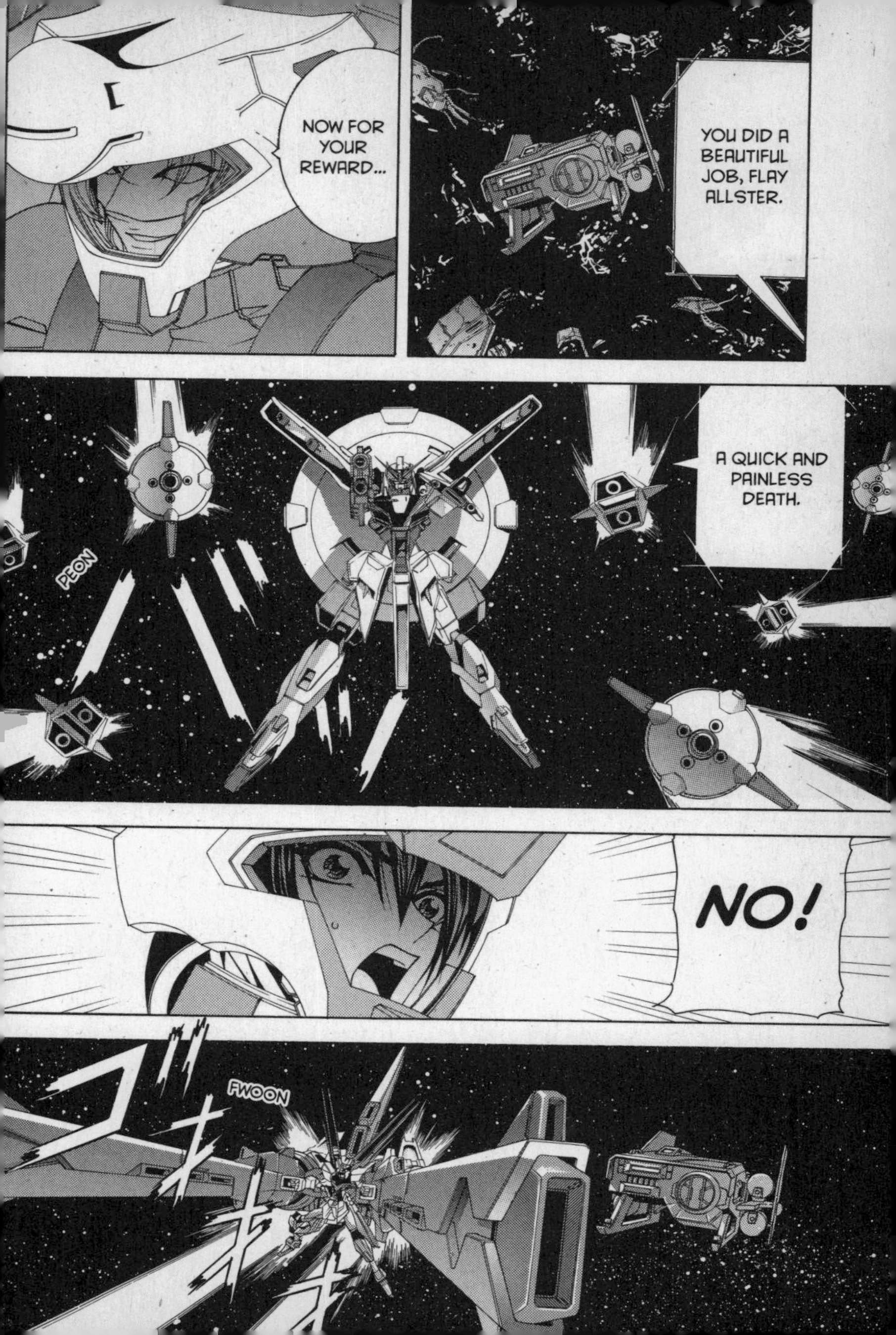
YOU DID A BEAUTIFUL JOB, FLAY ALLSTER.
NOW FOR YOUR REWARD...
A QUICK AND PAINLESS DEATH.
PEON
NO!
FWOON

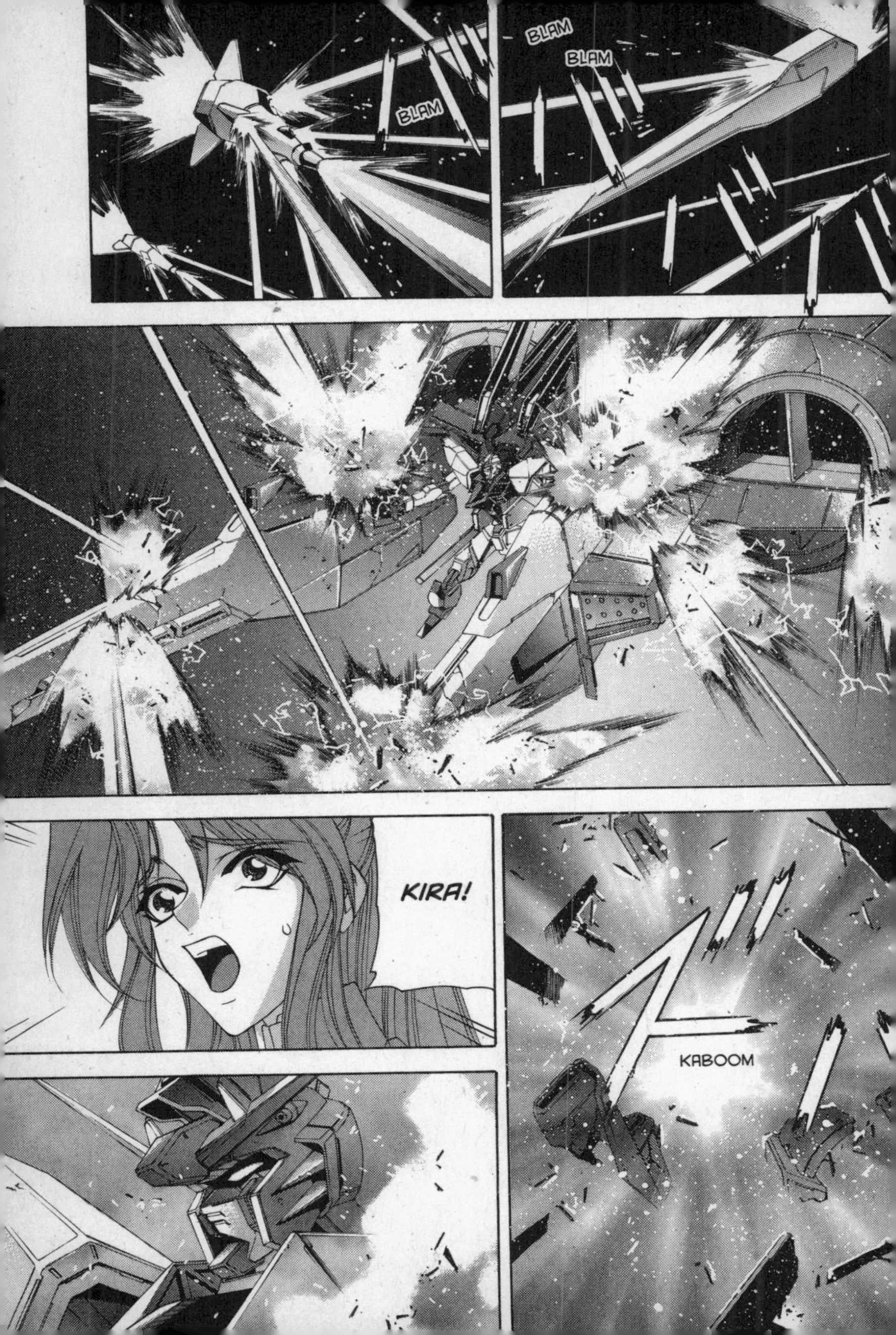
BLAM
BLAM
BLAM
KABOOM
KIRA!

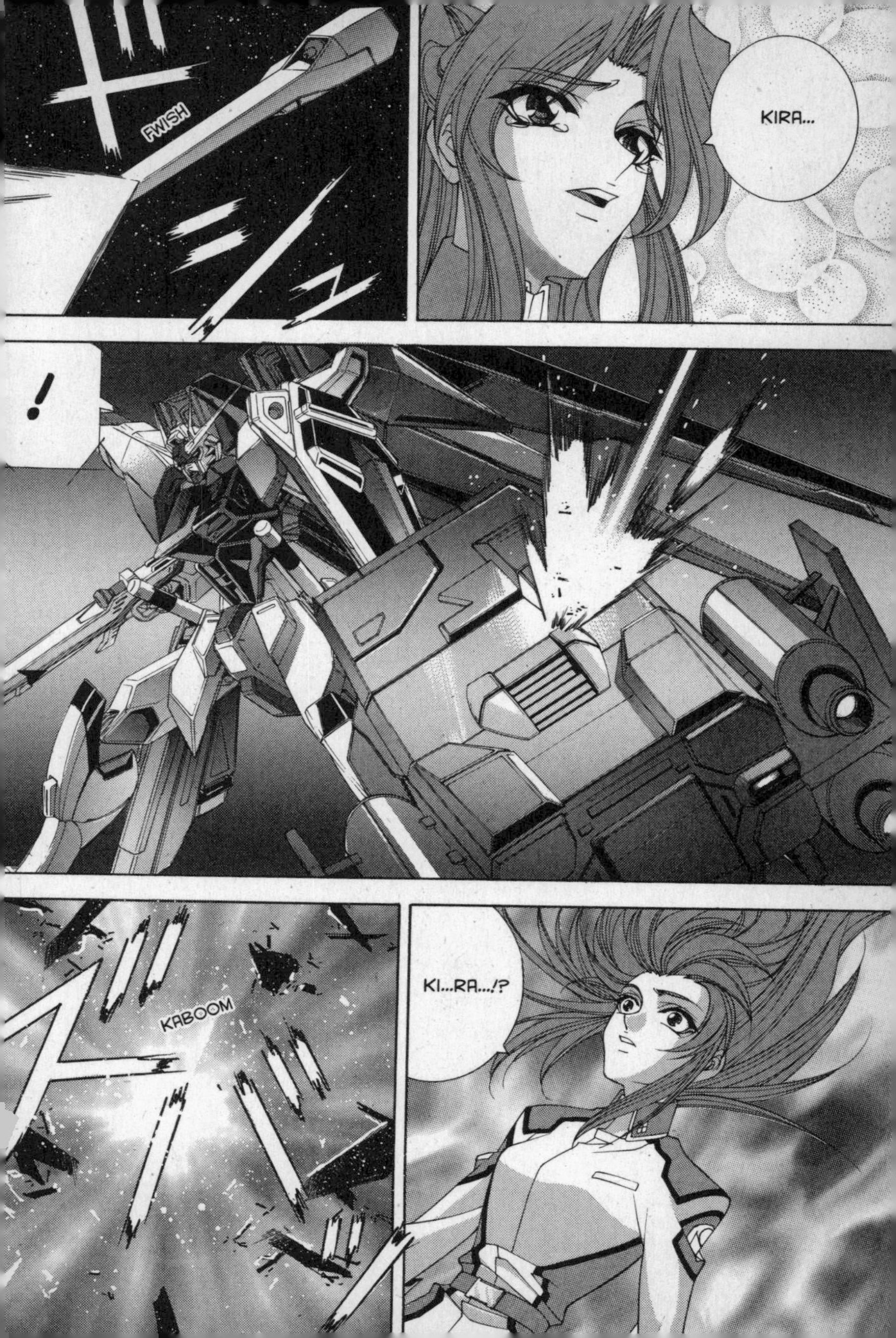
KIRA...
FWISH
!
KI...RA...!?
KABOOM

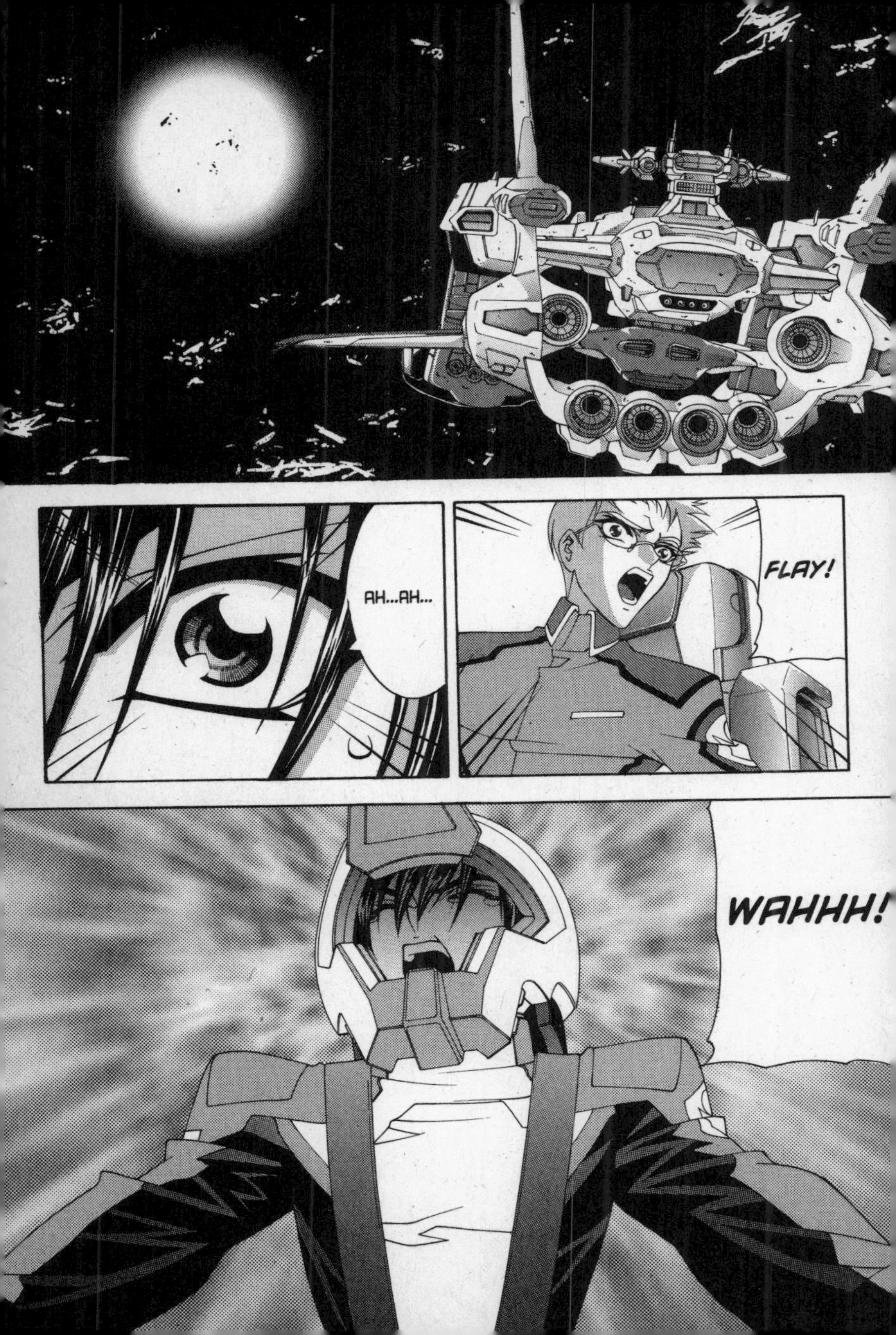
FLAY!
AH...AH...
WAHHH!

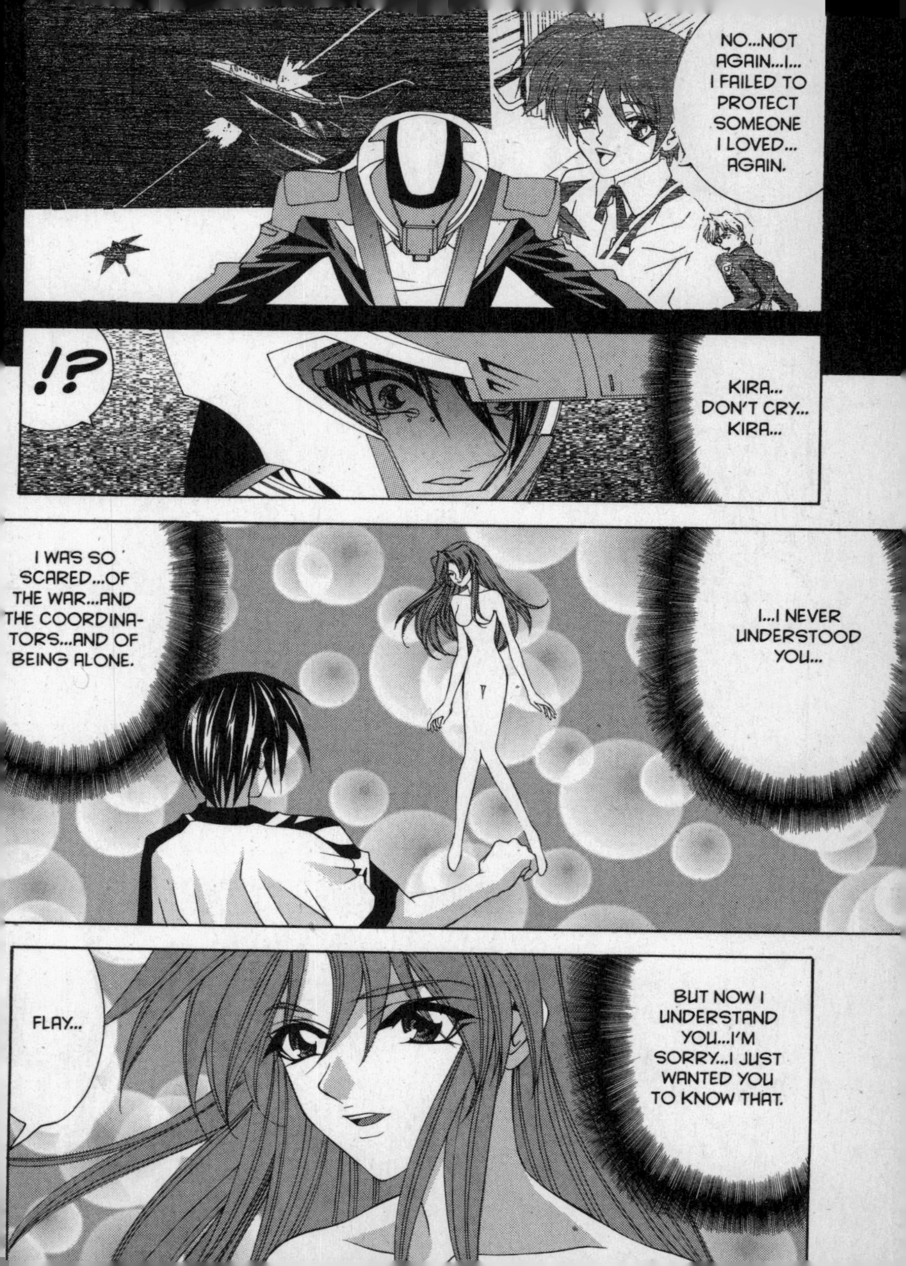
NO...NOT AGAIN...I... I FAILED TO PROTECT SOMEONE I LOVED... AGAIN.
KIRA... DON'T CRY... KIRA...
!?
I...I NEVER UNDERSTOOD YOU...
I WAS SO SCARED...OF THE WAR...AND THE COORDINATORS...AND OF BEING ALONE.
BUT NOW I UNDERSTAND YOU...I'M SORRY...I JUST WANTED YOU TO KNOW THAT.
FLAY...

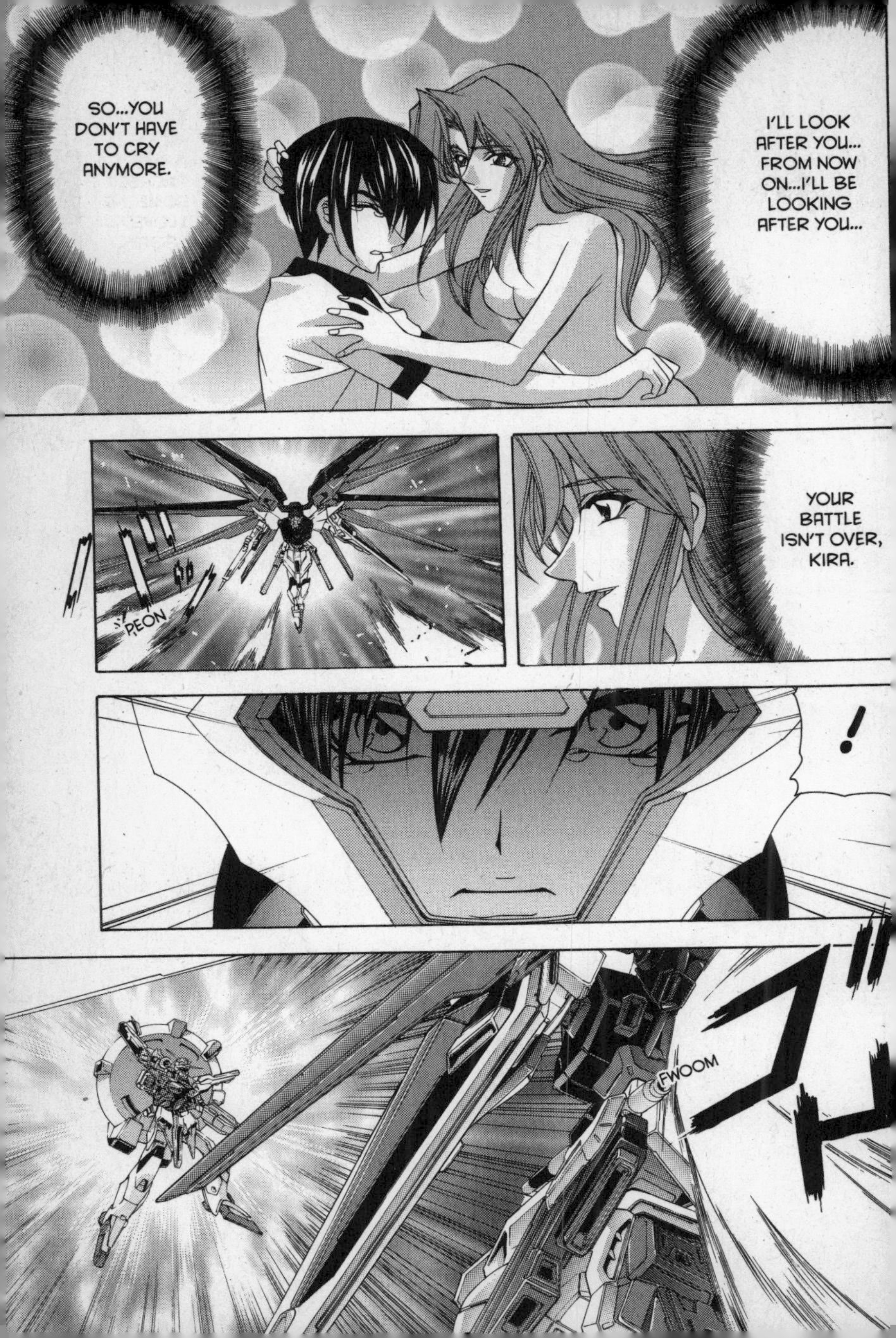
I'LL LOOK AFTER YOU... FROM NOW ON...I'LL BE LOOKING AFTER YOU...
SO...YOU DON'T HAVE TO CRY ANYMORE.
YOUR BATTLE ISN'T OVER, KIRA.
PEON
!
FWOOM

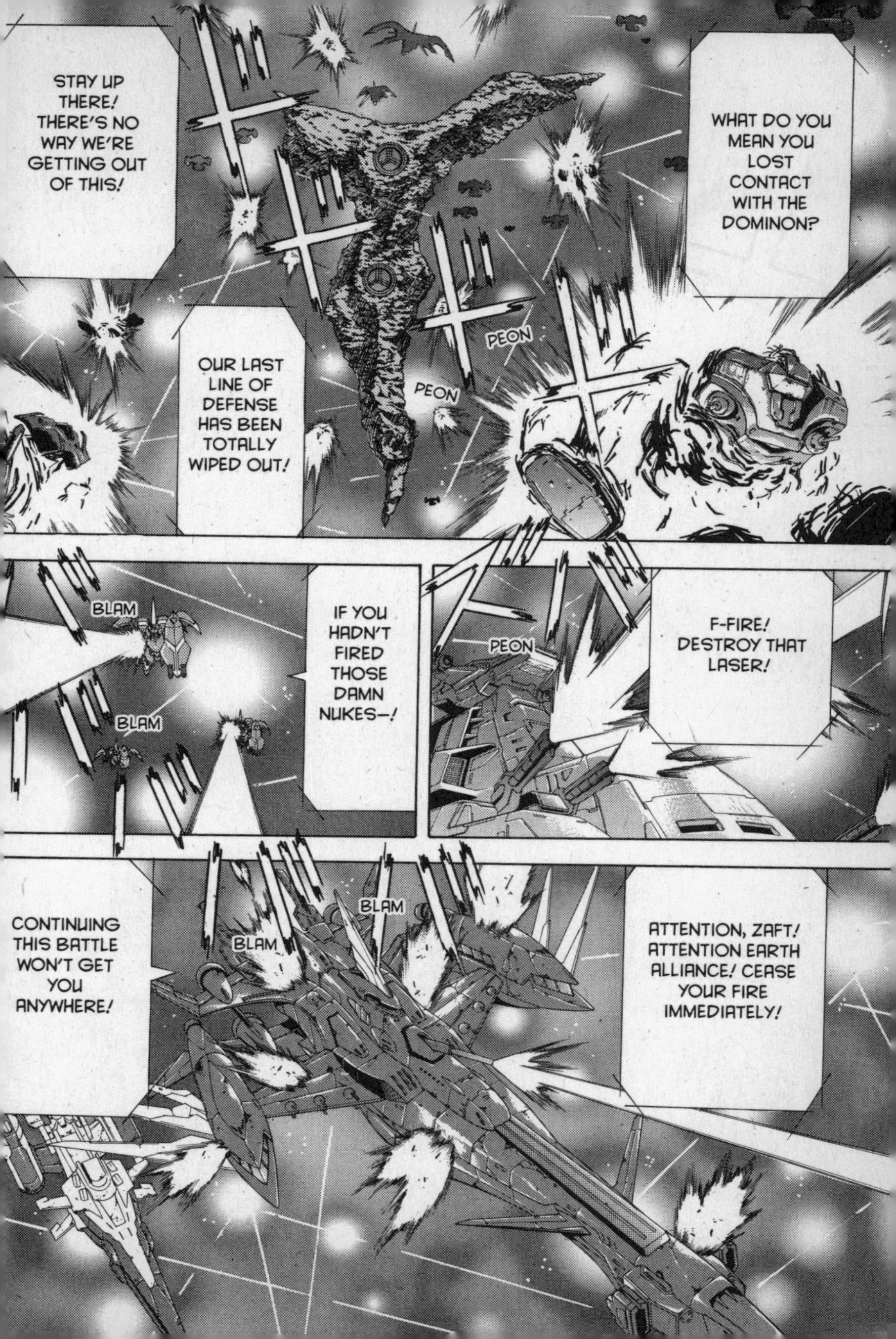
WHAT DO YOU MEAN YOU LOST CONTACT WITH THE DOMINON?
STAY UP THERE! THERE'S NO WAY WE'RE GETTING OUT OF THIS!
PEON
PEON
OUR LAST LINE OF DEFENSE HAS BEEN TOTALLY WIPED OUT!
F-FIRE! DESTROY THAT LASER!
PEON
IF YOU HADN'T FIRED THOSE DAMN NUKES—!
BLAM
BLAM
ATTENTION, ZAFT! ATTENTION EARTH ALLIANCE! CEASE YOUR FIRE IMMEDIATELY!
BLAM
BLAM
CONTINUING THIS BATTLE WON'T GET YOU ANYWHERE!

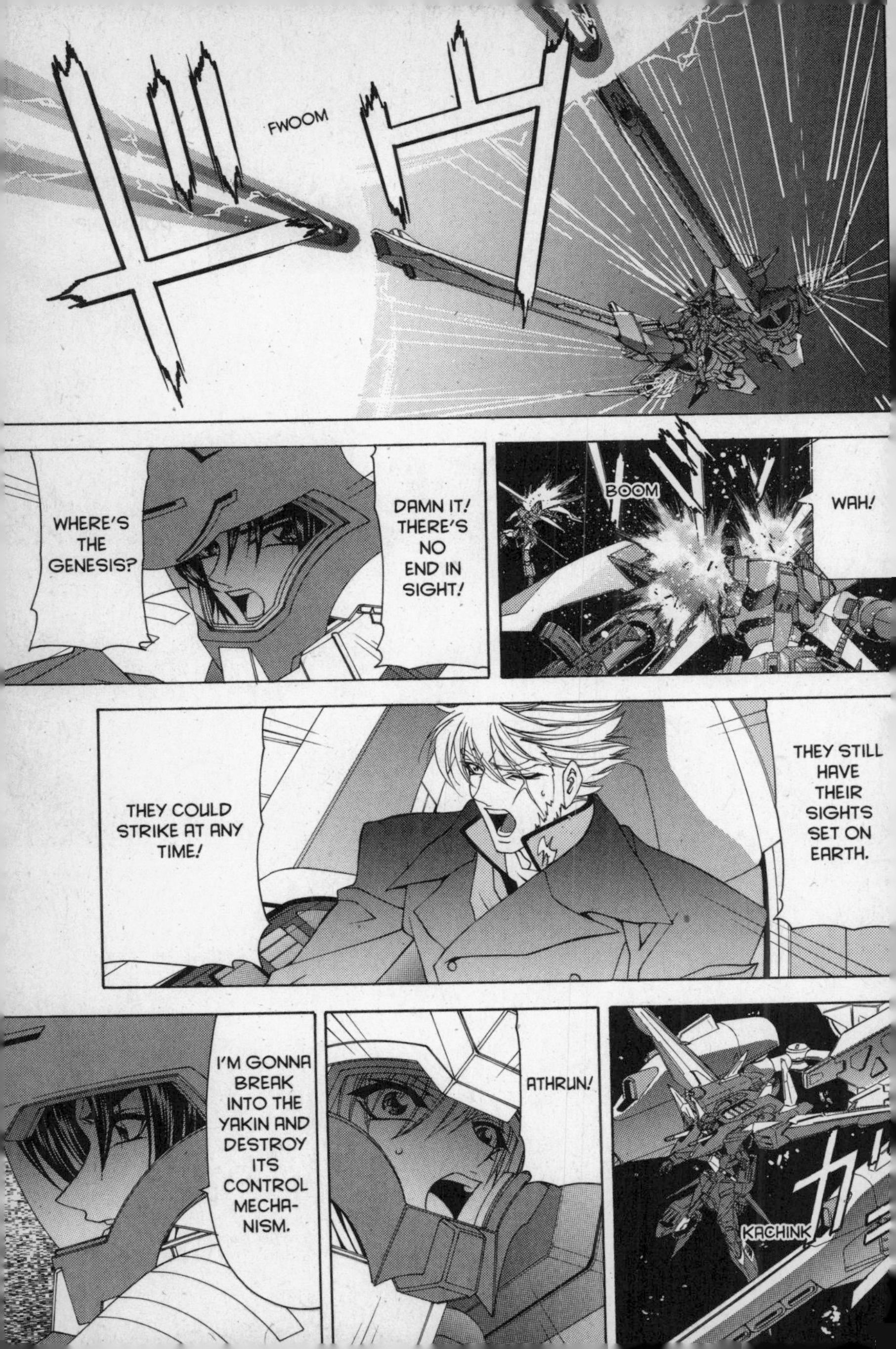
FWOOM
BOOM
WAH!
DAMN IT! THERE'S NO END IN SIGHT!
WHERE'S THE GENESIS?
THEY STILL HAVE THEIR SIGHTS SET ON EARTH.
THEY COULD STRIKE AT ANY TIME!
KACHINK
ATHRUN!
I'M GONNA BREAK INTO THE YAKIN AND DESTROY ITS CONTROL MECHA-NISM.

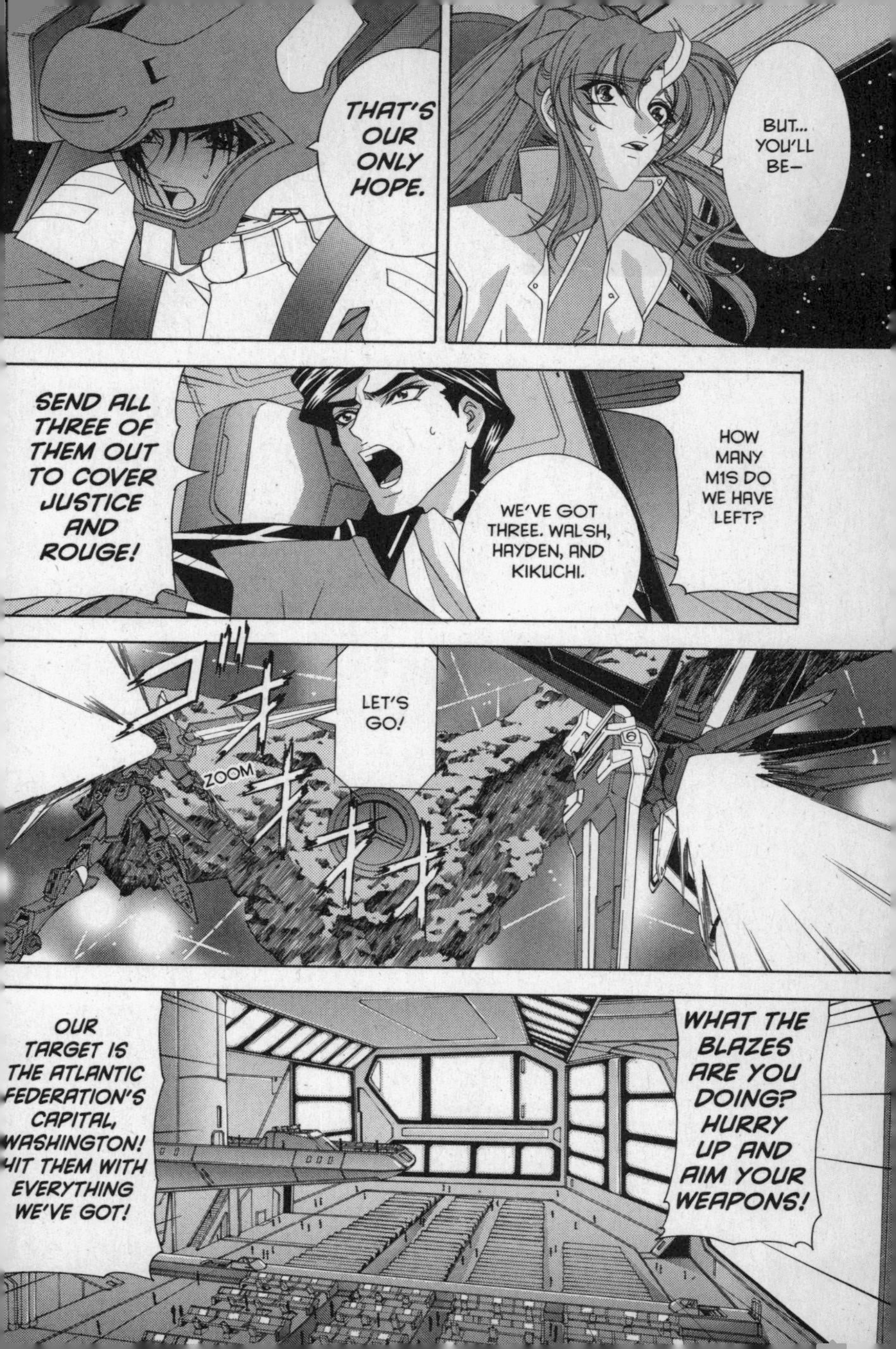
BUT... YOU'LL BE—
THAT'S OUR ONLY HOPE.
HOW MANY M1S DO WE HAVE LEFT?
WE'VE GOT THREE. WALSH, HAYDEN, AND KIKUCHI.
SEND ALL THREE OF THEM OUT TO COVER JUSTICE AND ROUGE!
LET'S GO!
ZOOM
WHAT THE BLAZES ARE YOU DOING? HURRY UP AND AIM YOUR WEAPONS!
OUR TARGET IS THE ATLANTIC FEDERATION'S CAPITAL, WASHINGTON! HIT THEM WITH EVERYTHING WE'VE GOT!

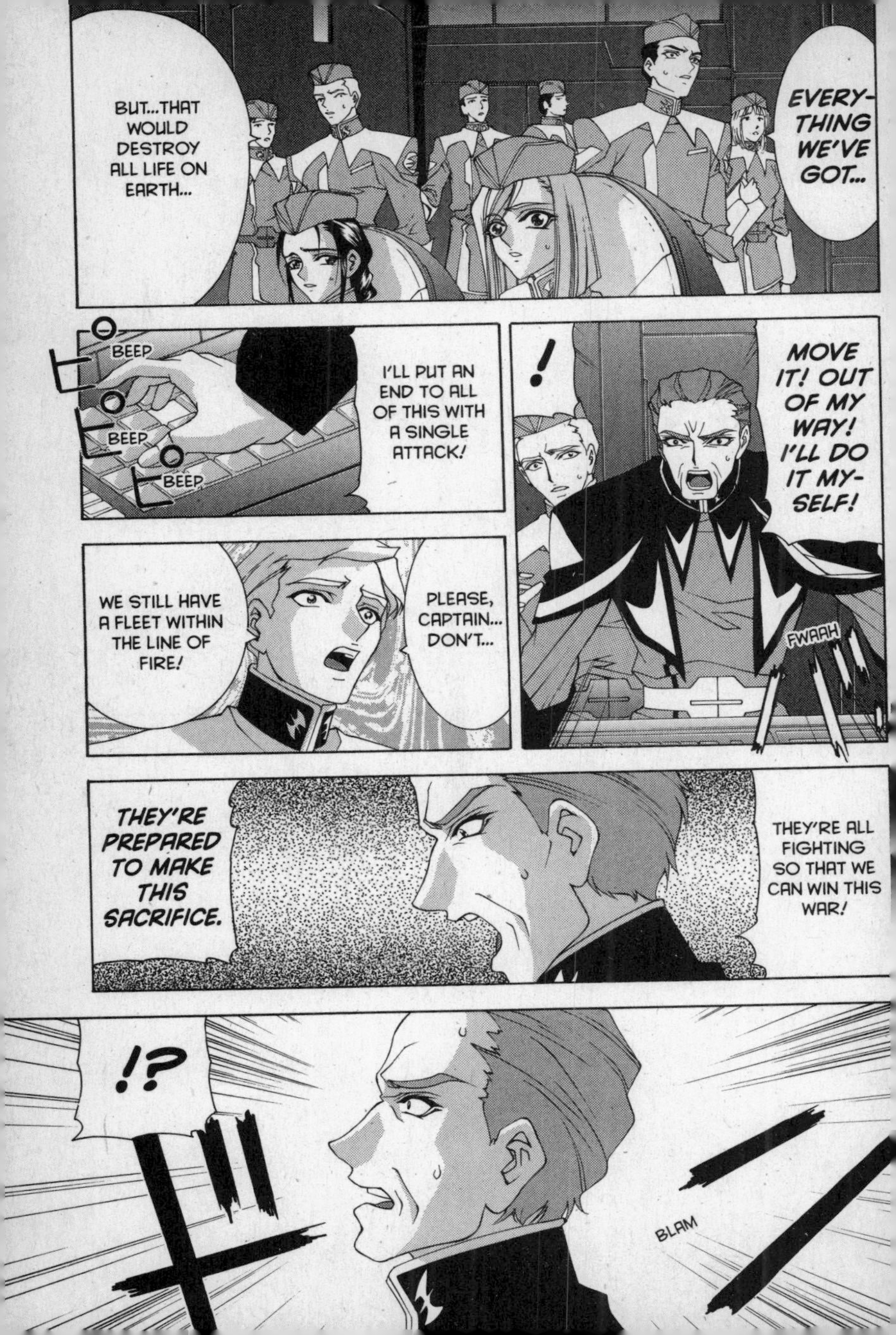
EVERY-THING WE'VE GOT...
BUT...THAT WOULD DESTROY ALL LIFE ON EARTH...
MOVE IT! OUT OF MY WAY! I'LL DO IT MY-SELF!
!
FWAAH
I'LL PUT AN END TO ALL OF THIS WITH A SINGLE ATTACK!
BEEP
BEEP
BEEP
PLEASE, CAPTAIN... DON'T...
WE STILL HAVE A FLEET WITHIN THE LINE OF FIRE!
THEY'RE ALL FIGHTING SO THAT WE CAN WIN THIS WAR!
THEY'RE PREPARED TO MAKE THIS SACRIFICE.
!?
BLAM

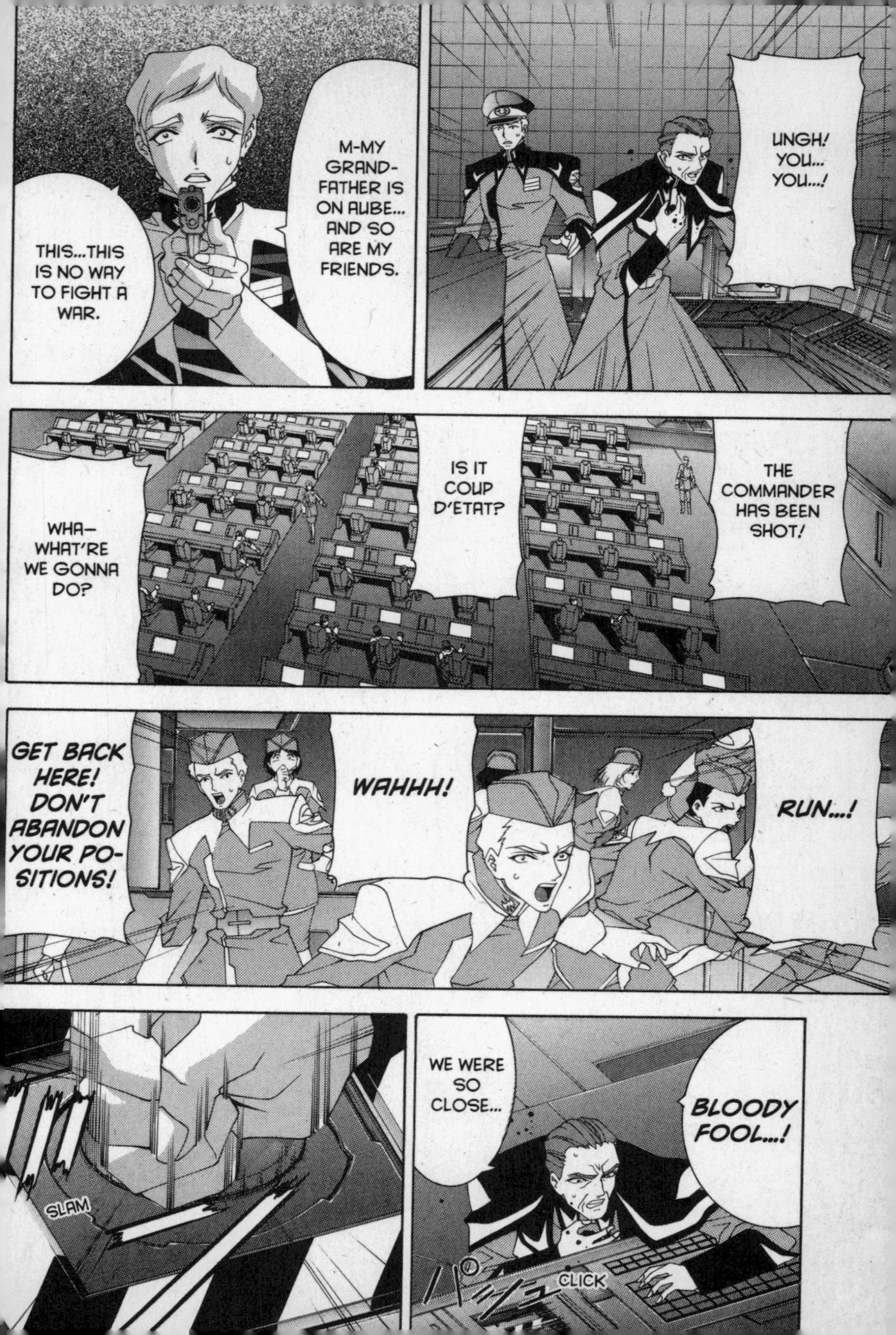
UNGH! YOU... YOU...!
M-MY GRAND-FATHER IS ON AUBE... AND SO ARE MY FRIENDS.
THIS...THIS IS NO WAY TO FIGHT A WAR.
THE COMMANDER HAS BEEN SHOT!
IS IT COUP D'ETAT?
WHA-WHAT'RE WE GONNA DO?
RUN...!
WAHHH!
GET BACK HERE! DON'T ABANDON YOUR PO-SITIONS!
WE WERE SO CLOSE...
BLOODY FOOL...!
CLICK
SLAM

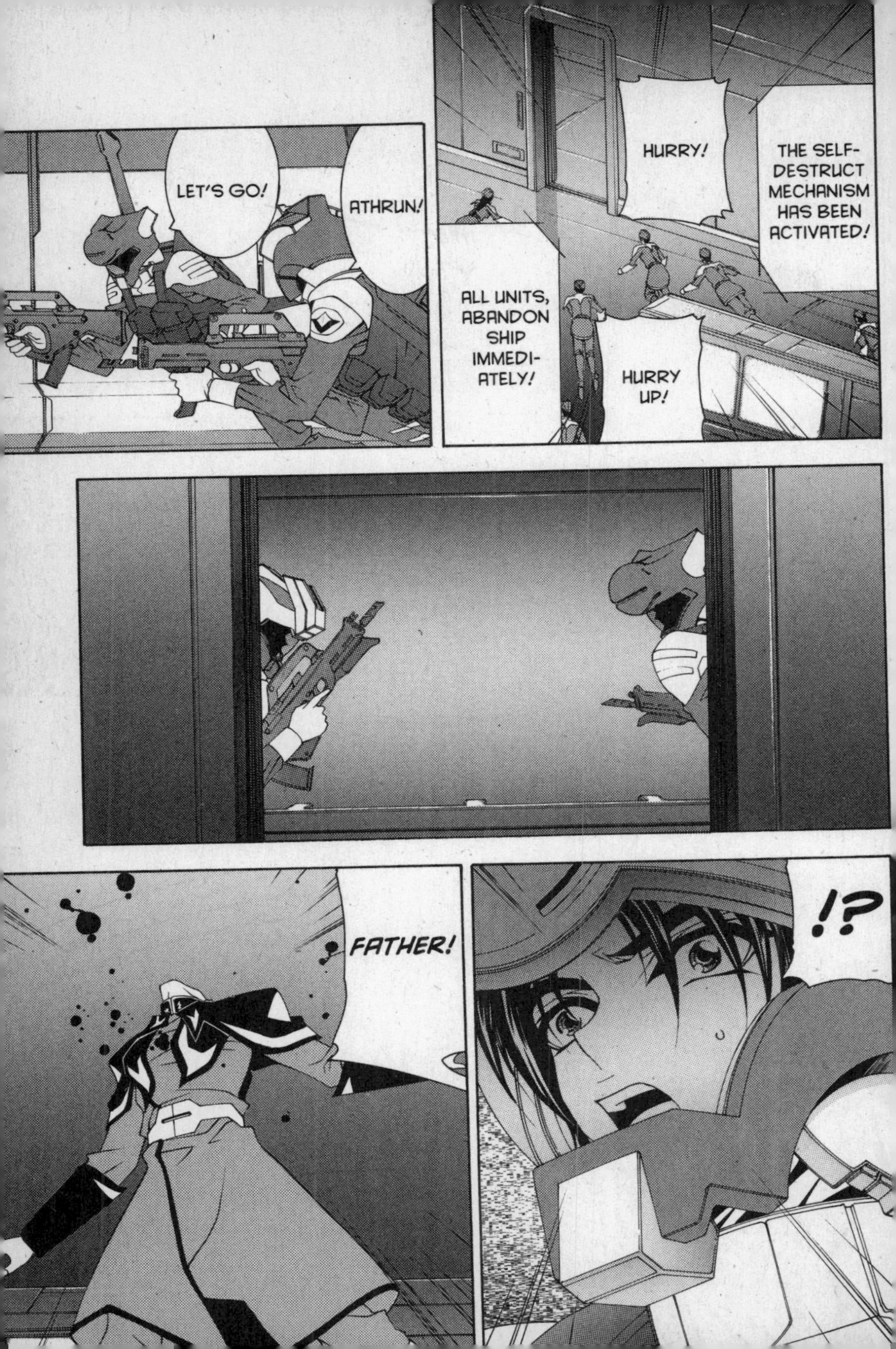
THE SELF-DESTRUCT MECHANISM HAS BEEN ACTIVATED!
HURRY!
ALL UNITS, ABANDON SHIP IMMEDI-ATELY!
HURRY UP!
ATHRUN!
LET'S GO!
!?
FATHER!

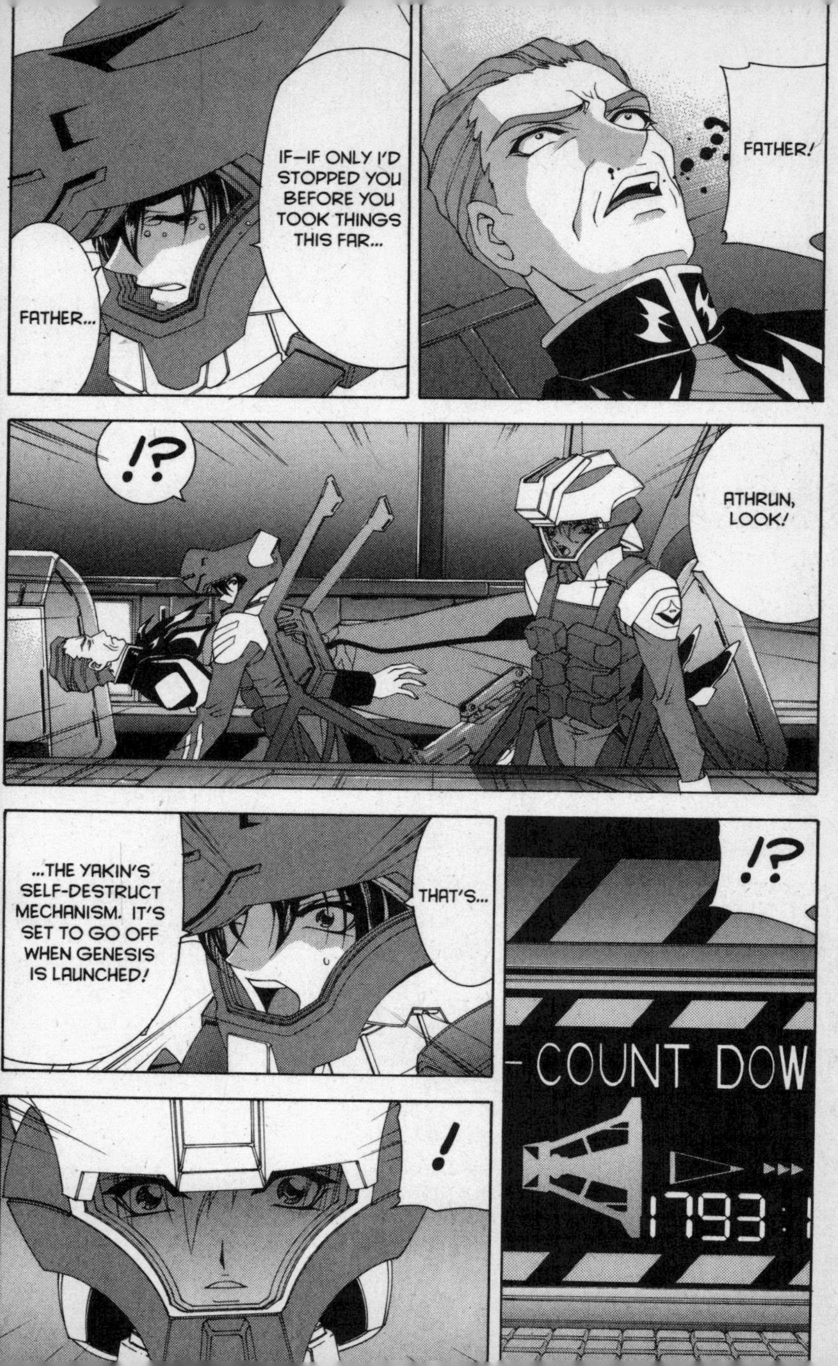
FATHER!
IF—IF ONLY I'D STOPPED YOU BEFORE YOU TOOK THINGS THIS FAR...
FATHER...
ATHRUN, LOOK!
!?
!?
COUNT DOW
1793 :
THAT'S...
...THE YAKIN'S SELF-DESTRUCT MECHANISM. IT'S SET TO GO OFF WHEN GENESIS IS LAUNCHED!
!

WHAT'RE YOU DOING, ATHRUN?

ZOOM

WHAT?

I'M GONNA USE JUSTICE TO SET OFF A NUCLEAR EXPLOSION INSIDE OF GENESIS.

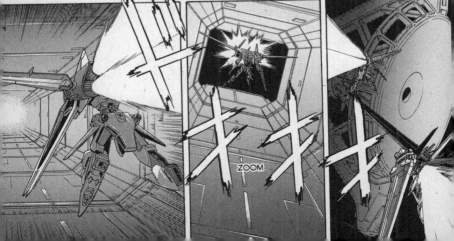

ZOOM

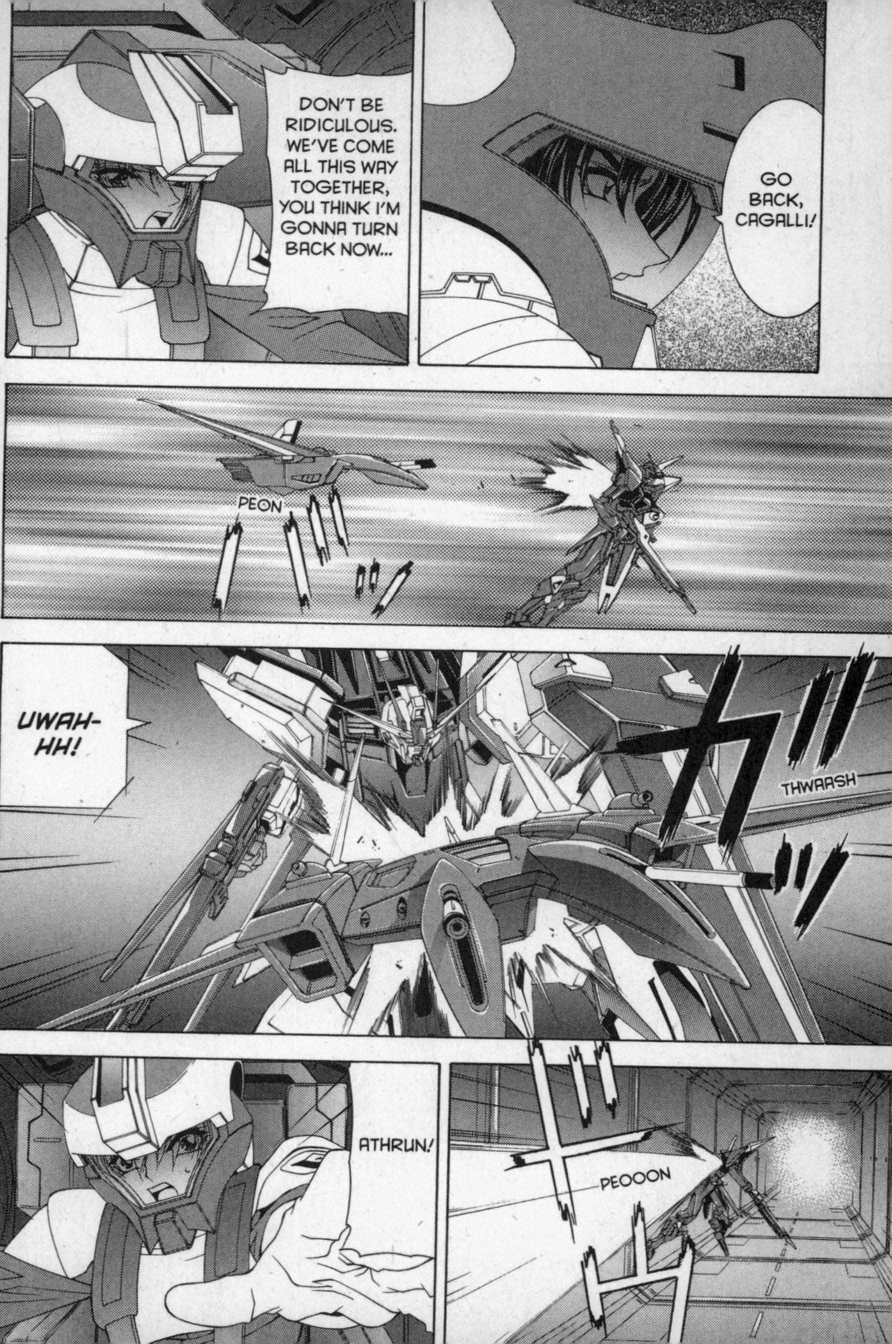
GO BACK, CAGALLI!
DON'T BE RIDICULOUS. WE'VE COME ALL THIS WAY TOGETHER, YOU THINK I'M GONNA TURN BACK NOW...
PEON
THWAASH
UWAH-HH!
PEOOON
ATHRUN!

THIS MUST
BE THE
CORE OF
GENESIS....

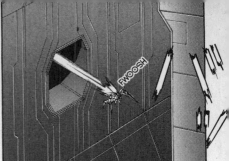

FWOOSH

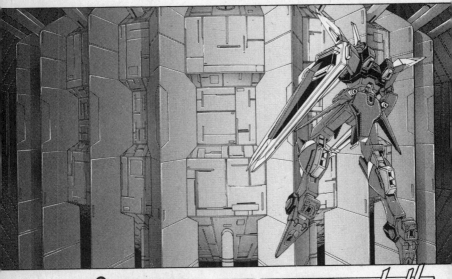

BEEP

BEEP

BEEP

ATHRUN!

KACHINK

CAGALLI?

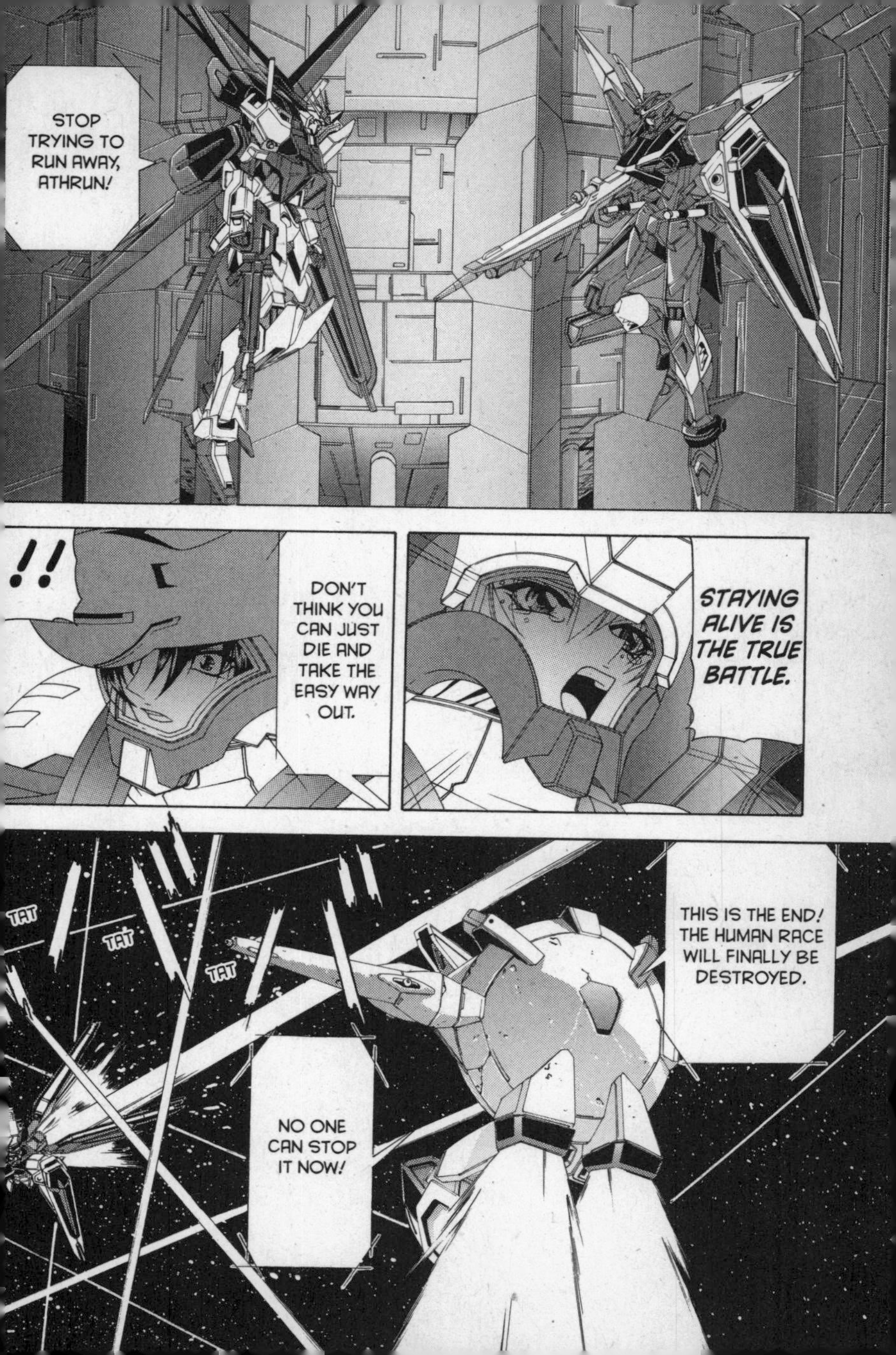
STOP TRYING TO RUN AWAY, ATHRUN!
STAYING ALIVE IS THE TRUE BATTLE.
DON'T THINK YOU CAN JUST DIE AND TAKE THE EASY WAY OUT.
!!
THIS IS THE END! THE HUMAN RACE WILL FINALLY BE DESTROYED.
NO ONE CAN STOP IT NOW!
TAT
TAT
TAT

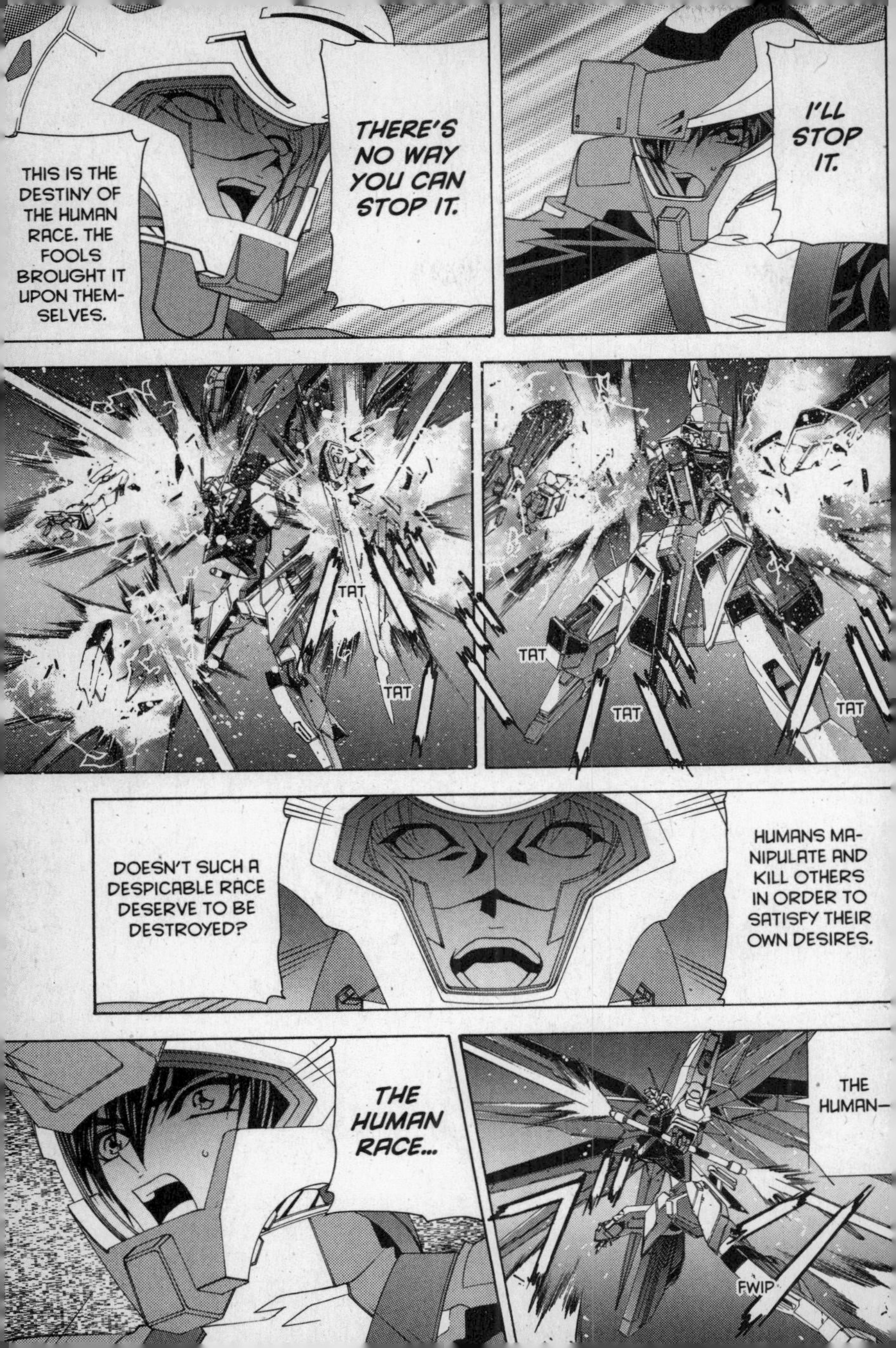
I'LL STOP IT.
THERE'S NO WAY YOU CAN STOP IT.
THIS IS THE DESTINY OF THE HUMAN RACE. THE FOOLS BROUGHT IT UPON THEM-SELVES.
TAT
TAT
TAT
TAT
TAT
HUMANS MA-NIPULATE AND KILL OTHERS IN ORDER TO SATISFY THEIR OWN DESIRES.
DOESN'T SUCH A DESPICABLE RACE DESERVE TO BE DESTROYED?
THE HUMAN—
FWIP
THE HUMAN RACE...

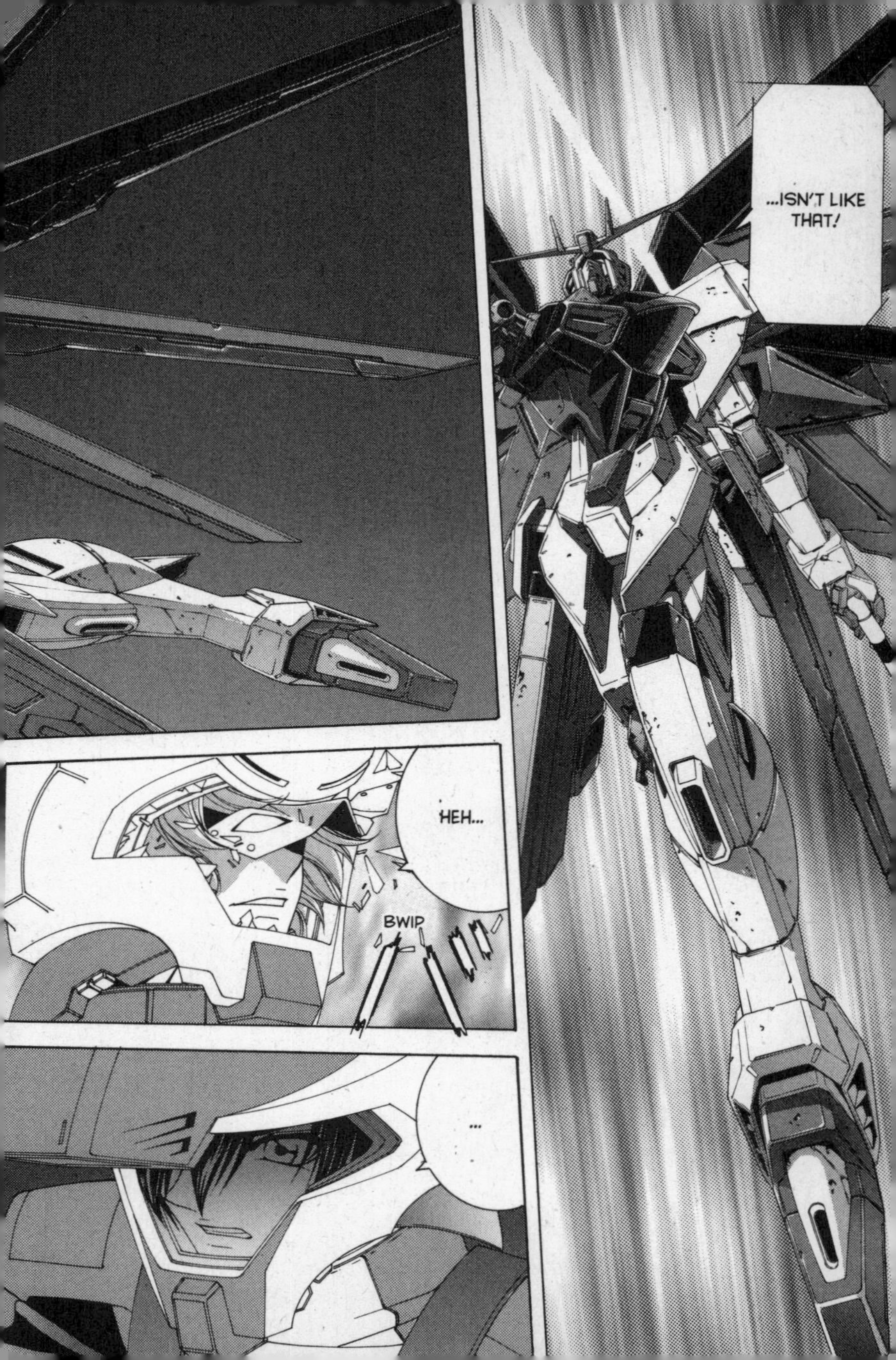
...ISN'T LIKE THAT!
HEH...
BWIP
...

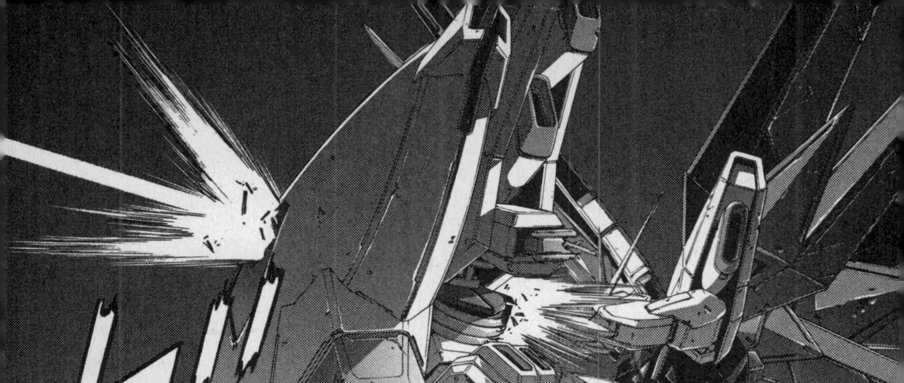
KASHACK
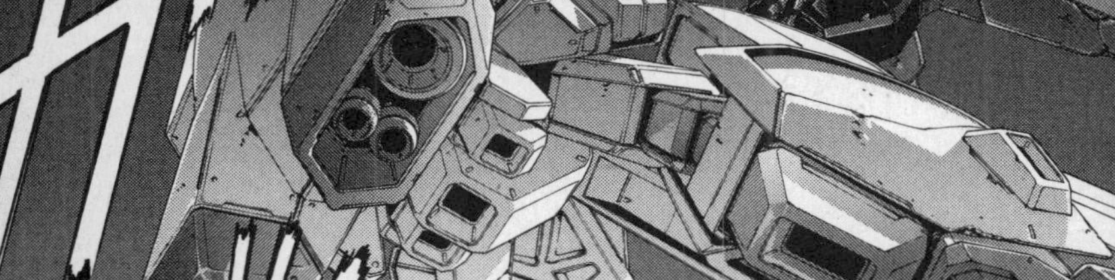
BEEP
COUNT DOWN
0000:000
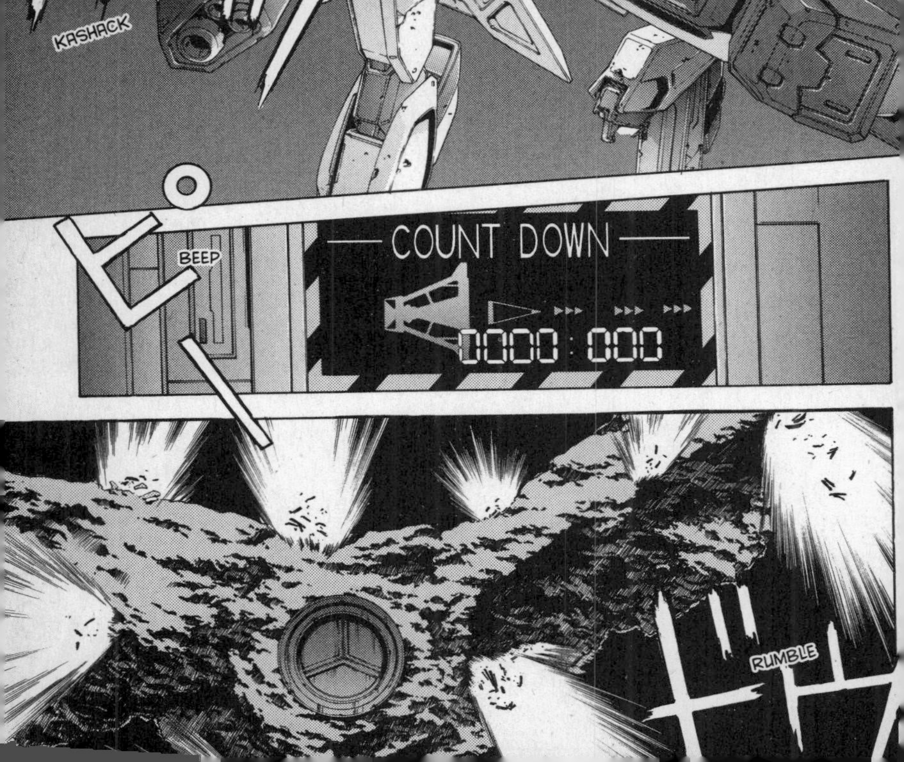
RUMBLE

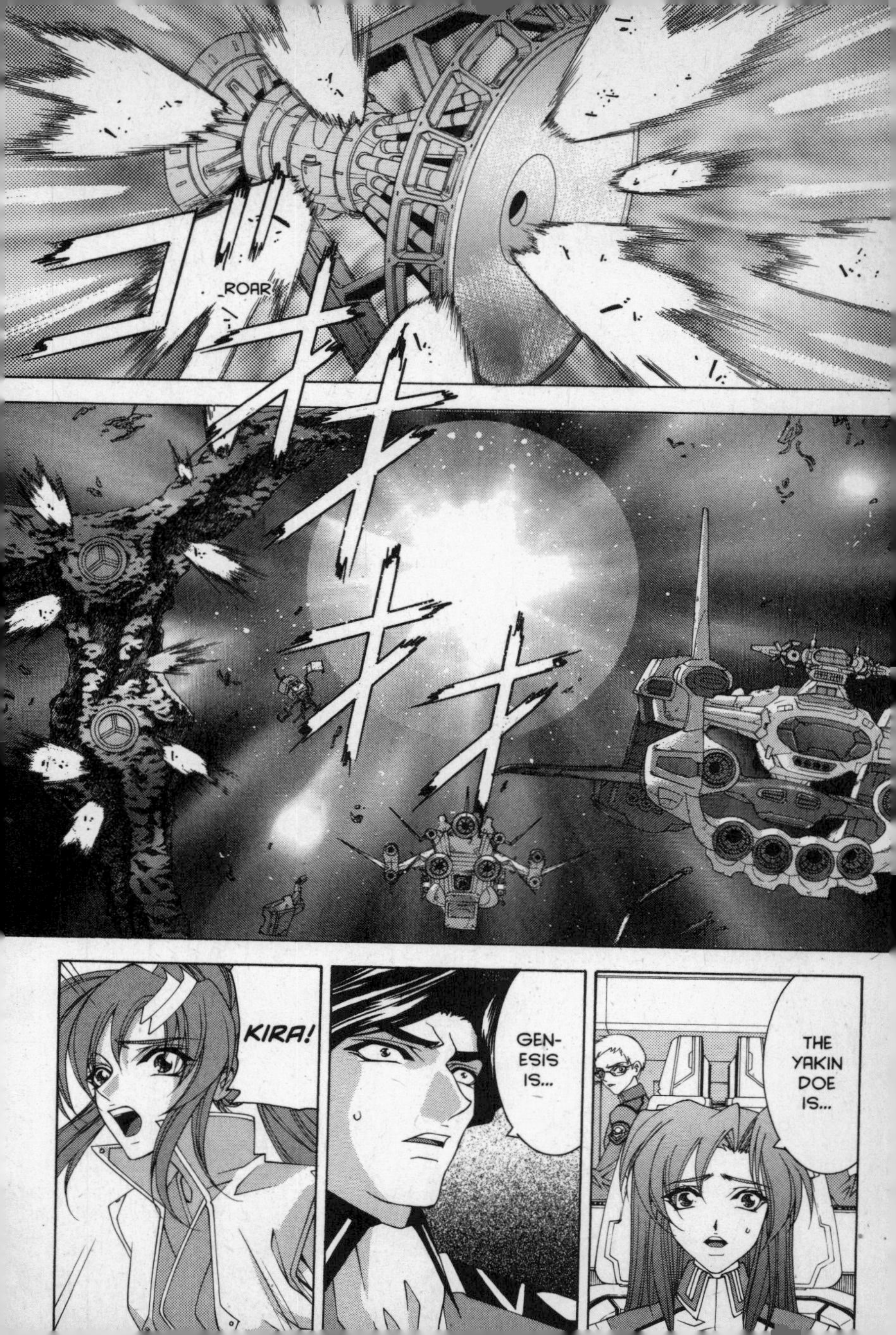
ROAR
THE YAKIN DOE IS...
GEN- ESIS IS...
KIRA!

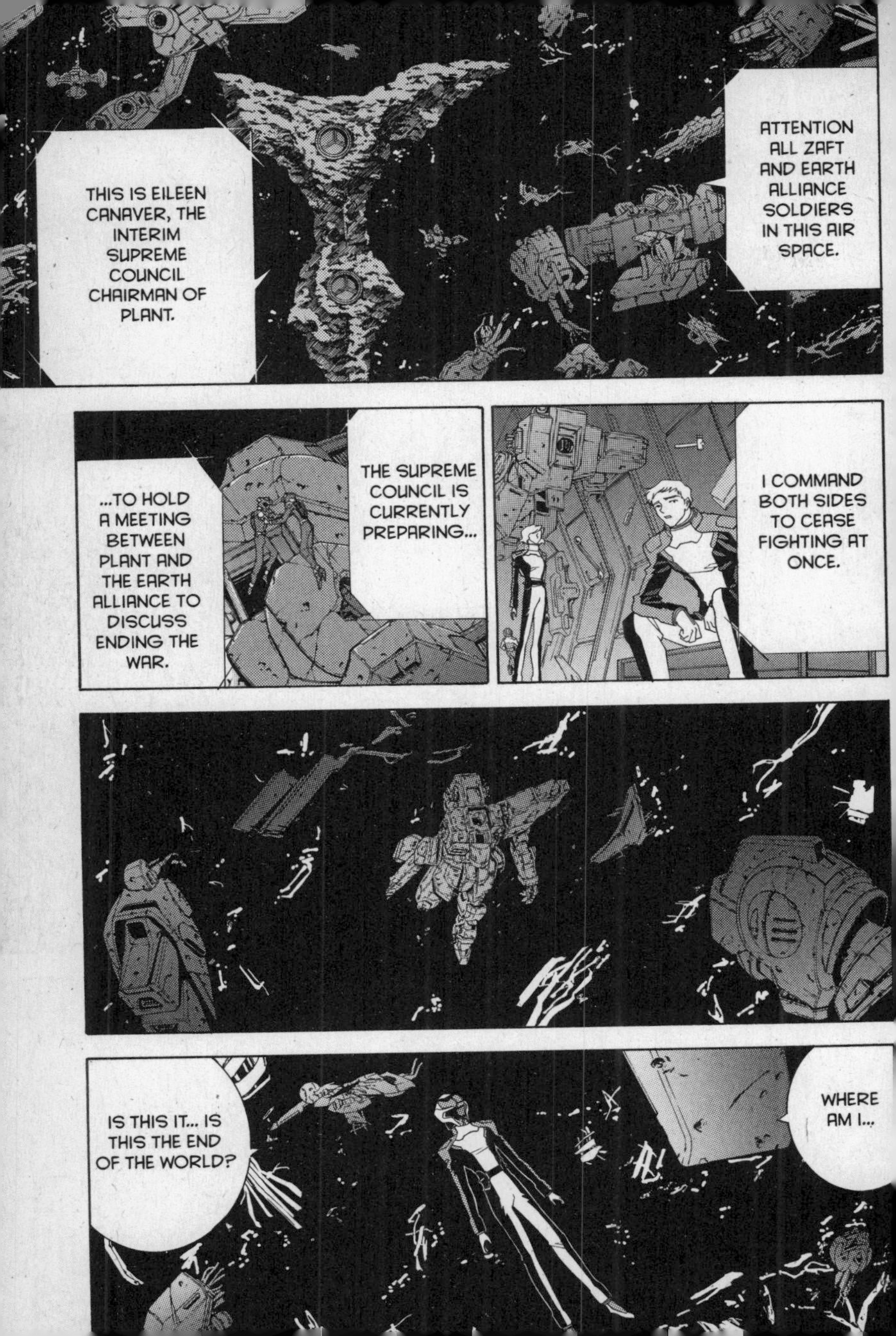
ATTENTION ALL ZAFT AND EARTH ALLIANCE SOLDIERS IN THIS AIR SPACE.
THIS IS EILEEN CANAVER, THE INTERIM SUPREME COUNCIL CHAIRMAN OF PLANT.
I COMMAND BOTH SIDES TO CEASE FIGHTING AT ONCE.
THE SUPREME COUNCIL IS CURRENTLY PREPARING...
...TO HOLD A MEETING BETWEEN PLANT AND THE EARTH ALLIANCE TO DISCUSS ENDING THE WAR.
WHERE AM I...
IS THIS IT... IS THIS THE END OF THE WORLD?

AM I...

...DEAD?

BIRDY?

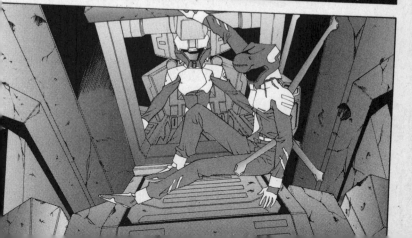

KIRA...

KIRA...

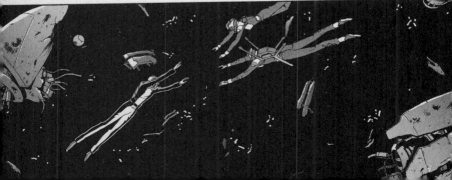

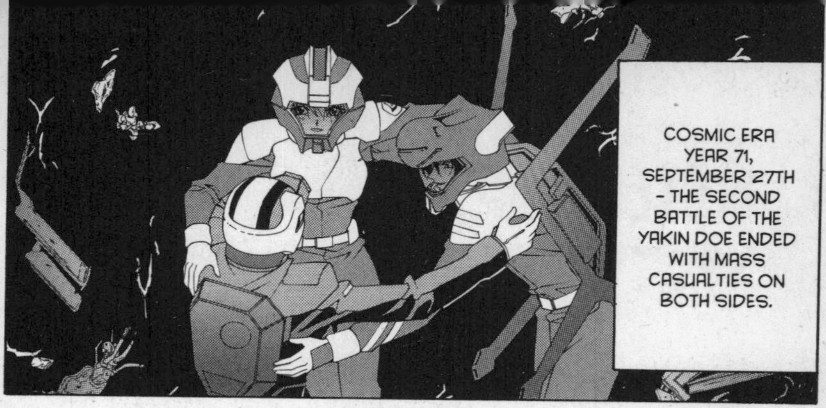
COSMIC ERA YEAR 71, SEPTEMBER 27TH - THE SECOND BATTLE OF THE YAKIN DOE ENDED WITH MASS CASUALTIES ON BOTH SIDES.

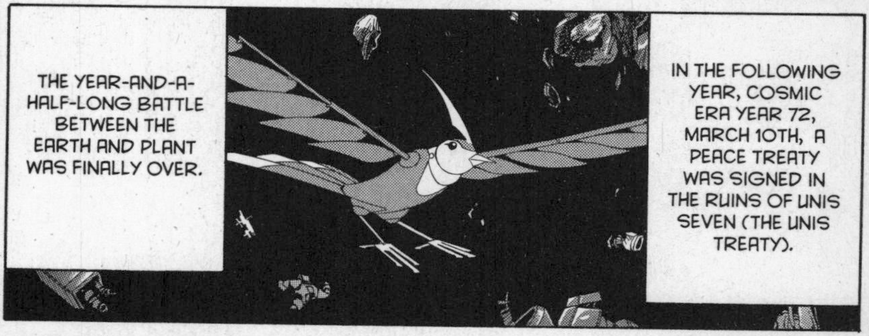
THE YEAR-AND-A-HALF-LONG BATTLE BETWEEN THE EARTH AND PLANT WAS FINALLY OVER.
IN THE FOLLOWING YEAR, COSMIC ERA YEAR 72, MARCH 10TH, A PEACE TREATY WAS SIGNED IN THE RUINS OF UNIS SEVEN (THE UNIS TREATY).

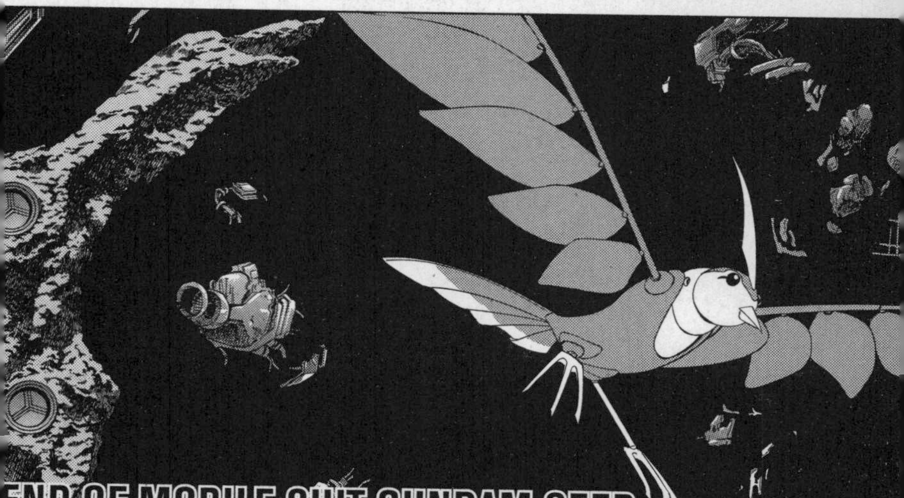
END OF MOBILE SUIT GUNDAM SEED

ZGMF-X ARMED MODULE

METEOR

THIS MODULE WAS BUILT ESPECIALLY FOR FREEDOM AND JUSTICE IN ORDER TO PROVIDE THEM WITH GREATER THERMAL POWER.

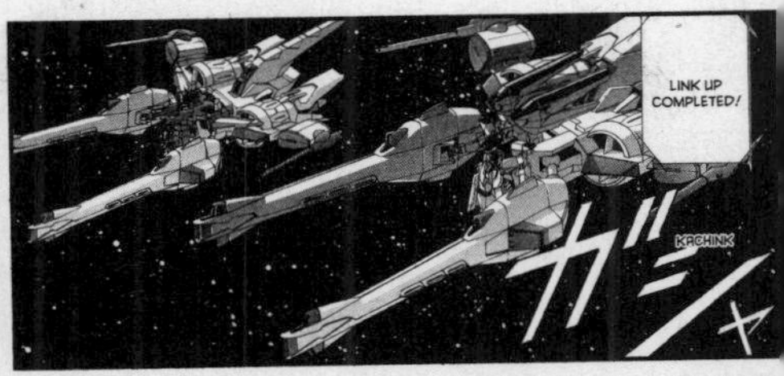
LINK UP COMPLETED!
KACHINK
ガシャ

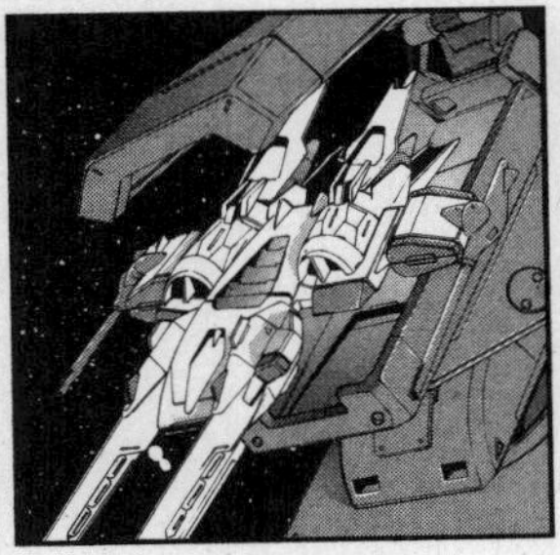

THE GENESIS TRANSPORTS THE ZGMF-X. FREEDOM'S UNIT IS MOUNTED ON THE LEFT SIDE OF THE SHIP WHILE JUSTICE IS ON THE RIGHT.

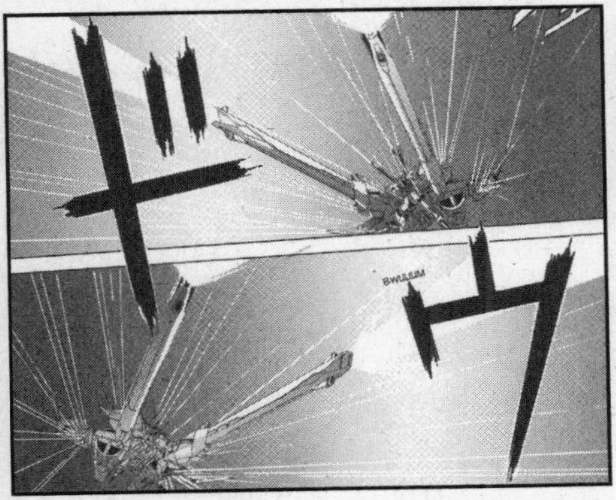
BWUUUM

THE BEAM-

120-CENTIMETER-WIDE, HIGH ENERGY CONVERGENCE BEAM

A LARGE BEAM CANNON LOCATED ON BOTH ARMS OF THE MOBILE SUITS. IT CAN BE MOVED IN CONJUNCTION WITH THE MOBILE SUITS' ARMS.

93.7-CENTIMETER-WIDE, HIGH ENERGY CONVERGENCE BEAM

A BEAM CANNON LOCATED ON BOTH WINGS OF THE MOBILE SUIT.

60 CENTIMETER ANTI SHIP MISSILE - THERE ARE 34 MISSILE CANNONS LOCATED ON EACH SIDE OF THE METEOR UNIT, AND NINE LOCATED ON THE METEOR'S TAIL. IT'S CAPABLE OF SHOOTING 77 MISSILES AT ONCE.

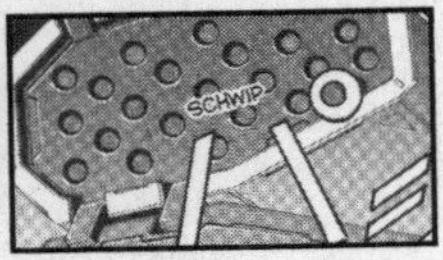
SCHWIP

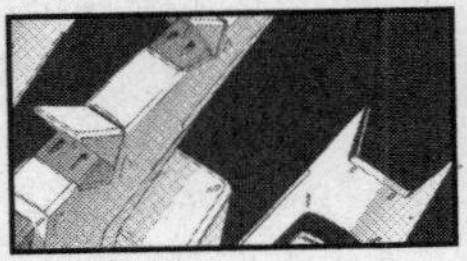

METEOR DATA

LENGTH: 99.46 METERS
WIDTH: 60.12 METERS
WEIGHT: 552.42 TONS

LEFT SIDE: CODE 01 (FREEDOM)
RIGHT SIDE: CODE 02 (JUSTICE)

MA-X 200 BEAM SWORD- A LARGE BEAM SABER THAT CAN BE MOVED IN CONJUNCTION WITH BOTH ARMS. IT HAS A VERY LONG RANGE, AND CAN TAKE OUT THE ENEMY IN ONE SHOT.

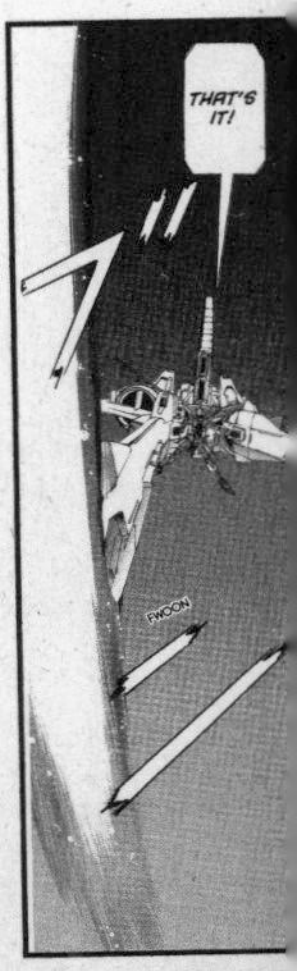
THAT'S IT!
FWOON

WE FINALLY MADE IT TO THE FINAL BOOK OF GUNDAM SEED. WE OWE IT ALL TO YOU, THE READERS. AT FIRST I WAS A BIT OVERWHELMED TO BE TAKING ON A SERIES AS FAMOUS AS GUNDAM, BUT IT ACTUALLY WAS A GREAT LEARNING EXPERIENCE FOR ME. I'M REALLY GLAD TO HAVE GOTTEN A CHANCE TO WORK ON THIS PROJECT. THIS IS THE END OF GUNDAM SEED, BUT THE STORY CONTINUES IN GUNDAM SEED DESTINY. I HOPE YOU'LL ENJOY IT.

HEISEI YEAR 17 – JANUARY 21ST

MASATSUGU
IWASE

—ASSISTING STAFF—

MAMORU OOISHI,
SUIGUN KAWANO,
TSUYOSHI ISOMOTO,
RYO YAMANE,
HIROMI YAMANE,
KOUTARO NIKKO,
YOUSUKE IMAJI,
AKIHIRO YAMAZAKI,
KENYA AZUMA,
AKIHITO IKEDA

AND THANK YOU TO EVERYBODY ELSE WHO HELPED OUT.

THANK YOU FOR READING GUNDAM SEED!

About the Creators

Yoshiyuki Tomino

Gundam was created by Yoshiyuki Tomino. Prior to Gundam,
Tomino had worked on the original *Astro Boy* anime, as well as
Princess Knight and *Brave Raideen*, among others. In 1979, he
created and directed *Mobile Suit Gundam*, the very first in a long
line of Gundam series. The show was not immediately popular
and was forced to cut its number of episodes before going off the
air, but as with the American show *Star Trek*, the fans still had
something to say on the matter. By 1981, the demand for Gundam
was so high that Tomino oversaw the re-release of the animation as
three theatrical movies (a practice still common in Japan, and rarely
if ever seen in the United States). It was now official: Gundam was
a blockbuster.

Tomino would go on to direct many Gundam series, including
Gundam ZZ, *Char's Counterattack*, *Gundam F91* and *Victory
Gundam*, all of which contributed to the rich history of the
vast Gundam universe. In addition to Gundam, Tomino created
Xabungle, *L.Gaim*, *Dunbine*, and *Garzey's Wing*. His most recent
anime is *Brain Powered*, which was released by Geneon in the
United States.

About the Creators (continued)

Masatsugu Iwase

Masatsugu Iwase writes and draws the manga adaptation of *Gundam SEED*. It is his first work published in the United States. The manga creator is better known in Japan, however, for his work on *Calm Breaker*, a hilarious parody of anime, manga, and Japanese pop culture.

A Brief History of Gundam, Part 5
By Mark Simmons

SEEDS OF DESTINY

The story of *Mobile Suit Gundam SEED* ends with this volume, but the saga of the Cosmic Era continues. The world of *Gundam SEED* has already been enlarged and expanded through spinoff stories like *Gundam SEED Astray* and the Mobile Suit Variation series, and now it's gone one step further with the launch of a sequel TV series, which made its Japanese debut on October 9, 2004. Picking up two years after the conclusion of the original series, *Gundam SEED Destiny* features both an extensive cast of new characters and the return of some old favorites, who are forced to reenter the battlefield as the world slides once again into global war.

A Rare Honor

Although the *Gundam* saga has been going for more than twenty-five years, it's unusual for an individual series to receive a direct sequel. 1985's *Zeta Gundam* served as a continuation of the original *Mobile Suit Gundam* series, with starring roles for a few of the earlier show's cast members and guest appearances by many more. Zeta's unfinished story continued into the followup series *Gundam ZZ*—although most of its characters didn't—and the 1988 movie *Char's Counterattack* then concluded the adventures of the original Gundam cast.

Otherwise, the only example of a true sequel in the quarter-century history of the *Gundam* franchise would be *Gundam Wing: Endless Waltz*, a three-episode video series (later compiled into a movie) which served as an epilogue to the popular *Gundam Wing* TV series. It's thus a major distinction for *Gundam SEED* to be given what amounts to a second season. Unlike *Endless Waltz*, this sequel is a full-length TV series, the kind of full-scale followup that hasn't been seen since the days of *Zeta Gundam* and *Gundam ZZ* almost two decades earlier.

A Brief History of Gundam, Part 5

Momentary Peace

At the end of *Gundam SEED*, the war between the Earth Alliance and the PLANTs—between Naturals and Coordinators—seems to have reached a conclusion. The extremist leaders who seized control of both sides and attempted to carry out mass genocide have been eliminated, giving the moderates a chance to call a ceasefire and begin peace negotiations.

Although the fighting ends with the fierce battle at Jachin Due, the war itself will not be formally concluded for another six months. The Junius Treaty, signed on March 10, C.E. 72, establishes the terms for peace between the PLANTs and the nations of the Earth Alliance. In order to prevent the kind of devastation seen in the final days of the war, this treaty prohibits all military use of the Neutron Jammer Canceler, bans Mirage Colloid stealth technology, and sets limits on the number of mobile suits each side can maintain.

A Brief History of Gundam, Part 5 (continued)

Back to the Battlefield

This peaceful interlude, however, proves to be brief. No sooner have the terms of the Junius Treaty been set than both sides begin developing a new generation of weapons, hoping to obtain the maximum possible military advantage within the treaty's restrictive rules. With Earth's nations and the forces of ZAFT engaged in an ongoing arms race, it seems only a matter of time until open warfare resumes.

This, then, is the setting for *Gundam SEED Destiny*. By the time the new story begins, in October of C.E. 73, ZAFT's arms buildup is in full swing. ZAFT has assembled an army of mobile suits at the newly constructed PLANT known as Armory One, including a handful of powerful new Gundams and a formidable warship to carry them. It's here that the new conflict will begin, and it's here that two of *Gundam SEED's* heroes will find themselves drawn once again into the battle...

Honorifics Explained

Throughout the Del Rey Manga books, you will find Japanese honorifics left intact in the translations. For those not familiar with how the Japanese use honorifics, and, more important, how they differ from American honorifics, we present this brief overview.

Politeness has always been a critical facet of Japanese culture. Ever since the feudal era, when Japan was a highly stratified society, use of honorifics—which can be defined as polite speech that indicates relationship or status—has played an essential role in the Japanese language. When addressing someone in Japanese, an honorific usually takes the form of a suffix attached to one's name (e.g. "Asuna-san"), as a title at the end of one's name, or in place of the name itself (e.g. "Negi-sensei" or simply "Sensei!").

Honorifics can be expressions of respect or endearment. In the context of manga and anime, honorifics give insight into the nature of the relationship between characters. Many translations into English leave out these important honorifics, and therefore distort the feel of the original Japanese. Because Japanese honorifics contain nuances that English honorifics lack, it is our policy at Del Rey not to translate them. Here, instead, is a guide to some of the honorifics you may encounter in Del Rey Manga.

-*san*: This is the most common honorific and is equivalent to Mr., Miss, Ms., Mrs., etc. It is the all-purpose honorific and can be used in any situation where politeness is required.

-*sama*: This is one level higher than -*san*. It is used to confer great respect.

-*dono*: This comes from the word *tono*, which means *lord*. It is an even higher level than -*sama* and confers utmost respect.

-*kun*: This suffix is used at the end of boys' names to express familiarity or endearment. It is also sometimes used by men among friends, or when addressing someone younger or of a lower station.

-*chan:* This is used to express endearment, mostly toward girls. It is also used for little boys, pets, and between lovers. It gives a sense of childish cuteness.

Bozu: This is an informal way to refer to a boy, similar to the English terms "kid" or "squirt."

Sempai: This title suggests that the addressee is one's senior in a group or organization. It is most often used in a school setting, where underclassmen refer to their upperclassmen as *sempai*. It can also be used in the workplace, such as when a newer employee addresses an employee who has seniority in the company.

Kohai: This is the opposite of -*sempai*, and is used toward underclassmen in school or newcomers in the workplace. It connotes that the addressee is of a lower station.

Sensei: Literally meaning "one who has come before," this title is used for teachers, doctors, or masters of any profession or art.

-[blank]: This is usually forgotten on these lists, but it's perhaps the most significant difference between Japanese and English. The lack of honorific means that the speaker has permission to address the person in a very intimate way. Usually, only family, spouses, or very close friends have this kind of license. Known as *yobisute,* it can be gratifying when someone who has earned the intimacy starts to call one by one's name without an honorific. But when that intimacy hasn't been earned, it can also be insulting.

Gacha Gacha

BY HIROYUKI TAMAKOSHI

SECRET CRUSH

Lately, Kouhei can't get his friend Kurara out of his mind. Even though he has known her since elementary school, all of a sudden, ever since she came back from summer vacation, he has been crushing on her . . . hard.

But something is different about Kurara—lately she has been acting very unusual. Sometimes she seems wholesome, pure, and innocent, and other times she is extremely forward and unabashed. Kouhei soon learns that Kurara has multiple personalities—and decides to help her keep her secret from their classmates. But Kouhei soon finds himself struggling between helping her as a friend, and trying to win her heart . . . which is a challenge, since she has many!

Ages: 16+

Includes special extras after the story!

VOLUME 1: On sale August 30, 2005

For more information and to sign up for Del Rey's manga e-newsletter, visit www.delreymanga.com

Sugar Sugar Rune

BY MOYOCO ANNO VOLUME 1

QUEEN OF HEARTS

Little witch-girls Chocolat and Vanilla are best friends, but only one of them can be Queen of the Magic World. To determine who deserves the title, they must go to the Human World and enter a strange competition. Whoever attracts the most human boys wins!

Here's how it works: When a boy falls for a witch-girl, she utters a few mystic words and the boy's heart will be hers in jewel-like form. It may sound simple, but winning hearts is tricky business. While Chocolat had no problem enticing witch-boys with her forthright personality, human boys seem to be drawn to shy and modest girls like Vanilla. And to make matters worse, Chocolat is finding herself increasingly drawn to the cool and mysterious Pierre—who feels nothing for her! The girls had planned to be best friends forever, but both of them want to be Queen. Will their rivalry ruin their friendship?

Sugar Sugar Rune

1

Moyoco Anno

Ages: 10 +

Includes special extras after the story!

VOLUME 1: On sale September 27, 2005

For more information and to sign up for Del Rey's manga e-newsletter, visit www.delreymanga.com

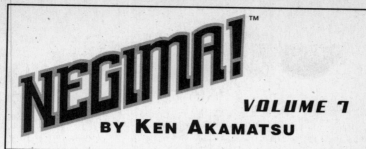

NEGIMA!™

VOLUME 7

BY KEN AKAMATSU

IT'S TRAINING TIME!

7
NEGIMA!™
MAGISTER NEGI MAGI
KEN AKAMATSU

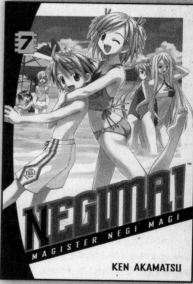

After their adventures on a school trip to Kyoto, you'd think that Negi and his students would want to rest. But now that they're back at Mahora Academy, relaxation is pretty low on the list! First there are Asuna's dreams, which hint at a deeper relationship between Negi and his father of which she is unaware. Then Negi starts a quest to improve his abilities. To do this, the teacher will need to become a student—and Negi's students will become his teachers.

Ku Fei is a master of every martial art imaginable, but can she teach Negi the skill he needs to survive? And there's only one magic user at Mahora Academy with abilities that surpass Negi's own. Dark Evangeline might train him, but only at a price—and does Negi really want to be Evangeline's personal slave?!

Ages: 16+

Includes special extras after the story!

VOLUME 7: On sale September 27, 2005

DEL REY

For more information and to sign up for Del Rey's manga e-newsletter, visit www.delreymanga.com

VOLUME 5

BY SATOMI IKEZAWA

TAKING MATTERS TO NEW HEIGHTS

Master manipulator Megumi Hano—Hano-chan—is enraged by her failure to bring down timid Yaya Higuchi and her alter ego, the confident and boisterous Nana. So Hano-chan decides to take the ultimate revenge. Using the singing contract that Yaya desperately wishes to null and void as a means to her mean-spirited ends, Hano-chan makes her an offer. She will rip it up . . . if Yaya agrees to play a little game with her. If Yaya can catch Hano-chan and steal the contract, Hano will cancel the agreement and return the application fee. Sounds simple, yes? But there's a little hitch. Yaya must chase Hano while skydiving!

Ages: 16+

Includes special extras after the story!

VOLUME 5: On sale September 27, 2005

For more information and to sign up for Del Rey's manga e-newsletter, visit www.delreymanga.com

GENSHIKEN

The Society for the Study of Modern Visual Culture

VOLUME 3
BY KIO SHIMOKU

Kanji Sasahara's annoyingly normal little sister, Keiko, has fallen for video game master Kousaka. And now she's willing to do whatever it takes to steal him away from his girlfriend, Saki Kasukabe . . . even if it means becoming a fangirl herself! But as a wise member of the Genshiken once said: "You don't become an otaku by trying." So Saki teaches Keiko-chan what dating a rabid fan truly means . . . and it ain't pretty. Just to add to the craziness, there's plastic modeling mayhem (don't ask), the challenge of Kanji's first PC, and Saki's penchant for pyromania. Looks like things are heating up!

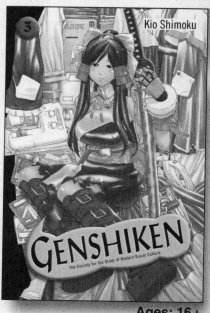

Ages: 16 +

Includes special extras after the story!

VOLUME 3: On sale October 25, 2005

For more information and to sign up for Del Rey's manga e-newsletter, visit www.delreymanga.com

TOMARE!

[STOP!]

You're going the wrong way!

Manga is a completely different type of reading experience.

To start at the *beginning*, go to the *end*!

That's right! Authentic manga is read the traditic
way—from right to left. Exactly the *opposite*
books are read. It's easy to follow: Just go t
book, and read each page—and each par
side, starting at the top right. Now y
it was meant to be.